*Parties, Slavery, and the Union*
*in Antebellum Georgia*

# Parties, Slavery, and the Union in Antebellum Georgia

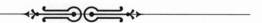

## ANTHONY GENE CAREY

The University of Georgia Press    *Athens and London*

© 1997 by the University of Georgia Press
Athens, Georgia 30602
All rights reserved
Set in Ehrhardt by G&S Typesetters, Inc.
Printed and bound by Braun-Brumfield, Inc.
The paper in this book meets the guidelines for permanence and
durability of the Committee on Production Guidelines for Book
Longevity of the Council on Library Resources.

Printed in the United States of America

01   00   99   98   97   C   5   4   3   2   1

*Library of Congress Cataloging in Publication Data*

Carey, Anthony Gene.
Parties, slavery, and the Union in antebellum Georgia / Anthony
Gene Carey.
p.   cm.
Includes bibliographical references and index.
ISBN 0-8203-1898-1 (alk. paper)
1. Georgia—Politics and government—1775–1865.
2. Political parties—Georgia—History—19th century.   I. Title.
F290.C37     1997
324.2758′009′034—dc20          96-30786

*British Library Cataloging in Publication Data available*

For Layne

# CONTENTS

# TABLES

# PREFACE

This is a book about party politics. Matters defined and discussed by other scholars as "political," from local quarrels over the location of roads to contested gender relations, are considered here only as they relate to the foundations of Georgia society and to partisan politics. Slavery is, throughout the book, treated as a massive reality, as an institution that shaped every aspect of life and thought. My contentions about the centrality of gender relations, specifically about the enormous power that white men wielded as heads of households, are based mostly on arguments made and evidence uncovered by other scholars. I outline my understanding of the salient features of Georgia society—of its "political" arrangements in the broad sense—in chapter 1, and then focus on linking that understanding to the history of the state's political parties.[1]

The reason for my focus on political parties is rather simple: from the early 1830s to the end of the nineteenth century, parties controlled the political life of the nation and captured the loyalties of white—and, after the Civil War, black—men as they never had before and never have since. Examining, in a single state, how political parties arose, how they functioned, how they attracted voters, how they handled various issues over time, how they fit into the national party system, and how sectional conflict disrupted the party system is a worthwhile undertaking, and more than enough to handle in one book.

My reasons for choosing Georgia are simple as well: it was a vital state, relatively little has been published about its antebellum political history, and I attended graduate school at Emory University in Atlanta. Georgia is, I submit, about as representative, or unrepresentative, as any other state in the sprawling, diverse Union in the years before the Civil War.

There is something in this book to displease nearly everyone engaged in the debate over the nature of the Jacksonian parties, a debate that tends to run toward extremes. Edward Pessen flayed Jacksonians and frequently dismissed the idea that significant differences separated Whigs from Democrats, particularly at the leadership level. Pessen liked to find exceptions to other scholars' generalizations, exceptions that he believed disproved rules and displayed Whig and Democratic hypocrisy. Joel Silbey, in contrast, has long contended that party battles had meaning, that the parties offered distinct alternatives, and that party loyalty—based on coherent choices made by enthusiastic citizens—was the most important force in nineteenth-century politics. With Pessen gone and few or none ready to take his place, interpretations that portray the parties as ideological vehicles seem clearly in the ascendant. Historians searching for deep meaning in politics have found it, and in some formulations, Whigs and Democrats appear as exponents of rival worldviews or as class parties struggling for or against capitalism.[2]

Scholars intent on discovering the *essence* of Whiggery or Democracy, however, overgeneralize to simplify complex realities. The Jacksonian parties were electoral *and* ideological, in different measures at different times and in different ways. As electoral coalitions with ideological stances, they were neither programmatic parties devoted to rigid principles and unchanging policy agendas, nor mere machines cynically managed to amass votes. The parties adhered to general positions and tried to enact favored policies while also pragmatically adjusting to events and working to maximize electoral advantages. Over the decades, issues changed, the political balance altered, and the country was transformed economically and socially. What it meant to be a Whig or a Democrat necessarily varied with time and place. Emphasizing a single, practically timeless key to understanding the country's partisan divisions, be that key ethnocultural antagonisms, as once was fashionable, or divergent reactions to the market economy, as is currently the rage, sacrifices too much for the sake of thematic coherence.[3]

In many respects, parties in antebellum Georgia functioned as electoral coalitions. On questions of state policy particularly, Whigs and Democrats seldom adopted consistent stances or articulated alternative philosophies. Statewide coalitional parties embraced diverse interests, and the dangers of conflict within rather than between parties made leaders wary of stirring up strife over state questions. Politicians, indeed, usually dismissed state issues as irrelevant to party divisions, and neither Whigs nor Democrats let intraparty differences over state questions interfere with the pursuit of electoral victory. The parties, for example, typically focused far more on what sort of signal the outcome of a gubernatorial election might send to Washington than on that election's potential impact on state policy. Even on national issues, the parties had a checkered record. Party differences over the tariff were more rhetorical than real, and the national bank issue was only briefly important in Georgia. On the problem of slavery in the territories, the parties diverged sharply on strategy and in their respective choices of northern allies, but they agreed on the substance of southern rights and on the necessity for defending slavery. And political leaders, of course, repeatedly resorted to obfuscation and evasion on the territorial issue in desperate efforts to keep the national parties and the Union together.

Dwelling simply on the programmatic shortcomings of Georgia parties, however, misses a crucial point: the parties were most ideological on the matters on which they fundamentally agreed. Both parties articulated an elaborate defense of a rural, agricultural southern society based on slavery. Both justified and protected the supremacy of white men. Both contrasted the South favorably with the North and vowed to shield the South from outside enemies and antislavery agitators. Both eulogized the Constitution, extolled the virtues of the founders, and offered American liberty as an example for the world. Both promised economic prosperity and promoted economic opportunity. The parties did not need to differ always and sharply to merit devotion, nor did they have to be remarkably effective at enacting specific policies. They could and did earn voters' trust by expressing the core values of the white men who ruled Georgia. Laws not subject to partisan debate, like those that enslaved African Americans, subordinated women, and enfranchised white men, were profoundly ideological and formed the foundation of society.

A balanced view of the Jacksonian parties, then, concedes much to consensus and to the parties' roles as electoral organizations, while still maintaining that the parties spoke to voters and that party differences existed and mattered. The Georgia parties presented, at times, contrasting economic views and policies, and Whigs' antiparty sentiments consistently distinguished them from partisans of the national Democracy. Calhounite Democrats frequently pushed southern party ideas that challenged the legitimacy of the national party system. Whigs criticized the Mexican War; Democrats offered the controversial doctrine of popular sovereignty as a solution for the problem of slavery in the territories. Former Whigs halfheartedly embraced nativist proposals in the mid-1850s, while Democrats denounced northern Know-Nothings as abolitionists. In special instances in 1850–52 and 1860–61, state parties fractured over issues involving slavery and the Union, and new coalitions arose to offer voters significant choices on weighty matters. Georgians and Georgia parties, in short, differed more than enough to keep party conflict alive for three decades.

The republican political culture, moreover, tended to magnify even slight party differences and to encourage partisan mindsets that invested political activity with meaning. If one accepted, as many antebellum Georgia voters did, that opponents were corrupt office seekers whose shady maneuverings would undermine public virtue and erode liberty, then political contests became struggles that required involvement and affected the country's fate. In an era when parties were new and anxieties about the future of the Republic were often acute, unjaded voters believed that their parties could solve problems and express social values. That antebellum Americans sometimes overestimated the significance of their choices and overrated their party's adherence to principle did not change the fact that party loyalties were deeply felt and powerfully shaped voting behavior.[4]

The complicated question of how and why voters formed such lasting party loyalties is addressed, if not fully answered, in this book. Many factors—economic interests, slaveholding, regional antagonisms, family influence, neighborhood ties, political traditions, and personal sentiments among them—influenced voters' allegiances. No neat overall theory can explain how Georgians, much less all Americans, chose between the parties, and no such theory is offered here. My explanations for voting behavior are multicausal and, I think, appropriately tentative. No systematic means of measuring public opinion existed in nineteenth-century America. Explanations of past voting behavior therefore are informed guesses, a fact that scholars ought to admit more readily. One conclusion that can safely be drawn about the Jacksonian parties is that they attracted support from a cross section of the voting public. Broad generalizations about what Whigs thought or what made men Democrats are useful—one could not write textbooks or teach survey courses without them—but subject to countless qualifications. In arguing that the Georgia parties were similar, though hardly identical, in composition, and that party divisions only partially reflected social cleavages, I avoid constructing artificial dichotomies not supported by the infuriatingly fragmentary evidence. Scholars who find my approach unsatisfying are invited to try to formulate more sweeping conclusions that will fit the Georgia evidence.

A major argument of this book is that Georgia, and by extension every other state, had a unique party system. Geographic, demographic, economic, and historical factors distinctively shaped each state's politics, even though all states shared elements of a national political culture. Georgia and Massachusetts Whigs, for example, had ideas and goals in common that allowed them to work together, for a time, in a national Whig party; one can discern similarities that formed the basis for the Whig alliance. But Georgia Whigs were, at bottom, more like Georgia Democrats than they were like any party of New Englanders. The sort of reform impulses, antislavery sentiments, ethnocultural tensions, and class conflicts that figured prominently in politics in the Northeast had no real counterparts in Georgia. Few planters or yeomen walked the streets of Boston or New York City, and Georgia's primary working class consisted of native-born African Americans, not foreign-born Democrats. The diversity of antebellum America precluded political conflicts and partisan divisions in Georgia, or any other state, from mirroring those elsewhere.[5]

It mattered immensely that Georgia was a Deep South state with a slave population that exceeded 40 percent and an enormous investment in cotton agriculture (see chapter 1). I argue, along with William Cooper and others, that the defense of slavery and white men's liberty was paramount in southern politics. Georgians did not, however, always fixate on the "politics of slavery"; other concerns frequently engaged the parties, especially in the years before the Wilmot Proviso. Slavery issues, furthermore, were not as salient in upper South states such as Virginia, Tennessee, and North Carolina as they were in Georgia, a fact that white Georgians knew well. Cooper's thesis regarding the "politics of slavery" clearly applies better to Georgia and the rest of the Deep South than to the perimeter South. I also contend that the phenomenon that Cooper identifies is not a unique politics of slavery but a variation of a political dynamic that operated nationwide. Antebellum politicians were adept at finding enemies—often Northerners found Southerners and vice versa—and identifying threats to fundamental institutions. Northern Republicans who denounced the "Slave Power" and defended free labor practiced their own version of the politics of slavery, and southern Democrats attacked northern Whigs for other things—tariff protectionism and advocacy of the second Bank of the United States, to name two— besides Whigs' antislavery proclivities. The politics of slavery, broadly considered, was the politics of antebellum America: parties everywhere used extremes to define differences.[6]

The stake that all white men had in preserving slavery and the democratic thrust of party politics made George an imperfect "herrenvolk democracy," or, the term I prefer, a "white men's democracy." The character of antebellum Georgia society is discussed in chapter 1, but a few additional words are in order here. I agree with Elizabeth Fox-Genovese and Eugene D. Genovese that the Old South was a "discrete social formation" that "was in but not of the bourgeois world"—southern distinctiveness is central to this book. Paternalism permeated southern society and mediated relations between masters and slaves, and men and women. But paternalism did not extend with as much force into relations among white men. The democratic ideals of the Jacksonian era and the reality of yeoman independence limited the power of the planter class and ensured that Georgia's white men's government was based on white men's consent. Scant evidence—really no more than hints—exists of class conflict in party politics; Georgia parties issued few class appeals and routinely affirmed the unity of white men. Planter-politicians seldom controverted the fiction that all white men were equal; yeomen who recognized inequality acted within the major parties anyway, and no state political movement in the antebellum period remotely menaced slavery. The state of Georgia and Georgia's parties were, to be sure, run in the interests of planters and slaveholders, but they also served the interests of other white men. Antebellum Georgia society was, objectively, immensely unequal and riven by class, but white men perceived the world through ideological filters that made distinctions of race and gender paramount.[7]

Given the influential nature of Steven Hahn's work, the place of upcountry and mountain yeomen in Georgia politics and society deserves further comment. Hahn shows that upcountry yeomen shied away from market agriculture to varying degrees, that they valued their independence, and that the upcountry differed economically and demographically from the black belt. Despite his assertions, however, Hahn does not and cannot demonstrate that differing levels of market involvement or slaveholding consistently determined political behavior. North Georgia was Democratic, and the black belt was Whiggish, although one would not want to overestimate the degree of the difference. Whigs were numerous in the upcountry, and planters led the black belt Democracy. North Georgia Democrats were among the champions of the Central Bank of Georgia, they strongly backed the state-owned Western & Atlantic Railroad built through Cherokee Georgia, and many of them clamored for private railroad development in the 1850s. North Georgia farmers exploited the opportunities that the Western & Atlantic created, and their political representatives evinced little resistance to the spread of the market economy (see chapter 5). On matters related to slavery, north Georgia and black belt Democrats differed repeatedly over means but never over ends, and a majority of upcountry voters backed immediate secession (see chapter 8). Many of Hahn's conclusions about the distinctiveness of upcountry society and politics, in short, seem overstated and based more on what theoretically ought to have been the case than on what antebellum evidence reveals actually was the case.[8]

Previous books on Georgia politics are a mixed lot. The earliest, Ulrich B. Phillips's *Georgia and State Rights,* remains surprisingly useful considering that it is nearly a century old. Phillips concentrates on the period before 1840, is strong on details, and emphasizes, as I do, the importance of national issues in shaping Georgia party alignments. I dissent from his Progressive interpretation of state party conflict and treat white Georgians' commitment to state rights as what it mostly was, a commitment to maintain slavery. Horace Montgomery's idiosyncratic *Cracker Parties* sacrifices substance for color, dwells on personalities, and seldom goes much below the surface of political events. Richard Shryock's *Georgia and the Union in 1850* has much to recommend it, althought it at times borders on economic determinism and vastly overstresses prosperity as a cause of conservatism in 1850. Shryock, interestingly, exhibits an understanding of the politics of slavery—he does not call it that—in his treatment of events preceding the 1850 crisis.[9]

Donald DeBats's 1973 dissertation, published in 1990 with small changes and an additional chapter on the state legislature, has specific strengths and general weaknesses. DeBats combines history and political science and utilizes political party models and theories of voting behavior. Most of the book examines Georgia parties as institutions and analyzes voting returns and census statistics. Many of DeBats's statistical findings, such as his conclusion that social and economic variables altogether explained only about one quarter of the variations in voting behavior, are exceedingly useful, and I gratefully borrow from his analysis in this book.

DeBats and I partially concur on many points. He treats the nullification era as the key formative period for Georgia parties, emphasizes the inchoate nature of the party system through much of the 1830s, reports the failure of state parties to divide clearly on economic issues, views national issues as crucial, pays due attention to the elements of party organization, stresses the influence of elites, and demonstrates that past partisan behavior was the best predictor of voting patterns in subsequent elections. DeBats makes valuable comments on all these subjects and more, and I take the similarities between his work and mine as evidence that we both have aspects of Georgia's political party history about right.[10]

DeBats, though, drastically overstates his thesis that elites led and masses followed in antebellum Georgia. He sees political communication as "essentially uni-directional," operating from the top down, and he writes "of a political style divorced from the social base of the citizenry." He portrays elections largely as scrambles for office by cynical politicians, and contends that the failure to address significant issues represented a severe flaw in the state party system. These claims are half truths at best, and however valuable his work is on specific points, overall DeBats offers a distorted, disjointed view of antebellum Georgia politics. His research in newspapers is weak, and his fondness for statistics and correlations draws him away from literary sources that might have given meaning to the numbers. He underappreciates the "southernness" of Georgia politics and fails to comprehend that the central ideological component of state politics was the defense of slavery and white men's liberty. In defining ideology mainly in economic terms, DeBats imposes his model of appropriate party differences on antebellum Georgians and misses much of significance. Apart from such fundamental disagreements, DeBats and I differ on countless lesser points that are of interest mostly to specialists, who, I trust, can sort out these matters for themselves.[11]

The sharpest historiographical clash occurs in chapter 8, in which I con-

tradict Michael Johnson's views on the secession of Georgia. Johnson's book
is well written, soundly researched, persistently argued, and, I contend, in-
terpretatively wrong. Without belaboring here controversial points that are
belabored elsewhere, let me say that Johnson's focus on a single episode cre-
ates problems of perspective, and that he pursues arguments in the face of
what I consider to be obviously contrary evidence. Johnson particularly fails
to grasp how white Georgians could be utterly committed to preserving
slavery yet disagree vehemently over how best to preserve it. He interprets
the debate between immediate secessionists and cooperationists as evidence
of a social crisis, and he insists that immediate secessionists, who feared that
nonslaveholders might prove disloyal to the peculiar institution, rushed
Georgia out of the Union to prevent what they saw as an impending internal
upheaval. In contrast, I stress that the political divisions present during the
secession winter were thoroughly familar to Georgians, who had lived with
variations of them for decades; that the campaign to elect delegates to the
secession convention was in basic respects like every other antebellum campaign; and that the act of secession was a logical, fitting culmination to all
that had gone before and the ultimate expression of white unity. In seceding
from the old Union, white Georgians were moving not toward some "patriarchal republic" but away from the hated Yankees into a proslavery, white
man's confederacy that in form closely resembled the government they were
leaving behind. Readers have, in this case, a clear choice between two radically divergent interpretations.[12]

I offer this book as a comprehensive, analytical narrative on party politics
in antebellum Georgia. Other such books on other southern states have contributed much to our understanding of antebellum politics and the Old
South, and I hope that readers will find my work similarly useful and mildly
entertaining. Instead of concentrating on a single, dominant thesis, this book
interweaves many arguments about the nature of the Georgia parties, Georgia society, antebellum political conflicts, the national party systems, and the
Old South. I can only hope that I have woven tolerably well.[13]

The first chapter, as noted above, gives an overview of Georgia society.
Chapter 2 examines the formation of the Georgia Jacksonian parties and
carries events forward to 1840. Chapters 3 and 4 chronicle the party struggles of the early 1840s and the beginnings of conflicts over slavery extension.

Then the narrative breaks for a more explicitly analytical fifth chapter that discusses the nature of the Georgia parties and various facets of state politics. Indeed, some readers may want to start in the middle, as all the other chapters rest ultimately on my overall understanding of Georgia politics. The story resumes in chapter 6 with the dealignment and realignment of Georgia parties during and after the crisis of 1850. Chapter 7 covers the mid-1850s and examines the impacts of the Kansas–Nebraska Act and "bleeding Kansas" on Georgia parties and the national party system. The final chapter builds toward secession.

# ACKNOWLEDGMENTS

My journey through antebellum Georgia politics began with a paper written for James L. Roark's seminar on the Old South at Emory University. He subsequently directed this study as a dissertation, suffered through draft chapters, and advised me on revisions for the book. There is much that I could say, but I will simply say that no student ever had a better, more genial mentor. Dan T. Carter shared his knowledge of the South and quizzed me in his kind and penetrating way about various parts of the dissertation. Elizabeth Fox-Genovese inspired me with her work, aided me with her comments, and will undoubtedly shudder at some of my conclusions. The same applies to Eugene D. Genovese. Frank L. Byrne, recently retired from Kent State University, once directed an astonishingly long master's thesis, written—before he made clear that it *would* be otherwise—almost entirely in passive voice. If the writing in this book is any better, I attribute much of the improvement to his enforcement of "Hesseltine's commandments," which I have since passed on to my own students. August Meier, also retired from Kent State, and John T. Hubbell, still active within limits, helped convince me to study the Old South and slavery.

Thanks also go to other friends, teachers, and critics scattered across the country: Jonathan Atkins, Andy Doyle, Virginia Gould, Lacy Ford, John DeJong, John Inscoe, Kent Leslie, John Merryman, Chris Owen, Jonathan Prude, John Rodrigue, Michael Schrier, Joe Thompson, Peter Wallenstein, Harry Watson, and all the rest. Colleagues and students in the Auburn University Department of History have been supportive, friendly, and wonderful to know; they have taught me much about more important things than Georgia politics.

Emory University funded my graduate study and my work on this project with a George W. Woodruff Fellowship and an Andrew W. Mellon Fellowship in Southern Studies. The Colonial Dames of Georgia granted me a generous dissertation award. Auburn University and the College of Liberal

Arts provided me with a research grant-in-aid and a summer stipend to help me complete this book; the Department of History also arranged a quarter's leave.

A portion of chapter 3 previously appeared as "'E Pluribus Unum': Georgia Politics and the Dynamics of the Jacksonian Party System, 1840–1844," *Georgia Historical Quarterly* 79 (Winter 1995): 810–41; a portion of chapter 7 was published previously as "Too Southern to Be Americans: Proslavery Politics and the Failure of the Know-Nothing Party in Georgia, 1854–1856," *Civil War History* 41 (March 1995): 22–40.

Malcolm Call and Kelly Caudle of the University of Georgia Press encouraged my work and guided me through the publication process. Melinda Conner, my copy editor, corrected slips and suggested many improvements.

Layne McDaniel has lived with this book for as long as I have, and I dedicate it to her, for all she means to me.

*Parties, Slavery, and the Union*
*in Antebellum Georgia*

# ONE

# *Surveying a White Men's Democracy*

Georgia throughout the antebellum period was a growing, diverse state, divided by nature and history into distinctive geographic and demographic regions. Most of its territory in the 1820s was wilderness; even relatively populous areas were sparsely settled, and the difficulties of travel by land or water kept most citizens in rural isolation. Then, over the decades, Georgians, black and white, tamed frontiers and carved out counties. The population swelled and shifted from east to west, the economy expanded, and railroad networks developed to link the state together. This conquering of space brought significant changes amidst great continuity. Society in 1860 remained rural, the economy, agricultural. From the coastal counties in the southeast through the central piedmont to Cherokee Georgia in the northwest, regional patterns of economic and social life set early persisted and shaped state politics.

Georgia's leading city and seaport, Savannah, lay in Chatham County, the northernmost in the tier of six coastal counties (map 1, tables 1–4). The first English colonists in Georgia had settled here, but by the 1830s the majority of the population was of African descent. Slaves far outnumbered whites in every coastal county, and black labor produced the abundant crops of rice and sea island cotton that sustained an export economy. Savannah merchants used their connections with Charleston, New York, and Europe to market staples and furnish planters' credit. Laborers loaded cotton on Savannah's wharves while slave and free artisans manufactured articles ranging from shoes to rice barrels in nearby shops. Part metropolis and part tropical plantation zone, the coastal region never contained more than a small fraction of Georgia's white population, but its elite merchants, wealthy planters, and eminent lawyers wielded disproportionate influence in state affairs.[1]

1

# Georgia Regions and Counties, 1860

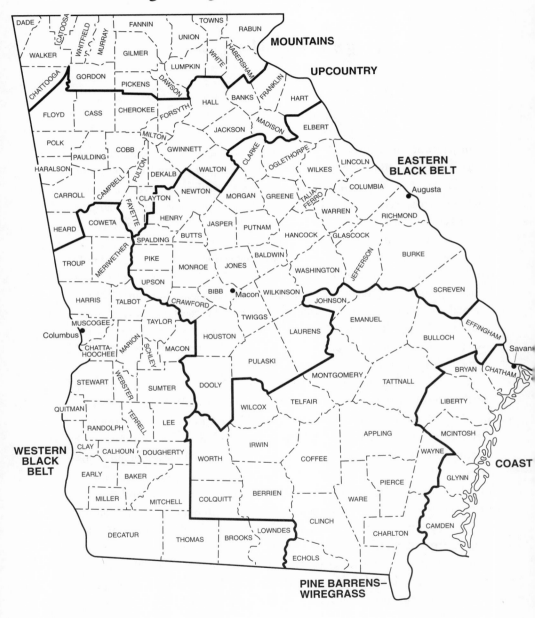

MOUNTAINS

UPCOUNTRY

EASTERN
BLACK BELT

WESTERN
BLACK
BELT

COAST

PINE BARRENS–
WIREGRASS

DADE
CATOOSA
WHITFIELD
MURRAY
FANNIN
TOWNS
UNION
RABUN
WALKER
GILMER
WHITE
HABERSHAM
LUMPKIN
CHATTOOGA
GORDON
DAWSON
FRANKLIN
PICKENS
HALL
BANKS
HART
FLOYD
CASS
CHEROKEE
FORSYTH
JACKSON
MADISON
ELBERT
POLK
MILTON
PAULDING
COBB
GWINNETT
CLARKE
OGLETHORPE
LINCOLN
HARALSON
CAMPBELL
FULTON
DEKALB
WALTON
WILKES
COLUMBIA
Augusta
CARROLL
CLAYTON
NEWTON
MORGAN
GREENE
TALIA-
FERRO
WARREN
RICHMOND
HEARD
COWETA
FAYETTE
HENRY
JASPER
PUTNAM
HANCOCK
GLASCOCK
BURKE
SPALDING
BUTTS
BALDWIN
SCREVEN
TROUP
MERIWETHER
PIKE
MONROE
JONES
WASHINGTON
JEFFERSON
UPSON
BIBB
Macon
WILKINSON
HARRIS
TALBOT
CRAWFORD
JOHNSON
MUSCOGEE
TAYLOR
TWIGGS
EMANUEL
EFFINGHAM
Columbus
CHATTA-
HOOCHEE
MARION
SCHLEY
MACON
HOUSTON
LAURENS
BULLOCH
Savan
STEWART
WEBSTER
SUMTER
DOOLY
PULASKI
MONTGOMERY
TATTNALL
BRYAN
CHATHAM
QUITMAN
TERRELL
LEE
WILCOX
TELFAIR
LIBERTY
RANDOLPH
CLAY
CALHOUN
DOUGHERTY
IRWIN
APPLING
MCINTOSH
WAYNE
EARLY
BAKER
WORTH
COFFEE
GLYNN
MILLER
MITCHELL
COLQUITT
BERRIEN
PIERCE
WARE
DECATUR
THOMAS
BROOKS
LOWNDES
CLINCH
CHARLTON
CAMDEN
ECHOLS

## Table 1. Population by Regions, 1830

|  | Total Population | White | Slave | % Slave | % of State Population |
|---|---|---|---|---|---|
| Mountains | 12,847 | 11,872 | 968 | 7.5 | 2.5 |
| Upcountry | 82,011 | 64,593 | 17,028 | 20.8 | 15.9 |
| Black belt | 364,878 | 196,645 | 166,825 | 45.7 | 70.6 |
| Pine barrens– |  |  |  |  |  |
| wiregrass | 18,445 | 14,009 | 4,350 | 23.6 | 3.6 |
| Coast | 38,642 | 9,687 | 28,352 | 73.4 | 7.5 |
| Total | 516,823 | 296,806 | 217,523 | 42.1 | 100.1 |

*Source: Fifth Census of the United States, 1830.*

*Note:* Percentage totals in tables may not equal 100 percent due to rounding.

## Table 2. Population by Regions, 1840

|  | Total Population | White | Slave | % Slave | % of State Population |
|---|---|---|---|---|---|
| Mountains | 37,301 | 32,872 | 4,358 | 11.7 | 5.4 |
| Upcountry | 119,855 | 94,803 | 24,986 | 20.8 | 17.3 |
| Black belt | 464,195 | 248,403 | 214,177 | 46.1 | 67.1 |
| Pine barrens– |  |  |  |  |  |
| wiregrass | 24,080 | 18,031 | 5,975 | 24.8 | 3.5 |
| Coast | 45,961 | 13,586 | 31,538 | 68.6 | 6.6 |
| Total | 691,392 | 407,695 | 281,034 | 40.6 | 99.9 |

*Source: Sixth Census of the United States, 1840.*

## Table 3. Population by Regions, 1850

| | Total Population | White | Slave | % Slave | % of State Population |
|---|---|---|---|---|---|
| Mountains | 78,993 | 69,918 | 8,995 | 11.4 | 8.7 |
| Upcountry | 168,361 | 131,510 | 36,632 | 21.8 | 18.6 |
| Black belt | 572,846 | 278,688 | 292,456 | 51.1 | 63.2 |
| Pine barrens– wiregrass | 33,455 | 25,047 | 8,321 | 24.9 | 3.7 |
| Coast | 52,530 | 16,409 | 35,278 | 67.2 | 5.8 |
| Total | 906,185 | 521,572 | 381,682 | 42.1 | 100 |

*Source: Seventh Census of the United States, 1850.*

## Table 4. Population by Regions, 1860

| | Total Population | White | Slave | % Slave | % of State Population |
|---|---|---|---|---|---|
| Mountains | 97,394 | 84,526 | 12,673 | 13.0 | 9.2 |
| Upcountry | 215,173 | 162,322 | 52,519 | 24.4 | 20.4 |
| Black belt | 626,742 | 277,254 | 347,452 | 55.4 | 59.3 |
| Pine barrens– wiregrass | 59,697 | 44,302 | 15,240 | 25.5 | 5.6 |
| Coast | 58,280 | 23,184 | 34,314 | 58.9 | 5.5 |
| Total | 1,057,286 | 591,588 | 462,198 | 43.7 | 100 |

*Source: Eighth Census of the United States, 1860.*

The politically and economically marginal pine barrens–wiregrass region formed a barrier between the coast and the rest of Georgia. Slaves comprised one quarter of the population, but the region was no plantation belt. The sandy, low hills covered with clumps of wiregrass and the swampy flatlands shaded by pine trees offered poor agricultural prospects. Other Georgians often ridiculed the supposedly ignorant and backward "pine woods boys," who earned a living through grazing livestock and exploiting the timber resources for lumber, tar, and turpentine. The absence of sizable towns and the scattering of farmsteads over a huge area gave much of the pine barrens–wiregrass an uninhabited look; it long remained the least developed region of the state.[2]

North of the pine barrens–wiregrass lay the red clay and sandy loam soils of the piedmont, the center of the state's population and wealth. Two out of every three Georgians in 1830 lived within a ninety-mile radius of the state capital at Milledgeville. Tobacco had been the main staple crop in the early years of white settlement, but the expansion of short-staple cotton production after the invention of the cotton gin rapidly transformed the piedmont into a cotton kingdom. In the mid-1820s, Georgia surpassed South Carolina to become, for a time, the leading cotton state, and the cotton crop mounted steadily from 90,000 bales in 1821 to 326,000 bales in 1839. The cotton crop reached market through the towns located on the fall lines of the major rivers: Augusta on the Savannah, Milledgeville on the Oconee, Macon on the Ocmulgee, and Columbus on the Chattahoochee. By the 1830s, erosion and constant cotton cultivation had already diminished the fertility of many eastern piedmont tracts. The resulting search for fresh lands moved slaveholders and their chattels ever westward during the antebellum period, creating a plantation belt that stretched from the Savannah River to the Alabama border.

An indistinct economic and demographic line separated the piedmont into upper and lower sections. The white yeoman farmers—nonslaveholders and small slaveholders who lived in the upper piedmont, or upcountry—grew mainly food crops and marketed their surplus produce; household subsistence was the focus of upcountry agriculture. Many farmers, to be sure, also raised a bale or two of cotton, even in the early years, and cotton production expanded over time. Although slaveless yeoman households predominated, slavery was hardly an insignificant factor: one out of every five upcountry residents was a slave. White upcountry families already comprised more than 20 percent of Georgia's white population in 1830, even though much of the region was still a frontier, and the upcountry's strength in terms of political leadership and voting numbers would increase throughout the last three antebellum decades.

Nonslaveholders also formed a majority of the white population in the lower piedmont, or black belt, region, but it was a land dominated by masters whose slaves tilled fields of cotton and corn. The older, eastern portion of the black belt was known colloquially as "middle Georgia." Slaves outnumbered whites in this area, which centered on Wilkes County. Georgians distinguished between middle Georgia and the newer counties in the west and the southwest near Columbus, which were just developing as cotton plantation lands. The size of black belt slaveholdings varied widely: most slave owners operated on a modest scale with one or two black families, although the largest planters owned several dozen slaves or more. More than any other set of men, the slaveholding lawyers and planters of the black belt controlled state politics. Leadership and votes from this large, rich region formed the foundation of every statewide political party in antebellum Georgia.[3]

Huge tracts of Georgia's territory were freshly settled—or, rather, re-settled—during the 1830s, following the removal of the Creek and Cherokee Indians. A series of cessions from the Creeks, culminating in 1827 with the extinguishment of the final Creek claims in Georgia, opened the way for a rush of emigration to the west and southwest. Meanwhile, the discovery of gold in northwest Georgia in 1829 prompted the state government to extend its laws over the Cherokee nation. Protracted, coercive treaty negotiations and Georgia's defiance of an adverse Supreme Court decision eventually forced the Cherokees to cede the remainder of their lands and move west of the Mississippi River. By the time the United States Army removed the last reluctant Cherokees in 1838, white settlers had already occupied much of the Indians' former domain.[4]

The western Creek lands quickly became part of the plantation belt, while white yeomen staked their claims to Cherokee Georgia. The final Cherokee cessions included several upcountry counties and most of the mountain region. The mountain counties stretching from the Appalachian Valley in the northwest to the Blue Ridge in the northeast featured marvelous scenery and fertile valley soils, but the short growing season and transportation problems limited the production of market crops. Most white families lived by raising corn and vegetables, running livestock, and hunting game. Household production remained an important part of mountain women's duties well after such traditions waned in other parts of America. Andrew Jackson Gass, whose family's political leanings might be surmised, remembered that during his boyhood in a Dade County cabin, his mother had sung him to sleep many times with her spinning wheel. Few mountain families owned a single slave, yet even here, slavery was a growing presence. The mountain population, very small in 1830, climbed steadily over the years, until mountain folk, too, exerted crucial influence in state politics.[5]

Frontier expansion and explosive population growth led to the creation of forty-six new counties between 1820 and 1840. The state disposed of these new lands through a lottery system that gave every adult white male taxpayer (and widows and other special persons) at least one chance to win the right to purchase homesteads for a few cents an acre. Not all the winners settled their parcels, of course, and land speculators and the wealthier farmers enlarged their holdings by purchasing claims. But the lottery initially helped to distribute land widely among the white population. Most white men had, and more aspired to, a freehold that would allow them to farm independently; independent landownership was the social ideal.[6]

Perhaps the most obvious fact about antebellum Georgia, and the most important, was that the white adult males who directly participated in politics were in themselves an elite. Society, in broad terms, was organized around farm households headed by white men, who ruled over their own families and held black families in bondage. Whatever the exceptions or limitations in individual cases, white men as a whole wielded immense social and economic power and zealously guarded their prerogatives. The denial of rights to others defined the boundaries of white men's sphere. White men excluded children, white women, and free blacks from voting or exercising other important rights, and slightly more than 40 percent of Georgians were legally chattel. Voters therefore amounted to little more than a tenth of the total population, and a statewide party majority could be fashioned by carrying the votes of a shade over 5 percent of all Georgians. Inequality was fundamental; white men controlled society and politics.[7]

The sovereign white men were southern–born, Protestant farmers residing on scattered homesteads and plantations. Just above 98 percent of

Georgia's white population in 1850 was native-born; almost three quarters had been born in the state, and nearly all of the rest were native Southerners, chiefly from North and South Carolina. More than eighty thousand male Georgians listed their occupation as farmer in the 1850 census. When farmers were combined with the more than ten thousand (mainly farm) laborers, nearly two thousand planters, and more than two thousand overseers, the proportion of adult white men officially recorded as being engaged primarily in agriculture neared 80 percent; the actual percentage was probably higher. The artisan trades, notably blacksmithing and carpentry, furnished employment for around ten thousand, while some four thousand worked as clerks or merchants. Industrial and manufacturing enterprises, apart from household production, were a comparatively small part of the state economy and were usually closely linked to the land. Saw and grist mills, as leading examples, were basically rural enterprises subsidiary to agriculture. Business, too, centered on marketing cotton and other staples and providing merchant goods for plantations and farms. Although small villages were scattered around the state, and the cities of Savannah, Augusta, Macon, Columbus, and, eventually, Atlanta reached appreciable size, fewer than 5 percent of Georgia whites in 1850 lived in towns with populations greater than two thousand—the overall population density was less than sixteen persons per square mile. People came to towns and tiny county seats infrequently, perhaps to buy a few supplies or to go to a Sunday meeting, or for men to vote or to attend court. In religion, the Baptist and Methodist churches claimed the allegiance of an overwhelming majority of churchgoing whites, with the Presbyterians a poor third.[8]

Class distinctions, in the sense of vast differences in wealth and perceived gradations in social status, separated white men into poorer tenants and laborers, yeomen, small slaveholders, and planters, with townsmen and artisans of various occupations falling somewhere toward the middle or upper range of the hierarchy. The poor whites at the bottom often struggled simply for something to eat and frequently moved from county to county (or from state to state) seeking fresh starts. The number of landless men grew over the antebellum period, and levels of farm tenancy on the eve of the Civil War ranged from less than 10 percent to nearly 40 percent, depending on the county, with the levels often highest in nonplantation areas. Many young landless men were still saving to buy homesteads or waiting to inherit from landholding relatives, but considerable numbers of truly poor whites had either permanently lost their land or had never owned an acre—and might never own one.[9]

Most white men, however, possessed at least enough property—typically a small farm, tools, and livestock—to provide an adequate living. Yeomen and their families, accustomed to hard toil and proud of their independence, formed a large part, and often a large majority, of the white population in counties across Georgia. Joe Free, whose parents, Peter and Ruthie, raised him in Cherokee Georgia, recalled that the family lived in a log house on 160 acres. Peter farmed and Ruthie made the family's clothes, among countless other household tasks. Everyone did their own work, as Joe Free remembered it; there were no slaves in his community. Charles Beasley's memories were much the same, except that plenty of slaveholders resided in black belt Clarke County, and lots more passed through while attending Franklin College (later the University of Georgia) at Athens. Beasley's family owned 40 acres and a three-room log house—not much by the standards of Clarke County planters, but enough to earn respect, and whites in the "neighborhood all mingled freely together." Once out from under their father's roof and settled on their own land, yeomen took neither orders easily nor insults lightly. A white man's honor meant something: a careless remark, if resented and not quickly withdrawn, might lose the offender his life in a duel or an eye in a brutal brawl. Lesser property, in the minds of yeomen, did not a lesser man make; those who worked honestly and protected their families were the equals of any man.[10]

Nonetheless, the top one or two deciles of property holders held a large share of the wealth in most Georgia counties—and, indeed, in most counties in antebellum America. A single adult slave was worth hundreds of dollars, and ownership of a few slaves made even a small slaveholder far wealthier than the average yeoman. James Haynes, born in the upcountry near Alpharetta, remembered that his father, Richard, worked several slaves on 300 acres. Richard also helped operate a cotton gin; his property holdings totaled around eight thousand dollars. An even greater disparity in wealth separated lawyer-planters such as Alexander Stephens, Robert Toombs, and Howell Cobb—the three most prominent politicians in Georgia during the 1840s and 1850s—from the common folk they represented. A year's income for such men might exceed what some poor whites earned in a lifetime.

Wealth meant public power: slaveholders, especially planters, held a disproportionate share of the political offices, and no internal political movement
ever remotely challenged the existence of slavery at any time during the
decades preceding the Civil War. Not all planters, much less all slaveholders,
became politicians, but no poor whites sat in Congress or lounged in the
governor's chair.[11]

For all the differences in wealth and power between white men, the lines
demarking classes blurred in everyday life. Many factors encouraged white
Georgians to see their neighbors as individuals grouped into households
rather than as members of a class. Regardless of region, occupation, or
wealth, the seasonal rhythms of agriculture—yearly rounds of cotton picking, corn shucking, and hog killing—shaped the lives of all. The inex-
haustible subject of weather and crops supplied topics suitable both for a
moment's conversation and for hours of mutual reflection on a rainy after-
noon. Rural churches and schools mixed adults and children from all ranks.
Women assembled, far too infrequently to suit them, for weddings, charity
functions, quiltings, and other social affairs. Men gathered, much more
regularly, to drink, gamble, and gossip in courthouse taverns, in crossroads
stores, at militia musters, on hunting trips, and, if need be, out behind
barns. Friendliness toward neighbors was important when neighbors were
scarce.

Despite the dispersed settlement and restless migration, the small size of
communities ensured that white men knew the other white men around
them. Strangers were few in a county such as coastal Glynn, where only 102
voters came to the polls in the 1840 presidential election. But even Muscogee County, the site of Columbus, returned only 1,855 votes that year—the
largest Georgia county total in a contest noted for vast turnouts. Although
the voting population increased considerably during the 1840s, both the
mean and the average number of voters per county remained below 1,000 at
the end of the decade. Just three counties returned more than 2,000 votes in
the 1848 presidential election; twenty counties returned less than 500 votes.
White men actually voted, moreover, at district polling places that brought
together only men from immediately surrounding neighborhoods—usually
a few score voters at most. The men who held offices and those who appeared at the polls were familiar faces rather than anonymous figures.[12]

Blood ties bound neighborhoods together and shaped political behavior.

Democratic politics in and around Appling County, for example, long centered on the Hall clan. The Georgia family patriarch was Lewis Hall, a Revolutionary War officer, holder of numerous Tattnall County posts, and the father of eighteen children by two wives. Two of Lewis Hall's sons, Instance and Seaborn, served multiple terms in the legislature; a third son, Enoch, was a county tax collector and inferior court justice. Furthermore, the Halls forged myriad links with the extensive Johnson family through marriage. Jehu Hall's wife was Catherine Johnson, the daughter of Malcolm, an inferior court justice for eleven years. Malcolm Johnson's brother, Duncan, was also an inferior court justice, a tax collector, and a state legislator for three terms. Moreover, Duncan Johnson and Instance Hall were brothers-in-law, having married sisters Lujoice and Drusilla Sellars. Finally, preparing for the next generation of officeholders, Instance Hall's daughter, Drusilla, married Obediah Johnson, the brother of Catherine Johnson Hall; and Lemuel Sellars, the brother of Lujoice and Drusilla, married Seaborn Hall's daughter, Elizabeth. Dense kinship networks among leading families played a crucial role in structuring county politics.[13]

The mercantile trades were highly competitive, and the struggle to control good land pitted men against one another, but no inevitable economic conflict existed between planters or between planters and lesser farmers. Most white men did not work directly for other, unrelated men; neither clashes between employers and employees nor competition among wage laborers was central to productive relations. Cotton planters' profits depended on the vagaries of world demand and supply, while most yeomen worried about securing household sufficiency and raising relatively small surpluses for sale in limited markets. On the local scale, farming could hardly be viewed as a zero-sum game: a timely rain that fell on a planter's cotton also watered a yeoman's corn. The uncharitable might pray for a Mississippi drought and an accompanying rise in crop prices, but a dry spell in Georgia imperiled everyone's livelihood. Finally, although classes intermingled in all counties, planters and yeomen tended to cluster in different regions. On an everyday basis, what happened on somebody else's land in another county a hundred or two hundred miles away scarcely concerned either black belt planters or north Georgia yeomen; all had their own work to do.

Coexistence and cooperation characterized much of economic life; deeply rooted patterns of exchange and obligation—not unique to rural Georgia—

knitted communities together. The likeliest sources of credit locally were neighbors with money or goods to spare. Banks, which were widely scattered in any case, mainly financed larger commercial activities. Alexander Stephens and his half-brother, Linton, for example, routinely aided poorer neighbors with a sack of corn or an odd dollar. Notes recording small loans appear in the estates of planters and yeomen alike, and a side of bacon bartered for some corn exemplified common exchanges between kin and acquaintances. Access to a planter's cotton gin or a gristmill allowed the average farmer to earn cash dollars to purchase tobacco, coffee, or miscellaneous store goods. A few days' labor from a yeoman's sons or a planter's slaves, to be repaid later in kind, could save a sick farmer's harvest and his family from disaster.[14]

Common political ideas and vocabulary—shared ways of thinking and talking about politics and society—further united white men. Antebellum parties, without exception, paid homage to the greatness of America's founders. White men especially venerated George Washington and Thomas Jefferson, and they accepted as truth the latter's states' rights, republican creed: that the federal government had limited powers, enumerated in the Constitution; that all powers not granted to the federal government were reserved to the states; and that only a strict construction of the Constitution could maintain the balance between state and federal powers. Government existed to protect the liberty, property, and civil equality of white men. Republics were fragile entities prone to corruption and decay, and concentrated power—political, economic, sectional, or conspiratorial—endangered liberty. Freedom's only sure protection lay in the vigilance of a virtuous, independent citizenry—ideally, a body of landholding farmers. Threats to liberty had to be met at the threshold; the unresisted loss of any right would lead to the loss of all rights, to slavery. Statesmen in a model republic did not seek office; they awaited the summons of the people. Once called to serve, leaders guarded liberty, promoted *the* public interest, and preserved a united, free commonwealth.[15]

Republican ideology remained the touchstone of Georgia's political culture long after it had been modified and compromised. From the 1820s on, politicians, regardless of their rhetorical disclaimers, avidly sought office without awaiting spontaneous invitations from the people—a candid observer in 1828 compared rival candidates to "ram goats contending for a stump." [16] Factions and parties divided white men politically throughout the antebellum period, and noisy clashes between contending interests belied the notion of a single public good. Men could and did fight to defend liberty in manifold, contradictory ways; some followed paths toward safety and prosperity that others contended would lead to inevitable doom. States' rights doctrines were far from timeless and could be conveniently construed to apply to changing circumstances and altered cases. Over time, fears of corruption and decay increasingly focused simply on political opponents, whose supposedly insidious plots could be labeled unrepublican.

Still, despite the widening gap between practice and theory, republican ideas retained force enough to set the parameters of political conflict. Obligatory talk of offices as unsolicited gifts from the people acknowledged that the great body of white men was the source of sovereign power. The persistence of antiparty spirit and paeans to nonpartisanship amidst bitter party warfare reflected the belief that white men could be united in pursuing common interests and upholding common values. Even as the legislature chartered ever more banks, corporations, and railroads, apprehensions lingered about the potentially evil influences of powerful institutions. Republican emphasis on minority rights, though diluted by a countervailing, growing commitment to majority rule, armed Georgia parties with ideological weapons to combat perceived northern aggressions. Most important, although white men redefined republicanism to legitimize partisan debate over means, they never permitted effective questioning of the ultimate end: preserving and reserving liberty for themselves. The lack of ready-made policy prescriptions, however, made applying received ideology to the problems of a white men's democracy an ongoing, contentious process. [17]

Above all, white men agreed that they were superior to, and ordained to rule over, the other sex and other races. "Order and subordination, according to the natural fitness of things," Alexander Stephens once said in Congress, "is the principle upon which the whole fabric of our southern institutions rests." Nodding toward the Declaration of Independence, Stephens conceded that, perhaps, in an ideal world, all men would be equally free— he did not contemplate women's freedom—but the "law of nature" in the world as it *was* dictated freedom for some and degrees of dependence for the many. "Do what you will," Stephens intoned, "a negro is a negro, and he will remain a negro still. In the social and political system of the South the negro is assigned to that subordinate position for which he is fitted by the laws of nature." Like the Jews of ancient times, southern slaveholders took their chattels "from the heathen tribes." "Men of our own blood and our own race, wherever born, or from whatever clime they come, are free and equal," Stephens boasted. "We have no castes or classes amongst white men." [18]

Alexander Stephens was but one of the believers. In the early decades of the nineteenth century, many white Southerners were willing, like Thomas Jefferson, to call slavery an evil and to contemplate its eventual elimination. Never, however, did such antislavery sentiments create significant white opposition to the institution in Georgia or prompt the state government to take action against slavery. Then, from the 1820s on, the rise of King Cotton, the emergence of immediate abolitionism in the North, and the general maturation of the Old South's slave society discouraged questioning, converted minds, and turned southern apologists toward an ever more aggressive defense of slavery. As a multifaceted proslavery ideology crystallized, a chorus of voices came to proclaim that continued freedom for white men depended on the perpetuation of African slavery. [19]

The founders of the nation, the *Augusta Chronicle & Sentinel* unhesitatingly declared in 1860, had held the "crude *opinion*" that slavery was wrong, and that lamentable error had led them to endorse the "*utter untruth*" about man's unalienable rights contained in Jefferson's Declaration. Otherwise wise men had failed to foresee "how vitally *all the interests* of civilization . . . would become wrapped up in and dependent upon the God-given institution of African slavery." Over time, the North had grown "rotten and corrupt," and the South had become "far purer, more enlightened, more moral, and in every respect more excellent than Northern" society. The "secret of the whole difference" lay in the keeping of "*negro slaves.*" All societies inevitably possessed working classes, degraded and ignorant laborers unfit to exercise the rights of citizenship. The great defect of northern capitalism was that ever larger numbers of nominally free laborers, white men, were reduced to wage slavery yet allowed to retain the ballot and war politically against their employers. Northern society, unless radically reformed, would inevitably collapse under its contradictions, but the southern regime of independent white men rested on a firmer foundation: the "*great laboring class*" was of a "different *caste* from the proprietary class—separate and distinct, and far apart as the poles." "The fact is," the *Chronicle & Sentinel* asserted, "African slavery is the very cornerstone of the Republic, and the only really conservative element in this government." [20]

The laws of nature and of God, as white Georgians came to understand them, sanctioned and recommended slavery. The conviction expressed by the *Augusta Chronicle* in 1835 that slavery was "a blessing, morally and physically, not only to the land in which it exists, but to the inferior race which it involves," waxed ever stronger. "History, whether sacred or profane," the *Augusta Constitutionalist* contended in 1853, "points to no era of the human race, when slavery did not exist." The "very nature and disposition of human beings" seemed to require "that there should be dominant and subject races," and the "time when that labor will be dispensed with cannot well be compassed by the imagination." Joseph Henry Lumpkin, one of the state's more learned and devout men, accepted it as an "undeniable truth, that no man is a believer in the Bible, who denies the lawfulness of negro slavery." Eugenius A. Nisbet, Lumpkin's judicial colleague, elaborated further in an 1852 decree from the state's supreme bench: "The curse of the Patriarch rests still upon the descendants of Ham. The Negro and his master are but fulfilling the divine appointment." Jesus Christ, rather than removing "the curse," had defined the obligations of master-slave relationships and had ordained slavery as an "Institution of Christianity." Alexander Stephens, in a farewell address delivered on his retirement from Congress in 1859, reassured white Georgians that slavery "rests upon principles that can never be successfully assailed by reason or argument"; it "will still grow stronger as discussion proceeds, and as time rolls on." "We hold our destiny in our own hands," Stephens concluded, "and in pursuing it to the end, we shall be but fulfilling a great mission in advancing a new order and a higher type of Christian civilization." [21]

The generally prosperous 1850s strengthened white men's faith in slavery and southern society. The state's population surpassed one million by 1860; black slaves comprised 43.7 percent of the total (see table 4, map 1). Except along the coast, where the concentration of slaves was already the highest in the state, the percentage of slaves in the population increased in every region between 1850 and 1860. White outmigration from the black belt made that region more than half slave, and almost 40 percent of the black belt's population in 1860 lived in the newer western cotton lands along the Flint River and the Alabama border—dramatic evidence of the vitality of slavery. Even large white population gains in the mountains and the upcountry, which brought north Georgia nearly to equality in white numbers with the black belt, failed to outpace the slave population's growth.

High cotton prices lured ever more farmers into growing the fleecy staple; total cotton production jumped 40.6 percent between 1850 and 1860. The number of bales raised nearly doubled in the mountains, slightly more than doubled in the upcountry, and almost quadrupled in the pine barrens– wiregrass. (Per capita gains in production amounted to 55.7 percent, 64.5 percent, and 117.9 percent in the three regions, respectively. The per capita increase in the black belt was 21.8 percent.) The black belt still accounted for more than four out of every five bales of cotton grown in 1860, but cotton growing had become an increasingly common venture for slaveholders and nonslaveholders alike—roughly two bales of cotton were raised for every three people in the state. The total corn crop, significantly, dropped 12.3 percent between 1850 and 1860. All of the decline, moreover, came in the upcountry and the black belt; the other three regions actually showed gains in per capita corn production. The expansion of slavery and cotton produc- tion increasingly tied the state's two main regions together, although it hardly obliterated distinctions between the black belt and the upcountry.[22]

Manufacturing development in the 1850s was considerable compared with neighboring states, but inconsequential compared with the North or Great Britain. A manufacturing labor force of 11,575 in 1860, 2,064 of whom were women, produced almost seventeen million dollars in goods. Sawmill workers alone comprised roughly 16 percent of manufacturing laborers. The "flagship" industry, cotton textiles, employed 2,813 hands, more than half of them women, in thirty-three factories. Although small country towns proliferated in the 1850s, in 1860 just 7.9 percent of the population and 8.6 percent of whites lived in towns with more than 2,000 people—fully a quar- ter of the town folk resided in Savannah. Aided by Atlanta's rapid growth as a railroad hub, the overall town population increased by about 3 percent after 1850, but Georgia remained decidedly rural. Citizens still could praise the enterprising spirit abroad in the "Empire State of the South" without feeling dislocated by the sort of drastic social and economic change that swept across the antebellum Northeast.[23]

White Georgians assuredly recognized the difference. Sectional conflict promoted an increasingly acute consciousness of southern identity, a recognition and celebration of the distinctiveness of southern society. Hostility toward Yankees, whom newspaperman J. Henly Smith roughly described as "the whole New England race," was especially pervasive. "The greatest calamity that ever happened to this country," Smith told Alexander Stephens, "was that the Mayflower, with all on board, was not swamped before they reached these shores." Northerners, many believed, were "trained to hate us! every school-book is filled with pictures of naked slaves toiling under the lash." Meddlesome and jealous northern critics refused to acknowledge that slavery and cotton had "produced the unparalleled prosperity of the southern States" and had placed the South "in a position more independent and commanding, than that of any other political community upon the face of the globe." Cotton furnished "the material basis of one-half the commerce of the world," the *Savannah Republican* exulted, and southern "institutions are as firmly fixed, and must endure as long, as commerce and manufactures flourish in the world." To strike at slavery was to attack the "main prop of national wealth and civilization." Yet strike outsiders did, and every blow heightened sensitivities, underscored the need for white unity, and alienated white men further from their northern brethren.[24]

White men in antebellum Georgia unquestionably had much to defend and to explain to an ever more hostile world. Unity was, of course, imperfect. The dominant ideology notwithstanding, white men were far from equal, and at various mental levels they knew it. Planters and politicians occasionally wondered about the loyalty of poor whites and yeomen. Mountain whites muttered about coastal nabobs, and upcountry leaders contested the black belt's political power. Neighborhoods were not idyllic places with frictionless human relations. Disagreements among whites over innumerable matters, large and small, sparked tensions. Nor were white men always and indisputably masters of their own households. Wives deserted husbands, husbands fled in shame, daughters bridled at paternal authority, and sons challenged fathers' judgment. Some slaves fought whippings, ran away, or killed their masters; and the others resisted bondage less dramatically, physically and psychologically, day after day over their lifetimes. The dominant ideology, again, notwithstanding, whites were never as sure as they wanted to be that slaves would not and could not—certainly, probably not—rise in rebellion. Indeed, terror over the thought at times brought quarreling whites suddenly together inside a circle of fear.

Conflicts between various opposing factions and parties produced the most obvious and extensive evidence of discord among white men, and those conflicts and that evidence form the substance of this book. Partisans argued over banks, tariffs, railroads, and countless other issues. Mostly, though, and most significantly, parties battled over how best to protect the institution of slavery and the white male–dominated society that slavery had shaped. White's men fundamental commitment to that fundamental goal sharply constricted political debate. Except in scattered instances, political leaders did not appeal to class differences among white men; on the contrary, they insistently denied that such differences existed. And in a crucial sense, they were right: white men in antebellum Georgia experienced a world riven primarily by race and gender, not by class. Maintaining boundaries that forced the vast majority of the population into relations of political, economic, and social dependence mattered more than differentiating between classes of independent white men. Whatever the wealth or status of individuals, white men collectively possessed rights and privileges that belonged to them alone.

# TWO

# "Animosities Which Neither Time nor Reflection Ever Healed": The Formation of Georgia's Jacksonian Parties

George Gilmer, a veteran factional warrior and seasoned officeholder who well knew the idiosyncrasies of Georgia politics, once described, in a single sentence, a formative process that transpired over more than a dozen years: "All in Georgia were Jackson men whilst Gen. Jackson was in office, the Clark party from choice, the Crawford party from necessity, so that the old factions began to lose their lines of demarcation, and new parties to be formed upon the general principles which divided the people of the United States."[1] During Andrew Jackson's presidency, the Troup and Clark factions that had controlled state politics for decades disintegrated, and new organizations, the Union and State Rights parties, emerged to claim the allegiance of white men. The fledgling parties slowly, haltingly aligned themselves with Democratic and Whig parties elsewhere until, by 1840, Georgians were enmeshed in the national Jacksonian party system.

The conflicts between Federalists and Republicans that defined the early political history of many states had little relevance within Georgia, where men engaged in their own peculiar quarrels. Overwhelming opposition to Alexander Hamilton's financial program and to other Federalist measures prevented the formation of an organized Federalist party; scattered areas along the coast, the cities of Savannah and Augusta, and a couple of piedmont counties constituted the only Federalist enclaves. Federalist strength peaked in 1796, when John Adams carried perhaps a quarter of the state vote, and declined rapidly thereafter. Acting with virtual unanimity in an era of vitriolic national debate, Georgia cast its electoral votes three times for Thomas Jefferson and twice for each succeeding member of the Virginia Dynasty.

Early Georgia politics revolved around personalities. The state's most important political figure at the turn of the century was James Jackson, a headstrong Revolutionary War hero from Savannah who served as governor, congressman, and United States senator. A personal faction composed of Jackson and his friends first organized during the furor over the Yazoo land frauds in the mid-1790s subsequently dominated state politics. Following Jackson's death in 1806, leadership of the faction passed to William H. Crawford and George M. Troup. Crawford was a native Virginian whose family had moved to Georgia in 1783 and had settled along the Broad River in the neighborhood of other Virginia emigrants. He rose quickly in politics and, after an apprenticeship in the state legislature, in 1807 took a seat in the United States Senate. Troup meanwhile focused on managing the state's affairs. Born in 1780 along the frontier in what became Alabama, Troup graduated from Princeton before beginning a career as a Savannah lawyer, gentleman planter, and political chieftain. Opposition to the Jackson-Crawford-Troup faction came from the allies of John Clark, the son of a Revolutionary War general and no stranger to dueling grounds and military camps. One opponent remembered Clark as a rowdy with "the temper of a clansman," who demanded that every man "be for or against him" and "suffered no one of any consequence to occupy middle ground."[2]

The animosities that divided Troupites and Clarkites were obscurely rooted in rivalries between piedmont settlers in the era immediately following the American Revolution. The area along the Broad River in Elbert and Wilkes Counties was settled chiefly by emigrants from Virginia and North Carolina, respectively, and each group developed its own network of personal alliances and kin relationships. Leaders of the Virginians, who were perhaps slightly wealthier and possessed greater pretensions to distinguished ancestry, looked down on North Carolinians generally and particularly detested John Clark. Over the years, contests for political offices and militia appointments, disputes over the Yazoo sales and other western land schemes, and numerous personal altercations deepened and widened the divisions between the two factions. Troupites, in general, amassed strength in the low country and in the easternmost counties of the developing black belt, while John Clark and his allies appealed to settlers on the expanding frontier. If Troupites and Clarkites were not always sure what they differed over, they did differ violently, as exemplified by the 1806 duel between John Clark and William Crawford in which the latter received a pistol ball that shattered his left wrist.[3]

Georgia partisans competed under the constitution of 1798, which, with amendments, served as the state's fundamental law until 1861. The constitution divided the state government into legislative, executive, and judicial branches and established the framework for county government. The eligible electorate, all white male taxpayers at least twenty-one years old, annually chose the members of the bicameral legislature. Every county had at least one member in the state house of representatives and the state senate, and additional seats in the house were apportioned according to a scale of representative population, which included all free white persons and "three-fifths of all the people of color." A state census taken every seven years provided the basis for apportionment, and senators and representatives had to meet property qualifications to be eligible for office.

The governor, who was also subject to property qualifications, was elected by the legislature to a two-year term. His duties included commanding the state militia, granting pardons, and appointing persons to fill vacant offices. The governor possessed the veto power, but the legislature could override his veto by a two-thirds vote of both houses. The judicial branch consisted of inferior and superior courts that met at least twice yearly in each county and of two justices of the peace in each militia district. Originally, the state legislature and the governor selected these officials, but constitutional amendments in the 1810s gave county voters the right to elect inferior court justices and justices of the peace. The inferior court justices tried civil cases, supervised road maintenance, distributed school funds, and generally managed county affairs.[4]

The legislature's dominance in state affairs long inhibited the development of political parties. Prominent men usually announced their candidacies, either in newspapers or by word of mouth, and ran for the legislature on their own merits without party distinctions. Close legislative races were rare; those counties with definite political leanings heavily favored either Troupites or Clarkites. Large-scale political organizations were unnecessary and unwanted, and the Troup and Clark factions were not parties in any meaningful sense. They lacked state- and, normally, county-level organization, followed no regular nominating procedures, and seldom fielded full tickets in any election. No differences on state policy consistently divided Troupites from Clarkites; factional lines in the legislature emerged primarily during contests over offices. The absence of any statewide gubernatorial or presidential races between 1800 and 1825 (the legislature also chose presidential electors) precludes an estimate of the two factions' popular strength during those years. Congressional elections did involve statewide voting under the general ticket system, but the voting totals display no party pattern. Around half of the eligible voters participated in an average congressional election, and voters often cast ballots only for a few popular favorites rather than for a full complement of candidates.

Factional divisions remained inchoate until a series of contests between 1819 and 1825 extended the Troup-Clark alignment throughout the state. George Troup lost the governorship to John Clark in both 1819 and 1821 before finally beating the Clarkite Matthew Talbot in the 1823 election. Along with consolidating factional lines in the legislature, these battles heightened public interest in state politics and led to an 1824 constitutional amendment that provided for the popular election of governors. That same year, Troupite leader William H. Crawford's candidacy shattered Georgia's heretofore monolithic front in presidential politics. Clarkites, unwilling to back an ancient enemy, turned to General Andrew Jackson, a legendary Indian fighter, the hero of the Battle of New Orleans, and a sometime Republican politician from Tennessee. Jackson's warm friendship with John Clark and his enmity for Crawford placed the presidential race within the familiar personal context of the Troup and Clark factions. The legislature decided the contest, giving Georgia's electoral votes to Crawford, but a constitutional amendment adopted soon afterward turned the selection of presidential electors over to the voters. Procedural changes that placed elections directly in the hands of the mass of white men compelled leaders to conduct statewide, popular campaigns for gubernatorial and presidential candidates and propelled them toward creating political organizations that united allies across county borders.[5]

The cohesive power of the Troup and Clark factions peaked in 1825, when the two leaders clashed for the last time. An observer remembered that the "virulence of party . . . pervaded every family, creating animosities which neither time nor reflection ever healed."[6] The campaign combined personal enmity with concerns about Indian removal, an issue of considerable importance to white men who coveted tribal lands. Governor Troup was engaged in a controversy with President John Quincy Adams over the dubious Treaty of Indian Springs, which had supposedly ceded the remainder of the Creek lands in Georgia. Troup's vehement insistence that Adams honor the treaty threatened to embroil Georgia in hostilities with the federal government. Clarkites, while wholeheartedly endorsing Creek removal, made criticism of Troup's impulsiveness their key issue. More than four-fifths of the eligible voters came to the polls and narrowly reelected Troup; a disappointed John Clark soon moved to Florida.

The waning of the Troup–Clark rivalry after 1825 coincided with the rise of Andrew Jackson as an overshadowing figure. With William Crawford sidelined by illness and defeat, the 1826 legislature almost unanimously endorsed Jackson for the presidency. The formation of two Jackson electoral tickets in 1828—the Troupite slate won—further demonstrated Old Hickory's appeal. Jackson's forceful personality, obsessive concern with honor, fabled military career, and status as a slaveholding planter made him a model of southern white manhood and brought him victory in Georgia. His championing of Cherokee removal then cemented a popularity that long forbade opposition; state political movements for the next eight years hinged on reactions to Jackson's conduct.[7]

Jackson's appointment of John MacPherson Berrien of Savannah as attorney general of the United States had important long-term consequences. Berrien's family, originally from New Jersey, had moved to Georgia when John was a child. A Princeton graduate at the age of fifteen, the intelligent, cultured Berrien had overcome the political persecution suffered by his Federalist father and had become a prominent Troupite even while retaining many of his father's political sympathies. Berrien was a wealthy rice planter and a respected lawyer, a habitually reserved man who was extremely conscious of his own rectitude. His selection for Jackson's cabinet was odd in that the two men could hardly have been more different, and ironic in that it would be Berrien who would ultimately raise a Georgia party in opposition to Jackson's Democratic legions.[8]

The turbulent early years of Jackson's presidency splintered the Troupite leadership and disrupted Georgia's outmoded factional system. Jealous competition between Secretary of State Martin Van Buren and Vice President John C. Calhoun, which found expression in the notorious Peggy Eaton affair that resulted in the early 1831 dissolution of the cabinet, ruined old political friendships. Calhoun's Clarkite allies, once attracted to him by his long-standing feud with William Crawford, disowned him when he broke with Jackson. John Berrien, unwillingly caught on Calhoun's losing side in the cabinet imbroglio, came home denouncing former Troupite favorite Martin Van Buren. While Berrien, wary of Jackson's popularity, covertly and futilely tried to rally an anti-Jackson Troupite nucleus, former governor John Forsyth emerged as the leader of the Troupites most devoted to Old Hickory.

Behind this welter of personal antagonisms lay the burgeoning controversy over the tariff. Congress had passed several protective tariff bills since the War of 1812, including the highly protective measure of 1828, the "Tariff of Abominations." Georgians had tolerated, occasionally even supported, earlier tariff bills for reasons related to national defense, but by 1828 the limit of patriotic altruism had been reached. White men committed to an agricultural slave economy came to view protective tariffs as unjust, unconstitutional taxes wrung from southern planters and farmers to bestow bounties on greedy northern manufacturers. The passage of the 1828 bill sparked several protest meetings in locations around the state, and John Berrien headed the politicians who noisily equated protectionism with robbery.

The question in Georgia was *how*, not *whether*, to oppose the 1828 tariff, and debates centered on problems of political tactics and constitutional theory surrounding John C. Calhoun's doctrine of nullification. Calhoun's ideas rested on familiar premises: the original sovereignty of the states, the formation of the Union as a compact, the necessity for strict construction of the Constitution, and the reserved rights of the states. From these first principles, Calhoun arrived at one conclusion that few white men in Georgia doubted by 1828: protective tariffs represented a congressional abuse of the limited grant of power to raise revenue and were therefore unconstitutional. Calhoun's proposed method for handling disputes regarding the rightful powers of the federal government, however, aroused vast controversy. The states, Calhoun declared, were the final arbiters of the constitutionality of federal laws. States, acting individually through state conventions, could interpose their authority, nullify unconstitutional federal acts, and prevent the execution of the offensive laws within their borders. If negotiation or constitutional amendments failed to resolve the conflict, the offended states could resort to secession.[9]

By mid-1831 it appeared likely that South Carolina might act on Calhoun's theories and attempt to nullify the 1828 tariff. Since Andrew Jackson loathed Calhoun and had publicly condemned nullification, any clash between South Carolina and the federal government portended a crisis of the Union. By bringing into conflict concerns over the protective tariff, allegiance to states' rights, love for the Union, and loyalty to Andrew Jackson, the nullification controversy sparked a realignment in which new political parties organized along ideological lines superseded the archaic Troup-Clark factions.

The Clarkites, who had faltered badly in recent state elections, moved first and decisively to embrace the cause of Andrew Jackson and the Union. One of Calhoun's erstwhile Clarkite friends, Milledgeville physician Tomlinson Fort, informed him that many citizens sensed a "powerful passion of disloyalty" behind nullification and were convinced that the doctrine amounted to a "virtual dissolution of the Union." State defiance of federal laws, Fort warned, could bring only anarchy and civil war. Quickly adding "Union" to the Clark name, Clark-Unionists caucused at Athens and nominated Wilson Lumpkin as their standard-bearer in the 1831 gubernatorial election.[10]

The Clark-Unionist critique of nullification emphasized the distinctions between Calhoun's doctrine and traditional states' rights principles. Insisting that only two parties, "the *Troup,* or *disunion* party, and the *Clark,* or *union* party," existed in Georgia, the *Milledgeville Federal Union* declared that Clark-Unionists were "the true State Rights party" that stood for "the *limited sovereignty* of the states and the *limited sovereignty* of the General Government." Under the federal system, Clarkites contended, the state and federal governments had separate and distinct powers and were sovereign within their respective spheres. Strict limitations on the power of the federal government, enshrined in the Constitution, protected minority interests while still allowing majority rule. The doctrine of nullification, in contrast, tolerated state defiance of federal laws, negated majority rule, and weakened the bonds of the Union. Tomlinson Fort admonished Calhoun that to "object to a majority passing laws to favor their own interests is to object to our system altogether." Clark-Unionists accordingly denounced South Carolinians and strove to link Troupite antitariff protestors such as John Berrien with disunionist radicalism.[11]

The Clark-Unionist challenge overpowered the staggering Troupites. George Gilmer secured the Troupite caucus nomination for governor, but Thomas Haynes briefly entered the race as the candidate of John Forsyth's dissident faction. John Berrien and other Troupites meanwhile continued to stir up antitariff feeling, although they disavowed any connection with nullification. Clark-Unionists persuaded enough voters that the Troupites were nullifying disunionists and enemies of Andrew Jackson to give Wilson Lumpkin a narrow triumph. The continued growth of frontier counties, where Andrew Jackson's appeal was strongest, aided the Clark-Unionists, as did their trumpeting of Unionist themes. Troupites fared best in old middle Georgia, their traditional stronghold, where antitariff feelings ran high among planters.[12]

The disintegration of the Troup faction continued apace following the 1831 defeat. A few Troupite leaders, along with scattered Clarkites such as John H. Howard of Columbus, openly embraced nullification. South Carolina nullifiers courted Georgians, and dinners at Hamburg, South Carolina, and Augusta in the spring of 1832 promoted antitariff cooperation. The most prominent Georgia nullifier was Congressman Augustin S. Clayton, a Troupite from Athens, who angrily charged that unconstitutional protective tariffs were impoverishing the staple-producing South; he and other hotspurs talked of secession as a legitimate response if their grievances remained unredressed. The Troupite *Columbus Enquirer* declared that the "tariff is now considered a question of right, and the [protective] system must be abandoned or the Union must and will be dissolved. The south will no longer submit."[13]

The activities of vocal nullifiers infuriated most Troupites, who disclaimed nullification sympathies and accused Clarkites of conjuring up false issues. The *Macon Georgia Messenger* blamed Troupite woes on the South Carolina troublemakers who had arrogantly assumed "the championship of State Rights" and jeopardized the antitariff cause. Clarkites well knew, the

*Milledgeville Southern Recorder* thought, that "not one man in twenty, perhaps not one in an hundred," in Georgia acknowledged the "right of nullification." Yet Clarkites persisted in "calling their political opponents Nullifiers, Disunionists, and Traitors."[14]

Tensions in the Troupite camp came to a head at the annual August commencement exercises at Franklin College in Athens, a traditional political gathering place. An aging William Crawford tried to unify the Troupites by calling a meeting of Jackson men opposed to nullification. The effort backfired, however, when John Berrien, Augustin Clayton, and several followers noisily interrupted the gathering. After the shouting and turmoil had driven away most of the original participants, Berrien and Clayton rammed through resolutions proposing a state antitariff convention in November and establishing a committee of correspondence that included themselves and other prominent Troupites.

No one, not even Berrien and Clayton, understood the precise purpose of the extralegal convention movement. Leaders vaguely vowed to resist protectionism and federal oppression, yet they skirted nullification and disguised any animus toward Andrew Jackson. Despite prevailing uncertainties, the committee of correspondence generated some enthusiasm for the convention and arranged October elections for county delegates. The antitariff campaign in turn persuaded Clark-Unionists to run opposing slates of convention candidates. In an acrimonious running debate, Clark-Unionists stressed the dangers of disunion and civil war inherent in nullification, while Berrien and others depicted Unionists as submissive slaves ready to bow under the yoke of federal tyranny.[15]

Andrew Jackson's veto of the recharter of the second Bank of the United States (BUS) had little impact on Georgians absorbed in their own controversies. Reactions to the veto did not—could not—break neatly along Troupite-Clarkite lines, because the BUS question had never been a source of state factional divisions. Troupites such as William Crawford, John Berrien, and Congressman Richard Henry Wilde were avid national bank proponents, but George Troup himself condemned the BUS, and Augustin Clayton aided Jackson's efforts to destroy it. Clarkites likewise held various views on the BUS. Just months before the BUS veto, the leading Clarkite organ, the *Milledgeville Federal Union,* opined that it would be "impossible prosperously to administer the fiscal interests of the country, or to regulate its currency" without a national bank. The Troupite *Georgia Journal*, in contrast, hailed the veto as a glorious victory over "monied capital" that had "restored the rights and interests of the farmers and all the other classes of industrious yeomanry of the country to their own keeping." Clark-Unionists, though, on their journey into the national Democratic party, would shortly adopt anti-BUS themes and become Georgia's staunchest foes of a national bank.[16]

Both Georgia factions backed Jackson's 1832 reelection bid and anathematized Kentuckian Henry Clay, the National Republican candidate and a recognized advocate of protective tariffs. Troupites and Clark-Unionists did, however, quarrel over the Democratic vice presidential candidate, Martin Van Buren. Several Troupite congressmen attended the inaugural Democratic national convention in 1832 and supported Van Buren's nomination. But Clark-Unionists, who despised Van Buren for his 1824 alliance with William Crawford, endorsed an alternative southern candidate, Philip P. Barbour of Virginia. Denying the authority of the national convention, Clark-Unionists attacked Van Buren, who was known for his sharp political tactics, as "a selfish calculator, a fawning courtier, [and] a flattering sycophant, utterly unworthy of the name of friend." He would be their presidential candidate four years hence.[17]

The 1832 congressional elections, held a month in advance of the November presidential balloting, revealed that ordinary voters accustomed to localized, personal politics lagged considerably behind leaders who were rapidly choosing up sides in a changing political climate. Voters adhered to the traditional practice of scattering their ballots among favorite candidates and elected two Clark-Unionists and seven Troupites. Of the latter, Augustin Clayton and Seaborn Jones were nullifiers; George Gilmer, Richard H. Wilde, and James M. Wayne opposed nullification; and Roger L. Gamble and Thomas F. Foster were noncommittal. The candidates' opinions on the BUS similarly ran the gamut. Along with their congressional victories, the Troupites carried the state for the Jackson–Van Buren presidential ticket. That the Troup faction could triumph even as it was collapsing from internal strife was a testament to the power of ancient loyalties.[18]

The long-awaited state convention that opened in Milledgeville on 12 November featured a showdown between rival Troupites. Troupite John Forsyth led largely Clark-Unionist forces in a move to expose the convention as an extralegal, unrepresentative body. When, after three days of debate, the convention rejected Forsyth's demand for an investigation of the delegates' credentials, he and fifty-three other delegates walked out. With John Berrien and Augustin Clayton left in charge, the convention quickly adopted a platform of extreme states' rights principles. Defining the Union as a confederacy of sovereign states, the convention declared that the federal government, a mere agent of the states, could not be the arbiter of its own powers. Although the delegates avoided the term *nullification,* they insisted that each state had the right to judge the constitutionality of federal laws. They did not, however, propose to act on these convictions. The convention pronounced protective tariffs unconstitutional, but announced that Georgians were willing to wait for gradual tariff reduction. When voters subsequently ignored a proposal for a southern antitariff convention, Berrien and Clayton's crusade reached a dead end.[19]

Shortly after Georgia's state convention adjourned, South Carolina adopted an ordinance of nullification that pledged state resistance to the enforcement of federal tariff laws after 1 February 1833. Andrew Jackson, responding in a 10 December proclamation, declared nullification "*incompatible with the existence of the Union*" and urged South Carolinians to abandon their folly. Jackson maintained that the Union antedated the Constitution and that the federal government operated "directly on the people individually." The American people constituted one nation, not a collection of citizens of separate states. The states were sovereign only insofar as they retained powers not delegated to the federal government. The Union was a binding compact; the Constitution recognized no right of state secession. Viewing South Carolina's course as revolutionary, Jackson asked Congress for authority to use force in suppressing the nullifiers.[20]

Jackson's proclamation, which contradicted cherished states' rights principles, raised howls of protest in his native section and laid the foundation for a viable anti-Jackson party in the South. Troupite editors Miller Grieve and Richard H. Orme of the *Milledgeville Southern Recorder* charged that Jackson's opinions were "utterly at variance with those which have distinguished the Democratic party of the Union, and in their claims of Federal power, go far beyond what has ever been claimed by Daniel Webster himself." Alfred H. Pemberton, an avowed nullifier and the editor of the *Augusta Chronicle,* branded Jackson a "*Hypocrite, Usurper, and Tyrant.*" He warned

Georgians that there was "now no choice, but *liberty* or *slavery*"—failure to resist Jackson and his proclamation equaled submission to oppression. Many feared that the rashness displayed in Jackson's "*incendiary* Proclamation" presaged a bloody attempt to coerce South Carolina. Reasoning from the republican premise that tyranny was progressive, Troupites cautioned that even if the nullification crisis were resolved peacefully, the tenets of Jackson's proclamation could still serve to legitimize future federal aggression.[21]

The state's ongoing conflict with the Supreme Court over Cherokee removal made the specter of federal coercion peculiarly menacing. In the case of *Worcester* v. *Georgia,* decided in early 1832, the Supreme Court had overturned the convictions of two white missionaries, Samuel A. Worcester and Elizer Butler, who had been imprisoned for violating a Georgia statute that prohibited whites from residing in Cherokee territory without state permission. The Court, moreover, had generally upheld Cherokee sovereignty and had voided state laws that applied to Cherokee lands. Governor Wilson Lumpkin, following the state's established policy of ignoring Supreme Court proceedings in Indian matters, nonetheless kept the missionaries behind bars and continued enforcing the disputed laws. Although Troupites readily drew parallels between Georgia's intransigence and South Carolina nullification, Clark-Unionists distinguished between defying the Supreme Court and nullifying acts of Congress and praised Lumpkin for asserting the state's rights in a dispute that did not involve "the interests of any other state, nor the welfare of the Union." Lumpkin released the missionaries only after President Jackson's studied inaction had vitiated the *Worcester* decision, an outcome that cemented relations between Clark-Unionists and national Jacksonians and undercut Troupite efforts to generate sympathy for South Carolina.[22]

The climax of the nullification crisis came in March 1833, when Congress passed a compromise tariff bill that gradually reduced duties over a nine-year period and seemingly abandoned the principle of protection. Along with the tariff, Congress enacted a Force Bill, which granted the president the power to use the army and navy to enforce federal laws. South Carolinians, disgruntled but partially victorious, thereafter rescinded their original nullification ordinance and symbolically nullified the Force Bill. Clark-Unionists congratulated themselves for backing Jackson, while most Troupites, who execrated the "*bloody enforcing bill*" and deplored the president's conduct, still remained reluctant to break completely with Jackson. Congressman James M. Wayne and Senator John Forsyth had already deserted over nullification, and many more of the rank and file would surely follow if the Troupites abandoned Old Hickory.[23]

Short on options, the Troupites tried relying on a familiar name in 1833 and nominated William Crawford's son, Joel, for the governorship. His candidacy promptly aroused criticism. Extremist states' rights men and a few nullifiers, including some former Clarkites, complained that Crawford "was nominated merely as a Troup man," without regard for principles. Others, usually called Troup-Unionists, worried that the younger Crawford might secretly be a nullifier. Crawford's ambiguous public statements scarcely clarified his views on nullification, Andrew Jackson, or anything else. Enthusiastic Clark-Unionists reprised familiar antinullification themes, exploited Troupite dissension, and returned Governor Wilson Lumpkin to office by a handsome majority.[24]

That defeat finished the Troup faction as such and led to an overhaul of the state's political organizations. William Crawford, Augustin Clayton, Seaborn Jones, Richard W. Habersham, Absalom H. Chappell, and other prominent Troupites met in Milledgeville on 13 November 1833 and formed the State Rights party in open opposition to Andrew Jackson. Focusing totally on national issues, they enumerated the consolidationist errors of Jackson's proclamation, urged Georgians to sustain Jeffersonian principles, and demanded the immediate repeal of the Force Bill. The meeting also appointed a state central committee of thirteen that included such diverse figures as Joel Crawford and old Clarkite nullifier John H. Howard, and asked State Rights supporters to organize similar county organizations. Except for a smattering of Clarkite converts, the State Rights party consisted of Troup men.

Clark-Unionists gathered a week later and established the Union Democratic Republican party—the Georgia branch of the national Democracy. Unionists attacked nullification, outlined their understanding of states' rights principles, and proclaimed unswerving allegiance to Andrew Jackson. A subsequent meeting selected a state central committee composed of Clarkite stalwarts such as Tomlinson Fort, John A. Cuthbert, Augustus H. Kenan, and Charles J. McDonald. The Unionists called for the creation of county organizations and recommended that the party prepare to send delegates to the 1836 national Democratic convention. The mass of Clarkites—along with such Troupite leaders as James Wayne, John Forsyth, Seaton

Grantland, and a relatively small, scattered, yet important contingent of Troupite voters—formed the core of the Union party.[25]

As a new era in state politics began, the untested parties immediately confronted the issue of Andrew Jackson's removal of government deposits from the Bank of the United States. On 1 October 1833, the Jackson administration had announced that future federal revenues would be deposited in selected state banks, so-called pets, rather than in the BUS. The payment of federal expenditures from existing accounts was intended to exhaust government funds in the BUS well before the bank's charter expired in 1836. Jackson's bold executive action, taken against the advice of Congress and his cabinet, created intense controversy.[26]

State Rights men charged that Jackson's latest "dangerous assumption of power" violated Congress's constitutional prerogatives and constituted part of a plot to seize control of the Treasury and erect a tyranny. Jackson's arrogant impetuosity was the crucial issue; the State Rights party did not defend the BUS or recommend restoring the deposits. Drawing on ideas central to the American Revolution, State Rights men limned an ominous portrait of an untrammeled executive "corrupting the principles of the people" and destroying civil liberties. Opposition to excessive presidential power, which became a staple theme of anti-Democratic forces in Georgia, dovetailed neatly with the State Rights party's commitment to limit the scope of the federal government.[27]

During the 1834 congressional campaign, State Rights men emphasized their determination to resist federal encroachments by defending the right of secession. The recognition of secession as a constitutional right, the State Rights party contended, would reinforce the idea that the Union was a limited compact and thereby check federal usurpations. State Rights men contrasted their position with that of Union-Democrats, most of whom grounded the right of secession in the Lockean right of revolution. This heretical doctrine, the *Milledgeville Southern Recorder* warned, would brand those who resisted federal tyranny as traitors possessing nothing more than "the glorious privilege of the slave, to rebel against his master." Unfortunately for the State Rights party, their congressional candidates presented a broken front on the secession question just as they had on nullification, and the intricate, abstract nature of the issue limited its popular appeal.[28]

Loyalty to Jackson rather than fundamental opposition to a national bank shaped the Union-Democrats' stand on deposit removal. Like Jackson himself, they defended the deposit removal as necessary to protect the federal government from the insidious influence of a corrupt political machine. Unionists also strove to prove that the State Rights party was guilty of associating with Henry Clay, Daniel Webster, and assorted other anti-Jackson, pro-BUS leaders whose nationalist programs repelled Georgians. Still, as an economic matter, Jackson's bank war troubled Unionists. Many were skeptical of the pet bank experiment, and some suggested, as had Jackson himself on occasion, that a modified national bank would serve the national interest by stabilizing the currency.

Union-Democrats, stressing that only radicals bent on disrupting the Union would encourage debates about secession, easily defeated the State Rights party on its chosen issue. Unionists gained a large majority in the state legislature and elected their congressional candidates by an average of four thousand votes. The division along pro-Jackson and anti-Jackson lines and the organizational work of county leaders since November 1833 had caused the new party system to take root. Instead of splitting their ballots among favorites, most voters uniformly supported all of their party's congressional candidates, producing the first party-line vote in a Georgia congressional election.[29]

The problem of selecting Andrew Jackson's successor next engaged the parties' attention. The disparate anti-Democratic forces lacked national organization and relied on regional candidates. Senator Hugh Lawson White of Tennessee was the leading southern candidate, while Daniel Webster of Massachusetts and William Henry Harrison of Ohio emerged as the favorites among anti-Jacksonians in the northern and western states. Democrats, for their part, nominated Jackson's choice, Martin Van Buren, at their May 1835 Democratic national convention. Unionists, who had previously backed only Southerners for the presidency and had repudiated Van Buren's 1832 vice presidential nomination, not surprisingly balked at accepting the New Yorker. Van Buren had some strong boosters among the Troup-Unionists allied with John Forsyth, Jackson's new secretary of state, but many Clark-Unionists despised the New Yorker because of his past fondness for William Crawford. Persistent carping about Van Buren, coupled with criticism of convention "*trickery*," undermined unity and hindered campaign efforts.[30]

Some Union-Democratic leaders met these objections by articulating a novel—for Georgia—rationale for supporting Van Buren: party loyalty. John A. Cuthbert, the editor of the *Milledgeville Federal Union*, defended the legitimacy of the Baltimore convention by distinguishing between caucuses dominated by "a few leading men" and larger, representative gatherings that derived their "authority from the will of the people." Party organization, Cuthbert argued, was indispensable for success and provided the sole effective means of ascertaining and implementing the popular will. Georgians could no longer base political alignments simply on "ambitious rivalry" and "violent personal hostility." Martin Van Buren was more than an individual politician; he was the candidate of the national Democratic party. The *Macon Georgia Telegraph* acknowledged that Unionists might have preferred someone other than Van Buren, but they had to waive their "individual preferences and objections to the choice of the majority of the party." Uttering a sentiment that would have been unthinkable only a few years before, the *Telegraph*'s editor concluded: "With us, love of party is synonymous with love of country." [31]

Cuthbert and others interpreted one of Van Buren's supposed weaknesses, his northern nativity, as a token of strength. Cuthbert identified sectional political blocs as the bane of the Republic and proclaimed that the "reciprocal affection of the members of a party, extending through all the states, is a most valuable safeguard to the Union." Without national parties to bind the nation together, Cuthbert presciently explained, the "shock of a presidential election would always endanger the existence of the government." The *Athens Southern Banner* echoed that the national Democratic party was the "greatest barrier" to sectional discord. As long as the national Democracy maintained "its influence and ascendency," there would be "little danger to apprehend from fanaticism, whether northern or southern—political or religious." Although far from all Union-Democrats shared this faith by 1835, the belief that the national Democratic party was the foremost defender of the South and the great bulwark of the Union rapidly gained credence and became the cardinal principle of the Georgia Democracy down to the Civil War. [32]

While Unionists struggled to reconcile themselves to Van Buren, the State Rights party's standing as an independent organization unlinked to other anti-Democratic state parties created difficulties in adopting Hugh Lawson White as its candidate. Except for his rejection of Van Buren, White had toed the Jacksonian mark and had endorsed all of Old Hickory's major policies—even the Force Bill. The party would probably have backed George Troup had he had any support elsewhere, but political realities finally compelled State Rights men to embrace White. They did so with deep misgivings, however, and many editors frankly stated that White was "chosen as an evil; but as an evil the least we can choose under the circumstances."[33]

Both parties swallowed fears of party machinery and held state conventions in 1835. When the State Rights party gathered in mid-June at Milledgeville, former Troupite congressman Roger L. Gamble used his opening address to reassure delegates that the convention was legitimate and had "emanated from the spontaneous action of the people, the acknowledged source of all power." The convention, hoping to dodge controversy, passed over nullifier Augustin Clayton and instead nominated a mainstream Athens Troupite, Charles Dougherty, for the governorship. Qualms about Hugh Lawson White were evident in a conditional endorsement of him over Van Buren, "if the contest should be between those two." The Union party met some two weeks later and ratified Van Buren's Baltimore nomination. A party caucus had previously chosen William Schley, an Augusta lawyer of Clarkite background, as the Union gubernatorial candidate.[34]

The 1835 campaign once again raised the ghosts of the nullification era. Schley and Dougherty were rather colorless figures, and no state issues as yet divided the parties. Union-Democrats rehashed familiar and still effective warnings about anti-Jackson radicals, while the State Rights party worked to expose traces of Federalism in Schley's past. Schley won by more than two thousand votes, apparently confirming that the Union party controlled the state.[35]

Rising tensions over abolitionism, however, made Martin Van Buren vulnerable and brought slavery issues to the forefront in the 1836 presidential race. White Georgians condemned the publication of William Lloyd Garrison's *Liberator* and shuddered at Nat Turner's rebellion, but through the early 1830s state politicians only infrequently and indirectly mentioned slavery issues. Then, around mid-1834, antiabolitionist mobs disturbed the peace in New York and other northern cities, and the prospect of continuing agitation became suddenly more alarming. Abolitionists escalated their efforts in 1835 through mass mailings to the South and petitions to Congress, and several Georgia county meetings demanded that the federal and state governments suppress the antislavery onslaught. Expressing the common view that slavery was nobody's business but their own, white citizens in Washington County insisted that "all we request at the hands of the Northern people is exemption from insult and dictation—is to be let alone." The nagging suspicion that another Nat Turner might be hoeing cotton in some Georgia field usually inhibited newspaper editors from discussing the potential for slave insurrections, but one writer ventured to applaud the seizure of abolitionist pamphlets designed "to destroy the lives of our whole white population—men, women, and children, and lay waste the country." As fear and outrage united white society, one State Rights man summoned the parties to stave off "ABOLITION! *present and immediate* ABOLITION of every SOUTHERN SLAVE!!"[36]

The State Rights party extolled Hugh Lawson White's virtues as an independent southern candidate and presented the presidential race as "*emphatically* a struggle of the unofficial sovereign people, against the strides of power,—a conflict between party dictation and the inestimable right of free selection." In utterly rejecting the concepts of national party organization and party loyalty, the State Rights party depicted Union-Democrats as selfish politicians wholly subservient to their treacherous northern allies. Only slavish devotion to party could explain the Unionists' adoption of Van Buren, "whom but yesterday they unsparingly covered with abuse, spat upon, denounced and decried as the very incarnation of fiendism." The 1836 State Rights convention—tellingly designated the "anti–Van Buren" convention—proclaimed that the New Yorker was unfit to receive "the free suffrage of a Southern slaveholder." Eugenius A. Nisbet, a State Rights candidate for Congress, lamented that "one of the prime errors of the day" was the unwarranted "reliance which Southern politicians place in others for their protection." Another congressional candidate, Edward J. Black, labeled Van Buren "an ultimate abolitionist in principle, and an advocate of free negro suffrage," and alleged that Van Buren's running mate, Richard Johnson of Kentucky, had "been wedded to two negro women, and is now honored by a half dozen mulatto children." Why would any white man, the *Columbus Enquirer* wondered, support "General Jackson's *dog*," a stranger "who would trample upon every Southern institution and violate every notion of policy and propriety, in abolishing slavery and making free negroes equal to white men," over an honorable southern gentleman like Hugh Lawson White?[37]

Union-Democrats retorted that the militant prosouthernism of State Rights men was a sham, a device employed by desperate politicians gambling for power. Intersectional comity, achieved through the brotherhood of the national Democracy, offered the surest remedy for abolition agitation. The extremism of the Garrisons and the Calhouns stood in sharp contrast to the calm statesmanship of Martin Van Buren, who respected the rights of both North and South. Unless one believed that Andrew Jackson would betray his homeland, Democrats averred, his chosen successor had to be sound on slavery. Union-Democrats also suggested that White was a stalking-horse for more sinister figures; anti-Democratic forces were actually planning to coalesce around William Henry Harrison, "a federalist and an abolitionist." White himself was scarcely beyond reproach; Union-Democrats alleged that he had served as an attorney for a Tennessee abolition society and had once walked to "the Ballot Box, ARM AND ARM WITH A FREE NEGRO."[38]

Union-Democrats swept the October congressional races and elected a majority of state legislators, but the presidential balloting proved that Van Buren was a feeble substitute for Old Hickory. Several Unionist defectors accepted slots on the White electoral ticket, and White carried Georgia by some seventeen hundred votes. About two-thirds of the eligible voters came to the polls, considerably fewer than in the 1835 gubernatorial contest, and the turnout decline hit Unionists disproportionately hard. (From a longer-term perspective, however, the turnout in 1836 signaled a significant increase in popular interest in presidential politics—only about one-third of the voters had participated in the 1828 and 1832 presidential elections.) Although the State Rights party posted gains in all five regions of the state, voting shifts were particularly crucial in the black belt, which cast two-thirds of the state vote. Democrats suffered a net loss of more than three thousand black belt votes and carried just 40.7 percent of the regional vote. Across the state, thousands of Union-Democrats either stayed home or supported White, and the State Rights party's prosouthern campaign told most heavily in the slave-rich black belt.[39]

The 1836 campaign presaged the future of Georgia politics. Both parties concentrated on issues that appealed to the values white men held in common. The State Rights party and Union-Democrats alike defended the Union, the South, the Constitution, republicanism, Republicanism, democracy, state rights, and slavery; both abhorred abolitionism, aristocracy, free blacks, Indians, disunionism, and Federalism.[40] Since specific policy disagreements over matters such as the BUS or the tariff were slight at this early point, the two parties differed most significantly in their attitudes toward the rise of political parties. Union-Democrats more enthusiastically embraced party organization, forged ties to Andrew Jackson's national Democracy, and saw their strategy vindicated with Van Buren's national triumph. State Rights men spurned connections with other anti-Jacksonians, celebrated their own uniquely pure devotion to southern interests, and presented the corruption and subserviency fostered by the national Democratic party as a grave threat to the South and the safety of slavery. This debate over whether exclusively sectional state parties or national party alliances offered the best protection for the South would continue for the next twenty-five years. Also enduring would be the power of the slavery-related issues first widely aired in 1836; no subsequent presidential candidate would escape a searching examination of his soundness on slavery.

Martin Van Buren had barely settled into the White House when a financial crisis raised banking and currency issues to the top of the political agenda. Americans prospered during the 1830s as the supply of currency expanded, land values soared, and abundant credit drove prices upward. The rush to settle former Indian lands and to expand cotton cultivation prompted frequent comments about "the unnatural pitch to which the spirit of speculation had elevated the price of land, negroes, and produce and labor of every description." Cotton prices approximately doubled between 1831 and 1836, reaching upward of sixteen cents a pound in the latter year, and merchants in fall-line towns thrived on the cotton trade. John Basil Lamar, the young scion of a wealthy and influential planter clan, described the feverish harvest-time activity in the central town of Macon. Men scurried back and forth, "each intent on swindling somebody & to enrich himself, [while] drays [were] rushing by with cotton for the boats, & returning with boxes and barrels." The "streets choked up with waggons [*sic*] & carts" and the toots of passing steamboats contributed to the "melee of a commercial place" that Lamar found "gloriously exciting."[41]

A March 1837 wave of bank suspensions busted the boom and began a period of price deflation and economic sluggishness that would last until the mid–1840s. Georgia banks, following those in New York and other financial centers, suspended specie payments and called in loans. The precipitous decline in commodity prices threatened debtors, large and small, with bankruptcy. The causes of the panic of 1837 were complex and international in scope: the accumulated debt burden and the huge increase in the volume of paper currency during the 1830s exacerbated larger problems involving trade imbalances and specie flows between the United States and England. Andrew Jackson's war against the BUS and his Specie Circular of July 1836 helped undermine public confidence in paper money and banks. At the first signs of trouble, Americans made uneasy by the long speculative boom were all too ready to curtail credit operations and hoard specie.

Georgia's banking system was among the stablest in the South. At the beginning of the panic, the state's twenty-one commercial banks and sixteen additional branches had almost nine million dollars in banknotes in circulation and slightly more than three million dollars in specie reserves. Some of the railroad corporations created in the mid–1830s also operated banks, the most prominent of which were the Central of Georgia Railroad Bank and the Georgia Railroad Bank. Most banks were located in cities and towns involved in the cotton trade; Savannah and Augusta possessed by far the largest banking capital. Institutions such as the Planters' Bank and the Bank of the State of Georgia, both based in Savannah, and the Bank of Augusta had been in operation for more than two decades, but most banks had been chartered since 1825 to accommodate the state's frontier and economic expansion. Banks dealt mainly in short-term commercial loans and bills of exchange. Their charters generally prohibited them from owning real estate or other property, except in cases of foreclosure, and placed limits on their specie reserves and note issues. State banknotes were the money used for everyday financial transactions. The volume of note issues exceeded specie reserves by severalfold, and state law made charter forfeiture the ultimate penalty for banks that refused to redeem notes in specie.

The only public banking institution was the state-owned Central Bank of Georgia, established in 1828 and located in Milledgeville. Operated by three directors appointed by the governor, the Central Bank's capital consisted of assorted state funds and state stock in private banks. The bank made long-term agricultural loans—not normally handled by private banks—

apportioned according to county population and limited to $2,500 per individual borrower. Unlike private banks, the Central Bank's note issues were restricted to the amount of specie and notes of specie-paying banks actually in its vaults. The Central Bank had enjoyed broad political support: John Clark had championed it, and its charter bill had passed the legislature by nearly a two-thirds majority. Planters and farmers from credit-starved frontier counties were the Central Bank's strongest backers, while its opponents had come primarily from counties around Macon, Savannah, and Augusta, which already had access to banking capital.[42]

Georgians held complex and contradictory opinions about banks. Banking operations proceeded in normal times virtually without recorded comment, but periodic crises awakened latent hostility. An observer noted that there was "no one subject, upon which every one is more ready, and fewer able, to express an opinion, than that of *Banks*." Anyone who lost money in a bank failure or held a depreciated bank bill became "a judge of the whole banking system," and the sins of individual banks made the public intolerant "of all monied institutions whatsoever." Denunciations of banks as dangerous monopolies and sermons on the dangers of enslavement to debt dropped easily from the lips of white men schooled in republican principles, and all party leaders could ring the changes on antibanking arguments. Banks, moreover, often were distant and mysterious institutions; citizens in the mountains or other remote parts of the state resided far from any chartered bank. Making banks the scapegoats for larger economic problems was, in short, a ubiquitous and popular procedure.[43]

At the same time, white men ranging from the wealthiest planters to the poorest tenant farmers needed credit in a seasonal agricultural economy. Neighbors enmeshed themselves in webs of debt—scores of personal promissory notes that functioned as a kind of currency—and unpaid obligations sometimes stood for years. The cotton trade, the lifeblood of the state's economy, rested on a banking and credit system that spanned the Atlantic Ocean and made cotton prices in Liverpool, England, of the utmost concern to planters on the outskirts of Milledgeville. Myron Bartlett, the Union-Democratic editor of the *Macon Georgia Telegraph*, expressed Georgians' ambivalence toward these facts of life. He was "as opposed as any one to building up 'monopolies,'" but "all the Banks combined" lacked the resources to buy the cotton grown around Macon, and the city plainly required more banking facilities. The Democratic *Augusta Constitutionalist*, while likewise "not very friendly to banks," opined that the banking system was "so engrafted into all our business transactions, that it cannot be abandoned without material injury to the great interests of the country."[44]

However much the public and political leaders bemoaned the existence of banks, they tended to defend their local institutions. The State Rights *Macon Georgia Messenger,* for example, alleged that the "selfish, imbecile, shameless and abandoned management" of Union-Democratic directors had turned the Central Bank into "a powerful instrument of corruption." But its party ally, the *Milledgeville Southern Recorder,* thought that the Central Bank—located a few blocks away—represented "an almost unparalleled instance of skillful and successful banking." The Democratic *Milledgeville Federal Union* shifted its position on the Central Bank whenever a new editor came aboard. Tomlinson Fort founded the paper, and the Central Bank initially appeared in its pages as a monster that bled money "from the poor and embarrassed, to loan it to the rich." Fort later became a Central Bank director, John Cuthbert assumed control of the paper, and the two engaged in a violent quarrel over Fort's appointment of his brother-in-law to a bank post. During Cuthbert's tenure, the *Federal Union* repeatedly warned of evils and corruption stemming from the Central Bank. When Cuthbert retired in April 1837, John G. Park, the new editor and sometime state comptroller, opined that the beneficent Central Bank deserved "the fostering care and protection of the people."[45]

Conflicting and variable attitudes made concerted party action on either state or national banking policy extraordinarily difficult, and often impossible. Lacking a history of agreement on banking issues, which had never served as tests of political fellowship, State Rights men and Union-Democrats struggled throughout the late 1830s to establish coherent dividing lines between the parties. Martin Van Buren, at least, provided a reference point. He called a special session of Congress in September 1837 and proposed that the federal government divorce itself from banks by allowing government officers to collect public funds and keep them in their own vaults. Congress struggled for the next three years over whether to enact Van Buren's independent treasury, or subtreasury, system. Both Georgia parties invariably treated national banking policy as a problem of *political* economy, inseparable from general attitudes toward the federal government and the Democratic party in power.[46]

The special congressional session opened too late to have much impact on the issues discussed in the 1837 gubernatorial contest between the incumbent, William Schley, and George Gilmer. The State Rights party reiterated charges that Schley was a Federalist, and Unionists responded with criticism of Gilmer's supposed coddling of the Cherokees during his previous term as governor. Reprising 1836 themes, State Rights newspapers claimed that the "true question at issue" in the gubernatorial election was "Van Buren or anti–Van Buren." The onus of carrying Van Buren once again "drove from the party many of its warmest friends," and Schley lost by a little more than seven hundred votes. Voters, energized by the panic and traditionally more interested in state elections, turned out in huge numbers—about 86 percent—and cast twenty thousand more ballots than in the 1836 presidential election. Voting shifts between 1835 and 1837 were slight but significant: Schley ran worse in every region, and his share of the statewide vote tumbled from 52.2 to 49.4 percent—Van Buren had carried just 48.2 percent.[47]

When earnest debate over the subtreasury began, Union-Democrats tried to reduce the issue to a straightforward choice between Van Buren's measure and a national bank. An *"entire and eternal separation,* of BANK and STATE" would purify the federal government and end the corrupting influence of monopolistic banks. Unless the vital link that connected government officials to scheming private bankers could be broken, "a moneyed aristocracy would wield the destinies of the Nation." The creation of a gigantic new national bank, whose tentacles would invade the halls of power and ensnare formerly free white men, would inevitably follow the defeat of the subtreasury proposal. Liberty was at stake, Democrats warned, and they called on voters to make the subtreasury a *"test question"* and to rally under the *"new banner."* [48]

Despite their hostility toward a national bank and their distrust of bankers, Democrats disclaimed any desire to abolish banks or paper currency. A broad gulf separated Georgia partisans from radical agrarian and Locofoco Democrats clustered in the western and northern states. Georgia Democrats wanted "to regulate and reform" banks, not "to crush the paper system, and return to the good old days of hard money." Banking was "as legitimate and as lawful a business as planting cotton or making bricks," the *Macon Georgia Telegraph* asserted. The people possessed "too much good sense" for "Locofoco doctrines" to "prevail in Georgia." The idea of relying on gold and silver to furnish a circulating medium seemed fantastic and chimerical.

When Georgia Democrats declared, as they often did, that they were "hard money men," they meant that they wished to see no paper currency tolerated that did not have a specie basis.[49]

The state economy's dependence on the credit system inhibited wholesale assaults on banking and mercantile interests. Democrats did not intend "to disturb the harmony and goodwill" that prevailed "between the various classes of the community" or to damage the "industry of the country." Debt could enslave, but credit could liberate. "Credit is the wealth of the poor man," the *Milledgeville Federal Union* explained; "it is the lever of power in the hands of enterprize [*sic*] and industry; it is the destroyer of the aristocracy of wealth, it is the stimulant which has caused our people to do more in less time than ever was achieved by any other people." Union-Democrats who wanted prosperity without problems envisioned the subtreasury operating like a sanitized BUS. The government would be insulated from corruption, but the subtreasury would work as a regulator to ensure that state banks maintained adequate specie reserves and provided sound paper currency.[50]

State Rights men, who lacked the guideposts that national party membership provided for Democrats, went many separate ways on national banking questions. Most vehemently opposed the subtreasury plan, fearing that it would swell executive patronage and ultimately lead to despotism. They already blamed the panic on Andrew Jackson's destructive economic experiments, and they had no intention of letting Van Buren's party henchmen guard the public coffers. John Berrien and Ambrose Baber of Macon, who were most closely in touch with northern Whigs, cautiously advanced the possibility of cooperating in the growing movement for a new national bank. Long-standing objections about constitutionality and expediency, however, precluded the party from following that course. Indeed, several former nullifiers professed themselves more ready to swallow the subtreasury than to join the hated consolidationist northern Whigs in creating a national bank.

The positions of the party's congressional candidates revealed a tripartite division. The extreme states' rights group—Mark Anthony Cooper, Edward J. Black, and Walter T. Colquitt—were rising youngsters who had sympathized with nullification in 1832 and had long admired John C. Calhoun. Influenced by Calhoun's advocacy of the subtreasury and his odd rapprochement with Van Buren, they were willing to give the New Yorker's subtreasury idea a fair hearing. Most important, Cooper, Black, and Colquitt wholly opposed a national bank and saw northern Whigs as implacable enemies of the South and states' rights. Van Buren's faults seemed modest in comparison.

A fence-sitting group, which represented the bulk of the State Rights party, included young Macon lawyer Eugenius A. Nisbet and Thomas Butler King, a coastal planter. While withholding all praise from Van Buren and his policies, King and Nisbet nonetheless called for the federal government to divorce itself from banks and to cease tampering with the currency. Neither man wanted a national bank, and each seemed to suggest that, in lieu of any other alternative, the federal government should continue depositing its funds in selected state banks—hardly an effective plan for separation.

Only Richard W. Habersham among the State Rights candidates advocated a national bank. A lawyer-planter from a distinguished Savannah family and a good friend of John Berrien, Habersham had supported the second Bank of the United States and believed that only a national bank could satisfactorily manage government funds and stabilize the currency. Habersham considered the subtreasury plan a foolhardy attempt to establish a specie currency and deplored the pet bank system. A national bank, which could provide a single currency that circulated at par throughout the United States, would lower the cost of monetary exchanges and greatly benefit merchants and planters heavily enmeshed in the market economy. Habersham's arguments were somewhat beside the point, however, since other State Rights spokesmen rested their objections to a national bank primarily on political and constitutional grounds.[51]

State Rights men did not let disagreements over "the minor consideration of the monetary system" unduly distract them in the 1838 campaign. Relentless attacks on Martin Van Buren and Democratic party dictation spelled success for the entire State Rights congressional ticket. The parties refused to offer clear alternative stands on national economic issues, but the lack of such distinctions apparently mattered little to most voters. Durable loyalties that dated back to the nullification era and beyond still controlled political behavior and held state parties—especially the State Rights party—outside the mainstream of the emerging national party system. The parties had evolved to express broad attitudes and to function as electoral organizations; they were less effective as vehicles for the enactment of specific policies. Vows to protect independent white men from the potential ravages of Van Burenism thus were platform enough for a State Rights party that maintained no pretense of harmony on economic questions.[52]

Although the panic eased during 1838 and most Georgia banks resumed specie payments, the recovery proved fleeting. State banks suspended specie payments periodically from May through September 1839 before joining in a national bank suspension in October. Despite worsening conditions and mounting public impatience, the state parties hesitated to pursue solutions for banking difficulties. Some leaders proposed that the legislature mandate a resumption of specie payments. Others sensibly observed that fiats from the Georgia legislature could not cure international financial troubles. Conflicts between larger city banks in Augusta and Savannah and smaller country banks further muddled matters. Union and State Rights newspapers in Milledgeville and Macon complained that city banks were profiting from the general distress by demanding prompt note settlements and heavily discounting the notes of country banks. Friends of country banks feared that a resumption law would drain specie from local institutions, and the commercial community generally apprehended catastrophe if Georgia banks were forced to resume specie payments while banks in other states remained suspended. So, although the suspensions were illegal and could have voided the banks' charters, state officials and politicians were disposed to forgo drastic measures and to suffer through the 1839 crisis.[53]

The 1839 gubernatorial campaign illustrated how normal party operations were only loosely related to problems of state governance. Charles Dougherty, who had been defeated in 1835, once again bore the State Rights standard; his opponent was an old Clarkite, Charles J. McDonald. Of Scottish ancestry, the red-haired, blue-eyed McDonald was a Bibb County planter who had graduated from South Carolina College before embarking on a successful career in law and politics. The parties rarely discussed any current state questions, least of all state banking issues, and dwelt instead on cleavages based on national politics. The State Rights *Macon Georgia Messenger,* for example, urged voters who were "comparatively indifferent to State Politics, but who are opposed to the [Van Buren] administration, to remain firm to their principles." Unionists countered by trying to link the State Rights party with northern antislavery men, tariff supporters, and national bank advocates—northern Whigs, in other words.[54]

The charismatic McDonald triumphed by slightly more than two thousand votes in an exceptionally quiet campaign. Voter turnout remained around 80 percent, but a drop in the State Rights black belt vote, a voting surge in the newly organized mountain counties, and a better Democratic showing in the pine barrens—wiregrass cost the State Rights party the election. Both parties' total vote increased as a result of population growth in north Georgia, but Democrats benefited more because they typically carried at least 60 percent of the upcountry vote and close to 75 percent of the mountain vote. With the advancing years, the voting power of north Georgia—the northwest Cherokee country had only recently been opened to white settlement—became an ever more important factor in politics.

Once in office, McDonald persuaded the Democratic majority in the state legislature to act on banking. Unable to agree on a resumption measure aimed at private banks, Democrats instead expanded the operations of the state-owned Central Bank. State Rights legislators, who correctly observed that the bank was already overburdened with state debts, strongly opposed the Democratic bill that allowed Central Bank directors to double the volume of Central Bank notes in circulation (note issues had been restricted to the amount of capital on hand). The inflationary plan to counteract the credit shortage with emissions of state paper money was promptly executed by the Central Bank's directors, who sold state stock in private banks to raise funds for widespread loan distributions. The Central Bank shortly thereafter suspended specie payments and descended toward financial ruin. The Democratic answer to the problem of irredeemable paper currency was, in short, more of the same, and the 1839 Central Bank expansion would provoke much subsequent controversy.[55]

In the winter of 1839–40, though, presidential campaign preparations overshadowed all other political matters. Union-Democrats had already endorsed Martin Van Buren, and they participated in the May 1840 Democratic national convention that unanimously nominated him for a second term. Anti-Democratic forces, known as Whigs in most of the nation, finally developed enough confidence in their prospects for unity to hold a national convention in Harrisburg, Pennsylvania, in December 1839. Henry Clay, the southern favorite and the recognized champion of Whiggery, seemed the logical preconvention choice, but the nomination went to William Henry

Harrison, a military hero with fewer enemies and uncertain principles. A southern states' rights Whig, John Tyler of Virginia, filled the vice presidential slot.[56]

The formation of the national Whig party underscored the anomalous position of Georgia's State Rights men, who stubbornly refused to send delegates to Harrisburg. Like other states (except South Carolina), Georgia had two well-established parties, one of which was aligned with the national Democracy. But aside from common opposition to the Democracy and some shared antiparty feelings, State Rights men recognized no connection between themselves and national Whigs. The peculiar Troup-Clark legacy, the absence of Federalist antecedents, and the continued salience of nullification-era issues all contributed to the unique parochialism of the State Rights party. Considerations of political conscience, economic interest, and southern feeling forbade the advocacy of national Whig notions of enlarging federal power to promote economic development and national welfare; the State Rights party had been founded to combat such consolidationist heresies. The advent of a national two-party system, then, by no means guaranteed that the State Rights party would cast its lot with national Whigs. Whether State Rights men would remain isolated or join in supporting Harrison was a pivotal, and still undecided, question.[57]

The State Rights party initially looked to George M. Troup as a presidential candidate and insisted that it could not endorse Clay, Harrison, or Van Buren without betraying its heritage. Troup had a powerful and familiar name that was as likely as any to bring victory, and his candidacy would allow the State Rights men to postpone making possibly irrevocable and disastrous decisions regarding the subtreasury and national party affiliation. With Troup, in other words, the party could continue to disclaim "all identity with the Northern Whigs" and still contribute to the defeat of Van Buren. At the December 1839 State Rights convention, which met nearly two weeks after the Whig national convention, party members unanimously refused to support either Van Buren or Harrison.[58]

That verdict dissatisfied John Berrien and several other prominent leaders who had gradually migrated toward an alliance with the national Whig party. Berrien's group included Congressmen Richard W. Habersham and William C. Dawson, both of whom enjoyed good relations with Whigs in

Washington; Augusta lawyer Charles J. Jenkins; Ambrose Baber of Macon; and Iverson L. Harris, Berrien's political lieutenant in Milledgeville. These men found Whig economic programs, particularly the idea of a national bank, somewhat attractive, but more important was their shared conviction that the State Rights party could not stand on the sidelines—hamstrung by internal divisions—while Van Buren and his economic depression ravaged the country. Reflecting this viewpoint, the *Savannah Republican* criticized the movement for Troup as an absurd return to the issueless days of "one man parties." If State Rights men could not at least agree on opposing Van Buren and the subtreasury, the time clearly had come for a "re-organization of parties." [59]

Simultaneously, at the party's other pole, Congressmen Mark A. Cooper, Walter T. Colquitt, and Edward J. Black were edging ever closer to the Democrats. Along with others soon to be known as Calhounites, Cooper, Colquitt, and Black echoed John C. Calhoun's indictment of national parties as antirepublican institutions inimical to southern interests and stressed the need to resist every form of consolidation. They viewed northern Whigs in particular as almost satanic in their propensities for evil. In an April 1840 circular, Mark Cooper warned his constituents that some State Rights leaders were succumbing to the "centralizing influence of [national] parties" and trying "to amalgamate you with the Whigs, on mere feelings of opposition" to Van Buren. Contending that Democratic policies most closely matched State Rights principles, Cooper, Black, and Colquitt increasingly cooperated with congressional Democrats and professed leanings toward Van Buren. Their course, which contemplated transforming Georgia into a one-party state—like South Carolina—loosely linked to the national Democracy, sent shock waves reverberating through the State Rights ranks.[60]

Calhounite efforts to propel the State Rights party "into the support of Mr. Van Buren" backfired, creating a climate in which John Berrien's forces could successfully mount a countermovement for William Henry Harrison. Through private correspondence and editorials elicited from often reluctant party journalists, Berrien, William Dawson, Iverson Harris, and others assured party members that Harrison was the most available candidate, was sound on slavery, and would carry on the crusade against Van Buren's spoilsmen. A June "anti–Van Buren convention," which John Berrien chaired, revealed the changes wrought by the threat of creeping Van Burenism. The convention formed a Harrison and Tyler electoral ticket and selectively reorganized the State Rights party's leadership. Cooper, Colquitt, and Black were denied renomination for Congress, while the party retained incumbent Harrison supporters Richard Habersham, William Dawson, and Thomas Butler King. The adoption of Harrison and the expulsion of the Calhounites signaled a fundamental change in the nature of the State Rights party, which had finally moved toward finding a niche within the national party system.[61]

Democrats swiftly corraled the displaced State Rights dissidents. At a July state convention, Cooper, Black, and Colquitt accepted spots on the Democratic congressional slate opened through the prearranged resignations of three old Unionists. Another trio of State Rights men occupied vacated positions on the Van Buren electoral ticket. In welcoming Calhounite accessions, Union-Democrats got both more and less than they expected. The Calhounites were a rather small, quarrelsome crew whose influence depended more on talent than numbers, and they remained a distinct faction long after their absorption into state Democratic parties across the South.[62]

The 1840 contest generated unprecedented excitement. Ordinary white men had turned out in large numbers in state elections before, but never had they participated so actively in politics. The popular campaign techniques of the antebellum era—mass rallies, barbecues, stump speeches, slogans, banners, and assorted hoopla—became permanent fixtures during and after the 1840 canvass. Harrison boosters organized dozens of Tippecanoe and Log Cabin clubs, and tens of thousands of campaign documents flooded the state. The August Harrison convention in Macon, one of many mass rallies, lasted three days. Several thousand people feasted on pork and corn bread, listened to a procession of speakers on the scattered platforms, and marched with banners bearing slogans such as "Purge the Public Offices" and "Harrison, Tyler and Reform."[63]

If the atmosphere was different in 1840, the issues were strikingly similar to those of earlier elections. State Rights men portrayed the subtreasury plan and Secretary of War Joel Poinsett's proposal to reorganize and reform the state militias as interrelated attempts to raise a standing army and unite "the purse and the sword." Van Buren, if not checked, would soon be "assuming the purple and wearing the crown." Van Buren's history of "successful craft, hypocrisy, cunning, intrigue and knavery" demonstrated that he would, if necessary, overthrow the Constitution to retain power; his "whole life" was nothing but "a libel upon our country." Since State Rights men had scant knowledge of Harrison's views on national banks, tariffs, or other such questions, they lauded his military accomplishments and praised his simple, scrupulous honesty. Harrison's promises to curb the abuse of party patronage, to exercise the veto power with restraint, and to limit himself to one term in office meshed perfectly with the State Rights critique of Van Burenism. The State Rights party, in essence, pledged to prevent the establishment of a one-party monarchy in which Democratic presidents wielding vast patronage passed the mantle to chosen successors.[64]

The dire economic situation heightened concerns about corruption and decay, and the State Rights party's official address summarized the disastrous effects of Democrats' tampering with the national economy. Andrew Jackson's spiteful transfer of government deposits from the BUS to reckless state banks had "flooded" the nation with "Bank paper." When the bubble burst, Van Buren invented a subtreasury plan (finally enacted into law in July 1840) to "banish *credit*" and establish a "metallic currency." These capricious, calamitous maneuvers were the source of the nation's economic woes. Although they advanced no specific policies, State Rights men confidently declared that Harrison's steady hand on the financial helm would restore prosperity: the banking and credit system simply needed time to recover from Democratic bungling.[65]

Democrats understandably deflected discussion away from Van Buren's economic record and concentrated on denouncing Harrison and the motley Whig coalition. Harrison men, Democrats contended, acted on "no principle" and were "Federalists in one State, anti-masons in another, republicans in a third, abolitionists in a fourth, and we know not what in the rest." A Harrison victory would mean the erection of another monster national bank, the levying of protective tariffs, and the escalation of assaults on slavery. Proud southern congressmen, unwilling to witness the destruction of their homeland, would depart from Washington in disgust, and the Union would be practically dissolved.[66]

Democrats, most notably John Forsyth, stressed a fundamental difference between the Whig and Democratic organizations. Martin Van Buren was the candidate of the Democratic party in "ALL the States," Forsyth declared, and he was "equally acceptable" to Jacksonians everywhere. William Henry Harrison was merely the candidate of those parties who could be "brought to act against the present administration by the common instinct of hatred." Harrison had been nominated over southern opposition at the Whig national convention, and his northern backers expressed contempt for southern principles and institutions. Forsyth concluded that the State Rights alliance with northern Whiggery, a marriage of convenience preserved through hypocrisy and evasion, ought to outrage every honest white man in Georgia.[67]

George Troup, who renounced the State Rights party when it adopted Harrison, rightly observed that the parties spent the summer "cutting one another[']s throats in the controversy as to which of the two belongs the higher degree of abolitionism." Column headings such as "Van Buren Now and Always an Abolitionist" ran constantly in the State Rights party's newspapers. Democrats reported that news of Harrison's candidacy had nearly incited slave revolts in Louisiana and that Harrison had belonged to an abolition society fifty years ago (his more recent imprecations against abolitionism were deemed "very immaterial"). Harrison lived in a mansion rather than a log cabin, but without African slaves; he preferred "poor white men and women" for servants. Neither candidate was an abolitionist or anything like one, but both parties implicitly assumed that the slightest antislavery taint tarnished candidates in the eyes of white men devoted to defending slavery.[68]

The weight of the depression, Van Buren's lasting unpopularity, and the powerful State Rights campaign crushed the Democrats. After the Democrats relinquished control of the legislature and lost the congressional races in October, Harrison amassed a November majority of more than 8,000 votes, the largest margin in the history of the Union-Democratic and State Rights parties. Compared with the 1839 election, the Democratic party's share of the vote declined 7.3 percent in the mountains, 5.3 percent in the upcountry, 7.2 percent in the black belt, 23.9 percent in the pine barrens—wiregrass, and 1.7 percent along the coast. The State Rights party altogether gained nearly 10,500 votes between 1839 and 1840. Given the high voter turnout in previous state elections, increased participation was less of a factor in Harrison's victory in Georgia than it was in many other states. The leap in turnout from 62 percent in 1836 to 85 percent in 1840, however, signified that voters had mentally integrated state and national politics and had come to share their leaders' intense concern over presidential elections.

The 1840 campaign, a landmark in political history, had particularly immense significance in Georgia. Within the span of a few months, the State Rights party had purged its Calhounite wing, endorsed a national candidate, and won a smashing victory. A party born to defy Andrew Jackson and raised to loathe Martin Van Buren suddenly had its own president. For better or worse, the State Rights party's fortunes would henceforth be linked to those of the Harrison administration and the national Whig party. No one knew how far cooperation with northern Whigs might extend or what such cooperation might cost, but the State Rights party certainly would never be the same.

Union-Democrats who had staked their all on the national party experienced doubts about the investment. Thrilling memories of Old Hickory and the nullification era hardly compensated for losing four of the last five statewide elections. Unlike State Rights men, Democrats were very familiar with the often painful accommodations that a national party alliance required. They had taken their old Calhounite enemies aboard to aid Martin Van Buren, and satisfying the newcomers—who were instinctive leaders and recalcitrant followers—would prove a monumental challenge for the original Unionists. Democrats would also have to defend their Central Bank handiwork against the incoming State Rights majority in the legislature; sharp skirmishes over state economic policy lay immediately ahead.

In a long letter to John Berrien, Charles J. Jenkins reflected on the uncertainties facing a State Rights party that had assumed power "under adverse circumstances." Democratic "misrule" had placed the Central Bank in financial peril, but it was not their "abuse of power at home but their connection with Federal maladministration" that had caused the Democrats' overthrow. The voters who had "devolved upon" the State Rights party the "imperative duty of correcting the errors of our predecessors" possessed neither a "distinct perception of those errors" nor a clear understanding of "the means necessary to be used in their correction." If the party tried to "temporise to retain power," state interests would suffer. Decisive action, though, might alienate voters. "Is there any judicious course," Jenkins wondered, "uniting fidelity to our trust & a due regard to the perpetuation of Party ascendecey?" Fresh off a stunning triumph, the State Rights party was about to confront one of the dilemmas of American politics: how to reconcile party electoral imperatives with responsible governance.[69]

# THREE

# *From Tyler to Texas:*
# *Jacksonian Parties at Their Zenith*

The history of the Georgia parties in the early 1840s illustrates the tensions inherent in the state-based structure of Jacksonian politics. Following a decade of sifting and experimentation, the Georgia Whig and Democratic parties emerged in the early 1840s as well-developed organizations integrated into the national party system.[1] Cooperation with Whigs and Democrats elsewhere necessitated many compromises, however, and the terms of Georgians' national party allegiances were mutable and conditional. The problem of managing national-state party relations, particularly affiliations with northern allies, was central in antebellum Georgia politics. The difficulties involved in being Democrats, yet *Georgia* Democrats, and Whigs, yet *Georgia* Whigs, were never more apparent than during John Tyler's presidency, when the tariff, presidential politics, and Texas annexation tested Georgians' commitment to the national party system.

The search for solutions to banking problems preoccupied the 1840 legislature. The political options regarding suspended private banks remained basically twofold: pass a resumption law or do nothing. The former seemed the popular course, given the general belief that the banks' refusal to redeem their notes in specie constituted swindling, but legislators who understood banking affairs—relatively few—realized that mandated resumption would force banks to reduce loans drastically, thereby worsening the credit shortage. Acting on Governor Charles McDonald's advice, large majorities in both branches of the legislature passed a bill that set 1 February 1841 as the date for the resumption of specie payments. Banks that failed to resume faced lawsuits leading to the loss of their charters.

Legislators next dealt with the Central Bank and state finances. Money from land sales had swelled the Central Bank's coffers during the mid-1830s, and the bank had undertaken large loan distributions to the public. The state simultaneously had embarked on building the Western & Atlantic Railroad in northwest Georgia, an ongoing project that consumed considerable state funds. The flush times between 1835 and 1838 had also led the legislature to cease collecting state taxes. The onset of the depression made these past policies unworkable, however, and after the 1839 Democratic legislature enlarged the Central Bank's note-issuing powers, the bank became the chief target of Whig complaints about Democratic financial mismanagement.

Following the 1839 act, the Central Bank's total circulation vaulted from $65,000 to more than $1 million. The bank's assets existed mostly on paper, and its failure to maintain specie payments caused its notes to depreciate.[2] Whigs most sharply criticized the Central Bank's "legalized shin-plaster system" of "irredeemable paper," but both parties acknowledged that the state lacked the means to restore the bank's credit. Charles McDonald noted that past exactions on the Central Bank had almost exhausted its resources, and he recommended resuming the collection of state taxes to ensure the redemption of the bank's outstanding notes. Both the Whig majority and the Democratic minority reports from the house committee on the Central Bank called for the repeal of the 1839 act expanding note issues, and indeed, for the repeal of the bank's charter—the Democratic report concluded that the bank had "been of decided injury to the finances and the credit of the State."[3]

Bipartisan agreement proved transitory. Though bereft of funds, the Central Bank remained a powerful source of political capital. Before Whigs could mature their Central Bank plans, Governor McDonald dropped a political bombshell in a special message to the legislature. He lamented the meager 1840 cotton crop and the prevailing economic distress and urged legislators to provide "relief" for the people. When pressed for specific proposals, McDonald suggested selling state bonds to fund further Central Bank loan distributions. Outraged Whigs scorned the idea of pledging "the property and labor of the whole people, to raise money to supply the private wants of a portion only, of the people." McDonald's relief notions would increase taxes, necessitate state borrowing, and "operate so as to legislate money from one citizen's pocket, to those of another"—exactly the sort of legislative favoritism that Democrats supposedly abhorred. Democratic tinkering with the Central Bank had already ruined the state's credit anyway and made relief impossible. Whigs repealed the Central Bank legislation of 1839 and authorized the issuance of state bonds to redeem notes already circulating. Although the Whig bill simply repaired damage and returned the bank to its old basis, it met nearly unanimous Democratic opposition. McDonald's timely plea for relief drew sharp party lines on the Central Bank issue and transformed an apparent Whig victory on policy into a Democratic political boon.[4]

Rather than serving as remedies, the acts of 1840 made the currency situation worse. Private banks resumed specie payments by the 1 February deadline, but nearly all the banks outside Savannah and Augusta soon suspended again. Most Georgia banks could not operate for long paying out specie while banks in other states remained suspended. The Savannah and Augusta banks saved themselves by rapidly curtailing circulation. The Bank of Augusta, for example, capitalized at $1.2 million, had just over $73,000 in circulation at the end of 1841, while the suspended Georgia Railroad Bank at Athens had issued almost $430,000 in notes on $600,000 capital. Specie-paying banks mainly took in and paid out the notes of suspended banks, ensuring that the most depreciated currency achieved the widest circulation.

The lack of a market for shaky Georgia state bonds doomed Whig attempts to revive the suspended Central Bank's credit. Another large state deficit and state debt obligations actually forced the bank to issue more notes, raising its circulation to nearly $1.5 million. Central Bank notes passed at a 16 percent discount (eighty-four cents on the dollar) in Macon in March 1841 and remained depreciated throughout the year. The *Southern Recorder* sorrowfully remarked that the people had less confidence in the state's banks than ever before. Some state banks were genuinely unsound, but most of the trouble stemmed from the "unparalleled pressure in money matters" everywhere, and the people saw the "little money coming into their possession" taken from them "by the depreciation of the bills."[5]

Democrats, ignoring the overwhelming vote for the specie resumption bill in the 1840 legislature, scorned Whigs for bullying unprepared private banks into resuming specie payments. Whigs had "promised to revive the credit system—to foster the Banks, and make money plenty," but instead they had "closed up the Banks, deranged and depreciated the currency, and made money so scarce, that none can be borrowed." The callous, parsimonious Whig legislators who had denied the people relief from the Central Bank cared not that credit was "the poor man's greatest blessing" and a powerful means "of lessening the aristocratic power of the wealthy." Whigs would rather see farmers ground into the dirt than part with a penny of state money.[6]

The *Milledgeville Federal Union,* owned by Central Bank Director Tomlinson Fort, unsurprisingly led Democrats in defending the Central Bank and promoting relief. The paper proudly asserted in August 1841 that Georgians considered "Central Bank bills the best to be had in the country" and used them almost exclusively. The editor had a point of sorts: the flood of Central Bank paper had practically driven the notes of specie-paying banks out of circulation. Other banks exchanged Central Bank bills only at a discount, and the depreciation of Central Bank paper represented a loss to all its holders. The state government suffered along with individuals. Since Central Bank bills could be purchased cheaply but were received at face value for the payment of state taxes, the state collected precious revenues chiefly in the form of its own depreciated notes.[7]

Along with having to endure Democratic taunts about relief in 1841, Whigs experienced a disappointing beginning in their relationship with the national party. William Henry Harrison died in April after only a month in office, and John Tyler, a strict constructionist of the Virginia Old Republican school, assumed the presidency. When a special session of Congress, called by Harrison, convened on 31 May, Senator Henry Clay directed the Whig majority's efforts to enact an economic program. After scoring victories on several minor measures, Whigs foundered on the national bank question. Tyler had loathed the second Bank of the United States, and attempts to create a new national bank that would not violate his constitutional scruples proved fruitless. Tyler vetoed a first bank bill on 16 August; a second, somewhat revised bill met a similar fate three weeks later. Most of the cabinet then resigned, and a subsequent congressional Whig address read Tyler out of the party.

The Georgia Whig delegation in Congress, with newly elected Senator

John Berrien in the van, abandoned all opposition to a national bank and cooperated enthusiastically in the effort to overcome Tyler. Following Harrison's election, Berrien's forces had rallied the Georgia party behind the idea of a national bank; Whigs even came to claim, falsely, that the 1840 election had constituted a referendum on the question. Tyler's veto binge thus stunned state Whigs and compromised their stance on the two national issues—the creation of a national bank and the limitation of executive power—that most clearly divided the Georgia parties.[8]

The relief issue and Tyler's apostasy kept Whigs on the defensive throughout the 1841 campaign. Governor Charles McDonald sought another term for the Democrats; Congressman William C. Dawson was the Whig nominee. Crying that Whigs had failed to restore prosperity, Democrats pledged to end the persecution of state banks and make credit plenty. A typical Democratic handbill touting relief promised that Floyd County voters would receive thirty-six dollars apiece if the Central Bank made another loan distribution. The Whigs spent too much time grousing about Democratic demagogy while their opponents swept the field. McDonald reversed the verdict of 1840, capturing the state by more than four thousand votes only a year after Harrison had rolled up an eight-thousand-vote Whig majority. With McDonald safely returned to office and a sizable new Democratic majority in the legislature, the Democrats had an opportunity to bring relief.[9]

Events in Milledgeville again demonstrated that politics was one thing and policy another. In his annual message, McDonald admitted that the Central Bank, given its deplorable condition, could not "minister to the public relief." The burden of paying state appropriations had led to the "utter annihilation of its means." Whig moaning over state finances, McDonald alleged, had damaged the state's credit and had prevented the sale of state bonds that could have improved the bank's situation. Democrats nonetheless doggedly reversed the work of the 1840 legislature and reexpanded the Central Bank's note-issuing powers. They also negated their own legislation, however, by prohibiting the Central Bank from making new loans until the unforeseeable day when it could maintain its existing notes at par with those of specie-paying banks. To reduce the bank's circulation, Democrats offered citizens the opportunity to exchange Central Bank notes at par for state bonds bearing 8 percent interest, merely another version of the plan enacted by the previous Whig legislature. Finally, the legislature granted private banks a brief reprieve from the 1840 law mandating a resumption of specie payments—the sum total of the Democrats' relief.[10]

The urgent need to find another political leader in the wake of the Tyler fiasco forced Georgia Whigs into the heretofore unimaginable step of nominating Henry Clay for the presidency at their June 1842 state convention. Although Clay had greatly modified his stance on the tariff and other matters over the years, his lasting identification with the nationalist economic measures that the State Rights party had opposed throughout the 1830s exposed Georgians to charges of gross inconsistency. The party had, however, already advanced too far to retreat from a Whig alliance. Once Clay's nomination placed the erstwhile State Rights party firmly in the Whig camp, the challenge became how to make national Whig doctrines, particularly the idea of a protective tariff, politically palatable in Georgia. Or, as Clay himself more accurately put it, Georgia Whigs faced the "difficulty of opposing the Tariff, and at the same time maintaining their Whig connection." [11]

Since their days under the British colonial system, Americans had believed that tariffs could foster or stunt manufacturing growth, aid or injure agricultural interests, and favor one section or another. After the War of 1812, many Southerners had joined in promoting higher tariffs to develop national independence in manufacturing, but this spirit had waned steadily during the 1820s. The nullification controversy had thoroughly inculcated one idea among Georgians: high tariffs discriminated against the agricultural South. The planters and farmers of Georgia, Whig and Democrat, favored low tariffs, and every politician in the state knew it.

Two more immediate factors enhanced the tariff's importance in the early 1840s. One, the most obvious, was the lamentable state of the economy. Bank contractions and the resulting deflation drove down the prices of property and products and mercilessly squeezed debtors. Citizens in several counties suppressed sales of property condemned for debt, a crowd in Americus destroyed court records and kidnapped a deputy sheriff, and some sheriffs abandoned their offices rather than face community hostility. Businessman, planter, and Democratic politician John B. Lamar reported that nearly everyone in Macon was "broke & ruined." The "country is so much in debt, & is so reckless & desperate," Lamar wrote, "that I fear sometimes that it is all going hell-wards." Economic disaster inclined many Georgians to look toward changes in tariff policy to relieve their afflictions.[12]

The other pressing factor was the sharp decline in imports and the gradual reduction of duties under the compromise tariff of 1833, which had run the federal government deep into debt. The final set of tariff reductions, scheduled for July 1842, promised to worsen the deficit. The country required new tariff legislation, and the burden of producing it fell on the Tyler administration and the Whig congressional majority. Northern Whigs predictably demanded increased duties to ease the fiscal crisis and to provide protection for home industry—a call that Georgians just as predictably resisted.

During congressional debates over a new tariff, Georgia Whigs unfurled their states' rights colors and revived arguments from the nullification era. James A. Meriwether, a lawyer-planter from a distinguished Wilkes County family, considered protective tariffs unconstitutional in principle and unjust in practice. Meriwether believed that protectionism offered needless bounties to greedy manufacturers and raised consumer prices on imported goods. He rejected the favorite protectionist contention that high tariff rates ultimately lowered prices by encouraging industrial efficiency and domestic competition. In laying tariffs for revenue, Meriwether concluded, Congress could discriminate among items to provide "incidental" protection, nothing more. Richard W. Habersham charged that protectionists had framed the 1842 bill to make "*protection the principal,* and revenue the *incident,* instead of making *revenue the principal, and protection the incident.*" After serving as a member of the committee that drew up the tariff bill, Habersham opposed the majority Whig measure and defended the Democratic minority report.[13]

Even such defiant stands failed to satisfy Georgia Democrats, who urged their opponents to sever all connections with northern Whigs. Mark Cooper and Edward Black, back in Congress as Democrats, led the verbal onslaught. The tariff was "a question mainly between North and South," Cooper declared. The "interests of both parties in Georgia, as planters and farmers, are identical," he reasoned, and the "best interest of both parties" dictated "uncompromising opposition" to Henry Clay and the Whigs.[14] Edward Black likewise wondered how Georgia Whigs could ignore the "evidence before [them] that the Whigs of the North and East advocate doctrines at war with the views, and feelings, and interests of both parties in Georgia." Whig Lott Warren, in turn, scolded Black for daring to "make party speeches here, on a question in which there is no difference in opinion with us in Georgia."[15]

Every Georgian voting, Whig or Democrat, senator or representative, opposed the final passage of the 1842 tariff. The bill was primarily a Whig measure, and it returned tariff duties to the comparatively high 1832 levels. Only the support of key northern Democrats such as Senators James Buchanan of Pennsylvania and Silas Wright of New York, however, allowed the bill to squeak through both the House and the Senate by a single vote.[16]

When the 1842 bill became law, Georgia Whigs rushed to prove that high duties did not necessarily a protective tariff make. The 1842 tariff was, as the phrase went, "a revenue tariff with incidental protection," and this semantic formula or some variation of it became a Whig chant.[17] The logic was that the federal government's need for revenue required "as high a duty as any friend of his country can desire for the protection of any of its branches of production," and that high duties, if levied without protective intent, violated no cherished southern principles.[18]

The 1842 tariff had, moreover, been the work of Northerners; Whigs stressed that no one at home should be blamed for it. "The great body of the northern people of both parties are in favor of the [protective] tariff," the *Milledgeville Southern Recorder* declared, "and it is deceitful and inexcusable in our southern opponents to attempt to mislead our people on the subject." Whigs insisted that "*substantially* there is but little difference with us at the South in our *practical* views" on the tariff. Scoffing at Democratic calls for antitariff meetings, the *Augusta Chronicle & Sentinel* wondered who the Democrats intended to oppose, since there was "no tariff party in Georgia." Several editors, scorning the protectionist views of Horace Greeley and other northern Whigs, even endorsed "a tariff for revenue *only*," a doctrine long congenial to the national Democracy.[19]

Whigs' antiprotectionist bent left Democrats little distinctive ground to stand on. Democrats often declared that they favored free trade, but free trade in Georgia meant a revenue tariff with somewhat lower duties than those the Whigs proposed. The free trade idea advocated by some Democrats elsewhere—abolishing tariffs and instituting direct taxation—never received more than token support. The people of the South, the *Milledgeville Federal Union* opined, were "unanimously in favor of free trade," but adamantly opposed to direct taxation. The tariff system would therefore continue, and the duties necessary to support the government were high enough that "a tariff for revenue is inevitably a tariff for protection." Whigs never expressed the notion of incidental protection better themselves.[20]

Democrats nonetheless maximized minute differences in tariff policy by branding Georgia Whigs as the willing dupes of hostile outsiders. Rapacious northern Whigs aimed ultimately at pauperizing the South, Democrats warned, and thus there could be "no middle ground between an open avowal, and a total repudiation of the protective policy." The pusillanimous ruse of "incidental protection" touted by Whigs just sugared the poisoned draught of ruinous taxation. Their worship of Henry Clay had compelled good states' rights men to discover "beauties in a protective tariff, and benefits in a national bank, which were hidden from their view for more than twenty years." [21]

Georgians clung to their low-tariff views despite their acute awareness of the current economic difficulties. Newspaper editorials calling for crop diversification and more home industry were commonplace. "Cotton is a drug, and at a low price," the Whig *Savannah Republican* commented in early 1842, "and till we can turn our hands to something else, we must continue to languish." From the western edge of the state's cotton belt, the Democratic *Columbus Times* noted that the "gloom and prostration of the cotton growing interest" had prompted Georgians to consider economic pursuits other "than the everlasting and all absorbing routine of cotton making." Taking a break from blasts against Whig protectionism, the *Milledgeville Federal Union* confessed that "neither tariff laws or taxes differently imposed can much affect the condition of the South" so long as "*we raise for market nothing but cotton.*" [22]

Advice aplenty did remarkably little to persuade white men to alter their basic way of life. What Whigs and Democrats alike truly wanted was a revival of the agricultural economy that had previously brought prosperity to Georgia. Crop diversification and manufacturing development were grand things, if "the value of lands and negroes would be enhanced." Treasuring their status as masters, the planters who controlled most of the capital in Georgia invested in land and slaves rather than factories. Few yeoman farmers and farm laborers hungered to trade their life on the land, however difficult, for work tending machines. The Whig *Milledgeville Southern Recorder* fittingly observed that Georgians were "strictly an agricultural people. Manufactures of any sort are only resorted to to fill up rainy days when the pursuits of agriculture must be pretermitted." Georgia lacked a protariff constituency and any genuine commitment to industrialization; no basis existed for a tariff debate over economic fundamentals. [23]

The only essential distinction between the Georgia parties on the tariff issue lay in their choice of northern compatriots. Fortunately for Democrats, the bulk of their northern party wing opposed high tariffs, while Whigs had constantly to apologize for northern Whigs' protectionism. These national party differences, skillfully emphasized, defined state party lines. Opponents, whatever their stated position, could be made odious by attacking the views of northern Whigs and Democrats. Both parties had practiced this tactic throughout the 1830s on issues ranging from nullification to a national bank, and they had perfected it with assaults on the northern party wings on matters touching slavery. The drive to form party dichotomies created images of Whigs as rabid protectionists and of Democrats as reckless free traders bent on setting a swarm of direct tax gatherers on the people. Neither of these caricatures resembled Georgia Whigs and Democrats, but by employing symbols based on the national party extremes, state politicians drew party lines much more sharply than native differences between the parties justified. By declaring that *they* were *different* from their northern allies, and that only the opposition displayed a hideous national uniformity, state leaders both redefined issues to preserve strength at home and reinforced a national political framework in which each party reflexively opposed the other.[24]

The 1842 campaign illustrated how the depression years had broadened the party battlefront. Whigs aligned with the national party now had to parry Democratic thrusts against Henry Clay, national banks, and protective tariffs. However much the Georgia party tried to distance itself from northern Whigs, it could not overcome the reality that Whig control in Washington had not cured economic woes. A vow to curb the evils of the Central Bank was the Whigs' main positive issue. Democrats recalled broken Whig promises and retained the initiative throughout the contest, capturing substantial majorities in both branches of the legislature and electing every man on their congressional ticket. The state was swinging back and forth between party poles as voters sought some relief from their misery. Political skies certainly had brightened for Democrats since 1840, and they had targets like Henry Clay and northern Whigs in clear sight.[25]

The newfound Democratic confidence stemmed partly from the emergence of young, talented leaders. John H. Lumpkin, John B. Lamar, and Howell Cobb, all of whom won congressional seats in 1842, would wield great power in the Georgia Democratic party. John Lumpkin had particularly good political breeding; his uncles included former governor Wilson Lumpkin and noted jurist Joseph Henry Lumpkin. After acquiring a fine education at Franklin College and Yale, Lumpkin had moved to the Cherokee country in the mid-1830s and established a law practice in Rome. As a pragmatic, popular politician adept at local organizing, Lumpkin built a loyal constituency among the county notables and yeoman farmers of northwest Georgia. John Lamar, in contrast, lacked personal political ambitions and disdained glad-handing the masses. He pursued politics as a pastime, a diversion from managing his fortune in land and slaves, and he operated best in the circles of the black belt elite. Though influential in their own right, Lumpkin and Lamar were most important for the aid they rendered to the group's real politician.

Howell Cobb was gregarious, ambitious, generous, and calculating. Born in 1815 into a family that traced its roots back to early Virginia settlers, Cobb grew up near the town of Athens on the family estate of Cobbham. His father, John Addison Cobb, owned more than a hundred slaves, and the family's comfortable circumstances allowed the boys among the seven children to attend Franklin College. Howell began studying there at age thirteen, in 1829, and soon made his mark in both society and academics. He became president of the Phi Kappa debating society in his senior year and graduated fourth in his class. A couple of years later, while intermittently studying law in Athens, Cobb fell in love with and married Mary Ann Lamar, the daughter of a wealthy Bibb County planter and the sister of Cobb's college friend John Lamar. The marriage was fortunate for Cobb in several respects. He and Mary Ann were a loving couple; she was not only politically astute, but also willing to bear the burdens arising from Howell's political career. Mary Ann Lamar Cobb's legacy from her father included several plantations and some two hundred slaves. Her extensive family relations among the southern elite added to Howell's already formidable political connections. Not least, Cobb acquired the services of brother-in-law John, who managed his sister's properties and her husband's political business with uncommon ability.

Cobb passed the bar in February 1836 and entered a law partnership with another college mate, Junius Hillyer. Despite Cobb's ample means, the late 1830s were difficult years for the young lawyer. His practice with Hillyer grew slowly, and Cobb squandered huge sums on a farm in Walton County and on a mansion near Athens. His father's fortunes declined during the depression, and Cobb eventually had to assume many of his father's obligations and to sell family property to meet debts. Nevertheless, he found time for politics. His family had mainly been Troupites, but Cobb entered politics in the nullification era as a Unionist and a devoted supporter of Martin Van Buren. During his political apprenticeship, Cobb served in various minor posts in party affairs, made a reputation as a stump speaker in the 1840 campaign, and ran unsuccessfully for the legislature in Whiggish Clarke County. His selection as a candidate for Congress rewarded his talents and acknowledged his social standing. After a taste of Washington, Cobb's ambition for national honors drove him ever onward and eventually made him the leading Democrat in Georgia.[26]

Governor Charles McDonald, the most prominent Democrat in Georgia in 1842, had bad news for the incoming legislature. The failure of state bond sales and the practically universal payment of state taxes in depreciated Central Bank notes had produced a fiscal crisis; a tax increase was imperative to maintain the state's solvency. He recommended repealing much of the past Central Bank legislation and making the bank responsible only for redeeming its own notes and bonds. The Central Bank should not, McDonald emphasized, issue another dollar in loans.

Democratic legislators grudgingly took most of the prescribed medicine. A Central Bank bill prohibited it from extending new loans, left it to tend to its own obligations, and transferred all of the state's other financial business to the treasury. Nearly two-fifths of house Whigs voted for the bill when they found that they could get nothing better, but some Whigs formally protested using future taxes to pay Central Bank debts. The legislation nevertheless accomplished the Whig goal of ending the bank's active career; it would wind up its affairs, burn its bills as loans were collected, and pass from the political scene.

Legislators, reluctant to tax for any purpose at any time, strongly resisted McDonald's call for increased revenues. Democrats had howled about the 20 percent tax hike voted by the 1840 Whig legislature; they had even tried to repeal it a year later, only to meet McDonald's veto. Democrats tinkered with tax bills for nearly two months until McDonald finally threatened to block the appropriations bill—meaning no pay for legislators. Then they joined a minority of Whigs to boost tax rates 25 percent. The tax struggle, like that over the Central Bank, was a storm before a calm; the rates set in 1842 remained in place through the end of the decade.[27]

With the state decks cleared, the parties turned their attention to presidential politics. Both parties looked toward the 1844 race as the greatest trial yet on the issues of the Jacksonian party system. Georgia Whigs had, of course, cast their lot with Henry Clay, the overwhelming choice for the national party's nomination. State Democrats, meanwhile, became engaged in a quarrel over the presidential pretensions of Martin Van Buren and John C. Calhoun. Having lost the state in 1836 and 1840, few Georgia Democrats relished the prospect of another Van Buren run. Their opinions notwithstanding, the New Yorker was a northern favorite and the presumptive 1844 nominee. Calhoun's Democratic credentials were dubious, given his authorship of nullification, his enmity for Andrew Jackson, and his early flirtations with Whiggery. But some prominent Southerners were willing to follow nearly anywhere Calhoun led, and his aspirations for 1844 created trouble in Georgia.

The Calhoun–Van Buren rivalry exposed two fundamental cleavages in the state's Democratic coalition: the division between the black belt and north Georgia, and the overlapping, but not identical, clash between original Unionists and Calhounite Democrats of 1840 vintage. Most of the party's voting strength and many of its prominent figures hailed from the black belt. Black belt Democrats were, however, a minority within their own region, where Whigs were the dominant party. Mountain and upcountry Democrats of north Georgia were fewer in absolute numbers than their black belt brethren, but they formed the party's backbone. Lastingly devoted to Old Hickory, small farmers in many north Georgia counties supplied huge majorities for the Democracy, often overcoming the party's weakness in the black belt to produce victories in statewide elections. Harmonious cooperation between the black belt and north Georgia wings was thus essential for the party's success.[28]

Calhounites, unfortunately, did not work well with others. Their defining characteristics were their virulent antiparty spirit, their emphasis on southern unity, and their willingness to attack the national party system to promote sectional goals. Edward Black, Mark Anthony Cooper, and Senator-elect Walter Colquitt—chosen by the 1842 legislature—were the leading

Georgia disciples of the South Carolina statesman, but behind this trio stood men such as *Augusta Constitutionalist* editor James Gardner, Jr., John H. Howard of Columbus, Milledgeville's Tomlinson Fort, and former governor Wilson Lumpkin. Fort and Lumpkin, like several other old Clark-Unionists, had first befriended Calhoun during his early days as a national figure and were returning to the South Carolinian after closing the rift over nullification. Most, though far from all, Calhounites hailed from the black belt, and their headstrong drive for party leadership brought them into conflict with north Georgia Jacksonians.[29]

Toward the end of 1841, Wilson Lumpkin, John H. Howard, Edward Black, and other Calhounites launched a covert campaign to further Calhoun's presidential hopes. The Calhounites' strategy involved altering Democratic party nominating procedures and electing national convention delegates by districts. These delegates would then vote individually at the convention, breaking Van Buren's presumed hold on state delegations voting as blocs. Advised by Calhoun himself, and working in concert with Calhounites in several other states, the Georgia clique soon gained momentum. Editors William S. Rogers and John G. Park of the *Milledgeville Federal Union* endorsed Calhoun in December 1842, and William C. Daniell, a wealthy planter-physician, former State Rights man, and uncle of Mark Cooper, worked throughout early 1843 to engineer Calhoun's nomination at the June Democratic state convention. Daniell and various coadjutors shrewdly concentrated on organizing pro-Calhoun delegations from Whiggish black belt counties that seldom sent delegates to Democratic state conventions.[30]

Despite warnings from original Unionists that an attempt to force John Calhoun on the party might prove "disastrous to the Democracy of the State," the Calhounites staged a successful state convention coup. Tomlinson Fort presided, and a committee report declared that John C. Calhoun was the "first choice" of the Georgia Democracy and instructed national convention delegates to support the South Carolinian. Although Howell Cobb rose to defend Martin Van Buren, the convention set aside a substitute resolution nominating the New Yorker. The convention then adopted the pro-Calhoun report by a 101 to 63 vote, with black belt delegations furnishing the margin of victory. The Calhounites likewise triumphed in the race for the gubernatorial nomination when Mark Anthony Cooper narrowly defeated an original Union man, Hiram Warner, on the fifth ballot.[31]

The nominations of the prophet of nullification for the presidency and a former nullifier for governor provoked an immediate and violent reaction. Veteran Democrats bewailed the seeming reversal of fortune and the revival of South Carolina heresies. One stalwart Jacksonian, James P. Simmons, typically complained that the Union party of 1832 and 1833 had been "swallowed up" by Calhounites and transformed into a "Nullification party." Regular Democrats, well aware of the Calhounites' inveterate hostility toward party organizations, feared that the Calhounites' rise would threaten the integrity of the national Democracy. Several north Georgia Democratic editors virtually repudiated the Calhoun endorsement, and grumbling about Cooper's candidacy pervaded the mountains and the upcountry.[32]

To oppose Cooper, the 1843 Whig state convention unanimously nominated George W. Crawford, an Augusta lawyer-planter, a veteran state legislator who had helped lead the fight against the Central Bank, and a distant relative of William H. Crawford. George Crawford was John Berrien's favorite candidate, and the 1843 convention marked the pinnacle of Berrien's power in the Georgia Whig party. Berrien presided as the Whigs chose national convention delegates pledged to his friend, Henry Clay; he received a complimentary nomination for the vice presidency; he gave the closing speech; and he drafted the convention's address to the voters. But as the man who had done the most to guide the State Rights–Whig party along its tortuous course relaxed in the president's chair, the successors to his crown sat before him.[33]

Robert Augustus Toombs and Alexander Hamilton Stephens were nothing alike and had much in common. Both were children of old middle Georgia: Toombs, the elder by two years, was born in 1810 into a Wilkes County plantation family; Stephens was the son of a pious schoolteacher who worked his farm along with a handful of slaves. Though Toombs's father died in 1815 and Stephens was orphaned in 1826, both youngsters gained an education and attended Franklin College. Toombs entered at age fourteen and exited three and a half years later, expelled for accumulated infractions that ranged from swearing to assaulting his enemies with knives, hatchets, and pistols. After managing to graduate from Union College in New York, Toombs went to the University of Virginia law school, where he completed his first and only year tied for last in his class. A special act of the Georgia legislature allowed Toombs, who was not yet twenty-one, to take a March

1830 bar examination before Judge William Crawford—he passed in spite of his legal training. Later that year, he married Julia Ann DuBose, the daughter of a Lincoln County planter.

Stephens came to Athens the fall after Toombs had left it, carried books instead of weapons, and graduated in 1832 as the class valedictorian. He found college society very congenial, and his standing within it fed his already considerable ego. Scholarship was, however, no substitute for inherited wealth. When his college chums headed back to their family plantations after graduation, Stephens crushingly realized that he was still just a poor boy with limited prospects. He muddled along for many months in teaching jobs he hated before resolving to make a career as a lawyer. He, too, passed an examination given by the venerable William Crawford, in July 1834, and duly entered the legal profession.

The two men became close friends while riding the law circuits. The strong, boisterous, profane Toombs and the frail, melancholy, puritanical Stephens made far different but equally memorable impressions on their legal colleagues. Stephens's high-pitched voice and talent for pathos moved juries; Toombs hammered away at salient points and seemed to command favorable verdicts. Traveling and rooming together, they increasingly consulted each other on matters of law, politics, and life. Headstrong Robert sometimes even heeded Alex, the only person outside of Toombs's immediate family who ever exercised much influence over him. Stephens, a lifelong bachelor, had a circle of friends in his hometown of Crawfordville, but his political and personal alliance with Toombs was central to his public career.

They went to the legislature together in 1836, Toombs from Wilkes County and Stephens from Taliaferro. Except for 1841, when neither sought election, they returned to the legislature each year until they moved on to higher offices. Gradually ascending the ladder of party leadership, by the early 1840s they were among the handful of Whigs who directed the party's action in the legislature. Toombs battled Governor McDonald over relief and the Central Bank. In national affairs, Stephens drafted a Whig report outlining the party's stand on a national bank, an incidental protective tariff, and a limitation of the veto power. The 1843 Whig convention recognized these efforts by nominating Stephens for Congress and choosing Toombs as a national convention delegate.[34]

During the 1843 campaign, Whigs exploited jealousies over the Calhoun and Cooper nominations to promote disaffection among old Union-Democrats. They also flayed the McDonald administration and the Central Bank, portraying Crawford as a potential financial savior. Democrats, wary of mentioning the presidential question and reluctant to discuss the dismal economic affairs of the state, put up a rather feeble fight.[35]

On election day, many north Georgia Jacksonians shunned a Democratic party headed by Mark Cooper and John Calhoun. Crawford outpolled Cooper by some 3,600 votes statewide, and Cooper came as close to losing the mountains and the upcountry as any Democratic gubernatorial candidate ever had. McDonald had carried 65.2 percent of the north Georgia vote in 1841; Cooper received only 55.6 percent. In the black belt, where Calhounites had hoped to attract many old State Rights men, Cooper instead ran some 2,800 votes behind McDonald's previous showing. To cap off the Whig triumph, Alexander Stephens and Absalom H. Chappell captured vacant seats in Congress, and the party won a majority in both branches of the legislature. Whigs united behind the popular Crawford would have given the Democrats a close race in any case, but the Calhoun-Cooper nominations amounted to self-destruction.

A December Democratic convention read the lessons contained in the voting returns and hastily jettisoned John C. Calhoun. Those assembled rebuked the Calhounites for their "'*manworship*,' that fatal disease, which destroys the purity of a party, and directs the devotion of its members from principles, and directs it to a human creature (whom there [*sic*] senseless worship would erect into a demi-God)." The convention effectively rescinded Calhoun's nomination by omitting instructions for Georgia delegates, leaving them free to support any candidate at the Baltimore national convention. Martin Van Buren's few devoted allies gloated over the result. *Athens Southern Banner* editor Albon Chase assured Howell Cobb that the Baltimore nominee, the "favorite of the party throughout the Union," would be "our friend Van."[36]

Most Democrats were not in such a festive mood. They realized that membership in a national party entailed sacrifices, but a quadrennial dose of Martin Van Buren was too much for many to stomach. Van Buren's supposed dalliances with the abolitionists, his lackluster administration, his paltering on the tariff, and his reputation as a political trickster who was a "greater lover of office than of his country" had crippled him in Georgia.

Milledge H. Gathright, an original Union Democrat from Dahlonega, lamented that if Van Buren ran again, "the old slanders & abuse against him in 1840 will again be made; & it will be impossible to convince the people of Ga of their falsehood." John Calhoun was the wrong man, but Georgia Democrats had not abandoned thoughts of finding a substitute for Martin Van Buren.[37]

Whigs, on the other hand, hated to think that Van Buren might *not* receive the Democratic nomination. George Crawford exulted that Van Buren's "political transgressions" were "so freshly buried" that resurrecting them would be "an easy task." Whigs confidently assumed that Democratic divisions would produce a Clay landslide, and the Kentuckian's triumphal tour through Georgia in March 1844 further enhanced their optimism.[38]

But the Whigs reckoned without considering John Tyler's novel problem. The president had no party yet wanted to remain president, a difficulty perhaps soluble if the right hobby, like the annexation of Texas, could be mounted. Tyler and his secretary of state, fellow Virginian Abel Upshur, surreptitiously explored the prospects for annexation for many months before the project broke into the open in early 1844. When a freak cannon explosion during a Potomac cruise killed Upshur, Tyler replaced him with none other than John Calhoun, who had publicly abandoned his presidential bid. After assuming control of foreign affairs on 1 April, Calhoun concluded an annexation treaty with startling speed. Although Tyler's reelection chances remained moribund, the revival of the long dormant annexation question badly scrambled everyone's plans for the presidential race.

The Texas annexation fever that hit Georgia around the middle of April 1844 heartened state Democrats. Here at last, many thought, was an issue so appealing to Southerners that even Van Buren could ride it to victory. Texas annexation offered the opportunity to acquire open land, increase the political power of the South, expand the domain of American freedom, and extend the institution of slavery. The annexation question, moreover, rapidly became a test of northern respect for southern rights and institutions. The addition of a vast new slaveholding region to the Union—either with northern assistance or over northern objections—would demonstrate the South's continuing strength within the Union and provide additional guarantees for the future safety of slavery. A large majority of white men favored Texas annexation, and Thomas R. R. Cobb reported to his older brother

Howell that the "Texas question is exciting much attention in all minds & the feeling is strong that *now* or *never* are we to throw our protection over her. I tell you if Van Buren, is unequivocal in his approbation of the measure, Georgia is his."[39]

Martin Van Buren was, however, seldom unequivocal about anything, and Democrats worried that delay in advocating annexation might surrender the initiative to the Whigs. Lest Van Buren vacillate, the *Milledgeville Federal Union* delivered an ultimatum: "We consider the opinion of Mr. Van Buren himself, public and notorious; he has been and we have no doubt is decidedly in favor of annexation. If he is not, we are not in his favor."[40]

Whig leaders considered the source in reacting to the Texas issue. They thought that Tyler and Calhoun had contrived the Texas project to serve their own treacherous purposes; nothing those two did could redound to the advantage of the Whig party. While waiting to hear Henry Clay's views on Texas annexation, editors and politicians maintained silence or issued ambiguous comments. Editors Miller Grieve and Richard Orme of the *Milledgeville Southern Recorder,* for example, pronounced themselves "decidedly in favor of annexation" but cautioned against efforts to "*force* the question to a conclusion" prematurely.[41]

On 27 April, Clay and Van Buren published letters announcing their views on Texas annexation. Both men deprecated hasty action, citing the risk of war with Mexico, while still offering the hope of ultimate annexation. The Whig national convention met just four days after the publication of Clay's letter and unanimously nominated him for the presidency. The Democratic national convention was another month away, however, and proannexation southern Democrats quickly coordinated a drive to dump the New Yorker.[42]

Some Georgia Democrats still clung to Van Buren and opposed making the immediate annexation of Texas a party test. Albon Chase, for one, urged Georgians not to be "swallowed up in the whirlpool of sectional interest and fanatical prejudice." Whether their concerns were legitimate or not, many Northerners, even some Democrats, had qualms about Texas and the accession of slave territory. "The Texas question is obliged to injure us," Chase reasoned, "for if Mr. Van Buren had come out the advocate of immediate annexation, he would have lost more at the North than he will now at the South. My advice is that we prevent as far as possible making it a party question." The Democracy could lose several southern states and still capture the presidency, and Chase was willing to sacrifice Georgia and postpone annexation to promote national victory.[43]

Most Democrats were not so obliging; they threatened to abandon the national party unless the Baltimore convention ditched Van Buren. The *Macon Georgia Telegraph* became "deeply indignant at seeing Mr. Van Buren quibbling over words and technicalities" and demanded a proannexation candidate. Calhounite William C. Daniell alleged that Van Buren had crafted his letter "to please the abolitionists," and his colleague, William L. Mitchell, stated simply, "It is a sine qua non that our candidate should be in favor of the immediate annexation of Texas." Even stalwart Jacksonians such as Howell Cobb and Charles McDonald disowned Van Buren and talked of running a third candidate in the South.[44]

Not for the first or last time, Southerners bent the national Democracy to their will at the Baltimore convention. Although a majority of the delegates were pledged to support Van Buren on the first ballot, the Georgia delegation and nearly all others from the slave states voted to sustain the two-thirds rule to block Van Buren. The New Yorker's name was withdrawn after eight ballots, and the convention unanimously nominated James K. Polk of Tennessee on a platform recommending the immediate annexation of Texas. Polk had not been a prominent candidate before the convention, but Georgia Democrats gleefully received a nomination they "had not thought of" as the "best which could have been made." The *Milledgeville Federal Union* spoke for the whole Georgia Democracy in saying, "Candor will allow that we have suddenly been rescued from a very great dilemma."[45]

Whigs were left in an awkward position. John Berrien, Alexander Stephens, and others had known Clay's opinions beforehand, and they had agreed that annexation could be safely delayed. Rather than opposing annexation per se, as many northern Whigs did, Georgia Whigs objected only to immediate annexation—and not always even to that. When Clay's Texas letter first appeared, the *Southern Recorder* admitted to differing with the Kentuckian over immediate annexation, but assured Georgians that political considerations would not long impede the "colonization and civilization of the American South and West." The editors thought that Whigs, while not opposing "ultimate annexation," should assume "as the party ground the position in favor of that measure when the country requires it, and when it can be properly effected." The Whig state convention in June took precisely this tack in a resolution calling for "the annexation of Texas to the United States, at the earliest practicable period, consistent with the honor and good faith of the nation." The "earliest practicable period," most Whigs stressed, would arrive shortly after Henry Clay moved into the White House. Downplaying Texas and emphasizing Clay's superior experience and reputation seemed a foolproof plan, unless Democrats used the annexation issue "to circumscribe the presidential question, into a mere Southern and sectional effort." [46]

Some Georgia Whigs did express reservations about annexation similar to those found in northern Whig journals. "Old Thirteen," a correspondent of the *Savannah Republican,* complained that "continual and enormous additions of territory, destroy all identity of country—extinguish patriotism and make cosmopolites of us all." Annexation would "drain the older States of valuable population and immense capital" and would make the nation too "unwieldy" to be governable. Extending American institutions would pervert them by breaking attachments to home and place; the powerful centripetal "*passion* for change and restless movement" threatened societal stability.[47]

Other Whigs charged that northern Democrats had acquiesced in annexation only as a ploy to ruin the older slave states. Given low cotton prices, swelling production from the fertile lands of Alabama and Mississippi, and the prospect of more cotton to come from Texas, some Whigs in the eastern cotton belt wondered whether Texas annexation represented a sectional boon or an economic bust. The *Savannah Republican* warned that the lure of Texas land would drain masters and slaves from the upper South, gradually leading to "abolition in Virginia, Maryland, Delaware, Kentucky and Missouri—and *amalgamation* beyond the *Rio Bravo!!*" A glutted cotton market and a mass exodus for Texas could compel even Georgia masters to confront the question of what to do "with slavery if slave labour is rendered valueless?"[48]

Senator John Berrien was easily the most vocal of all Georgia Whigs in opposing immediate annexation. Annexation would not meaningfully increase southern political power, Berrien believed, because Texas's huge and varied territory would be divided into several free and slave states. Northern manufacturing and commercial interests would gain more from developing

Texas markets than the South would benefit from extending slavery. Berrien also deeply distrusted John Tyler; he feared that the president's headlong rush to seize Texas would instigate war with Mexico. Prudence, caution, and negotiations offered an honorable alternative to greedily wresting territory from a weaker neighbor. Arguments like Berrien's proved persuasive in the short run: in early June, the Senate defeated Tyler's Texas treaty by a 35-to-16 vote.[49]

Democrats scorned Whig temporizing and insisted that every "*friend* of the Annexation of Texas is in favor of immediate action." Drawing on concerns raised earlier by John Calhoun, Democrats warned of a British plot to snatch Texas and transform it into a free-soil haven for runaway slaves. Democrats maintained that only "party discipline" prevented southern Whigs from demanding immediate annexation; they had to bow to a northern "opposition founded on slavery alone." Henry Clay's attempts to appease antislavery feeling among northern Whigs betrayed a willingness to "surrender the south to the demon of abolition." "Alas! poor Southern Whiggery!" the *Athens Southern Banner* exclaimed. "Compelled to follow your Northern leaders against all your old principles, and yet trying to conceal your true position!" Make no mistake, it blared, "THE ELECTION OF HENRY CLAY IS THE DEATH KNELL OF TEXAS ANNEXATION." [50]

Many Democrats, particularly Calhounites, desperately wanted Texas. If Texas were not annexed, Matthew H. McAllister of Savannah predicted, "the interests and political importance of the Southwestern and Southern States will be doomed to encounter gradual decay and ultimately certain dissolution." Edward Black told John Calhoun that "the ultimate prosperity—perhaps the very existence, of the South depends in great degree" on Texas annexation. Former governor Wilson Lumpkin believed that Texas "must speedily become a part & portion, of our great confederacy—or the abolition spirit, will destroy our beloved institutions." Northerners' refusal to support Texas annexation because of slavery, Calhounites contended, would be an insult to every southern man and a violation of the South's equal rights in the Union. Texas was a vital test case for Calhounites, a portent of the future course of sectional relations.[51]

Torn between irreconcilable state and national party imperatives, Whigs lost the prosouthern high ground by trying to make timing the issue on Texas annexation. Their ties to Henry Clay and northern Whigs precluded them from echoing Democrats' calls for immediate annexation, yet they did not want to, and politically could not afford to, turn their backs on the Lone Star Republic. It was the sad and ultimately fatal misfortune of Georgia Whigs to have northern allies who never sided with the South in any controversy involving slavery.

Texas annexation was the new, volatile issue in 1844, but it was just part of the story. The tariff remained important despite the revelation that James Polk would have made a good Georgia Whig. In June, Polk released his so-called Kane letter, which informed a Pennsylvania Democrat that he favored a tariff with "moderate discriminating duties" that would "afford reasonable incidental protection to our home industry." Polk's employment of Whig phraseology to woo the northern protectionist vote embarrassed Democrats, and Whigs seized on the Kane letter as evidence that the Democrats had gulled Georgians. Although Whigs hoped that the tariff issue would fade away after Polk's missive, the Kane letter actually did nothing to silence Democrats' howling about Whig protectionism.[52]

Whigs and Democrats eventually ranged over all the issues of the Jacksonian party system: nullification, a national bank, the subtreasury, the Central Bank, the limitation of executive power, the evils of party dictation, and more figured in the canvass. The campaign was overwhelmingly negative; both parties concentrated on blasting the opposition. Whigs discovered thirty reasons for not electing James Polk, including the allegations that his grandfather had been a Tory during the Revolution and that Polk himself had shirked service during the War of 1812. But Democrats still preferred Polk over the "ambitious, unprincipled, arbitrary, artful, tyrannical demagogue, Henry Clay." Each party accused the other of inconsistency and documented northern opposition heresies to reinforce every stereotype that defined party differences.[53]

The negative issue that surpassed all others was the taint of abolitionism. Both northern party wings courted the small abolitionist vote during 1844, and Georgia newspapers printed extracts from northern opposition papers touting either Polk or Clay as antislavery candidates. A week before the election, the *Macon Georgia Messenger* featured several "news" items with headings such as "Polk in Favor of Abolition Petitions" and "Proof Positive of the Coalition between Locofocoism and Abolitionism." Democrats incessantly preached that "the strength of the whig party is at the North, and under influences adverse to southern principles, institutions and interests." "Are not the proofs overwhelming," the *Augusta Constitutionalist* asked, "of the northern whig leaders being abolitionists themselves, or making the greatest exertions to complete the treaty between them and the abolitionists?" The notion of guilt by association was integral to Georgia party competition; it mattered not that Polk and Clay were southern slaveholders.[54]

The October congressional elections, the first ever held under the district system, highlighted two central characteristics of Georgia politics: close statewide competition and significant differences in party strength between regions. Alexander Stephens and Robert Toombs handily carried the seventh and eighth districts in the eastern cotton belt, while John Lumpkin and Howell Cobb amassed large majorities in the fifth and sixth districts in north Georgia. The other four races were much closer. Washington Poe, a well-known Macon Whig, won by fewer than 150 votes in the second district in the southwestern black belt. In the third and fourth districts, which embraced the west-central black belt and two upcountry counties, Democrats Seaborn Jones, an old State Rights man, and Hugh A. Haralson gained narrow triumphs. The huge and sparsely populated first district, composed of coastal and pine barrens – wiregrass counties, went to Whig Thomas Butler King. The parties thus elected four congressmen apiece; the statewide Democratic majority was some 2,300 votes.

Ninety percent of Georgia's eligible voters went to the polls in the November election, and 51.2 percent of them voted for James K. Polk, who won Georgia with 44,153 votes to Clay's 42,115. North Georgia Democrats returned to their traditional form after the party shook off John Calhoun; Polk carried 68.1 percent of the mountain vote and 61.1 percent in the upcountry. A 25.8 percent increase in north Georgia turnout, amounting to 5,727 more voters than in 1843, was a major cause of Polk's triumph. Democrats also posted a slight increase, 1.7 percent, over their black belt totals the year before. The more telling point of comparison, however, was between 1840 and 1844. Statewide, Polk tallied 12,170 votes more than had Martin Van Buren; Clay bettered William Henry Harrison by only 1,771 votes. Given the intense partisan loyalties of the era, which ensured that most voters would retain their allegiances year after year, the net Democratic gain of more than 10,000 votes between 1840 and 1844 was startling. Although both parties played full hands in 1844, the Democrats held Texas, the ace of trumps.

The 1844 presidential election marked the zenith of the Jacksonian party system. The national Whig and Democratic parties were more closely matched and battled on a broader range of issues than ever before, and a few thousand votes decided the outcome. Polk won New York, Pennsylvania, and Virginia by thin margins, and with them, the election. Voting patterns in the South mainly mirrored those in Georgia: Clay's totals barely, if at all, exceeded Harrison's, while Polk gained thousands of votes over Van Buren's showing. The Texas issue and campaign excitement brought out multitudes of new voters and past nonvoters, who helped carry Polk into the White House.[55]

Georgia Whigs' manifold sacrifices seemed all for naught. The *Savannah Republican* rightly declared that "the Whigs have never been half so strongly united as at the present moment, even under their present defeat." Georgia Whigs had struggled for four years to adapt their views to those of the national party on a national bank, the tariff, and Texas annexation, only to falter at the polls. John Berrien complained that unprincipled Democrats had elected a candidate whose "chief recommendation" had been "his insignificance." That Polk could best the great Henry Clay was enough to "shake our confidence in our institutions."[56]

The verdict rendered in November 1844 ended an era of party history: perennial Jacksonian economic issues soon lost their salience. The tariff would inspire a bit more antebellum controversy, but not for decades would it regain the importance it had had in the early 1840s. John Tyler had already practically killed the national bank question, and Clay's defeat delivered the coup de grâce. Beginning in 1846 with the introduction of the Wilmot Proviso, the parameters of party competition rapidly constricted, until debates revolved almost solely around a small constellation of issues concerning southern rights, the protection of slavery, and the future of the Union. What had been intermittent shouts about abolitionism became protracted screams.

# FOUR

# Detours Around the Territorial Impasse, 1844-1848

Georgians mostly slumbered through 1845 "in a state of bankruptcy as to political feeling," but the Mexican War, the centerpoint of James K. Polk's administration, rekindled partisan passions and sparked an explosive conflict over the status of slavery in the territories acquired from Mexico.[1] The territorial issue split both national parties along sectional lines, and compromise efforts repeatedly failed either to settle the slavery question or to heal party breaches. In the 1848 presidential election, Whigs and Democrats temporarily surmounted their divisions by running Janus-faced campaigns: proslavery in the South and antislavery in the North. But such evasive tactics postponed rather than prevented the cataclysmic reckoning that in 1850 would disrupt Georgia's Jacksonian party system.

When Congress convened in December 1844, Texas annexation arose again to haunt the Georgia Whig leadership. John Tyler and assorted Democrats advanced the idea of annexing Texas through a joint resolution, which would avoid the constitutional requirement of a two-thirds majority in the Senate to confirm treaties. A majority of southern Whigs in the House, including Alexander Stephens and Duncan Clinch of Georgia, then maneuvered to steal the annexation issue by supporting Tennessee Whig Milton Brown's resolution to admit Texas immediately as a state. Stephens favored annexation as a means of augmenting the South's political power, and he contended that an independent Texas fell within the scope of Congress's constitutional authority to admit new states. Stephens's course outraged Senator John Berrien, who believed that a treaty was the sole constitutional means of acquiring foreign territory. He warned that constitutional laxity condoned by southern men in the scramble for Texas might someday recoil on the minority South and furnish precedents for federal action against slavery. On a more personal level, Berrien and his friends feared a Stephens plot to supplant Berrien as party leader.[2]

Whigs wanted to rid themselves of the Texas question, but backing annexation entailed alienating northern Whigs, and opposing it risked political suicide at home. Robert Toombs regretted that northern Whigs were "foolishly not to say wickedly narrowing it down to a single question of pro & anti slavery." If Texas annexation became a purely sectional question, Toombs thought that "its [southern] opponents must needs be swept from the political boards." A Milledgeville Whig similarly cautioned John Berrien that Texas "was in our way last year, it is in our way now and it will be a thorn in our side until it is, as you say, put to rest in some way."[3]

Berrien's refusal to relent on annexation seemed to many to be just the latest of the aging senator's errors. During a northern campaign tour in 1844, Berrien had hewed rather too closely to the northern Whig tariff line, verging on outright endorsement of protectionism. This brand of Whiggery had always repelled a Georgia party accustomed to speaking with a southern accent. Henry Clay's subsequent defeat had encouraged "a disposition to carp at your course," Charles Jenkins informed Berrien, "some saying that you had much better have been at your Post in Georgia last summer taking care of your own state—others that at the North you too strongly advocated the Tariff." Grievances against Berrien smoldered long after Congress disposed of Texas annexation, and the senator's allies rightly feared that his critics would grab at the first opportunity to unseat him.[4]

Whig leaders masked their disagreements during the 1845 campaign. The gradual upturn in the state's economy and the successful liquidation of the Central Bank made George Crawford a popular governor and the party's unanimous choice for a second term. The Whig convention, recognizing that it "would be worse than madness" to revisit the issues of 1844, avoided any mention of national politics. The Democrats nominated Matthew Hall McAllister of Savannah for governor, adopted the 1844 national Democratic platform as their creed, and ignored state concerns.[5]

The parties thus talked past each other in a peculiar contest. Democrats touted Polk, Texas, and the glory of the national Democracy. Insofar as they discussed state measures, they defended the Central Bank and gave the 1842 Democratic legislature credit for restoring the state's solvency. The Democratic newspapers depicted John Berrien as a raving protectionist and recalled that he had appeared on a Boston platform with the notorious Kentucky abolitionist, Cassius M. Clay. While urging the election of a Democratic legislature to end Berrien's career, Democrats also stressed that a McAllister victory would second the rebuke given to Henry Clay. Whigs recounted the financial horrors of the McDonald administrations and chastised Democrats for dragging national politics into a state election. In pleas for upcountry and mountain votes, Whigs characterized McAllister as an arrogant coastal nabob who dined with dictatorial Calhounites such as Mark Cooper and William Daniell. Elect McAllister, the *Athens Southern Whig* warned, "and you have an aristocracy settled upon you forever." [6]

Whig attacks on McAllister and Crawford's strong record as governor tipped the balance in another extremely close election. A few hundred additional Whig votes and a 4,500-vote drop in the Democratic total from 1844 gave Crawford a second term. The parties simply switched positions; Whigs carried 51.2 percent of the vote in 1845 after Democrats had captured 51.0 percent a year earlier. Some Whigs returned to their party after casting a vote for Polk and Texas, and Democratic leaders failed to match the 1844 enthusiasm that had produced a full turnout. Crawford ran ahead of Whig legislative tickets in many counties, a result Alexander Stephens ungenerously attributed "to the weight of Berrien." [7]

John Berrien's trial on charges of resembling a northern Whig took place during the first two weeks of the 1845 legislative session. The Whigs had a majority on joint ballot, but the Democratic senate majority could have blocked a resolution to elect a United States senator. Instead, on 6 November, six Democratic senators, gambling that disputes over Berrien would shatter the Whig party, instigated a resolution to bring on the senatorial election and thereby forced Whigs to join them in its passage. A Whig party caucus held that evening nominated Charles Dougherty for senator. On hearing the news, John Berrien resigned his seat, a move that sobered Whigs and commenced a scramble to avoid a party schism. In a straight party vote on 13 November, the legislature reelected Berrien to serve his unexpired term; Charles Dougherty received a superior court judgeship as a consolation prize. Democratic senators then tired of the sport and blocked further attempts to fill the 1847 Senate seat. Berrien's firm yet conciliatory speech delivered to a Whig meeting just prior to his reelection defended his opposition to Texas annexation and denied that he had ever advocated a tariff solely for protection. Although Berrien survived this challenge, his days as the champion of the Georgia Whig party were ended.[8]

The year 1846 was a watershed in American history. President James K. Polk and the Democratic majority in Congress passed an overhauled version of Martin Van Buren's subtreasury and a new tariff bill. In foreign affairs, Polk contested Great Britain's claims to Oregon and engaged the United States in a controversial war with Mexico. The Mexican War was for Polk what Texas had been for John Tyler, a powerful lever that triggered all sorts of intended and unintended consequences.

Aside from occasional excitement over war rumors, Georgians found Oregon too remote for serious concern. Robert Toombs expressed a common attitude when he said that he did not "want a foot of Oregon or an acre of any other country, especially without 'niggers.'" In a December 1845 message, Polk upheld America's title to the entire Oregon territory and recommended notifying Great Britain that the United States wanted to terminate the joint occupancy agreement and achieve a permanent settlement. Congressional debate over whether or not notice should be given dragged on for months. Whigs nationwide feared war and favored compromise, most likely a division of the territory along the forty-ninth parallel, and they scorned what they saw as Polk's belligerent, bluffing tactics. Georgia Democrats in Congress likewise desired conciliation, although Howell Cobb worried that northern Democrats would feel betrayed if Polk bartered away part of Oregon. The controversy ebbed once Congress authorized Polk to give notice and negotiations ensued, and Georgians quietly accepted the subsequent agreement to divide Oregon with Great Britain.[9]

The Mexican War, brought on by Mexico's bitterness over the annexation of Texas and by Polk's aggressive actions, was a different matter. Polk, an ardent expansionist, was determined to maintain Texas's questionable claim that its western boundary was the Rio Grande. Following Texas annexation, Polk ordered General Zachary Taylor to march his army into disputed territory and set up camp on the east bank of the Rio Grande. The move led to an altercation on 25 April 1846 between Mexican forces and American troops stationed on the eastern side of the river. After receiving word of the encounter on 9 May, Polk informed Congress that a state of war existed, that the Mexicans had "invaded our territory and shed the blood of our fellow-citizens on our own soil." Democrats enshrined Polk's version of events—which absolved him of blame and fastened the guilt on Mexico—in the preamble of a bill to raise men and supplies for Taylor's army. Democrats rammed the bill through Congress, although most Whigs supported it to avoid appearing unpatriotic. Alexander Stephens and John Berrien, however, were among the Whigs who balked at the war bill's preamble and abstained from voting.[10]

The battlefield war against Mexico, though not James Polk's diplomatic and military policy, enjoyed lasting support in Georgia. Feelings of superiority based on racial and religious prejudices—Mexico was, of course, a Catholic country—helped justify the nation's course and inspired confidence in American arms. Whether or not they favored the war, most Georgians had little doubt that the United States would prevail over Mexico.[11]

Public concern for the safety of Taylor's army initially muzzled Whigs and postponed political skirmishing over the hostilities. When partisan forbearance ceased around mid-June, John Berrien and Alexander Stephens led Whigs in condemning Polk's blunders. Stephens's indictment charged the war to Polk's "imprudence, indiscretion, and mismanagement" and alleged that the president could have "easily avoided" war "without any detriment to our rights, interests, or honor as a nation." The unilateral attempt to settle the Texas boundary by "taking military possession of the disputed territory" had sparked the conflict and had usurped Congress's power to declare war. Stephens pledged to support an "active prosecution" of the war "to a speedy and honorable termination," but he refused to sanction the manner in which the war had been brought about. Turning to the problem of war aims, Stephens wanted "to know if this is to be a *war for conquest,* and whether this is the object for which it is to be waged. If so I protest against that part of it." While "no enemy to the extension of our domain," Stephens believed that republics ought to expand peacefully to preserve the purity of free institutions. Any conquests made under Polk's impulsive leadership would only expand the reach of despotism. "Fields of blood and carnage may make men brave and heroic," Stephens concluded, "but seldom tend to make nations either good, virtuous or great." Although Georgia Whigs understandably avoided echoing northern Whigs' complaints that the conflict was a direct result of Texas annexation and that it was being waged to extend slavery, they otherwise stood unreservedly alongside their northern brethren in opposition to Polk's war.[12]

Democrats, who cited Mexico's insolence as the chief cause of the war, defended Polk and proclaimed that the Whig criticism bordered on treason. John Lamar observed that the tone of Whig "editorials and conversations on the subject of the administration and the war generally is of such a virulent character as to be actually loathesome." War enthusiasm and Whig attacks bound Democrats together; even John Calhoun's denunciation of the war failed to shake party unity. Although Georgia Democrats undoubtedly favored expansion, few at the outset comprehended Polk's consuming desire for territorial accessions. Democrats looked, rather, for a short, glorious war that would humble Mexico and vindicate American honor.[13]

As party conflict over the Mexican War opened, Democratic victories in Congress closed discussions of the national economic issues of the Jacksonian era in Georgia. Democrats established an independent treasury, making specie the medium for government transactions, and enacted a new tariff that lowered most duties. Polk's veto of a major bill appropriating money for the improvement of rivers and harbors dismayed northern Democrats but drew applause from Georgians, who objected on constitutional and practical grounds to federal projects designed to benefit mainly the North and the West. The Georgia Whig delegation opposed most of the Democratic program, but the fire had gone out of these issues. The passage of the independent treasury elicited scarcely any comment from the Whig press, and scattered sniping at the 1846 tariff represented last shots, not an opening salvo.

An amendment that failed to pass proved vastly more important than the Democratic successes. Near the close of the congressional session in early August 1846, Polk asked Congress to appropriate two million dollars for use in negotiating territorial accessions from Mexico. Debate had barely begun when David Wilmot, a Democratic congressman from Pennsylvania, offered an amendment to the appropriation bill that proposed to bar slavery from any territory acquired from Mexico. The Wilmot Proviso instantly split the House of Representatives along sectional lines, and the northern majority— with Whigs and Democrats voting together—passed the appropriation bill with the Wilmot Proviso attached. Congress adjourned before the Senate could act, but the Wilmot Proviso nonetheless demonstrated its potential for polarizing the sections and disorganizing the parties.[14]

This brief episode occurred too late to affect the Georgia congressional elections. The Mexican War had temporarily eclipsed politics as a topic of conversation, and voter turnout was just above 60 percent, lower than it had been in any election since the formation of the Jacksonian parties. With no following presidential contest and no legislative races because of the switch to biennial sessions, voters in less competitive districts had little incentive to come to the polls. Alexander Stephens, Robert Toombs, and Thomas Butler King defended their course on the Mexican War and won easily. No Whig candidate dared to challenge John H. Lumpkin in the fifth district, and Howell Cobb carried the sixth handily. The other districts were again closely contested. Victories by Democrats Hugh Haralson and Alfred Iverson, and Whig John W. Jones, left the congressional delegation split evenly between the parties.[15]

The gravity of the Wilmot Proviso question became more apparent when Congress reconvened. Northern attempts to pass the proviso infuriated Southerners, and vitriolic debates over the future of slavery in territories not yet acquired dominated congressional sessions. Ingrained constitutionalism encouraged rigid resistance to compromise. Day after day, the disputants bludgeoned one another with dogmatic arguments elucidating constitutional theories regarding congressional power over slavery in the territories. Such debates were destined to be divisive and inconclusive because the passages in the Constitution that mentioned territorial matters said nothing definite on the mooted points.

Congress's checkered record on territorial slavery could be construed to support innumerable contradictory theories. The Northwest Ordinance had prohibited slavery in territories north of the Ohio River and east of the Mississippi. In areas south and southwest of the Ohio River, Congress had erected no barriers against slavery, and territorial residents had adopted the institution. The Missouri Compromise of 1820 had banned slavery in the part of the Louisiana Purchase lying north of the latitude line of 36°30′, but had left the remainder of the territory open to slavery. Congress had employed the Missouri Compromise line again in framing the joint resolution to annex Texas. Historically, then, Congress had prohibited slavery in some territories, had allowed it in others, and had divided the Louisiana Purchase—the policy had been to have no fixed policy.

The Wilmot Proviso thus proposed to do two novel things: prohibit slavery south of the Missouri Compromise line and make congressional exclusion of slavery the single, permanent territorial policy. The proviso itself, to be sure, encompassed only the prospective Mexican cessions, but its northern proponents intended to apply congressional bans on slavery to all future acquisitions as well.

Southerners found that prospect intolerable and advanced a contrary doctrine, best formulated by John C. Calhoun. In Calhoun's view, the territories were the common property of the states and of the citizens of the several states, and he believed that the Constitution enjoined Congress to provide equal protection for the rights and property of all citizens. Therefore, congressional prohibition of slavery in the territories, a discriminatory act that impaired slaveholders' rights in the common national domain, was unconstitutional. Calhoun also thought that territorial governments, which were created by Congress, lacked constitutional power to prohibit slavery. Only existing states or territorial conventions framing constitutions for statehood could legitimately decide the status of slavery. The institution of slavery, Calhoun concluded, did and had to exist in every parcel of American ground still in the territorial stage—and thus unconstitutional were the Wilmot Proviso, the Missouri Compromise line, and all kindred measures.[16]

Calhoun established in logic a position often defended in rage. The Wilmot Proviso represented an assault on southern white men's identity as well as on slavery—not that the two were truly separable. Congressman Seaborn Jones proclaimed that honor, justice, equality, and, indeed, survival were at stake in the controversy. Self-respect forbade submission to a proviso that sought to brand Southerners as inferiors whose institutions merited contempt. Never, never would Northerners insult and endanger the South by blocking the expansion of slavery and precluding the admission of new slave states. The *Milledgeville Southern Recorder* urged Georgians to "stand up for those rights—rights which they must either maintain, or cease to be, as a people." The Wilmot Proviso indicted them "for the crime of being Southern people," and they had to resist this opprobrium or "sacrifice themselves, their section, and the rights of their children who are to follow after them."[17]

Republican precepts taught that submission to initial antislavery encroachments would promote further northern assaults, leading ultimately to the abolition of slavery. In all sectional controversies, white men insisted that they could allow no outside power, foreign or domestic, to tamper with slavery. Georgians' "highest political duty," George Gilmer had observed in 1837, was to limit the federal government "to legislation upon the general subjects specified in the Constitution," leaving "unimpaired the rights of the States and the people." The South's "peculiar domestic relations, slave labor, and its productions," were in "constant danger of being sacrificed to selfish cupidity, or the zeal of fanaticism," and could be protected only by "unceasing vigilance." Richard D. Arnold, a wealthy Savannah physician who was several times mayor of that city, spoke for legions of white men when he emphasized that "our domestic concerns are for us to manage." Everything—"life and property, safety and security"—depended on preserving slavery. So "intimately is it mingled with our social conditions, so deeply has it taken root," Arnold observed, "that it would be impossible to eradicate it without upturning the foundations" of southern society.[18]

The conviction that upholding the *right* to extend slavery was essential to preserving the existing social order made the actual prospects for expanding slavery a rather peripheral concern. Although many Georgians hoped to add new slave states to augment the South's political power and always insisted on opening at least some of the new territory to slavery, Whigs and Democrats alike doubted whether slavery would ever be established in the arid Southwest. But even white men who had no direct interest in slavery or its expansion still thought southern rights in the territories were worth protecting. All white men valued the fundamental caste distinctions that separated them from black chattels. Acutely sensitive about their honor, their privileges, and their rights, Georgia voters were and intended to remain the equals of other white men in the Union; to tolerate less marked them as inferior. When Democrat Elihu S. Barclay reported in early 1848 that "there is considerable interest felt even in these mountains in regard to the action of Congress on the Slave question," he did not mean that the few Habersham County slaveholders were eager to be off for the Southwest. He meant that the Wilmot Proviso threatened the bedrock values that unified white men and buttressed their collective mastery.[19]

Even instantaneous, instinctive antagonism to the proviso, however, left open the political means and measure of resistance. Although no one knew it yet, the task for would-be compromisers, North and South, in early 1847 was essentially the same one they would face for the next fourteen years: how to steer the sections toward some middle ground and away from the antithetical Wilmot and Calhoun doctrines.

Whigs presented the simplest solution: no territory, no problem. At the beginning of 1847, Alexander Stephens and John Berrien offered House and Senate resolutions that renounced all intentions of acquiring Mexican territory, a position that became the national Whig party line. Removing Polk's territorial incentive, Whigs reasoned, would speedily end the war and avert the looming evils. Northern Whigs had supported the Wilmot Proviso unanimously; southern Whigs had opposed it equally solidly. Continued conflict would shatter the national Whig party, destroy the party system, and, ultimately, rend the Union. Berrien and Stephens embraced no-territory as a way to thwart Polk and elude shipwreck on the Wilmot Proviso.[20]

To Democrats, the no-territory policy represented a betrayal of national honor and national interests in expansion and a capitulation to northern Whig antislavery fanaticism. Their loathing for no-territory, however, did not supply much guidance in overcoming their own difficulties in developing an alternative territorial policy. Northern Democrats had displayed a distressing fondness for the Wilmot Proviso, and Georgians initially announced their willingness to accept any settlement that killed the proviso, opened some territory to slavery, and promoted national party harmony.

At first, Howell Cobb and others found the extension of the Missouri Compromise line to the Pacific Ocean an attractive alternative. Cobb contended that a permanent, unambiguous resolution of the controversy was worth waiving the right of Southerners to take slaves into all territories. The North would get Oregon, the South would receive most of any Mexican cession, and the nation would be better off for the bargain. Southern representatives almost unanimously supported various versions of Missouri Compromise line extension, but the northern House majority defeated every one and clung to the Wilmot Proviso. The Senate, in which the South had greater strength, in turn rejected House bills containing the Wilmot Proviso. As the congressional deadlock persisted through 1847, Georgia politicians pondered the territorial issue and reconsidered options.[21] As usual, presidential politics influenced their thinking.

The first gunfire along the Rio Grande had commenced the search for military candidates, and the Whigs had shortly espied General Zachary Taylor. Splendid early victories had made Taylor a hero, and the Louisiana planter's southern appeal glistened. Taylor had spent most of his adulthood in remote army camps, had never voted, and had only the dimmest grasp of political affairs. His lack of political credentials and political enemies enchanted many Whig leaders in both sections who were anxious to rebound from the seemingly conclusive defeat of Henry Clay's traditional Whiggery. An uncommitted candidate such as Taylor would allow Whigs to postpone territorial quarrels and concentrate on electoral victory. Most Georgia Whigs unhesitatingly assumed that Taylor's southern interests would dictate his political course, and the opinion rapidly developed that Taylor was "the man for the times" and "the only man in the nation stronger than Democracy & abolition united."[22]

Georgia Taylorites reworked a familiar plot and cast Taylor in the role pioneered by Hugh Lawson White and perfected by William Henry Harrison. Taylor was a "*Whig* in principle," yet thankfully "no *party* candidate." His popularity was "not the result of political management or trickery"; his election would "be by acclamation, and irrelative of party or party nominations." More precisely, Taylor was the "candidate of the Whig party by the acclamation of the people." However Taylorites labeled the Whig candidate who was not exactly a Whig or a candidate, they stressed that Taylor was a "true Southern patriot" who would protect southern rights and institutions. Rather than trust "another 'miserable slippery spawn of a midnight national caucus,'" southern Whigs and Democrats should adopt Taylor and form "a united front at home to the common enemy." Under Taylor, the *Macon Georgia Journal and Messenger* declared, "we would have nothing to fear from the question of territory."[23]

The Taylor image was so alluring that Calhounite Democrats contemplated kidnapping the general. In the spring of 1847, James Gardner of the *Augusta Constitutionalist* perused the scanty evidence available on Taylor's political leanings and pronounced the general a Democrat. Most of the editors who echoed Gardner merely relished tormenting Whigs, but Gardner

seriously advocated co-opting Taylor and emphasized "the necessity of having *a Southern candidate*" at a time of growing sectional strife. Gardner's
suggestions predictably irritated old Unionists. Hopkins Holsey, the new
editor of Howell Cobb's mouthpiece, the *Athens Southern Banner*, scolded
Gardner, and Cobb himself complained about "deranged" Democrats who
talked of nominating a "man with whose political principles, they are utterly
unacquainted & who is no doubt a whig." Cobb, Holsey, John Lumpkin,
and their allies planned to rely on the national Democratic party to heal
sectional divisions; they neither wanted nor needed a southern military
candidate.[24]

The 28 June Democratic state convention featured three interrelated contests. George W. B. Towns, a former congressman from Talbotton, bested
Herschel V. Johnson for the gubernatorial nomination. Johnson, though not
completely identified with the Calhounites, was a sometime editor of the
*Federal Union* and a confidant of Milledgeville Calhounites Tomlinson Fort
and David J. Bailey. The second contest, over Taylor and the presidency,
resulted in a Calhounite defeat. On Howell Cobb's urging, Democrats
spurned Taylor and affirmed their adherence to the national convention
mode of selecting candidates. The convention did, however, declare that
Democrats would reject any presidential candidate who refused to repudiate
the Wilmot Proviso.

The third and most important struggle concerned slavery in the territories. James Gardner and Edward Black championed the so-called Virginia
resolutions, which trumpeted John Calhoun's territorial doctrine and, crucially, disdained compromise. Howell Cobb and other original Unionists,
while not quarreling with the main points of the Virginia resolutions,
nonetheless insisted on an additional plank announcing their willingness to
accept an extension of the Missouri Compromise line. Proffering the compromise line again after repeated northern rejections seemed obsequious to
Calhounites, who had a point: if Northerners persistently adhered to the
Wilmot Proviso, pride and political necessity would harden Democrats' attitudes and foreclose possibilities for amicable compromise.[25]

Whigs, meanwhile, gave substance to familiar metaphors linking war and
politics. Their state convention recommended Zachary Taylor for the presidency and nominated Duncan L. Clinch for governor. Clinch, the "Hero of
Withlacoochee," enjoyed modest renown as a Seminole Indian fighter and

boasted a record of longevity in the United States Army rivaling Taylor's. The genial, unobtrusive, sixty-year-old retiree lived on a coastal rice plantation and owned some two hundred slaves. The Whigs issued few orders to their generals. The convention praised the Crawford administrations, ignored no-territory and the Mexican War, and condemned the Wilmot Proviso as "unequal, unjust, and unconstitutional."[26]

The parties contending in the 1847 contest could not effectively argue about the one issue that anyone really cared to argue about, slavery in the territories. Both Georgia parties unequivocally opposed the Wilmot Proviso, but neither could control its northern party wing, and neither national party had a definite, viable territorial policy—the triumphs of American armies in Mexico having outmoded the Whigs' no-territory solution. Under the circumstances, any promises, beyond the most general, made on the territorial issue might easily backfire, so the parties avoided commitments. Whigs ran what amounted to a presidential campaign, endlessly emphasizing that a vote for Duncan Clinch was a vote for Zachary Taylor. Democrats pleaded with voters to sustain Polk by supporting Towns. The governorship, largely a figurehead position in state affairs, was transformed into a post of supreme national power. The *Augusta Constitutionalist* asserted, for example, that electing a Democratic governor and state legislature would preserve the 1846 tariff, close the Mexican War, and secure the acquisition of territory "subject to the terms of the Missouri Compromise."[27]

George Towns felled the uninspiring Duncan Clinch by 43,228 votes to 41,936; turnout, as in 1845, was around 80 percent. The growth of the voting population in north Georgia, where roughly six out of ten voters were Democrats, was crucial to Towns's victory. Whigs also failed to rally their full black belt strength; Democrats gained 1,434 votes in that region. The most striking features of the election were the continuity of voting behavior and the closeness of the party competition. Towns's total constituted just 50.8 percent of the vote, and voting patterns in 1847 were virtually identical with those in 1845. The parties, in other words, tapped an immense reservoir of mutual antagonism and enduring voter loyalty in a canvass that served as an opening act for the main attraction, the 1848 presidential campaign.[28]

National affairs and preparations for the presidential campaign unsurprisingly consumed much of the legislature's session. First came the election of two United States senators: one to fill Berrien's seat immediately, the other to take office in March 1849. Despite Clinch's defeat, Whigs enjoyed a small majority in both branches. Rivalry between four Whig contenders— John Berrien, Charles Dougherty, George Crawford, and William C. Dawson—eventuated in contests between Berrien and Dougherty for Berrien's place, and between Crawford and Dawson for Walter Colquitt's seat. Berrien downed Dougherty in the Whig caucus and smoothly won reelection. Dawson, who controlled a handful of Whig legislators, used a threat to seek Democratic support to bluff his way past the more popular Crawford, gain the caucus nomination, and secure the other seat.

Then, in an attempt to refocus their party, the Whigs jettisoned issues that might impede Zachary Taylor's march. A series of senate resolutions disclaimed a desire to tamper with the 1846 tariff, pronounced a national bank dead, and abandoned the goal of modifying the presidential veto power. Distancing themselves from national Whig economic issues that had never been particularly attractive to Georgians allowed Whigs to return to essentials: opposition to tyrannical Democratic presidents and Democratic party dictation. Whigs had never wavered on these points, and Zachary Taylor, whom the resolutions nominated for the presidency, was a marvelous antiparty, anti-Democratic candidate—truly, the man of Georgia Whigs' dreams. The resolutions also grudgingly recognized that no-territory was a casualty of war. General Winfield Scott and his conquering army had been camped in Mexico City since September, and Whigs acknowledged that territorial accessions would probably serve as compensation for American claims against Mexico. Confidence in Zachary Taylor would have to suffice as a territorial policy for Georgia Whigs until northern and southern Whigs hammered out—if they could—a substitute for no-territory.

A unanimous senate declaration of southern solidarity against the Wilmot Proviso gave the misleading impression that white men thought as one on the territorial issue. Broad areas of agreement did exist, of course: Whigs and Democrats alike opposed the proviso and would shun any presidential candidate who favored congressional exclusion of slavery. Nearly all, moreover, accepted the theoretical validity of John Calhoun's analysis of southern rights in the territories. The mooted and vital question, however, was not what Georgians wanted or abstractly believed, but what sort of practical solution they would settle for as a means of ending the controversy. An attempt by Luther J. Glenn, one of Howell Cobb's friends, to insert a resolution affirming Georgians' satisfaction with Missouri Compromise line extension failed by a 26-to-20 vote, defeated by a nearly solid bloc of Whigs combined with a few Calhounite Democrats. Even while senators pledged their devotion to Calhoun's doctrine and total victory, they were anxiously calculating the prospects of reaching an accommodation with their northern party allies.[29]

Compromise-minded Democrats took a bold step at their December party convention. They omitted mentioning the Missouri Compromise line and instead endorsed popular sovereignty, the last of the basic solutions offered for the territorial problem. After conventionally asserting that congressional prohibition of slavery in the territories was unconstitutional, Democrats also emphasized that they had no wish for Congress to establish the institution of slavery in any territory. They asked only "that the inhabitants of each territory shall be left free to determine for themselves, whether the institution of slavery shall or shall not form a part of their social system." Congress should, in other words, rid itself of the divisive debate over slavery by letting territorial residents conduct the quarrel and decide for themselves.

The brief resolution on popular sovereignty left questions hanging, contradictions unexplored. If, as Democrats stated, Congress possessed "no power under the Constitution, to legislate in any way or manner" on slavery, then presumably neither did territorial legislatures, which owed their existence to Congress. Yet, perhaps territorial legislatures possessed powers to prohibit slavery that Congress lacked, a proposition that Democrats had already rejected and here did not explicitly advance. But if territorial legislatures could not prohibit slavery, what could territorial residents "be left free to determine"? Perhaps Democrats meant that territorial residents could make a decision on slavery at the time they framed a state constitution. No, Democrats did not say that either, a significant fact given that positions on slavery in the territories often hinged on nuances of language. What Democrats said and intended to say at their December convention was that they were willing to allow territorial residents to decide the fate of slavery during the territorial stage. This overture toward compromise contradicted the Calhoun doctrine and signaled a strong desire to harmonize relations with northern Democrats.[30]

Howell Cobb and north Georgians were the chief instigators of the switch to popular sovereignty. Even as the state Democratic convention met, Cobb's friend and favorite presidential candidate, Senator Lewis Cass of Michigan, was preparing to champion popular sovereignty in his so-called Nicholson letter. Since James Polk had ruled out a second term and Cass's main adversary, Secretary of State James Buchanan, had already advocated the extension of the Missouri Compromise line, an advance endorsement of popular sovereignty by Georgians aided Cass's bid for the presidential nomination. In any case, the resolution put Georgians in step with a general Democratic movement toward popular sovereignty, which was fundamentally a prescription for preserving the national Democratic party. As Hopkins Holsey phrased it, northern Democrats could choose whichever "they can stand better upon," the Missouri Compromise or popular sovereignty, and "Southern Democrats will be satisfied with either position." The paramount goal was to fix on a mutually acceptable territorial solution in time to crush the Whigs in the presidential election.[31]

Lewis Cass's explication of popular sovereignty was even more enigmatic than that of Georgia Democrats. Cass neglected to state whether either territorial legislatures or Congress could constitutionally prohibit slavery—though he hinted that legislatures could and that Congress could not. He forthrightly opposed the Wilmot Proviso and advised "leaving to the people of any territory . . . the right to regulate [slavery] themselves, under the general principles of the constitution." What these "general principles" were, of course, constituted the crux of the case, and Cass declined to elucidate them. The democratic notion of letting the people rule, without specifying when they could rule or what they could rule on, was the essence of popular sovereignty.[32]

While Democrats mended fences, some Whigs prepared to abandon the national party. A December meeting, billed as a nonpartisan gathering but actually controlled by Whig legislators and party stalwarts such as Miller Grieve of the *Milledgeville Southern Recorder*, nominated Zachary Taylor for president and scheduled a convention to select a Taylor electoral ticket. The date set, 5 June, was just two days before the opening of the Whig national convention. Taylorites intended to run their man and ignore the Philadelphia national convention, and the *Southern Recorder* even argued that a national nomination would endanger Taylor's election by "ranging the parties in strict party lines." The widespread feeling that the national Whig party was a bust reflected defeatism from 1844, disinterest in traditional economic questions, and sectional alienation caused by the Wilmot Proviso. Taylorites, in effect, wanted to split the national party themselves before northern Whigs did it for them.[33]

Discontent over Henry Clay's efforts to woo northern Whigs further fueled the Taylor fire. To bolster his still unannounced but widely anticipated candidacy, Clay delivered a November 1847 speech in Lexington, Kentucky, in which he called slavery an evil and announced his opposition to its extension. Clay had been saying similar things about slavery for half a century, and Georgia politicians had finally heard enough. Robert Toombs indignantly charged that Clay had "sold himself body and soul to the Northern Anti-slavery Whigs." The editor of the *Savannah Republican,* Joseph L. Locke, noted that the "belief that he [Clay] has *actually* joined the abolitionists is almost universal." Locke vowed to repudiate Clay if he were the national Whig nominee. Likewise ruminating on the Whigs' future, Iverson L. Harris declared that the "slavery question if agitated will admit of no further fraternity. It is a question of existence to Southern Whigs." "Depend upon it," Charles Jenkins notified John Berrien, "unless the Whig Party will take ground against the Wilmot Proviso, or present us a candidate above suspicion at the south, the Georgia Whigs will take this matter into their own hands."[34]

Whigs intensely debated boycotting the Philadelphia convention before finally rescheduling their state convention to allow time to choose national convention delegates. Notwithstanding the enthusiasm for Taylor, many were loath to forfeit their investment in Whig stock. The *Augusta Chronicle & Sentinel* castigated Taylorites who seemed "ready to form new political associations and resort to untried expedients, in the vain hope that the people can be easily led into any political absurdity, by a sort of 'spontaneous combustion.'" More influential than the *Chronicle*'s mutterings was the advice of Whig congressional leaders. John Berrien, a Clay supporter, strongly backed a national convention, as did Robert Toombs and Alexander Stephens. Stephens and Toombs thought that Taylor's popularity, always the overriding factor behind his candidacy, would compel reluctant northern Whigs to acquiesce in his nomination.[35]

Taylorites dominated the May Whig state convention. Taylor had finally avowed in late April that he was "a Whig, but not an ultra Whig," a bare admission that eased some Clay Whig consciences and posed additional obstacles to an independent Taylor movement. While naming Taylor as its first choice, the convention pledged to support the national party nominee, provided that his views accorded "with our own on the subject of the Wilmot Proviso and Southern Rights." Since Henry Clay had already flunked this test, the caveat set Zachary Taylor's nomination as the price of continued Whig allegiance to the national party.[36]

The national convention gave Georgians what they wanted: Zachary Taylor without baggage. Nearly unanimous southern support sustained Taylor, while Northerners who opposed the general failed to coalesce behind Clay or any other candidate. Taylor's popularity swayed undecided delegates and secured his nomination on the fourth ballot. The convention drafted no platform; Whigs would try to elect Taylor first and decide later what his election meant. Given the depth of the divisions over slavery in the territories, Whigs could hardly do otherwise and hope to preserve their party.

The three candidates for the Democratic nomination—Cass, Buchanan, and Levi Woodbury of New Hampshire—all favored territorial compromise and were unobjectionable to Southerners. If the national convention would let the territorial question alone, Hopkins Holsey thought, "Some may support the nominee for one reason, some for another, and the peculiar sectional views of every one" could "be left untouched." Cass's nomination thus satisfied Georgia Democrats, as did the national convention's refusal to take a definite stand on the territorial issue.[37]

When the national conventions detoured around the territorial impasse, the Georgia parties felt obliged to follow. The peace treaty with Mexico, which had been concluded in February, had given the United States an enormous expanse of territory stretching from Texas to the northern border of California. These territories, and Oregon as well, required organization, which in turn necessitated some decision on territorial slavery. This topic dominated the congressional session that extended from December 1847 to August 1848, and Georgians plagued by indecision over territorial policy proved unwilling and unprepared to issue ultimatums that would sever relations with their northern party compatriots.[38]

Calhounite Democrat James Gardner's quest for a viable territorial solution exemplified the difficulties involved in balancing southern rights and party imperatives. Gardner began 1848 with a headline in his *Augusta Constitutionalist* demanding "Equal Rights to the South in New Territory, or Disunion." This manifesto did not prevent him from finding Lewis Cass's ambiguous declarations on popular sovereignty congenial, however, at least until he came across the Alabama resolutions, a state Democratic platform that went as far as Southerners would ever go in proclaiming their rights in the territories. Alabama Democrats contended that the Constitution, which recognized slavery, automatically extended the institution to any conquered territory—slavery followed the flag. The direct corollary of this proposition, which Gardner warmly endorsed, was that Congress was obligated to provide legal support—a slave code, either through congressional acts or those of a territorial legislature—for slavery in the territories. The assertion that Congress actively had to protect slavery throughout the territorial stage was southern rights with a vengeance.

This position would never satisfy northern Democrats, and it did not satisfy Gardner for long. As the national convention neared, he reconciled himself to the "wide and radical differences of opinion" within the party on the territorial question and receded from demands for southern rights or disunion. After the Democratic national convention, just as the party appeared ready to rally around popular sovereignty, Gardner shifted to advocating Missouri Compromise line extension. By October, Gardner was—with no apparent sense of incongruity—touting Lewis Cass as the Missouri Compromise line candidate. Fellow editor Hopkins Holsey complained that Gardner had "boxed every point of the compass on the Slavery question," and publicly tried to call Gardner back to the popular sovereignty principle that slavery should be controlled "by the people of the territories themselves," a position that the June Democratic state convention had reaffirmed.[39]

But perhaps this was not the true ground. Georgia Democrats in Congress, reacting against northern provisoists and yielding to pressure from other Southerners, repeatedly denied that territorial legislatures could prohibit slavery. Over the protests of northern Democrats, Senator Herschel Johnson asserted, wrongly, that Lewis Cass and the Baltimore national convention had declared that neither Congress nor territorial legislatures could exclude slavery. The Constitution automatically extended to American territories and established slavery in them, Johnson averred, and the institution of slavery thus instantly established could not thereafter be prohibited until such time as the territories applied for statehood—it was the full length and breadth of John Calhoun's doctrine. Principle mattered: Johnson would oppose the Wilmot Proviso if Northerners sought to apply it to "the moon."[40] Johnson's construction of popular sovereignty was becoming *the* southern interpretation, but northern Democrats were just as surely forming a consensus that popular sovereignty was a free-soil doctrine that licensed territorial legislatures to prohibit slavery.

One fact explains these bold advances and awkward retreats: Georgians could not have it all their way on the territorial issue and have national parties too. Necessary concessions to northern feelings created ambiguities and diluted principles. In revealing back-to-back House speeches delivered on 1 July, Robert Toombs and Howell Cobb quarreled over whether a vague platform was better than none at all. Democratic platform planks, Toombs intoned, were patently "intended to be ambiguous—to cover up, under convenient generalities, the discordant sentiments of the Democratic party, in order that they might be expounded differently in different sections of the Union." The glory of the Whigs was that they could differ widely on principles without using "fraudulent platforms to conceal this difference." Their Janus-faced campaign at least made no pretense of harmony when none existed. Toombs's antipartyism followed Georgia Whig traditions, but it begged the question of how Whigs who were so honestly and openly divided over slavery could endure as one party.[41]

Howell Cobb denounced the "folly and attempted fraud" of the Whigs, "*an organized party,* whose only principle is, opposition *to party organization!*" The most devoted national Democrat in Georgia wholeheartedly believed that "party organization" was "the very corner-stone" of the political system. While the great national Democracy enunciated principles designed to bind the nation together, "double-dealing" Whigs were painting northern and southern faces on Zachary Taylor and perpetrating "a gross fraud and imposition upon the one or the other section of the Union." Everyone present in the House knew, of course, that Democrats were at loggerheads over popular sovereignty, but Cobb dodged persistent questioning, refused to interpret the national platform, and confidently reiterated assertions of Democratic unity. Perhaps Robert Toombs smiled at the performance.[42]

Northern and southern congressmen's inability to harmonize on any territorial formula spawned the Clayton Compromise. The crucial parts of this measure forbade the New Mexico and California territorial legislatures from passing laws on slavery and provided that persons held as slaves in these territories could bring freedom suits in federal courts. Congress expected the judicial process to yield a conclusive Supreme Court opinion on the status of slavery in the territories. The Clayton Compromise passed the Senate by a vote of 33 to 22; John Berrien and Herschel Johnson supported it. But a coalition of northern representatives and eight southern Whigs, led by Alexander Stephens, killed the bill immediately on its arrival in the House.

Tangled lines of reasoning strangled the Clayton Compromise. Alexander Stephens, who believed that the existence of slavery depended on local law, argued that preexisting Mexican bans on slavery, unless overturned by congressional legislation, would compel the Supreme Court to rule against slavery. John Berrien and others, however, contended that the Constitution had been automatically extended over the conquered Mexican territory, and that the general constitutional clauses that protected slavery would produce a verdict sanctioning slavery in the Southwest—indeed, everywhere in the common national domain.

The largely legalistic and theoretical dispute had practical implications. If Stephens was correct and slaveholders had no rights in the territories that a court would respect, then the South effectively had no rights at all. The reverse of the old legal maxim that there was no wrong without a remedy seemingly applied here: if the South had no remedy, then slavery exclusion was no wrong. Slaveholders would never go into the territories without adequate security for their property. Uncertainty regarding the validity of Mexican antislavery laws or the prospect of early antislavery votes by territorial legislatures would exclude slaveholders from the territories just as surely as would the Wilmot Proviso.

The conflict between Berrien and Stephens created a furor. An assortment of Berrien followers, Clay Whigs, and compromise advocates bewailed Stephens's intransigence. Democrats charged that the traitorous Stephens reasoned like a Wilmot Provisoist; his call for congressional legislation to open the Mexican cession to slavery invited the conclusion that Congress could also do the opposite and prohibit slavery. Stephens replied that Congress's power to protect slavery did not necessarily involve the power to prohibit it (a southern idea hardly original with Stephens), but he declined to answer directly whether Congress could constitutionally exclude slavery.

A last stab at compromise closed the marathon congressional session.

John Berrien and Herschel Johnson helped the Senate pass the long-delayed Oregon territorial bill with a clause providing for the extension of the Missouri Compromise line to the Pacific Ocean. All eight Georgia congressmen supported the extension clause when it came before the House, but it was once again defeated by northern votes. The Missouri Compromise line was too clear-cut for campaign circumstances and too unattractive to northern congressmen determined to enact the proviso. An Oregon bill that included a prohibition of slavery subsequently passed both chambers, leaving the Mexican cession alone unorganized. Since Northerners were unlikely ever to assent to a Missouri Compromise line extension that opened most of the remaining territory to slavery, the organization of Oregon dealt a mortal blow to Georgians' favorite practical territorial solution.[43]

After months of complicated wrangling, the parties returned to simple trademark themes in the presidential campaign. Taylor's peculiar candidacy only intensified the debate over contrasting conceptions of party that had long dominated the state's political discourse. Troublesome details of territorial policy were submerged in general vows to defend southern rights. Whigs and Democrats accepted their own parties' Janus-faced campaigning, yet they constantly raised alarms about the antislavery zealotry of the northern opposition. In charging forward behind Lewis Cass and Zachary Taylor, men known elsewhere as antislavery champions, Georgians gambled that Southerners could control whichever national party triumphed.

Whigs threw all their weight on their good Taylor leg and endowed their candidate with mystical powers. "Elect Gen. Taylor," Whigs urged, "and all sectional factions will be hushed into silence by those pure, uncompromising, invaluable qualities of the head and of heart, which prove him to be a second Washington." Taylor would rescue the nation from party domination and presidential despotism, restore the golden days of the early Republic, and replace sectional strife with blissful harmony. The Whigs' lack of a platform was a virtue: a "party which cannot be trusted without pledges, should not be trusted with them—for they are always made with a view to success." Like Taylor, George Washington and Thomas Jefferson had been "Southern men and slaveholders," the "highest pledge that could possibly be given."[44]

If Taylor was a conservative constitutionalist, Cass was a "time-serving, selfish politician," always chasing after majorities, tacking to meet every popular breeze, and lusting after office. "Changeling party hacks" such as Lewis Cass, who were "everything by turns and nothing long," were "offensive to all pure-minded men, of all parties and sections." The "great political chameleon" had "been on every side of every leading question" for more than three decades; he could hardly be trusted on the Wilmot Proviso.[45]

Whigs identified Cass as the political twin of Martin Van Buren, the wily New Yorker who now headed a northern Free Soil party dedicated to the Wilmot Proviso. The formation of the Free Soil party in 1848 sent a shiver through Southerners, and Whigs wondered why Van Buren's desertion did not silence Democratic prattle about "Northern gentlemen with *Southern principles.*" Case was another "*viper in disguise,*" another "Judas Iscariot" poised to betray the South. To prove that the national Democratic party consisted of liars and turncoats, Whigs thumbed through the northern press for antislavery editorials supporting Cass. As election day approached, extracts from these editorials filled Whig papers, crowding out almost all other material.[46]

The greatest Democratic lie of all, Whigs maintained, was popular sovereignty, or "Cass's Proviso." This doctrine was even more to be feared than Wilmot's, "inasmuch as it is more concealed from the public eye." Whigs emphasized the northern interpretation of popular sovereignty and claimed that instead of letting Congress prohibit slavery, Cass would let the "Indians, Negroes, and Mongrel half-breeds" of the territories enact "*their* laws" to prohibit it. Desert denizens, accustomed to living under Mexican laws prohibiting slavery, would never decide to establish the institution; popular sovereignty was a ruse to cheat Southerners out of their rights in the territories.[47]

Everything Cass did or said was claimed to be a product of his northern upbringing and northern prejudices. The mantra that Cass was not a Southerner, not a slaveholder, not one of us, was central to the Whig campaign. Alexander Stephens captured the gist: "Shall it be said that the South can not trust their peculiar interest in the hands of a cotton and sugar planter of L[ouisian]a, but must look for a man in Detroit who has not a feeling in common with them to take charge of their rights and interests?"[48]

Democrats deplored the Whigs' sectional ranting. If North and South embraced such extremism, it would "break up the organization of existing parties and forming [them] upon a sectional basis, would rend the Union."

Old Union-Democrat Hiram Warner believed that the "interests of the Southern states never can be promoted by threats, intimidations, or exclusive sectional selfishness." The Democrats occupied "a broad, national and anti-sectional position in the present canvass," James Gardner declared, and he condemned "sectional excitements, sectional prejudices, and sectional appeals, as the grounds on which the claims of a candidate are to be based." Cass, whatever his nativity, had behind him the national Democracy, united and strong, the ark of the Union and of southern rights.[49]

While assuming the high national ground, Democrats stressed that northern abolitionists ruled the Whig party. Vice presidential candidate Millard Fillmore of New York, who had a mildly antislavery record, was subjected to particularly harsh abuse, but Democrats attacked the whole Whig crew as "essentially a Northern party, residing at the North and animated by Northern sympathies and prejudices." Since the northern Whigs had, in truth, unflinchingly backed the Wilmot Proviso, Democrats easily found antislavery editorials to place under the heading "Gen. Taylor's Northern Face."[50]

Democrats used northern Whig effusions to construct a horrific scenario. The ignorant, no-veto general, a creature of his abolitionist handlers, would meekly sign a Wilmot Proviso rammed through Congress by northern Whigs. Then would come a national bank and a protective tariff, obnoxious measures that the Whigs had supposedly abandoned. At last, with all resistance crushed, Taylor and the Whigs would move toward military rule—the "habit of command," after all, had "an almost inevitable tendency to make men self willed and despotic." The sum of the Democratic indictment was that Whigs had no principles worth mentioning, no party organization worth respecting, and no candidate worthy of a white man's suffrage.[51]

Minimizing national Whiggery and maximizing Taylor worked wonders: voters streamed to the polls and gave Taylor the state by a margin of 47,539 to 44,791. Taylor's strengths as a Southerner, a slaveholder, a successful general, and an independent man greatly augmented the normal Whig party vote. Taylor captured normally Democratic voters in north Georgia and energized the Whigs' black belt faithful in a way not seen since the 1840 campaign. Whereas Henry Clay had captured only 31.9 and 39.9 percent of the vote in the mountains and the upcountry, respectively, Taylor carried 39.1 and 42.2 percent of a much larger overall vote in these two regions. Whigs also gained more than 3,000 votes over their 1844 showing in the black belt. Democratic leaders knew all too well what had happened. James F. Cooper, the superintendent of the United States mint at Dahlonega in north Georgia, told Howell Cobb that expectations of a large turnout had been "fully realized, but hundreds of democrats have come to the polls only to vote against us." [52]

Although the evasive strategies employed in 1848 kept the national parties together, relentless exploitation of sectional prejudices during the campaign hardened feelings and lessened subsequent chances for compromise. John B. Lamar had accurately predicted that if the parties postponed solving the "nigger question" until after the election, "the successful party will have no inducement, and the defeated party [will be] too much exasperated, to yield anything." As if to prove Lamar's point, Hopkins Holsey berated Georgia voters for "blindly" rushing, "in a fit of hero-worship, into the very crater of a volcano, which will either overwhelm them with degradation and a final emancipation of their slaves, or disrupture [*sic*] the ties of the political union, in a servile and civil war." [53]

When solid national Democrats such as Holsey started exploding, the rest of the Georgia Democratic party had to be nearing the flash point. Cass's galling defeat exhausted Calhounites' limited patience with the national Democracy and steeled their determination to settle for nothing less than the full measure of southern rights in the territories. The power of the territorial issue, moreover, ensured that Calhounites would not make their stand alone. Up to 1848, party interests and sectional interests had generally coincided for Georgia Democrats, and this happy circumstance had restricted the audience for periodic Calhounite appeals for a united southern front. Few had wanted a southern sectional party when a national party had suited just as well. But northern Democratic spines had stiffened recently, and a substantial body of New York Democrats had formed the Free Soil party instead of standing by their erstwhile southern friends. Once Congress reconvened, continued foot dragging on southern rights would drive tens of thousands of Georgia Democrats toward the Calhounites' southern party solution; some would even opt for disunion.

Whigs faced a fight over a payoff that could not be evenly split. Northern Whigs wedded to the Wilmot Proviso considered Taylor an antislavery candidate. Southern Whigs claimed the general as their man and saw him as their only hope for controlling the party. Both could not be right, and the Georgia Whig party would not survive Taylor's answer to the territorial question. The anomalous alliance with northern Whigs, so laboriously maintained, would soon be broken.

*William H. Crawford.* A key leader of the Troup faction and an important national figure before his unsuccessful bid for the presidency in 1824. (Courtesy of the Hargrett Rare Book and Manuscript Library, University of Georgia Libraries.)

*George M. Troup.* A feisty advocate of states' rights, Troup triumphed over his arch-rival, John Clark, in a memorable 1825 gubernatorial contest. (Courtesy of the Hargrett Rare Book and Manuscript Library, University of Georgia Libraries.)

*John MacPherson Berrien.* After his resignation from Andrew Jackson's cabinet, Berrien returned to Georgia to organize the State Rights – Whig party and later became an influential United States senator. (Courtesy of the Hargrett Rare Book and Manuscript Library, University of Georgia Libraries.)

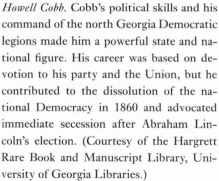

*Howell Cobb.* Cobb's political skills and his command of the north Georgia Democratic legions made him a powerful state and national figure. His career was based on devotion to his party and the Union, but he contributed to the dissolution of the national Democracy in 1860 and advocated immediate secession after Abraham Lincoln's election. (Courtesy of the Hargrett Rare Book and Manuscript Library, University of Georgia Libraries.)

*Joseph E. Brown.* After his election to the governorship in 1857, Brown quickly elevated himself into the front rank of state leaders. Even wilier in politics than he was pious in religion, he warred against Georgia's banks, played powerful politicians against one another, and appealed to the pride and the fears of north Georgia yeomen in an attempt to rally them behind immediate secession. (Courtesy of the Hargrett Rare Book and Manuscript Library, University of Georgia Libraries.)

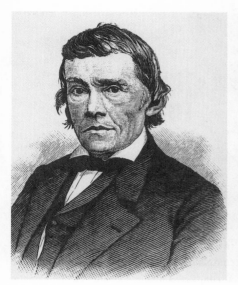

*Alexander H. Stephens.* Chronic illness and a melancholy disposition did not prevent "Little Aleck" from pursuing his large ambitions. A rising young Whig in the 1840s, he became in the next decade one of the nation's most prominent Democrats and played a significant role in battles over slavery in the territories. He retired from Congress in 1859, supported Stephen Douglas in the 1860 presidential campaign, and was Georgia's best-known opponent of immediate secession. (Courtesy of the Hargrett Rare Book and Manuscript Library, University of Georgia Libraries.)

*Robert Toombs.* He and Alexander Stephens were a potent political duo. As a Whig Congressman in the 1840s and a Democratic senator in the 1850s, Toombs earned a reputation as a slashing debater who relished a good fight and a strong drink. Yankees who challenged southern rights often felt the sting of his invective. (Courtesy of the Hargrett Rare Book and Manuscript Library, University of Georgia Libraries.)

*The Old Capitol at Milledgeville.* Completed in 1836, the building required almost immediate repairs and was the subject of frequent complaints. Much of the business of the state government and the state's political parties was conducted within its walls, and men on the road to higher office usually traveled through its legislative chambers. (Courtesy of the Hargrett Rare Book and Manuscript Library, University of Georgia Libraries.)

*A rally for southern independence, Savannah, 8 November 1860.* Abraham Lincoln's election aroused intense emotions and sparked a heated debate over how best to protect the South and slavery. While citizens at this rally cheered for immediate secession, others elsewhere counseled caution, delay, and cooperation. The state convention of January 1861 ultimately decided the issue. (Courtesy of the Hargrett Rare Book and Manuscript Library, University of Georgia Libraries.)

# FIVE

# "In Politics, We Are Party Men": Voting Patterns, the Legislature, and Party Organization

The partisan passions of nineteenth-century politics were then, and remain, difficult to explain. Men chose their parties based on family influences, county traditions, charismatic leaders, economic interests, religious views, and countless other factors; the precise reasons why millions of individuals nationwide became Democrats or Whigs are unknown and unknowable. In Georgia, especially, the parties were like tints and shades of a single color; they tended toward different ends of a spectrum and mixed elements in unequal measures, but their similarities remained striking. The nuances that distinguished the parties nonetheless mattered, and politicians labored to magnify and emphasize distinctions. The resulting polarization intensified partisanship and created an emotional political culture in which most proudly announced, as did a Macon editor in 1837, "that in politics, we are *party* men." Conventions, rallies, parades, speeches, and all the other party trappings of the Jacksonian era excited the vast majority of voters, inculcated lasting loyalties, and controlled the political life of the nation. Various elements of that party framework are the subjects of this chapter.[1]

The Georgia Jacksonian parties inherited habits of opposition that dated back at least to the late eighteenth century. These habits became entrenched over time and transcended transitory policy questions. Simply put, neither Georgia party could chart its course without constantly referring to its adversary's position. Linton Stephens's observation that "the opposition to enemies is much stronger than the adherence to friends" hits the crux: the parties existed in a symbiotic relationship in which their attacks on each other normally strengthened popular attachments to both. Robert Toombs certainly appreciated the value of promoting antagonism. As Whigs in Congress vacillated over whether to repeal a national bankruptcy law that they had previously enacted, Toombs told John Berrien that it would be "better for the country & the Whig party to stick to bad measures than to change them every moon." To have the Whigs correct themselves would weaken party lines. "If it be a bad measure as I think it is," Toombs advised, "then let the Locos repeal it." Toombs, in his own mind, smoothly reconciled his pragmatic counsel with a concluding condemnation of his Democratic counterparts in the state legislature as "the vilest crew of desperate, unprincipled scoundrels that ever deceived and betrayed an honest people."[2]

Toombs and his contemporaries unhesitatingly assailed the honesty and integrity of opponents and assumed that their adversaries were devious men who hid sinister motives behind a veil of hypocrisy. An arsenal of accusations, developed during the eighteenth century and widely employed in the Federalist-Republican battles of the 1790s, focused on the threat of subversion and made thwarting the evil designs of liberty's enemies a basic goal of politics. Whigs' self-professed conservatism, for example, found expression mainly through criticism of all things Democratic. After resisting "King" Andrew Jackson, Whigs railed against the party monarchy of Martin Van Buren and censured James Polk's tyrannical empire building. The *Milledgeville Southern Recorder,* while conceding that "diversities of opinion" and "peculiar sectional interests" kept the Whigs from enacting many positive measures, emphasized that Whigs were united in seeking "the entire overthrow and route [*sic*] of the Destructives." Similarly, Joseph Henry Lumpkin, Georgia's preeminent jurist, the brother of Wilson Lumpkin, and the uncle of John H. Lumpkin, forthrightly informed Howell Cobb that "Democracy & Infidelity are now & ever have been the Siamese Twins, one & indivisible." At some deep level, Lumpkin believed that his closest relatives and friends were implicated in a worldwide conspiracy to foster anarchy and irreligion that had begun during the French Revolution, had been carried on by Thomas Jefferson, and had been institutionalized in the national Democratic party.[3]

Lumpkin was hardly alone in his beliefs; both parties routinely leveled such charges. Whigs presented Martin Van Buren, the party trickster, as the archetypal Democrat and tirelessly repeated that the Democratic party was a desperate coalition of selfish, office-seeking demagogues that had "meta-morphosed" the government "into a political brothel." Democrats might pretend to love the people, but they really desired "to see the *rich grow richer and the poor grow poorer*," "to see an aristocracy of wealth springing up in the land, and the farmers and laborers sinking into tenants and *serfs*." Demo-crats, for their part, spread rumors in 1856 that if Millard Fillmore were elected president, his supporters planned to erect "*all over our country Cotton Factories, and all poor men who do not own land, with their wives and children, . . . will be forced to go to work in these Factories for* TEN CENTS *a day!*" Democrats routinely ridiculed the Whigs' "weathercock course" and catalogued all evidence of Whig hypocrisy: [4]

> Georgia Whigs have ever been *professedly* great sticklers for principle. Occu-pying this high vantage ground, and holding in utter detestation the spoils of office, their principles for the time being, have been the only principles worth possessing, and with equal boldness and apparent confidence in their correct-ness, they have repudiated on one day those they sustained on another, and vice versa advocated those they had hitherto denounced. In *all* their changes, they being the judges, they are always right; their opponents always wrong. They are always the conservative party, ever having in their ranks all the in-telligence, decency and patriotism of the country, while their opponents are always opposed to order and good government, led by demagogues and the associates of agrarians." [5]

Georgians obviously were prepared to believe the worst about their ene-mies. Intensely partisan feelings and language antedated the formation of the Jacksonian parties proper and laid foundations for a political culture in which Whigs and Democrats arrayed themselves into hostile phalanxes.

Like other successful American political parties, those in Georgia drew sup-port from every segment of the electorate. To appeal successfully to core constituencies—the planters, smaller slaveholders, yeomen, and farm la-borers who together comprised the great bulk of the adult white male population—the parties had to represent the common interests and reflect the common values of white men. The creation and maintenance of broad, powerful coalitions within the lower South's most competitive party system

## Table 5. Voting by Regions, 1835–1859

| | Whig Votes | Democratic Votes | % Democrat | % Whig Vote | % Democratic Vote | % of Total Vote |
|---|---|---|---|---|---|---|
| *1835–40* | | | | | | |
| Mountains | 5,407 | 13,867 | 71.9 | 3.4 | 9.0 | 6.1 |
| Upcountry | 26,416 | 39,607 | 60.0 | 16.5 | 25.7 | 21.0 |
| Black belt | 119,062 | 89,113 | 42.8 | 74.3 | 57.8 | 66.2 |
| Pine barrens– | | | | | | |
| wiregrass | 4,809 | 6,622 | 57.9 | 3.0 | 4.3 | 3.6 |
| Coast | 4,637 | 4,945 | 51.6 | 2.9 | 3.2 | 3.0 |
| Total | 160,331 | 154,154 | 49.0 | 100.1 | 100 | 99.9 |
| *1841–49* | | | | | | |
| Mountains | 19,703 | 36,243 | 64.8 | 6.8 | 12.5 | 9.7 |
| Upcountry | 56,937 | 81,792 | 59.0 | 19.7 | 28.1 | 23.9 |
| Black belt | 192,660 | 152,589 | 44.2 | 66.8 | 52.4 | 59.6 |
| Pine barrens– | | | | | | |
| wiregrass | 10,189 | 11,535 | 53.1 | 3.5 | 4.0 | 3.7 |
| Coast | 9,132 | 8,834 | 49.2 | 3.2 | 3.0 | 3.1 |
| Total | 288,621 | 290,993 | 50.2 | 100 | 100 | 100 |
| *1853–59* | | | | | | |
| Mountains | 24,804 | 50,052 | 66.9 | 10.2 | 15.7 | 13.3 |
| Upcountry | 55,178 | 90,975 | 62.2 | 22.6 | 28.5 | 25.9 |
| Black belt | 146,662 | 149,849 | 50.5 | 60.2 | 46.9 | 52.6 |
| Pine barrens– | | | | | | |
| wiregrass | 10,236 | 18,051 | 63.8 | 4.2 | 5.6 | 5.0 |
| Coast | 6,790 | 10,760 | 61.3 | 2.8 | 3.4 | 3.1 |
| Total | 243,670 | 319,687 | 56.7 | 100 | 100.1 | 99.9 |
| Grand total | 692,622 | 764,834 | 52.5 | | | |

*Sources:* Walter Dean Burnham, *Presidential Ballots, 1836–1892* (Baltimore: Johns Hopkins University Press, 1955); *Macon Georgia Messenger,* 16 Nov. 1837; *Milledgeville Southern Recorder,* 14 Nov. 1837, 9 Nov. 1841, 17 Oct. 1843, 21 Oct. 1845, 12 Oct. 1847, 25 Oct. 1853, 16 Oct., 4 Dec. 1855, 20 Oct. 1857; *Milledgeville Federal Union,* 31 Oct. 1835, 23 Oct. 1838, 16 Oct. 1849, 29 Nov. 1853, 25 Oct. 1859; *Augusta Chronicle & Sentinel,* 14 Nov. 1851.

required Whigs and Democrats to find alternative ways to defend black slavery and white men's liberty.

The parties grew from black belt bases. The black belt cast more than two-thirds of the state vote during the 1830s, and more than a generation later still contained more than half of Georgia's voters (tables 5–7). The early overweening power of the eastern black belt declined over time as settlement expanded into the western cotton lands and north Georgia, but the older section retained strength enough to account for a clear majority of the region's vote through the 1850s. Both halves of the black belt became blacker over time: the east acquired a slave majority in the 1840s, and the west followed a decade later. The combination of slaveholding wealth and voting numbers ensured that no political party could prosper without attracting extensive black belt support.[6]

State Rights–Whig ascendancy in the black belt during the 1830s and

*Table 6. Voting of Eastern and Western Black Belt Region, 1835–1859*

|  | Whig Votes | Democratic Votes | % Democrat | % of Black Belt Vote |
|---|---|---|---|---|
| *1835–40* |  |  |  |  |
| Eastern | 80,537 | 57,985 | 41.9 | 66.5 |
| Western | 38,525 | 31,128 | 44.7 | 33.5 |
| *1841–49* |  |  |  |  |
| Eastern | 122,985 | 92,931 | 43.0 | 62.5 |
| Western | 69,675 | 59,658 | 46.1 | 37.5 |
| *1853–59* |  |  |  |  |
| Eastern | 87,110 | 88,116 | 50.3 | 59.1 |
| Western | 59,552 | 61,733 | 50.9 | 40.9 |
| Total | 458,384 | 391,551 | 46.1 | 100 |

*Sources:* Walter Dean Burnham, *Presidential Ballots, 1836–1892* (Baltimore: Johns Hopkins University Press, 1955); *Macon Georgia Messenger,* 16 Nov. 1837; *Milledgeville Southern Recorder,* 14 Nov. 1837, 9 Nov. 1841, 17 Oct. 1843, 21 Oct. 1845, 12 Oct. 1847, 25 Oct. 1853, 16 Oct., 4 Dec. 1855, 20 Oct. 1857; *Milledgeville Federal Union,* 31 Oct. 1835, 23 Oct. 1838, 16 Oct. 1849, 29 Nov. 1853, 25 Oct. 1859; *Augusta Chronicle & Sentinel,* 14 Nov. 1851.

*Table 7. Population of Eastern and Western Black Belt Region, 1830–1860*

|          | Population | White   | Slave   | %<br>Slave | % of<br>Black Belt<br>Population |
|----------|-----------:|--------:|--------:|-----------:|--------------------------------:|
| *1830*   |            |         |         |            |                                 |
| Eastern  | 316,884    | 163,992 | 151,535 | 47.8       | 86.8                            |
| Western  | 47,994     | 32,653  | 15,290  | 31.9       | 13.2                            |
| *1840*   |            |         |         |            |                                 |
| Eastern  | 313,480    | 155,564 | 156,569 | 49.9       | 67.5                            |
| Western  | 150,715    | 92,839  | 57,608  | 38.2       | 32.5                            |
| *1850*   |            |         |         |            |                                 |
| Eastern  | 371,369    | 169,635 | 200,287 | 53.9       | 64.8                            |
| Western  | 201,477    | 109,053 | 92,169  | 45.7       | 35.2                            |
| *1860*   |            |         |         |            |                                 |
| Eastern  | 380,239    | 164,520 | 214,095 | 56.3       | 60.7                            |
| Western  | 246,503    | 112,734 | 133,357 | 54.1       | 39.3                            |

*Sources: Fifth Census of the United States, 1830; Sixth Census of the United States, 1840; Seventh Census of the United States, 1850; Eighth Census of the United States, 1860.*

1840s reflected the party's deeper roots and slightly greater devotion to regional interests. In early political conflicts between settled areas and the expanding frontier, the Troupite Virginians of old middle Georgia aligned against the Clarkite periphery and formed the nucleus of a lasting party. The State Rights party's antitariff crusade of the 1830s expressed the economic frustrations of cotton planters, and its simultaneous promotion of railroad projects and defense of state banking furthered important commercial interests. Then, in the great change that took place about 1840, the Whig party endorsed a national bank and suggested a modest program of economic development and diversification as cures for economic woes. The idea of harmony of interests (between capital and labor, agriculture and commerce, North and South), a notion propounded in much Whig literature, jibed well with the emerging paternalistic slaveholding ideology, reduced friction between farmers and merchants, and eased concerns over sectional conflict that could undermine slavery. Finally, Whigs' opposition to executive power and their persistent antiparty rhetoric upheld the ideals of free government and personal independence that so many white men valued. All in all, despite shifts and equivocations, Whig policies—as Georgians interpreted them—recognizably served the interests of black belt voters, who always formed a considerable majority of the party's constituents.

The Whigs were not, however, the *only* black belt party; Democrats carried well over 40 percent of the black belt vote even during the peak years of the Jacksonian party system, and they assumed majority status in the region in the 1850s. Compared with Whigs, Democrats emphasized protection and eschewed promotion. Although black belt Democrats endorsed railroads and shrank from full-scale assaults on state banks, they criticized both freely and vowed to curb corporate abuses. Similarly, Democrats warned that national banks and protective tariffs would injure southern agriculturalists and line the pockets of distant enemies. Democratic claims that government action, rather than benefiting all, tended merely to make certain rich men richer fit the prejudices of some suspicious planters and legions of middling white men. Above all, the Democracy presented itself as the premier defender of slavery, white liberty, the South, and the Union. The power that southern Democrats wielded in the national party, moreover, allowed them to make good many of their promises, a fact that lured thousands of reluctant former Whigs into the Democratic fold during the 1850s.

Whether Whig or Democratic sentiments predominated in a black belt county depended more on the date of settlement, local leadership, and tradition than on levels of slaveholding or other obvious economic factors. Slaveholders formed a large portion, sometimes a majority, of voters in black belt counties with vastly different political leanings. To give some examples, tax digests listed 655 slaveholders in Oglethorpe County in 1835; the county cast 638 votes in that year's state election. Wilkes County, with 550 slaveholders, polled 790 votes in the 1840 presidential contest, and fully 80 percent of farm households in nearby Taliaferro County owned slaves. In elections spanning two decades, the ratio of votes cast to slaveholders in Houston County ranged around two to one. While Oglethorpe was very strongly and Taliaferro was almost unanimously Whiggish, Wilkes and Houston were divided battlegrounds that often favored the Democracy. Clearly, to compete in black belt counties, both parties had to and did secure substantial support from slaveholders.[7]

The earliest to join and the last to leave the Whig party were the counties of old middle Georgia, where established leaders such as Alexander Stephens and Robert Toombs preserved old animosities. Farther west, in an area filled during Andrew Jackson's presidency, a bloc of counties on both sides of a diagonal line running from Coweta to Pulaski formed a Democratic black belt enclave. These counties (fourteen in all) were nearly identical with surrounding Whiggish counties, but they stood out from their neighbors in politics and furnished several prominent Democratic politicians. The slave population and level of cotton production in Butts County, for example, equaled that of many Whig strongholds, yet Butts consistently yielded Democratic majorities of better than 60 percent. To take an extreme case, the adjacent counties of Laurens and Twiggs had slave populations of 46.2 and 56.5 percent, respectively, in 1850, and Twiggs produced nearly three quarters of the enormous combined cotton crop of the two counties. Well over 90 percent of Laurens County voters were Whigs; Laurens went smoothly from being a banner Troupite county to being the strongest Whig county in the state. Voters in Twiggs County, on the other hand, returned Democratic majorities averaging about 55 percent. Generally, the farther away from eastern Troupite traditions, the weaker the Whig party became, and the steady transfer of population to the less Whiggish western black belt drained crucial strength from the party.

The accompanying growth in the mountains and the upcountry provided an even greater bonanza for the Democracy. The population of north Georgia more than tripled between 1830 and 1860, and the area's share of the state vote leaped from 27.1 percent to 39.2 percent. While the white population declined in the black belt in the 1850s, the mountains and the upcountry added forty-five thousand whites—and it was white sons who became voters. North Georgia Democrats practically matched their black belt brethren in voting numbers by the late 1850s and felt less inclined than ever to defer to them in party councils.

A bit more than six out of every ten voters in the mountains and the upcountry were Democrats. Andrew Jackson's military campaigns and removal policies had done much to wrest north Georgia from the Creeks and Cherokees, and the mountains and the upcountry were settled predominantly during his presidency. North Georgia contained tens of thousands of original Unionists who had bonded with Old Hickory's party in the early

1830s and ever after remained staunch Democrats. As they slowly passed from the scene, these men handed down Democratic traditions to subsequent generations. The Democracy's greater hostility to banks and corporations proved lastingly attractive in regions where both were few, and themes of states' rights and limited government matched the mood of countless yeomen who desired mostly to be left alone. The innumerable battles that north Georgia Democratic leaders fought against black belt Whigs and Democrats satisfied small farmers and poor whites who sometimes resented the pretensions of the planters to the south. The main outlets for regional and class animosities in state politics were, indeed, struggles for power within the Democratic party.

Whigs, initially hampered by voters' Clarkite proclivities and the damaging taint of nullification, never received many more than one out of every three north Georgia ballots. As everywhere, some planters, merchants, and yeomen viewed Whig economic programs positively, and the party convinced others of the Democracy's despotic tendencies. Overall, however, Whigs lacked historical foundations, leaders (a list of even marginally prominent mountain or upcountry Whigs would be very short), and sizable constituencies for policies and appeals that were tailored more to black belt audiences. Whigs managed to carry only one mountain county, Chattooga, in a state election, and Democratic mountain majorities often bulked absurdly large—eight Rabun County Whigs met more than three hundred of their Democratic neighbors at the polls in the 1841 election. Whigs, to be sure, triumphed occasionally in a handful of upcountry counties and held Democratic majorities to less than 60 percent in others. But in general, Whigs lost heavily for three decades; only in extraordinary instances, such as Mark Cooper's 1843 race or Zachary Taylor's no-party campaign, did they meaningfully erode Democratic margins in north Georgia.

The pine barrens–wiregrass and coastal regions also experienced growth, but together they cast, at most, 9 percent of the state vote. Before a swing toward the Democrats in the 1850s, results in these evenly divided regions had no appreciable impact on statewide contests. Savannah and Chatham County, which contained the lion's share of the white coastal population, started out Democratic, found Whig economic measures worthwhile in the 1840s, then returned to the Democratic column as the national Whig party collapsed and Democratic immigrants, chiefly Irish, poured into the city.

The huge and sparsely populated pine barrens–wiregrass counties tended to be dominated by local leadership cliques, and ridiculously lopsided elections were the norm. Montgomery and Tattnall Counties, old Troupite bastions, routinely produced Whig majorities exceeding 90 percent. In neighboring Bulloch County, in contrast, Whigs were shut out twice and felt thankful to poll totals exceeding single digits.

Close competition in gubernatorial and presidential races in Georgia—as in most other states—rested on a foundation of decidedly unequal county contests (tables 8 and 9). Counties initially developed particular styles in leadership and voting behavior, which then persisted over time and were only minimally affected by shifting populations, economic fortunes, and issues. Between 1835 and 1849, more than half of Georgia's ninety-three counties consistently gave better than 60 percent majorities for a single party; nearly one-third of the counties favored one party by thirty percentage points or more. Fifty-four counties (58.1 percent) returned either Whig or Democratic majorities exclusively; all but fifteen counties voted for a particular party at least three quarters of the time. Whether measured by the mean or the median, the typical gap between parties at the county level hovered around twenty percentage points. The pine barrens–wiregrass and the mountains were clearly the least competitive regions—the former

*Table 8. Party Majorities in County Voting, 1835–1849*

| County Type | No. of Counties | % Democratic Majorities |
|---|---|---|
| All Democratic | 28 | 100 |
| Usually Democratic | 21 | 77.4 |
| Usually Whig | 18 | 24.7 |
| All Whig | 26 | 0.0 |
| Total | 93 | 52.1 |

*Sources:* Walter Dean Burnham, *Presidential Ballots, 1836–1892* (Baltimore: Johns Hopkins University Press, 1955); *Macon Georgia Messenger,* 16 Nov. 1837; *Milledgeville Southern Recorder,* 14 Nov. 1837, 9 Nov. 1841, 17 Oct. 1843, 21 Oct. 1845, 12 Oct. 1847; *Milledgeville Federal Union,* 31 Oct. 1835, 23 Oct. 1838, 16 Oct. 1849; *Augusta Chronicle & Sentinel,* 14 Nov. 1851.

*Table 9. County Competitiveness: Percentage Differences between Party Totals, 1835–1859*

| | 1835–40 | | 1841–49 | | 1853–59 | |
|---|---|---|---|---|---|---|
| | Mean | Median | Mean | Median | Mean | Median |
| Mountains | 46.5 | 46.1 | 26.9 | 28.1 | 35.8 | 30.1 |
| Upcountry | 21.5 | 21.4 | 18.2 | 17.1 | 25.0 | 18.4 |
| Black belt | 25.4 | 18.9 | 21.6 | 12.0 | 18.4 | 15.3 |
| Pine barrens– | | | | | | |
| wiregrass | 51.8 | 49.7 | 38.9 | 26.6 | 42.2 | 39.1 |
| Coast | 23.0 | 17.6 | 21.3 | 11.9 | 26.9 | 18.6 |
| Total | 29.4 | 21.7 | 23.3 | 17.2 | 25.9 | 18.2 |

*Sources:* Walter Dean Burnham, *Presidential Ballots, 1836–1892* (Baltimore: Johns Hopkins University Press, 1955); *Macon Georgia Messenger,* 16 Nov. 1837; *Milledgeville Southern Recorder,* 14 Nov. 1837, 9 Nov. 1841, 17 Oct. 1843, 21 Oct. 1845, 12 Oct. 1847; *Milledgeville Federal Union,* 31 Oct. 1835, 23 Oct. 1838, 16 Oct. 1849; *Augusta Chronicle & Sentinel,* 14 Nov. 1851.

because of its odd mixture of wildly Whig and wildly Democratic counties, the latter because of Democratic dominance. The upcountry and the coast became considerably more competitive during the 1840s, before gaps widened again with Democratic advances in the 1850s. More important, competition increased in the black belt after the 1830s as less Whiggish western counties developed and Democrats rallied in the eastern section. Since, up to the 1850s, the parties frequently exchanged control of the state and just a couple of percentage points usually separated them, both the large party margins at the county level and the stability of county voting patterns were remarkable. In Georgia's highly partisan political culture, voters possessed a pride in their party attachments, a confidence in local leadership, and a contempt for the familiar opposition that kept them coming to the polls and casting party ballots.[8]

The conflict between the Whiggish black belt and the Democratic mountains and upcountry was the most important electoral division in antebellum Georgia, but, as noted above, the magnitude of the differences in party support can easily be overestimated. Particularly, despite superficial appearances, no clear relationship existed between levels of slaveholding and

*Table 10. Counties Ranked in Quartiles by Slave Population Percentages,*
*with Voting Results, 1835–1849*

| Quartile | Whig Counties | Democratic Counties | Median Slave % (Average) | Median Demo- cratic % (Average) | Mean Slave % (Average) | Mean Demo- cratic % (Average) |
|---|---|---|---|---|---|---|
| First | 17 | 6 | 61.7 | 40.5 | 63.4 | 39.6 |
| Second | 16 | 7 | 46.6 | 42.7 | 46.5 | 42.8 |
| Third | 10 | 13 | 32.2 | 50.2 | 31.5 | 49.7 |
| Fourth | 2 | 22 | 13.6 | 60.5 | 13.5 | 63.1 |
| Totals | 45 | 48 | 40.7 | 50.2 | 38.4 | 49.0 |

*Sources:* Walter Dean Burnham, *Presidential Ballots, 1836–1892* (Baltimore: Johns Hopkins University Press, 1955); *Macon Georgia Messenger,* 16 Nov. 1837; *Milledgeville Southern Recorder,* 14 Nov. 1837, 9 Nov. 1841, 17 Oct. 1843, 21 Oct. 1845, 12 Oct. 1847; *Milledgeville Federal Union,* 31 Oct. 1835, 23 Oct. 1838, 16 Oct. 1849; *Augusta Chronicle & Sentinel,* 14 Nov. 1851; *Sixth Census of the United States, 1840; Seventh Census of the United States, 1850.* The median and mean slave percentage averages are based on combined averages calculated from the United States Census population figures. Median and mean Democratic percentage averages are based on statewide elections from 1835 to 1849.

county voting behavior (table 10). Twenty-two of the twenty-four counties with the smallest slave population percentages were Democratic, and the Whigs controlled about three quarters of the black belt and coastal counties in the top two quartiles. Yet, within regions and between individual counties, levels of slaveholding alone explain next to nothing about the divergent voting patterns. Most of the Whig counties in the first quartile were, of course, in old middle Georgia; the low slaveholding Democratic counties were, also obviously, predominantly in north Georgia. The counties in the middle quartiles, lying mainly in the central and western black belt and in the pine barrens–wiregrass, lacked the historical legacies of either of those two distinctive areas and thus were almost equally divided between the parties. Counties in the same quartile with similar economic and demographic profiles voted differently—often very differently—because of their peculiar political cultures and structures. The underlying causes for enduring county voting patterns become understandable—though, inevitably, less than perfectly clear—only if one combines many factors such as region, tradition, leadership, and slaveholding and considers county results within the context of the larger, strikingly balanced, party system.[9]

Beginning in 1807, the Georgia state government conducted business in Milledgeville, a small commercial town located along the Oconee River in Baldwin County. Delays in establishing railroad connections doomed Milledgeville to remain a provincial capital; it had just over twenty-two hundred residents in 1850, nearly half of them slaves. Construction of the statehouse, begun in 1805, was not completed until 1836, and the legislative hall remained in disrepair until a thorough remodeling in the mid-1850s. The governor's mansion, finished in 1838, was palatial in design, but parsimonious legislators refused to provide funds to purchase adequate furnishings. The town's social season coincided with the meeting of the legislature, which opened its sessions in early November and adjourned around Christmas—though sessions ran longer as the years advanced. Legislators could display their refinement at formal dinners or at the governor's annual levee, but the everyday habits of rural society proved hard to break. As the slightly snobbish Richard Arnold of Savannah observed in 1837, in "both Halls of the Legislature the members sit with their hats on or walk about, or lounge about the fires, chewing, spitting, and smoking." The most popular tavern was the Big Indian, its doorway guarded by a wooden figure—scalping knife in hand—that faced across Greene Street toward the Presbyterian church. A generation of legislators enjoyed hospitality at ten cents a drink before the Big Indian was destroyed in an 1853 fire. Visitors so inclined could join "plenty of members of the legislature" at the faro table, betting "very high"; and the bordello district lay, conveniently, just two blocks south of the governor's mansion.[10]

If men's basic nature remained much the same, the composition and character of the legislature nonetheless changed markedly over time. Early nineteenth-century legislatures were stable bodies filled with incumbents and directed by experienced leaders; the average legislator could claim two or three (sometimes many more) terms of service. With the advent of the Jacksonian party system, however, the average tenure of legislators began to decline, and by the late 1850s it had fallen to just over a single term. Since no evidence suggests that incumbents either were consistently denied renomination or were defeated in massive numbers, the likelihood is that a winter or two in Milledgeville was simply enough for most men, and they declined to seek additional terms. Few compelling state issues arose to draw ambitious men to the capital, and many observers throughout the 1840s testified to the declining prestige of legislative service. Probably most important, the rise of parties made men more interchangeable. Candidates no longer ran on their own hook, and the party vote could be rallied for any number of suitable aspirants. The parties as institutions, rather than legislators as individuals, controlled proceedings and wielded power at both the state and county levels. Local party stalwarts could afford to and did take turns in the legislature.[11]

Although legislators increasingly came and went, a cadre of veterans still provided considerable continuity in leadership. A select group of 148 men who served four or more terms each during the 1840s amounted to just 5.5 percent of all legislators but served 26.8 percent of the total terms available. Somewhat more than half of the veterans were Democrats, mainly from the mountains and the upcountry; almost all the veteran Whigs hailed from the black belt.[12]

The veterans directed party activities and controlled much of the legislative business. Charles Jones Jenkins, the foremost Whig presence in the state house during much of the Jacksonian era, served ten terms between 1836 and 1849 and was four times chosen Speaker. Born in Beaufort District, South Carolina, Jenkins moved to Georgia while still a youth and later graduated from Union College in New York. After reading law with John M. Berrien, a kinsman, Jenkins set up his practice in Augusta, a city he would call home for the remainder of his life. A serious, religious man, Jenkins gained respect from friends and opponents alike, both in politics and before the bar. Jenkins's ally in Richmond County politics was another Augusta lawyer, Andrew Jackson Miller, who served a house term in 1836 and then represented Richmond County in the senate continuously from 1838 until his death in 1856. Often reelected with little or no opposition, Miller had a reputation as a master in framing bills, and he played an invaluable role in rallying Whig forces in the senate. Other outstanding Whig legislators included, of course, Alexander Stephens and Robert Toombs, both of whom spent six winters at Milledgeville. On the Democratic side, Joseph Dunagan, a perennial senator from Hall County during the Van Buren–Tyler years, frequently framed the obligatory resolutions on the state of the Republic that defined the party's positions on national affairs. The north Georgia Democracy furnished many veterans, including Robert M. Echols, elected senator from Walton County every year between 1836 and 1843, who helped shape Democratic policy on the Central Bank and other economic questions. Upcountry and mountain Democrats Horace W. Cannon of Rabun, John Carlton of Campbell, Dennis Carroll of Murray, and Johnson P. Wellborn of Union all served at least half a dozen terms.[13]

A large majority of the counties elected legislators from the same party year after year, seldom or never deviating in their partisan allegiance (table 11). In the 1830s, the forty-two most Democratic counties elected 33 Whigs and 535 Democrats; the thirty-one most Whiggish counties elected 20 Democrats and 475 Whigs—these two groups accounted for nearly 80 percent of the counties in the state. The same pattern held true throughout the

Table 11. *Counties Ranked by Tendency to Elect Democratic Legislators, 1836–1859*

|  | Range of Democratic Legislators (%) | No. of Counties | Whigs | Democrats | Total Democrats (%) | Avg. No. of Demo- crats per County |
|---|---|---|---|---|---|---|
| *1836–40* | 100–75 | 42 | 33 | 535 | 94.2 | 12.7 |
|  | 74.9–25 | 20 | 162 | 177 | 52.2 | 8.9 |
|  | 24.9–0 | 31 | 475 | 20 | 4.0 | 0.6 |
| *1841–49* | 100–75 | 44 | 58 | 496 | 89.5 | 11.3 |
|  | 74.9–25 | 18 | 143 | 133 | 48.2 | 7.4 |
|  | 24.9–0 | 31 | 425 | 32 | 7.0 | 1.0 |
| *1853–59* | 100–75 | 76 | 38 | 507 | 93.0 | 6.7 |
|  | 74.9–25 | 38 | 162 | 177 | 52.2 | 4.7 |
|  | 24.9–0 | 18 | 168 | 8 | 4.5 | 0.4 |

*Sources:* Georgia Official and Statistical Register, *1977–1978* (Atlanta: Perry Communications, 1978); *Journal of the House of Representatives of the State of Georgia, 1836–59; Journal of the Senate of the State of Georgia, 1835–59; Macon Georgia Messenger,* 27 Oct. 1836, 16 Nov. 1837, 18 Oct. 1838, 24 Oct. 1839; *Milledgeville Federal Union,* 20 Oct. 1840, 26 Oct. 1841, 25 Oct. 1842; *Milledgeville Southern Recorder,* 17 Oct. 1843, 21 Oct. 1845, 12 Oct. 1847, 9 Oct. 1849, 21 Oct. 1851, 25 Oct. 1853, 16 Oct. 1855, 20 Oct. 1857, 28 Oct. 1859.

*Note:* Legislators elected by the Union or Southern Rights parties in 1851 have been excluded.

Table 12. Representatives by Region and Period, 1836–1859

| | Whigs | Demo-crats | Total | % Demo-crats | % of All Legis-lators | % of All Whigs | % of All Demo-crats |
|---|---|---|---|---|---|---|---|
| *1836–40* | | | | | | | |
| Mountains | 5 | 53 | 59 | 89.8 | 6.2 | 1.1 | 10.9 |
| Upcountry | 21 | 161 | 183 | 88.0 | 19.3 | 4.6 | 33.1 |
| Black belt | 387 | 209 | 598 | 34.9 | 62.9 | 84.3 | 43.0 |
| Pine barrens– | | | | | | | |
| wiregrass | 19 | 30 | 50 | 60.0 | 5.3 | 4.1 | 6.2 |
| Coast | 27 | 33 | 60 | 55.0 | 6.3 | 5.9 | 6.8 |
| Total | 459 | 486 | 950 | 51.2 | 100 | 100 | 100 |
| *1841–49* | | | | | | | |
| Mountains | 11 | 62 | 74 | 83.8 | 7.3 | 2.2 | 12.3 |
| Upcountry | 35 | 152 | 188 | 80.9 | 18.6 | 6.9 | 30.2 |
| Black belt | 406 | 225 | 632 | 35.6 | 62.5 | 80.6 | 44.6 |
| Pine barrens– | | | | | | | |
| wiregrass | 23 | 37 | 60 | 61.7 | 5.9 | 4.6 | 7.3 |
| Coast | 29 | 28 | 57 | 49.1 | 5.6 | 5.8 | 5.6 |
| Total | 504 | 504 | 1,011 | 49.9 | 99.9 | 100.1 | 100 |
| *1853–59* | | | | | | | |
| Mountains | 12 | 52 | 65 | 80.0 | 10.7 | 5.5 | 13.5 |
| Upcountry | 19 | 98 | 117 | 83.8 | 19.2 | 8.7 | 25.5 |
| Black belt | 166 | 170 | 338 | 50.3 | 55.5 | 75.8 | 44.2 |
| Pine barrens– | | | | | | | |
| wiregrass | 17 | 43 | 61 | 70.5 | 10.0 | 7.8 | 11.2 |
| Coast | 5 | 22 | 28 | 78.6 | 4.6 | 2.3 | 5.7 |
| Total | 219 | 385 | 609 | 63.2 | 100 | 100.1 | 100.1 |
| Grand total | 1,182 | 1,375 | 2,570 | 53.5 | 100 | 100 | 100 |

*Sources: Georgia Official and Statistical Register, 1977–1978* (Atlanta: Perry Communications, 1978); *Journal of the House of Representatives of the State of Georgia, 1836–59; Journal of the Senate of the State of Georgia, 1835–59; Macon Georgia Messenger,* 27 Oct. 1836, 16 Nov. 1837, 18 Oct. 1838, 24 Oct. 1839; *Milledgeville Federal Union,* 20 Oct. 1840, 26 Oct. 1841, 25 Oct. 1842; *Milledgeville Southern Recorder,* 17 Oct. 1843, 21 Oct. 1845, 12 Oct. 1847, 9 Oct. 1849, 21 Oct. 1851, 25 Oct. 1853, 16 Oct. 1855, 20 Oct. 1857, 28 Oct. 1859.
*Note:* Legislators elected by the Union or Southern Rights parties in 1851 have been excluded.

1840s, until the addition of thirty-nine new, mainly Democratic counties and the dramatic decline of Whig strength altered alignments somewhat in the final antebellum decade. Still, at all times, the vast majority of legislators came from counties monopolized by one party.

Since a victory was a victory in a legislative race, no matter the size of the margin, regional differences in party representation in the legislature were considerably more marked than differences in regional voting patterns (tables 12 and 13). The black belt, which always elected more than half of the legislature, supplied more than three quarters of all Whig legislators; small wonder that Whig lawmakers guarded black belt interests. Sizable contingents of Democrats, however, also came from the black belt, and by the 1850s the majority of black belt legislators were Democrats. Mountain and upcountry Democrats filled well above 80 percent of their region's seats in Milledgeville and always accounted for more than a third of all Democratic legislators. The coast and the pine barrens–wiregrass, which sent small but not insignificant delegations to the house and elected a sizable part of the senate, usually favored Democrats—dramatically so in the 1850s—and furnished some very prominent legislators. (The notable leap in pine barrens–wiregrass representation in the 1850s resulted from the creation of ten new counties in the region.)

In terms of overall numbers, the parties remained locked in a stalemate for fifteen years, with the Democrats having only a slight edge, until the Whigs finally gave way in the 1850s. Control of the house changed hands regularly in the 1830s and 1840s, but the Whigs managed majorities in the senate only in 1840 and 1847—the populous, Whiggish black belt had less relative representation in the senate. Gaining control of the legislature before the 1850s depended on winning races in closely contested counties and thus adding a few doubtful seats to a much larger constant party base.

The scheme of legislative apportionment used in Georgia tended to promote party and regional balance. The basic plan, which operated from 1798 until 1843, gave each county one senator and at least one representative and allotted additional representatives according to a scale of population (counting the free population plus three-fifths of the African American population, free and slave, usually called—slightly inaccurately—the federal ratio), up to a maximum of four representatives per county. A state census taken every seven years provided data for reapportionments, and counties were limited

Table 13. Senators by Region and Period, 1836–1859

| | Whigs | Demo-crats | Total | % Demo-crats | % of All Legis-lators | % of All Whigs | % of All Demo-crats |
|---|---|---|---|---|---|---|---|
| *1836–43* | | | | | | | |
| Mountains | 4 | 62 | 67 | 92.5 | 9.1 | 1.2 | 15.4 |
| Upcountry | 12 | 124 | 136 | 91.2 | 18.5 | 3.6 | 30.8 |
| Black belt | 257 | 149 | 406 | 36.7 | 55.1 | 77.2 | 37.0 |
| Pine barrens– | | | | | | | |
| wiregrass | 33 | 47 | 80 | 58.8 | 10.9 | 9.9 | 11.7 |
| Coast | 27 | 21 | 48 | 43.8 | 6.5 | 8.1 | 5.2 |
| Total | 333 | 403 | 737 | 54.7 | 100.1 | 100 | 100.1 |
| *1845–49* | | | | | | | |
| All | 68 | 73 | 141 | 51.8 | 100 | 100 | 100 |
| *1853–59* | | | | | | | |
| Mountains | 9 | 48 | 57 | 84.2 | 12.4 | 6.0 | 15.6 |
| Upcountry | 10 | 73 | 83 | 88.0 | 18.0 | 6.7 | 23.8 |
| Black belt | 108 | 125 | 236 | 53.0 | 51.2 | 72.5 | 40.7 |
| Pine barrens– | | | | | | | |
| wiregrass | 18 | 42 | 61 | 68.9 | 13.2 | 12.1 | 13.7 |
| Coast | 4 | 19 | 24 | 79.2 | 5.2 | 2.7 | 6.2 |
| Total | 149 | 307 | 461 | 66.6 | 100 | 100 | 100 |
| Grand total | 550 | 783 | 1,339 | 58.5 | 100 | 100 | 100 |

*Sources: Georgia Official and Statistical Register, 1977–1978* (Atlanta: Perry Communications, 1978); *Journal of the House of Representatives of the State of Georgia,* 1836–59; *Journal of the Senate of the State of Georgia,* 1835–59; *Macon Georgia Messenger,* 27 Oct. 1836, 16 Nov. 1837, 18 Oct. 1838, 24 Oct. 1839; *Milledgeville Federal Union,* 20 Oct. 1840, 26 Oct. 1841, 25 Oct. 1842; *Milledgeville Southern Recorder,* 17 Oct. 1843, 21 Oct. 1845, 12 Oct. 1847, 9 Oct. 1849, 21 Oct. 1851, 25 Oct. 1853, 16 Oct. 1855, 20 Oct. 1857, 28 Oct. 1859.

*Note:* Legislators elected by the Union or Southern Rights parties in 1851 have been excluded. Senators were elected by districts from 1845 to 1849. Since several senate districts included counties from different regions, no regional analysis for those years was attempted.

to a maximum of two representatives beginning in 1845. Except for a brief experiment with senate districts between 1845 and 1851, Georgians acted on the assumption that "the different counties of the State . . . are composed of separate and distinct political communities, having separate and distinct local wants and interests, and are, therefore, entitled each to a separate and distinct representation in *both* branches of the Legislature."[14]

By tying representation both to counties and to population calculated by the federal ratio, Georgians fashioned a compromise that gave most white men's votes approximately equal weight in electing legislators. Whites in counties with large slave populations obviously reaped benefits from the federal ratio, but since every county was entitled to at least one representative, the smaller predominantly white counties also gained greater representation than their population warranted. The structure of the senate, in which each county, regardless of population, had one seat, further offset the effects of the federal ratio. Under the various federal ratio apportionments actually implemented, the pine barrens–wiregrass was overrepresented, especially in the senate, the mountain region was slightly overrepresented in both branches, the black belt and the upcountry were underrepresented, and the coast received its just deserts.

No region ever suffered severely or benefited tremendously from malapportionment. Indeed, if county lines had been completely ignored and a perfect system of apportionment had been established, using either the federal ratio or white population only as the basis, the strength of the various regions in the legislature would have scarcely changed. In 1840, for example, the upcountry held 18.7 percent of the seats in the legislature. Under a perfect federal ratio system, it would have had 19 percent of the seats; under a perfect white basis system, 23.3 percent. The black belt's share of legislators would have been no different under a perfect white basis than it was under the system in use, and the pine barrens–wiregrass and the coast would have lost several seats. By 1860, shifts in the population had made the black belt somewhat overrepresented measured against a perfect white basis, and the mountains and the upcountry were underrepresented. But again, the mere shifting around of a dozen or so seats would have been a sufficient remedy. Apportionment was as equal as it could be without obliterating county lines, and thus representation never became a potent issue in Georgia as it did in some other southern seaboard states.

The issue of representation attained significance periodically in the 1830s and early 1840s, when a series of contests pitted party against party and exposed regional divisions. Troup–State Rights leaders from the eastern black belt, apprehensive about the proliferation of frontier counties, complained frequently about the excessive size of the legislature and the expense of the sessions. Troupite pressure finally influenced the legislature to schedule a constitutional convention in May 1833 to consider reapportionment. The convention fashioned a plan that would have eliminated many house seats and would have halved the senate by erecting two-county districts. Most controversially, the convention proposed abandoning the federal ratio and making white population the basis for house apportionment. The whitest regions—the upcountry, the mountains, and the pine barrens—wiregrass—overwhelmingly supported the white basis, but it was black belt votes that actually swung the balance against the federal ratio. While Troupite black belt counties backed the federal ratio, more than two-thirds of the black belt delegates from Clarkite counties favored the white basis. The combined power of factional and regional animosities pushed the proposal through the convention, although the plan adopted would have produced only minuscule changes in relative regional representation.[15]

The ensuing referendum campaign—voters had to ratify or reject the convention's work—explored the ideologically charged issue of white male equality in a slave society. Opponents of reform, mainly Troupites, argued that overturning the federal ratio in Georgia would encourage northern fanatics to attack the three-fifths clause of the Constitution, the "rock on which is based the glory and independence of the slave holding states." The superiority of white men in Georgia, in other words, would not be secure unless the whole South retained the power to protect slavery. Clarkites, however, especially John Cuthbert, the militant editor of the *Milledgeville Federal Union*, hailed the convention plan as a guarantee that "every *white man* will *be* a *white man*, and not feel that he is reduced to the level of a slave, or a free negro!" Cuthbert denounced defenders of the federal ratio as elitist conspirators who wanted "to refuse to freemen who are poor, their equal rights in the republic," and "to perpetuate that aristocratic principle which maintains, that wealth is entitled to peculiar privileges." In the end, black belt and Troupite strength defeated reapportionment by a few thousand votes.[16]

There the matter rested until 1839, when legislators summoned another state convention to address the urgent need to reduce the size of the legislature. Reapportionment under the 1838 state census had increased the legislature to three hundred members, and per diem pay for lawmakers drained large sums from the state's shrinking treasury. The sessions of the 1839 convention were long and contentious; altogether the delegates considered some two dozen reapportionment plans. The time for serious debate regarding the federal ratio had, however, permanently passed. The threat of northern abolitionism and the march of the cotton belt westward consolidated the coastal and black belt counties, regardless of party, behind the federal ratio, and less than 30 percent of the convention displayed a fondness for the white basis—the only significant support came from mountain and upcountry Democrats. The Unionist majority in the convention eventually adopted a proposal that merely raised the population scale for house representation and organized two-county senate districts; the relative weight of regional representation remained undisturbed. The voters, who displayed little interest in the whole matter, overwhelmingly rejected the convention's work.[17]

The legislature itself finally broke the reapportionment deadlock. With the state practically bankrupt, Whigs and Democrats managed to work together to pass two constitutional amendments. The first, ratified in 1841, made legislative meetings biennial beginning with the 1843 session. The other, ratified in 1843 to take effect with the 1845 election, reduced the number of representatives by more than one-third and established forty-seven senate districts composed of two contiguous counties—except for Chatham, which alone formed a single district. Subsequent legislatures undermined these reforms; single counties started electing senators again in 1853 and the legislature swelled to more than three hundred members, but legislative apportionment was never again more than a peripheral issue in state politics.[18]

The typical legislator was a forty-year-old man, very probably born in Georgia and almost certainly born in the South, who farmed, practiced law, or combined the two vocations. Legislators were far wealthier than their average constituents; more than two-thirds of lawmakers in 1850 and 1860 were slaveholders, and a bit less than half of the slaveholders were planters. Whigs held slaves somewhat more often and in slightly larger numbers than did Democrats. Senators were marginally older than representatives, and the median slave holding in the senate was greater than in the house. Ownership of land and slaves clearly was an important qualification for legislative service, but nonslaveholders occupied seats, and tens of thousands of slaveholders never saw Milledgeville. Above all, men elected to the legislature had stature, a combination of achievement, connections, reputation, and character.[19]

Legislators often built on family traditions of officeholding and trained as militia officers, inferior court justices, and justices of the peace. Peter Cone of Bulloch County belonged to a prominent south Georgia family descended from North Carolinians. His uncle, William, represented Camden County in the legislature for thirteen terms and also served as a captain of the militia and a justice of the peace. Peter, similarly, was a county surveyor for eight years and a justice of the inferior court; people usually addressed him as General Cone, acknowledging his militia rank. Except for a brief sabbatical in the late 1840s, Peter Cone also was the senator from Bulloch County from the time of Andrew Jackson to the Civil War. James Fulwood, a Revolutionary soldier's son and a Ware County planter, spent four years in the senate in addition to serving as justice of the peace, inferior court justice, and Waresboro postmaster. His sister, Mary, was the bride of John Smith Henderson, militia captain, clerk and justice of the inferior court, and legislator. Another longtime Waresboro postmaster, Colonel Thomas Hilliard, at one time or another filled nearly every office in the county and enjoyed thirteen winters in Milledgeville. His (probably illegitimate) son, Cuyler W. Hilliard, was likewise a militia officer, justice of the peace, sometime postmaster, and senator. William Angus McDonald, another legislator who followed in his father's footsteps as an inferior court justice, took time enough away from legislating and preaching Methodism to raise his own constituency; his three wives blessed him with twenty-two children.[20]

Along with having family connections, a willingness to meet and greet voters helped. Many candidates treated; that is, they supplied voters with free drinks, sometimes even in defiance of laws that banned the practice. When John B. Lamar ran for a house seat in Bibb County in 1837, he asked Howell Cobb for a thousand-dollar loan to cover his anticipated expenses and allowed that he "would not be beaten for [$]1500 or [$]2000 and therefore am willing to lose that much." Ten years later and in another part of the state, a "Backwoods' Candidate" spent less and complained more. While delivering speeches at court sessions and militia musters, "Backwoods" encountered voters who "drank like horses" and expected their candidates to tipple too. One day, before mounting the stump, "Backwoods" dropped "into a doggery, and told the owner to set out a quart." When the voters insisted on enjoying his company as well as his liquor, "Backwoods" abandoned his "temperance pledge—sacrificed to expediency." Politics even intruded on the Sabbath. Come Sunday, "Backwoods" felt compelled to "go to [church] meeting" to shake hands with the county folk, but he "couldn't get out the carriage—they'd say I was an aristocrat and a *swell-head*." Few white Georgians could have missed the satirical point: by drinking convivially and worshipping humbly, regardless of his own inclinations, "Backwoods" surrendered to the people even as he sought to fool them.[21]

Who was manipulating whom during campaigns was never clear, but some managers certainly prided themselves on their ability to gull voters. One campaign report from John Hughes, a Whig correspondent of Congressman Thomas Butler King, oozed cynicism. At an Appling County militia parade in 1844, a Major Bacon spoke to the crowd of two hundred, and "in a little time had them all in good humour[,] he flattered them by telling them they were honest[,] and I really believe he got them to believe they were worthy men[,] and when he touched on the leading measures of the whig party they paid good attention[,] and I could frequently here [*sic*] them cry out that[']s the truth." Hughes went on to lament the "misfortune that we have not had Bacon in our pine woods one month sooner . . . [for] he is a popular man with these people and knows how to manage them." Most politicians did not share Hughes's jaundiced view of voters, but even the hypocrites recognized the necessity of praising the virtue of white men.[22]

Paying homage to rural values benefited Jacob Martin and many other candidates. Martin, of yeoman stock, mined for gold in the Cherokee country and taught school before adopting the law as a career. When friends drafted him to run in 1845 in the senate district comprising Pike and Monroe Counties, Martin found himself facing a planter who was more than willing to exploit prejudices against lawyers. One day, while Martin was on his way to a stump engagement, an idea struck him as he rode by his opponent's dilapidated homestead. When he stood before the voters, Martin downplayed his legal attainments, stressed his roots in the soil, and challenged his rival's agricultural credentials: "I passed his plantation this morning. I can beat him in grubbing [out stumps], in cutting and splitting rails, in hoeing and picking out cotton. I am a better farmer than he is. On one branch of a farmer's life alone to him I yield the palm. *He can beat me in raising hog-weed and crab-grass.*" Martin, only half in jest, asked the voters to compare the candidates' farms and then vote accordingly. He won the election.[23]

The most vivid surviving account of legislative campaigning in antebellum Georgia is a fictional one created by William Tappan Thompson in his collection of sketches, *Major Jones's Courtship*. Thompson, a newspaper editor who knew most of the major figures in state politics, ranked alongside his mentor, Augustus Baldwin Longstreet, at the top of the list of Georgia humorists. The title character, Major Joseph Jones, was a small planter whose purported letters kept Thompson apprised of the latest ridiculous happenings in the imaginary town of Pineville.[24]

In an August 1842 missive, Major Jones described a militia muster, which went "jest as I expected, only a thundering sight wurse!" Dressed in a gaudy—and overly snug—officer's uniform, Jones issued orders from horseback, or at least he did until random gunfire from the spirited regiment caused Jones's mount to throw him. The fall burst every seam of Jones's finery, but he gamely changed into farming clothes and reorganized the regiment. A march of a few hundred yards in an unrecognizable formation exhausted the militia's patience, and Jones glumly called for a rest break.[25]

> Bout this time out come a whole heap of fellers with sum candidates, what was runnin for the Legislater, and wanted I should let'em address the betallion. I told'em I didn't care so long as they didn't kick up no row.
>
> Well, the men wer all high up for hearin the speeches of the candidates, and got round'em thick as flies around a fat gourd. Ben Ansley—he's the poplarest candidate down here—begun the show by gittin on a stump, and takin his hat off right in the brilin hot sun.
>
> "Feller-citizens," ses he, "I spose you all know as how my friends is fotched me out to represent this county in the next Legislater, and I want to tell you what my principles is. I am posed to counterfit money and shinplasters; I am posed to abolition and free niggers, to the morus multicaulis and the Florida war, and all manner of shecoonery whatsumever! If I's lected your respectable representation, I shall go in for good money, twenty cents for cotton, and no taxes, and shall go for bolishin prisonment for debt and the Central Bank. I hope you'll all cum up to the poles of the lection, and vote like a patriot for you very humble servant—Amen."
>
> Then he jumped down and went around shakin hands. "Hurra for Ben

Ansley! Ansley for ever!" shouted every feller. "Down with the cussed bank—devil take the shinplasters and all the rale-roads!" ses Captain Skinner. "Silence for a speech from Squire Pettybone!" "Hurra for Pettybone!"

Squire Pettybone was a little short fat man, what had run afore, and knowed how to talk to the boys.

"Friends and feller-citizens," ses he, "I's once more a candidate for your sufferins, and I want to splain my sentiments to you. You've just hearn a grate deal about the Central Bank. I aint no bank man—I'm posed to all banks—but I is a friend to the pore man, and is always ready to stand up for his constitutional rights. When the Central Bank put out its money it was good, and rich men got it and made use of it when it was good; but now they want to buy it in for less nor what it's worth to pay their dets to the bank, and they is tryin to put it down, and make the pore man lose by it. What does they want to put the bank down for, if it aint to cheat the pore man who's got sum of it? If I's lected, I shall go for makin the banks redeem ther bills in silver and gold, or put every devil of 'em into the penitentiary to makin nigger shoes. I's a hard money man and in favor of the vetos. I goes for the pore man agin the rich, and if you lect me that's what I mean to do."

Then *he* begun shakin hands all round.[26]

The excitement generated by the speeches hurt discipline. Shouts for the candidates and curses on the opposition soon set the men of the regiment against each other in a free-for-all. Ansley, Pettybone, and Major Jones attempted to separate the mob, but "it wasn't no use to try to git'em into line agin." "The whole betallion was completely demoralized," Jones concluded, "so I turned 'em over to their captains, accordin to law, and aint 'sponsible for nothin that tuck place after I left."[27]

His exaggeration of underlying truths made Thompson's stories hilarious. Militia musters, which typically mixed a little training with a lot of drinking, attracted most of the white men in a district and thus were favorite occasions for campaign speech making. Ben Ansley and Squire Pettybone comically displayed the candidate's knack of supporting what no one opposed and opposing what no one supported—they affirmed white men's values. Neither man had a kind word for banks or worthless paper money; both endorsed "good money" and prosperity. The tellingly named Squire struck a few licks against the rich, and both despised "niggers." Some differences, to be sure, emerged. Pettybone, recognizably the Democrat in the piece, defended the Central Bank as the poor man's friend, but the Whig Ansley advocated its

destruction. When Ansley omitted any reference to a national bank, Pettybone made sure to register himself as "in favor of the vetos" of President
John Tyler in the 1841 bank fight. The rusticity of campaign rhetoric clearly
stands as the vignette's main theme. Rather than debating issues in fine de-
tail, Ansley and Pettybone appealed to general prejudices and vowed to protect white men from their enemies—a promise that, as William T. Thompson well knew, was the alpha and omega of campaign rhetoric in antebellum
Georgia.

Nelson Tift's true chronicle of his 1847 run for the house seat from Baker
County captured further peculiarities of local politics. Tift, a Connecticut
native, a self-made entrepreneur, and one of the founders of the town of
Albany, served as an inferior court justice, marched as a militia colonel, and
covered county events as the longtime editor of the *Albany Patriot*. Although
his personal fortune exceeded $200,000 by 1860, Tift was one of the more
radical Democrats in the state, a diehard enemy of the system of chartered
private banks.[28]

Tift's campaign, however, had little to do with banking or any other public policy question. Tift's quest began at a June convention, where he announced that he was tired of bowing to a "democratic party of the county
[that] has long been ruled or swayed by a few men who were then in office
and expectants of office." When the divided gathering deferred making a
nomination, Tift and his opponent, Dr. J. T. Sims, entered a kind of primitive primary contest, in which they courted the support of voters in the
various militia districts. Tift garnered the nomination on Sims's withdrawal,
but the victory proved only a prelude to greater troubles. Many leading
Democrats still harbored hostility toward him, and the partisans of Richard F. Lyon, Tift's Whig adversary, immediately began "using the most ne-
farious and contemptible means to defeat" him.[29]

Lyon and Tift compaigned extensively, both in person and in print, and
the battle waxed increasingly bitter. September found Tift gathering "cer-
tificates" from former employees to refute the newspaper "slander" that he
had "sent respectable white mechanics and labourers to my kitchen to eat
with negroes."[30] Tift, for his part, charged that Lyon had used his position
as an inferior court justice to solicit bribes from "two notorious counterfeit-
ers," whom Lyon had later released from jail. Tift also chided Lyon, who
worked as a "collecting attorney" for northern firms, for earning a living by

"applying the screws" to southern debtors.[31] Finally, on the weekend before the election, Tift returned to town after a campaign trip to discover an extra edition of the Whig *Albany Courier* containing allegations that he was "a defaulter to the poor school fund for $255." Tift quickly printed a handbill to correct the "infamous lie," but it "was too late to prevent all the mischief of the falsehood which had been in swift circulation for two or three days."

Tift endured "the most bitter malignity and the most base detraction" and braved "frequent threats that [he] would be attacked with weapons" to emerge triumphant by a little more than one hundred votes.[32] The issues that Tift faced on his path to Milledgeville mostly appealed to voters' emotions and moral instincts. To frame questions in ways that precluded debate and to convict the opposition of unpardonable offenses was good campaigning, pure and simple. If a candidate forced white laborers to eat with blacks or put poor men into the hands of greedy Yankees, he was detestable, not merely mistaken; he did not belong among honorable white men. Easily understandable and emotionally powerful issues reinvigorated party regulars and swayed the undecided, which was precisely why such issues were campaign staples.

Only a few odd souls ever suggested that Georgia party divisions could be or should be based on state policy concerns. Party platforms dwelt on national banks, tariffs, the Mexican War, the Wilmot Proviso, naturalization laws, Kansas, the annexation of Cuba, and a host of other issues outside the state government's purview. Aside from isolated controversies, party discussion of state matters virtually ceased once legislators left Milledgeville, and state issues played at most a minor role in determining political alignments.

Most of the legislative business in any session consisted of local bills, a fact that sparked frequent but unheeded complaints. As the *Savannah Republican* remarked in 1842, the passage of local bills was a "prolific source of County popularity," a way for legislators to show that they had "done something." There were "perpetually churches and academies to incorporate, ferries to be established, little towns to be incorporated, roads to be cut, suffering individuals to be relieved, names to be changed, and bastards to be legitimized." Consideration of uncontroversial local bills consumed days and weeks as legislators honed their oratorical skills in florid speeches aimed primarily at the ladies in the gallery. Although roads, churches, and ferries mattered greatly to communities, the routine satisfaction of local wants hardly provided issues for party debates.[33]

Each session began with days of balloting; the legislature elected officials ranging from clerks to superior court judges, and hundreds of office seekers traveled to Milledgeville seeking preferments. In filling just a few spots from a long list of offices available in 1849, the legislature altogether required thirty-one ballots to select seven officials from a total field of sixty-one candidates. Legislators also spent days, sometimes weeks, debating resolutions on the state of the Republic, which were usually among the first items introduced in any session. The parties battled to have their positions on national issues, as stated in their resolutions, adopted by the legislature and announced to the world as the solemn judgment of the people of Georgia. Conflicts over these symbolic pronouncements divided parties in the legislature more sharply and more consistently than any state issue ever did.[34]

The extremely restricted scope of state government, furthermore, limited the potential for party controversy. The great bulk of state law, apart from enactments with strictly local or individual applications, dealt with crime, property, land titles, court procedures, and slavery. Except for Indian removal, an issue settled by the mid-1830s, the only areas of state policy that provided substantial grist for party mills were banking, railroads, and taxation. The great era of debates over banking ended in 1843, although the panic of 1857 briefly revived dormant passions. Taxation and state assistance to railroads were inextricably linked because of the legislature's overriding devotion to tax-free finance. When the state received money from nontax sources (the sale of public lands and the distribution of the federal surplus revenue) in the 1830s, the legislature slashed taxes, and railroad projects proliferated. Once the surplus funds were exhausted, the legislature retrenched and hiked taxes, only to begin spreading largesse again in the prosperous 1850s. Both parties, reacting to changing economic conditions, had a hand in fashioning the notably cyclical state policies.[35]

The tax structure in place in the Jacksonian era dated back to the turn of the nineteenth century. Planters and slaveholders paid the most; levies on slaves alone amounted to nearly half of the total property taxes. Planters were, however, undertaxed relative to their total share of the state's wealth. Rural land was taxed much more lightly than town lots or merchant's stock, a discrimination against urban folk that pleased farmers. Every white male aged twenty-one to sixty was subject to an annual poll tax of thirty-nine cents, under the presumption that all white men should contribute something to support the government—a heavier poll tax punished free blacks. Specific taxes included duties on pleasure carriages. The tax system overall reflected the distribution of social and economic power: slave owners paid more because they had more, yeomen enjoyed relatively low rates on their farmland, and urban merchants faced the stiffest taxation.

Regardless of the details of the revenue system, white men in Georgia scarcely suffered from oppressive taxation. Laborers without property paid just the yearly poll tax, and even the rare planter with one hundred slaves under age sixty—worth tens of thousands of dollars—owed a mere $39 in taxes on his human chattel. The most heavily taxed county in the state in 1850, Richmond, which included the city of Augusta, paid a per capita tax of $1.20. With a state population of some 900,000 in 1849, Georgians paid a total of $265,433 in property taxes, about thirty cents per person. White men wanted and got a government that spent little and taxed less.[36]

Despite the minimal taxes, the system of specific rates, which taxed property according to type rather than value, struck many people as unequal and illogical, and political leaders intermittently discussed rate revisions and reform. Within narrow limits, Whigs, whose black belt constituents paid most of the state's bills, proved more willing than Democrats to support higher taxes. Specifically, Whigs saw the necessity of repairing the damage done to state finances by the panic of 1837 and by excessive reliance on borrowing. Once the fiscal situation improved in the mid-1840s, however, public and party interest in taxation issues all but evaporated. Governor George W. Towns, a Democrat, and a few others advocated thorough reform and the adoption of an ad valorem system, but the legislature, as it had for decades, preferred to suffer known evils rather than risk creating new ones.[37]

Ad valorem tax reform finally passed almost unnoticed amidst the turmoil following the Compromise of 1850. The unsettled political conditions broke long-standing deadlocks and allowed Union party coalitionists in the 1851 legislature to enact an ad valorem system that greatly reduced the tax rates on town property, shifted a small amount of the tax burden on slaves to taxes on rural land, and raised the total amount of state property taxes to $375,000. Legislators generally voted the economic interests of their counties. In the house, representatives from slave-rich black belt and coastal counties voted 45 to 11 for ad valorem. North Georgia and pine barrens–wiregrass representatives, whose constituents mainly owned land rather than slaves, opposed it 6 to 30. Regional divisions in the senate were less distinct. Senators whose districts included at least one mountain or upcountry county voted only 6 to 7 against ad valorem, coastal and pine barrens–wiregrass men opposed it 3 to 6, and black belt senators favored it by a 13 to 5 margin. Representatives and senators from counties with sizable towns—those with a population above two thousand—supported ad valorem by a 13 to 0 vote, with ten additional members absent.[38]

The adoption of the ad valorem system had little effect on most white Georgians. Town dwellers, especially merchants, received considerable relief, but they constituted a tiny part of the population. The proportion of state property revenues derived from the tax on slaves declined from 49.1 percent in 1849 to 42.3 percent in 1857, while the proportion of revenues derived from the rural land tax increased from 19.8 to 25.8 percent. While the shift may have hurt some large yeomen landholders who owned no slaves, it could not have altered planters' tax bills much—plantations included both valuable land and valuable slaves. Taxes overall remained strikingly low, especially given the rising land and slave values of the prosperous 1850s. According to the official reports, Georgians held more than $500 million in property in 1857; state property taxes totaled just under $425,000. Property taxes per capita in 1860 ranged from $0.11 in Gilmer County to $0.82 in Dougherty County. The per capita burden of *all* taxes paid in cash was lower in Georgia in 1860 than in any other state in the Union, just $0.75 compared with a national average of $2.91. Yearly income from the state-owned Western & Atlantic Railroad actually exceeded total state tax receipts by the late 1850s, and parties were less disposed than ever to argue about taxation.[39]

Before the coming of railroads, Georgians depended primarily on rough wagon roads and rivers for transportation. The expansion of white settlement in the 1820s and 1830s multiplied travel difficulties, which limited economic development and discouraged interregional trade. The legislature, recognizing needs and emboldened by flush times, caught railroad fever in the mid-1830s and laid the foundations of a state rail network. Legislators and promoters hoped that railroads would tie the state together, facilitate the transportation of cotton, open new markets, and tap western trade. Reflecting the black belt perspective, the *Macon Georgia Messenger* assumed that railroads would be "constructed mainly with a view to the transportation of the staple, which constitutes our principal wealth, to market." A Rome editor, on the other hand, predicted that railroads would bring the goods of the world to Cherokee Georgia and give farmers "the opportunity of supplying themselves upon the most advantageous terms." Merchants and mayors in Savannah, Augusta, Charleston, and other places dreamed grand dreams of commercial empire, and investment by towns and cities helped start many railroad enterprises.[40]

The Western & Atlantic Railroad system, the state's greatest antebellum project, took shape over more than a decade. The Central of Georgia Railroad and the Georgia Railroad, both chartered in 1833, built privately owned trunk lines, while the state constructed the Western & Atlantic trunk. The Central of Georgia, boosted by Macon townsmen and prominent coastal figures such as John M. Berrien, ran from Savannah up along the Ogeechee River and then through the south–central black belt to Macon. The Augusta to Athens route of the Georgia Railroad cut through the heart of old middle Georgia. The panic of 1837 slowed completion of the two lines: the Georgia Railroad did not extend its track to Athens until 1841, and the Central of Georgia reached Macon two years later. Plans for the Western & Atlantic itself, adopted in 1836, envisioned a railroad running from a point near the Chattahoochee River (the eventual site of Atlanta) to the Tennessee border near Chattanooga. Connections with private lines would then form a continuous rail route from the western states to Macon, Augusta, Savannah, and smaller towns. In the legislature, initial support for the W&A project came from counties and regions that stood to benefit directly; the fall line of the major rivers marked the division. Except for the counties due north of Augusta, which already had the Savannah River for transportation and would be bypassed by the rail lines, the upper black belt and north Georgia voted almost as a unit for the W&A proposal. The coastal region and a couple of counties along the Central of Georgia line also backed the W&A, but otherwise the southern and western parts of the state opposed it.[41]

When the state's fiscal crisis forced a suspension of work on the W&A in 1841, the project suddenly became a controversial party issue. Whigs, who emerged as the W&A's champions during George Crawford's first administration, supported a series of bills in the 1840s that authorized further construction and appropriated additional funds. Although most Democratic legislators opposed these measures, mountain and upcountry Democrats cast crucial votes to sustain railroad development in their regions. Eight north Georgia Democratic senators provided the margin of victory for an 1843 W&A bill, and nearly 40 percent of the Democratic senators backed 1847 appropriations. Aside from the effect of regional economic interests, hostility between north Georgia and black belt Democrats stemming from the 1843 and 1844 campaigns helped produce intraparty divisions.[42]

As the long recession lifted in the late 1840s, the W&A extended track through Marietta and Dalton to the terminus at Chattanooga. The connection of private lines to the W&A at Atlanta and the long-awaited arrival of the W&A in Chattanooga in 1850 completed the original plan of trunk lines and established continuous rail connections from the Tennessee border to the gulf coast—a host of shorter feeder lines were either already completed, under construction, or projected. By that time, however, older sections of the W&A had already fallen into disrepair, and the 1851 legislature voted a final appropriation of $525,000 to refurbish the whole line. The voting on this measure revealed that the W&A's geographical base of support had scarcely changed over fifteen years. Black belt and north Georgia counties located anywhere near the trunk lines overwhelmingly supported the appropriation. Southern and western counties distant from the existing lines heavily opposed the bill and, instead, pushed for state support for their own projects.[43]

The costs and benefits of the trunk system were unevenly distributed. The state directly appropriated almost $4.5 million for the W&A; the cities of Savannah, Augusta, and Macon invested nearly $1 million in the Central of Georgia and the Georgia Railroad. Much of the private investment came from slaveholders who received railroad stock as payment for employing their chattel in grading roadbeds or cutting timber. Cities, especially Macon, Savannah, and, later, Atlanta, profited from trade on the W&A; market-oriented farmers who lived near the rail lines also enjoyed cheaper, more convenient transportation. To be sure, some planters and yeomen complained when railroads divided their farms, when locomotives killed cattle, or when rumblings and roars disturbed the peace of once quiet local communities. But voices raised against railroads were easily drowned out by others crying for extensions and spurs to connect every hamlet of a few hundred souls to the trunk lines.[44]

Most of the areas missed by the original W&A system had only to wait for the 1850s boom. Democratic legislatures presided over an orgy of construction that more than doubled Georgia's track mileage—bringing the total to 1,404 miles, second only to Virginia in the South. Spurs linked towns such as Milledgeville and Athens to the Central of Georgia and the Georgia Railroad. The Southwestern Railroad ran from the hub at Macon through the western black belt to Albany, and then on to connections at the Alabama border. The Muscogee Railroad, which joined the Southwestern near Macon, tied Columbus to the rest of the state. The most important project was another trunk line, the Atlantic & Gulf Railroad, chartered in 1856 and supported by $1 million in state aid. Conceived as a southern counterpart to the Western & Atlantic, the Atlantic & Gulf extended two existing lines from Brunswick and Savannah and aimed at connecting these seaports to the fertile southwestern cotton belt—it was, however, completed only as far as Thomasville before the Civil War. By then, only extreme northeast Georgia and the central pine barrens–wiregrass still lacked convenient railroad connections.

Railroad politics in the 1850s primarily involved shifting competition among regional blocs. Legislators from both parties drifted back and forth, supporting some railroads and opposing others according to their changing perceptions of local and state interests. The prime example of such contests was south Georgia's triumph over the bulk of northern counties that opposed state aid for the Atlantic & Gulf trunk line. Governors Howell Cobb, Herschel Johnson, and Joseph Brown, all Democrats, used W&A patronage to procure political influence, and the American-Opposition party campaigned desultorily and ineffectually on corruption issues. In a reversal of the old Whig position, American gubernatorial candidates in 1855 and 1857 advocated selling the Western & Atlantic to private interests to remove it from political control. Many Democrats, conversely, reversed their earlier criticism of the W&A as the railroad began to reap huge profits. Income from the Western & Atlantic, which exceeded $400,000 a year in 1859 and 1860, even allowed the state belatedly to establish a system of common school education. In sum, with railroads as with taxation, fiscal exigencies, political circumstances, and clashes between competing interests—rather than between contrasting party ideologies—determined state policy.[45]

Political parties, in theory, were "representatives of the popular will" that, after engaging in a "free and honest interchange of information" and arriving "at the knowledge of what that will is," gave "that will shape and form and substantial efficacy." Experience, however, belied facile assumptions regarding a single popular will, and public opinion on matters such as who should occupy the Georgia governorship was more created than discovered. Instead of merely reflecting the popular will, the parties mediated between competing wills, narrowed options, and concentrated support behind certain choices. Newspaperman Cornelius R. Hanleiter came close to describing the reality when he spoke of conventions as "the proper way of ascertaining the popular will—or I might say, of giving direction to the popular will." More pointedly yet, Charles J. Jenkins worried in 1847 that few of the "leading men" would attend the Whig state convention, and that without their "controlling influence" the nattering of "second & third rate politicians" would prove disruptive. Within party organizations, some interpreters exerted more power than others, and the goal of controlling merged with the ideal of ascertaining the popular will.[46]

Parties as institutions rested on popular consent, even though the operations of party machinery sharply limited popular choice. As voluntary organizations, their existence depended on attracting allegiance. They were not recognized or regulated by law in any meaningful way, and the parties themselves determined nearly all the important matters that affected them, including the timing, composition, and legitimacy of conventions. Custom thus defined party practices and party regularity. Party organization arose and persisted because coordination, concentration, and coercion of opinion produced what leaders and voters wanted: victories. After conventions had done their work, party voters typically supported the nominee; the parties could not have survived otherwise. Control over party machinery gave politicians enormous, but not unlimited, power. Public feelings counted and unconditional loyalty could not be assumed. Misconduct and manipulation could bring discord and defeat, and the need for popular ratification of party decisions continually checked leadership prerogatives.[47]

Party organization worked upward from the precinct and county levels.

Local leadership was, in a sense, self-selected: any man so inclined could participate in party affairs. Of course, citizens with greater means, leisure, and education predominated. Inner circles of county partisans seldom numbered more than a few dozen men, if that many, and only a handful of these were truly influential politicians. County meetings typically were small gatherings that often served to ratify decisions made beforehand. Party gatherings were open to the public, and surprises sometimes occurred, but the intensity of party competition encouraged circumspection, private negotiation, and public displays of harmony. The rule, as Savannah Democrat Richard Arnold stated it, was to "fight in committee & behind the curtain. If the jackasses prevail against you yield, but stick to your party." [48]

County party operations were usually so routine that only significant flare-ups attracted attention. One such row erupted at the 1840 State Rights party convention in Taliaferro County. Alexander Stephens and Simpson Fouche, who had feuded for years, found themselves at odds in the debate over whether their party should support William Henry Harrison. Fouche and his allies, in not uncommon fashion, called a party meeting on short notice with little publicity in the hope of sending a county delegation to the state convention to oppose Harrison. Alexander Stephens caught wind of the coup, confronted some two dozen Fouche men assembled for the convention, and denounced "them from A to Izzard." To no avail, however; the Fouche majority smoothly proceeded to elect their slate of delegates. Another case, also reported by Alexander Stephens, involved "violent opposition" among Greene County Whigs to the candidacy of Thomas Stocks, who was seeking an eighteenth term as state senator. Stocks's extraordinarily long tenure and his staunch opposition to Texas annexation had aroused resentment, and another Whig candidate, James B. Nickelson, entered the race. Democrats, who were vastly outnumbered in the district, opportunistically supported Nickelson and helped disgruntled Whigs humble Thomas Stocks, whose decades of service proved no insurance against sudden popular disfavor. [49]

Records of the congressional district nominating conventions, an innovation adopted in 1844, provide a convenient sampling of convention scenarios. Elite figures, selected through preliminary county conventions, generally attended these district gatherings. Even with hosts of contentious, ambitious politicians present, however, the proceedings of most 1844 meetings were formalities. Fourth district Whigs chose John J. Floyd without dissent; those in the fifth district unanimously nominated Dr. H. V. M. Miller. Democrats unanimously chose Absalom Janes to oppose Alexander Stephens in the seventh district, while third district Democratic delegates all favored renegade former Whig congressman Absalom H. Chappell. Just 133 delegates, who collectively spoke for forty counties, attended the four conventions. Even smaller conventions were common, especially in uncompetitive districts. At the 1846 Democratic convention in the eighth district, all nine delegates gave Robert W. Flournoy their best wishes in his improbable bid to unseat Robert Toombs.[50]

Producing such harmony required backstage maneuvering. Incumbents, particularly, liked to take the field early and thereby quell opposition. Congressman Thomas Butler King repeatedly used the power of his incumbency to thwart fellow Whig James L. Seward of Thomas County. The huge first district, which King represented through most of the 1840s, covered eighteen counties chiefly in the pine barrens–wiregrass and coastal regions. A few active politicians wielded enormous influence in the sparsely settled district, and whispering campaigns among local leaders constituted Seward's main campaign tactic. In both 1846 and 1848, Seward worked to foster resentment against King and against coastal monopolization of the congressional seat (King was a sea island planter). King's intense lobbying of potential district delegates countered Seward's accusations, and King captured both nominations with minimal discussion at the actual conventions. Few facts about the ongoing rivalry between King and Seward ever received public notice.[51]

Incumbents sometimes contrived, as Howell Cobb did in 1846, to escape conventions by engineering "spontaneous" nominations. Cobb had *Southern Banner* editor Albon Chase avoid mentioning the congressional nomination altogether, so as not to excite expectations of a contest. Numerous private letters from Cobb's friends to party stalwarts, proclaiming him as the obvious choice, helped dissuade General William B. Wofford, a venerable Habersham County Democrat, from offering a challenge. Around mid-June, when all was in readiness, editor Milledge H. Gathright of the *Dahlonega Watchman* began publicizing Cobb's candidacy. Gathright, instead of Albon Chase, took the initiative for fear that the "hue & cry of 'Athens cliques' & 'Athens dictation' would be raised" if the *Southern Banner* endorsed Cobb first. Party newspapers hailed Cobb's smooth reelection as an unsolicited call to service emanating from a grateful public.[52]

Even when nominations were openly contested, the convention process tended to place power in a few hands. The thirty-seven delegates who assembled in Cassville in June 1844 met to anoint a congressman, since Democratic dominance in the fifth district, Cherokee Georgia, made nomination equivalent to election. Both John H. Lumpkin and William Henry Stiles, incumbents who had been elected two years earlier under the general ticket system, resided in the district and, problematically, desired second terms. The novel competition brought the cream of the Cherokee Democracy to the convention and split them evenly, forcing chairman Kinchen Rambo to cast the deciding ballot. Rambo's single vote sank Stiles and continued John Lumpkin's congressional career. Rambo may have been the kingmaker, but without Lumpkin's tremendous popularity in the Cherokee country the nomination would never have been made, and that same popularity ensured public acceptance of the narrow verdict.[53]

The public's distrust of conventions and party organization diminished over time but never died. The residual antiparty sentiment rested on images of conventions—or, pejoratively, "caucuses"—as cabals designed to impose undesirable candidates on the people, notions with enough semblance of truth to remain plausible. One party worker, for example, reported simply that a "great many" Democrats in his county were "death against nominations." In another case, Jackson County Democrats met at least three times in 1845 in an unsuccessful effort to settle on a slate of candidates for state representative. The Jackson County party had such "an utter horror of *caucuses*," editor Albon Chase observed disapprovingly, "and they are so fearful that any plan by which a *nomination* is made, will be stigmatised as a *caucus*, that they seldom dare attempt it." Resistance to conventions appeared most often in counties with huge partisan majorities, where no threat of defeat through division existed to encourage party regularity. Party editors frequently complained about "supernumerary candidates" in the most Democratic counties of north Georgia and inveighed against selfish aspirants "who have the vanity to imagine that they are somebody when their neighbors think they are nobody." When Alexander Stephens retired from the legislature in 1843 to run for Congress, at least four senate candidates and five house contenders—probably all Whigs—grasped the opportunity to run;

they could have divided the Whig vote equally and still have defeated any Democratic candidate.[54]

State conventions decided major questions and provided campaign cues for county partisans. Each party held one or two state conventions annually: winter conventions during the legislative session (usually in December), and larger, general conventions in June or July. Winter conventions were attended mainly by state legislators already in Milledgeville and thus included proportionally more representatives from the strongest party areas—north Georgia for the Democrats and the black belt for the Whigs. At least three quarters of the counties usually sent delegations, chosen at local meetings, to the summer state conventions. To illustrate the contrast, the December 1840 "Harrison and State Rights" convention included just fifty-eight county delegations and had only ten delegations from north Georgia; nearly four of every five delegates were Whig state legislators. The June 1843 Whig convention, however, was attended by seventy-six county delegations, nineteen of them representing north Georgia.[55]

The winter and summer conventions also performed different functions. Whig December conventions, with some exceptions during the 1830s, laid plans and nominated congressional candidates to run under the general ticket system. More significant steps, such as the nomination of William Henry Harrison in 1840 or of Henry Clay in 1842, Whigs reserved for June conventions. Democratic winter conventions sometimes nominated gubernatorial candidates—as in the 1837, 1839, and 1841 races—and also chose national convention delegates. Beginning in 1843, both Democrats and Whigs invariably made gubernatorial nominations at spring or summer conventions held during the election year. Summer conventions served as the major forums for party pronouncements on issues; Democrats, most noticeably, often reiterated their national convention platform in toto.[56]

While the Whigs reconciled themselves to state convention customs, the Democrats quarreled repeatedly over questions of structure and legitimacy. Basically, the practice of holding two quite different conventions institutionalized the rivalry between north Georgia and black belt Democrats. For practical reasons associated with traveling, north Georgians, who sent hosts of legislators to the capital, tended to control winter gatherings, while black belt forces bulked large at the summer conventions. North Georgians resented, at times bitterly, yielding power to a handful of Democrats from

Whig-dominated black belt counties, but black belt resistance stymied proposals for weighting convention representation toward Democratic strongholds. The unresolved disputes over the relative authority of the two conventions eventually exploded with disastrous effect in 1859–60. The voice of the Georgia Democracy, in short, changed with the seasons, and succeeding conventions could work at cross purposes, as when the December 1843 convention rescinded John C. Calhoun's June 1843 presidential nomination.[57]

The predominance of black belt planters among gubernatorial standard-bearers reflected the weight of the black belt in conventions and in politics generally. From the advent of the party system, just two Whig (to be precise, anti-Democratic) candidates—Duncan L. Clinch in 1847 and Warren Akin in 1859—hailed from outside the black belt, and most came from in or around old middle Georgia. Of Democratic nominees, only Joseph Brown qualified as a genuine representative of north Georgia, although Mark A. Cooper and Charles McDonald (in his 1851 race) maintained upcountry residences. Every other Democratic candidate except Matthew H. McAllister of Savannah lived in the black belt. Electability was, if possible, an even more pressing consideration in gubernatorial races than in other contests; the candidates came from where most of the voters were.

Nomination by conventions was a consensual process in which party elites proposed and the people disposed. Party leaders possessed the initiative in deciding most matters, but concern for party welfare encouraged cautious conservatism in selecting candidates and charting courses of action. The purpose of organization, after all, was to unite, not divide, the party.

Newspaper editors were spokesmen for the parties, and they controlled the means of mass communication among a scattered, rural people. Most newspapers were printed on one folded, oversized sheet of paper that had space for two pages of news items and two pages of advertising; some Savannah and Augusta papers were larger. Regular fare included original editorials, reprints of congressional speeches, proceedings of the legislature, notices of party meetings, letters from candidates or pseudonymous correspondents, and voluminous clippings from other newspapers. More occasional pieces focused on agriculture, railroad development, and commercial affairs. European, chiefly British, news and national items appeared more frequently as fast oceanic steamers and the telegraph improved communications in the late 1840s. Many papers were ephemeral, and even the major ones regularly changed hands and names. Both parties maintained papers in the major towns throughout the antebellum years, and these served as the leading party organs. The 1850 census listed twenty political newspapers in Georgia, mostly weeklies, with a total circulation of 20,900—altogether amounting to nearly 1.5 million copies of political newspapers printed annually.[58]

Newspapers reflected, in approximate order of importance, general party views, the opinions of editors and associated politicians, and the interests and prejudices of special constituencies. The *Athens Southern Banner*, first under the editorship of Albon Chase and later under Hopkins Holsey and others, usually spoke for Howell Cobb and for the bulk of the north Georgia Democratic yeomanry, who accepted the preservation of the national Democracy and the Union as paramount and inseparable goals. The *Milledgeville Federal Union* and the *Columbus Times*, in contrast, vented strong sectional feelings. Tomlinson Fort, Herschel V. Johnson, David C. Campbell, and other Calhounite sympathizers either owned or edited the *Federal Union* at various times, and they all feuded with Albon Chase over Calhoun's pretensions to Democratic leadership. The *Times,* particularly under the editorship of John Forsyth, Jr., was a radical southern and ambivalently Democratic sheet that provided a forum for Columbus hotspurs such as John H. Howard and Alfred Iverson. The most influential Georgia Democratic organ, the *Augusta Constitutionalist,* which James Gardner, Jr., controlled from 1842 on, shifted ground repeatedly on questions of southern rights and national party relations, but maintained a probanking, prodevelopment stance that served black belt and city commercial interests.

Among Whig sheets, the *Augusta Chronicle & Sentinel* adhered to the conservative national Whig line and came closest to echoing the Whig press elsewhere on issues such as the tariff and a national bank. Editors Miller Grieve and Richard H. Orme of the *Milledgeville Southern Recorder* charted a middle course on Texas annexation, the tariff, and most other questions in an effort to minimize discord. The *Savannah Republican*, more than most papers, carried news besides politics—particularly market, crop, and financial information related to business in the port city. The *Republican* opposed the Democratic party first, last, and always; it was flexible regarding means and issues.

One editor idealistically described members of the press as "sentinel[s] upon the watch-tower of liberty," whose duty was "*to instruct and warn the people*—to guard them against foes within and from assaults without." Warn they certainly did, if only about threats that originated beyond their party's walls. As honest men placed in positions that involved cynicism, hypocrisy, and prevarication, editors struggled with considerable success to convince themselves and others that serving party also meant serving truth and country. Editors did not report the news objectively, they adorned selected facts with extravagant rhetoric in arguing their party's case. The newspaper fraternity barred no holds, and editors readily admitted—after campaigns were over—that "greater latitude is claimed and exercised, as a matter of propriety, in printed newspaper articles, than any gentleman of sense and good manners would think of exercising in ordinary oral debate, or private and social conversation." The *Columbus Enquirer* observed in 1834 that "political lying" among the "Corps Editorial" had become "a matter of course—a part, and indeed the most material of their duties." Calumny was "the habit of the American press," the *Athens Southern Banner* remarked, and "newspaper abuse means nothing more than that the person attacked is on a different side in politics from the Editor: and newspaper laudations mean that he is on the same side." Editors were indeed like sentinels whose words were weapons wielded in a partisan cause.[59]

Newspapers shaped more than presented public opinion, although they did some of both. Most households did not subscribe to party newspapers, but the press was nonetheless influential. Men read the papers at post offices, shared them at taverns and courthouses, browsed through used copies at home, and received free campaign editions distributed by the parties. Milledgeville, let alone Washington, was mighty distant from most rural neighborhoods, and newspapers provided basic knowledge of the outside world. Alexander Stephens explained that "the *newspapers* in this country are the *senses* of the public. They have no other communications with men than by the *press* except in their own persons or individual correspondence." All the more important, then, that news filtered through a partisan screen portrayed a partisan world. Calculated repetition of editorial comment and political matter ensured that men who saw even a handful of issues a year knew the party line, and the near party monopoly on political information reinforced existing prejudices and solidified party attachments. A minor battle at the Summerville post office nicely illustrates the political value of controlling information. A Whig complained in 1844 that the Democratic postmaster had hoarded the mails throughout the campaign, so that "a paper of any importance could not be got out of this office untill [*sic*] some of their party read it—, and generally had the first news and was prepared to defeat us on all occasions." [60]

However much independence might be extolled in the abstract, editors could display it only sparingly. Any scribe who advanced beyond what voters and politicians would support risked losing precious patronage—editing was hardly a lucrative profession—and, ultimately, banishment. The Richmond (County) Hussars militia company once found the pronullification views expressed in Alfred H. Pemberton's *Augusta Chronicle* so offensive that they first stripped him of his lieutenancy and finally expelled him. When the editor of the *Athens Southern Whig* stepped out of line in 1845, Charles J. Jenkins pronounced him "a wrong-headed foolish man" who prided "himself in differing from others & conceives that by being impracticable he entitles himself to the reputation of being independent & manly." The *Columbus Enquirer*'s adamant opposition to William Henry Harrison inspired local Whigs to arrange a change of editorship, freeing the way for a Harrison endorsement—some of the original editors, presumably chastened, returned to manage the ensuing campaign. Excessive attachment to either independence or consistency, another rhetorically prized trait, shortened a lot of editorial careers. [61]

Editors provided services to the party besides printing regular issues. They also produced campaign editions, compilations of choice propaganda that politicians purchased in bulk. Single subscriptions good for several months cost from fifty cents to one dollar, with discounts for larger lots of ten, twenty, or a hundred. The issuance of campaign editions began around 1840 and soon became the universal practice. Francis S. Bartow, John Berrien's son-in-law, and Thomas Butler King, for example, purchased one thousand copies of the *Savannah Republican* in 1845 and mailed them to county committees for "effective distribution." Editors also printed election tickets—there were no official ballots—that served as the main voting instruments and promoted adherence to nominees. Voters could, however, write their own ballots or scratch a ticket—that is, cross out the names of undesirable candidates. Nominees or campaign committees paid for ballots at prices ranging from one to five dollars per thousand, and party workers handed out ballots at the polls. Distinctively marked or colored ballots, the most common kind by the 1840s, made enforcing party discipline easier.[62]

By lending their columns, editors allowed politicians to speak directly to the people, either through formal campaign letters or in the ubiquitous pseudonymous contributions. Writing under names such as "Piney Woods" or "An Old State Rights Man" shielded leaders from criticism if their opinions proved unpopular and permitted unrestrained attacks on enemies. Still, abuse of such letters created innumerable controversies. When Herschel V. Johnson, as "Baldwin," reviewed Alexander Stephens's supposedly mendacious statements on the Mexican War in 1846, Stephens managed to uncover Johnson's identity and demanded a public retraction. (Etiquette required editors to protect correspondents' anonymity unless an offended party perceived an affront to honor that might justify murdering the correspondent in a duel.) After Johnson refused to retract, Stephens challenged him to a duel, an invitation that Johnson spurned. An infuriated Stephens then published the correspondence relating to the affair, further embarrassing both men, who did not speak to each other for the next nine years.[63]

An unwillingness either to forgo billingsgate or to disregard honor sometimes made editing a surprisingly dangerous profession. *Georgia Telegraph* editor Philemon Tracy, fed up with L. W. F. Andrews of the *Georgia Citizen,* a "blackguard" who "made slander the business of his life," meted out savage vengeance when he encountered his reviler on the streets of Macon. Andrews used his cane to parry Tracy's initial blows, but Tracy soon wrested it away and proceeded to beat Andrews senseless. Tersely summarizing the affray with evident satisfaction, Tracy explained that he had "determined to flog him—to flog him publicly—to flog him severely—and I accordingly did flog him." The Macon city court fined Tracy ten dollars, a small price for revenge, and cleared his brother, Edward D. Tracy, and all others of complicity in the premeditated assault. Although Tracy regarded the incident as a purely personal affair, the bloody fight between two editors indicates how easily political conflicts could get out of hand.[64]

The violent language, and sometimes action, of politics reflected norms separate from the ordinary courtesies of society. Honorable men did not libel and abuse one another, except in politics. Conventions of politics demanded that editors' fervor exceed reasonable bounds and legitimated ad hominem

attacks and blatant misrepresentations that were impermissible in other con-
texts. What best served the parties did not always serve the truth, and an
editor's responsibility to the party was primary.

The ability to provide rewards for the faithful in the form of postmaster-
ships, public printing contracts, legislative clerkships, and other patronage
posts was essential to party organization. The number of positions available
never remotely approached the number of applicants who considered themselves deserving, and office seekers besieged state legislators and prominent
politicians, begging to receive patronage plums. Knowing the right people
vastly improved an applicant's prospects. One of the approximately five
hundred postmasters in the state in 1842, for example, was Aaron Grier of
Raytown, Taliaferro County. A fine man, and by all odds a competent postmaster, Grier also happened to be the kindly uncle who had raised Alexander Stephens. Unless a choice was this obvious, party brokers sifted information and tailored appointments to try to please as many people as
possible. Often, local committees canvassed claims and forwarded recom-
mendations, and patronage decisions affected the morale of county partisans. A Darien Whig complained to John Berrien in 1850 that the party had
"worked for the Last 20 years to Get a whig President . . . [and] Still a Loco
foco is allowed to Hold the Custom House"; "our friends is So Dis Heartened untill we Can Hardely Get the whigs to the Poles." Not only appointments but also removals could galvanize local parties. Democrat James F.
Cooper, the superintendent of the branch mint at Dahlonega, resolved in
1849 to retain his position until the ax inevitably fell. Since Cooper had
"faithfully performed" his duties, he and other Democratic leaders felt that
his "decapitation" would "furnish capital to be used in future campaigns
under the old cry of 'proscription for opinion.'"[65]

Indeed, patronage issues provided abundant campaign fodder. Both
Whigs and Democrats eloquently labeled their opponents unprincipled office seekers and promised reform every time election day drew near. Voters
undoubtedly gave some credence to such rhetoric; politicians gave none at
all. John Berrien, a man about as idealistic as a successful politician could be
and a prime mover in the "Harrison and Reform" campaign of 1840, busily
set about divvying up the spoils once Harrison triumphed. In a long letter
to his friend Ambrose Baber, Berrien explained that some Democratic incumbents would be suffered to remain in place briefly, simply "to authorize

the presumption that removals have not been made without consideration." Republican injunctions aside, offices not sought were never held, proper partisan affiliation was a prerequisite for appointive posts, and both parties expected a general housecleaning whenever power changed hands. Campaign pledges to the contrary were disingenuous, to say the least.[66]

A dispute over the Augusta post office exemplifies both the practical importance of patronage and the calculated use of rhetoric to conceal partisan motives. General Thomas Glascock, a former congressman and state legislator, and one of the most prominent Democrats in the Augusta area, contrived to keep his postmastership through John Tyler's years of quasi-Whig rule. The bargain that Glascock struck, which required that he employ Whig clerks, irritated some of his fellow Democrats, and they took the opportunity afforded by James Polk's election to inaugurate a crusade to have Glascock sacked. Pro- and anti-Glascock factions developed, and each side stated its case in a petition to the postmaster general. An extraordinary public meeting then passed resolutions demanding Glascock's ouster. John Phinizy, Jr., informed Howell Cobb that the anti-Glascock meeting had copies of its resolutions printed and "sent to most of the prominent Democratic members of Congress," to apprise the influential of the circumstances in this consequential case.[67]

The resolutions of the anti-Glascock clique proceeded from the democratic principle that the parties and the people had an indefeasible right to choose the officers who would implement their wishes—as if a postmastership was a policy-making position. The Whig letter sorters were "offensive to the democratic party, for their violent and proscriptive spirit" and were, moreover, greedy men "only bent on the spoils of office." Glascock's refusal to dismiss at least some of his Whig clerks and hire Democrats instead constituted "*a deliberate insult to the party.*" The aggrieved petitioners desired Glascock's removal and the appointment of "a successor who will respect party practice, and retain his office by the party's will."[68] In this case as in others, control of offices mattered greatly to the men involved, and verbiage about patronage reform and opposition corruption only thinly disguised personal and partisan motives.

Incoming governor George Gilmer assured listeners that his office had been "conferred, not assumed, nor sought for; that in the canvass I left the election to the free and unbiassed [*sic*] suffrages of the people." Gilmer's self-congratulatory remarks contained some truth when he uttered them in 1837, but the partisan descendants of Gilmer's generation made seeking office into a quasi science and paid, at most, rhetorical homage to older republican visions. Retiring Congressman Eugenius A. Nisbet conceded in 1841 that he had received his commission as much through his "own solicitation" as at the people's behest. He had craved the "honor of a seat in Congress from my native State"; his candidacy had arisen from "longings after personal distinction."[69]

Conducting campaigns was the most basic function of party organizations, and the many types of campaign activities generated a voluminous public record: newspaper editorials, convention proceedings, printed speeches, accounts of parades, and many other materials. Less well documented, but at least as important, were the mundane efforts of local partisans. By the 1840s, nearly every county convention appointed committees to rally voters, and, collectively, party committeemen probably contacted most of the voters in Georgia during campaigns. Alfred Iverson reported that Muscogee County Democrats, shocked by their dismal performance in the 1848 congressional elections, resolved to do better in the presidential contest. Although Muscogee had one of the state's largest voting populations, Democrats planned to "send our strongest men into every district and ride from house to house the week before the election and see every Democrat and arrange to bring out every one to the polls. We are also writing to our leading men in the other counties and sending out missionaries." At the same time, James F. Cooper informed Howell Cobb that Democrats had "succeeded in furnishing every point in Lumpkin and Union [Counties] with a full supply" of election tickets for Lewis Cass, "and we have the assurance that every Democratic voter will be seen by our committee men between now and the 7th November, and that all will be at the polls." Such face-to-face encounters, numerous as they were, inevitably left few lasting traces except in the minds of the individuals directly involved.[70]

Major politicians personally met and wooed thousands of voters. Once improvements in railroad transportation made wide-ranging campaigning feasible, leaders routinely spent weeks on speaking tours through distant counties. Alexander Stephens took countless trips, far and near; by the early 1850s, midway through his sixteen years in Congress, any voters in his district who had not yet glimpsed him must have been hiding from him. A personal touch could not work wonders, but it could certainly help. In urging Howell Cobb to attend the upcoming court session in Elbert County, Thomas W. Thomas related the instructive tale of Charles McDonald's 1841 visit to Elberton, the county seat. McDonald lodged with an eminent party member, and once "it was generally known that a live Governor was in town and that Governor the great inventor of Relief [loans from the Central Bank] crowds flocked to see him." McDonald "did the amiable as he well knows how, shook hands with everybody, took an interest in everybody's affairs[,] wife, children, crop, & [et]c.[,] said not a word about relief and after a day or two went quietly off." McDonald's total in the ensuing election was "at least 100 over the [Democratic] party vote at that time."[71]

McDonald eschewed speeches in this instance, but politicians and voters alike considered oratorical prowess to be telling evidence of greatness. Galleryites in Washington contentedly sat through days of Daniel Webster, and Georgians by the hundreds and thousands traveled to barbecues to listen to lesser lights. Successful use of oratory as a campaign tool was more a matter of style than of content. Politicians necessarily repeated themselves over and over again on the campaign trail, and banalities outnumbered profundities by a wide margin. Even the celebrated duo of Abraham Lincoln and Stephen Douglas said little or nothing new in their 1858 debates; the circumstances and the personages, rather than the words, created the drama. Unlike the coverage of the Lincoln-Douglas debates, common newspaper reports offered just brief summaries of remarks and focused on the speaker's appearance—his confident manner, his vigorous gestures, his booming voice. Signature phrases and stock anecdotes sounded fresh to new audiences and, if delivered with flair, convincingly demonstrated the orator's intelligence and wit. Speeches were for politicians what recitations were for schoolboys: tests of fitness that singled out some from their peers. Alexander Stephens, who was a marvel on the platform, well understood the significance of oratory in a political culture that tended to equate speaking with thinking and appearance with inner worth. On the occasion of his half-brother's maiden speech, Stephens advised him to make it a "rule of your life" to always "*appear well, and also to appear whenever you can with propriety.*"[72]

"One of the most amusing peculiarities of American politicians," Englishman James S. Buckingham observed, "is the extraordinary effects which they predict, or proclaim, of the delivery of remarkable speeches."

That politicians, whose careers depended on knowing the public, continued to wear out their vocal chords suggests that stump speaking at least rallied regular party voters and perhaps attracted some converts. Furthermore, the closeness of party competition, particularly in the 1830s and 1840s, meant that even if individual speeches swayed only handfuls of voters, the combined effects of hundreds of speeches could alter the outcome of a statewide election. Regardless of the precise impact of speechmaking, it unquestionably made politics more accessible to thousands of illiterate white men. The many voters who heard Robert Toombs in 1856, for example, received a briefing on the Democracy's interpretation of events in "bleeding Kansas," lessons on the horrors of Republican dogmas, and instructions to avoid casting a useless ballot for Millard Fillmore. Whether or not individual voters responded to such exhortations, white society as a whole clearly valued campaign oratory and learned something from it.[73]

Public speeches also provided precious entertainment and offered politicians a chance to display fellowship with voters. The several thousand persons who attended a two-day meeting in Athens in 1848, for example, ate voraciously, drank too freely, and listened to dozens of speeches. Howell Cobb himself delivered four addresses, only three of which were planned. Around two o'clock in the morning on the second day, Cobb was "aroused from my slumbers by the enthusiastic shouts of the democracy and was compelled to rise from my bed and give them a speech in my shirt tail." Voters intoxicated more with liquor than with politics probably recalled little about Cobb's oration, except that a wealthy planter-politician had complied with their summons and had joined in their fun. Cobb hoped, of course, that voters would cherish the image of a shirt-tailed fellow—just one of the boys—thundering words in the night.[74]

Aside from appearances on the stump, politicians, particularly those in Congress, conducted an enormous correspondence with their constituents. Alexander Stephens, who dispatched roughly two dozen letters a day, complained that he frequently wrote until his fingers ached. Congressmen also franked thousands of party documents during campaigns. Thomas Butler King sent "off Clay Almanac's by the dozen" in 1844, and Alexander Stephens routinely spent hundreds of dollars to print copies of his speeches. Robert Toombs, John Berrien, and most other prominent politicians maintained extensive mailing lists. Howell Cobb, the probable champion in this regard, had lists totaling thousands of names; most voters in his district received documents from him at one time or another. Whether it was the message that mattered or simply the favor itself, leaders believed that distributing literature influenced voters. Democratic editor Milledge H. Gathright of Dahlonega, one of the many adjutants who furnished addresses to Howell Cobb, urged Cobb to "deal out your documents with an unsparing hand." Receiving a document would "flatter the vanity" of a voter and "secure his personal friendship, and ten to one, if he ever has it in his power, he will repay it at the ballot box." The underlying proposition, that voters responded to personal gestures, seems indubitable.[75]

Documents, barbecues, election tickets, and the like cost money; wealthy politicians and party members footed the bills. When Hopkins Holsey's sniping at Howell Cobb became intolerable in 1853, Cobb arranged to buy Holsey's interest in the *Southern Banner.* Cobb's brother-in-law John B. Lamar supplied $1,500 of the $2,000 down payment, and Cobb, his brother Thomas R. R. Cobb, and their cousin James Jackson all contributed additional funds. Dr. Richard Arnold liberally subsidized the *Savannah Georgian,* the city's major Democratic newspaper, and he contributed around $2,000 to the party during the 1856 presidential campaign alone. The complaints of George W. Lamar, an Augusta representative of that farflung planter family, demonstrated that the parties depended on the largesse of select donors. Richmond County Democrats, Lamar lamented, had so "lost confidence" due to their minority position that they were "unwilling to aid even in exertions" during campaigns, and as "for *contribution,* they are entirely opposed." To help keep the party afloat, Lamar had donated several hundred dollars in both the 1844 and 1848 presidential elections, as well as giving smaller amounts to support county candidates. Although having the money to mount a decent campaign was important, the sums expended were comparatively minuscule; the economic and social power that leaders of landed wealth possessed influenced the political process far more than the dollars that went directly into campaign coffers.[76]

Electoral corruption, as understood by later generations, scarcely existed in antebellum Georgia. Parties sometimes bought votes on a small scale in Savannah, the city with the worst reputation. Francis S. Bartow, a Savannah Whig lawyer, told Howell Cobb in 1841 that the "floating vote of this county is exceedingly large, and its politics miserably corrupt. . . . Your friends the

Democrats are very active and are using money like water." Savannah even-tually employed rudimentary registration laws to curb such practices, but in nearly every other county white men voted without question. Authorities so seldom enforced eligibility laws—chiefly the requirement that taxes be paid—that prosecutions for illegal voting caused wonderment. Even if the parties had wanted to, they could not have tampered with elections in rural precincts: men knew one another, and partisans on both sides kept vigilant watch. Only in treating "floaters," men willing to trade votes for drinks, did the parties regularly verge on corrupting the franchise. Thomas W. Tho-mas, for example, half seriously resolved in 1857 to establish a Democratic tavern in Elbert County and to have it "well stocked before the next elec-tion," as the Whigs had "always controlled the two groceries in this county and through that means caught *every* floater." [77]

Antebellum election chicanery seems almost childish compared with the ballot-box stuffing and bribery so prevalent in the Gilded Age. In the Octo-ber 1840 election, some State Rights tricksters located a man of mixed race with very light skin and hurried him up to General Thomas Glascock, who "was much engaged [in] giving out tickets to the voters." Though Glascock denied giving a ballot to anyone "he supposed was a negro," two State Rights men rode through the streets crying that Glascock "was trying to get negroes votes taken, so the general was defeated." The parties sometimes fell victim to the temptations offered by printed ballots. During the 1856 Macon city election, Democrats discovered an opposition plot and replaced their previously printed tickets with new ones printed on yellow envelope paper. Despite their precautions, however, "bogus *Democratic* tickets came swarming forth like locusts." [78]

The following year, Oliver J. Porter, the Bibb County jailer, released three men from custody to cast American party ballots. When Democrats ob-jected, Porter explained that the men had been incarcerated only for failure to pay court costs, not for crimes, and that he had declined to let several other civic-minded criminals vote. Porter had, moreover, prudently sought legal advice from Thomas P. Stubbs, the American candidate for state sena-tor, who had assured him that prisoner voting was legal. Porter's actions might have been overlooked had not Stubbs defeated his Democratic rival, Nathan Bass, by exactly three votes. As it was, a week of wrangling between numerous ad hoc party committees failed to resolve the controversy. Finally, Nathan Bass, weary of the whole matter, called an end to Democratic protests and let Thomas Stubbs, the prisoners' favorite, take a seat in Milledgeville.[79]

A party system with roots deep in the past took definite form in the early 1830s and dominated the state's political life for nearly two decades. The crisis of 1850, however, disrupted the stability of the party system and raised the Democracy to supremacy. The era of closest party competition ended, but powerful partisan feelings endured.

# SIX

## Slavery and the Union, 1849–1853

The struggle over slavery in the territories resumed with even greater fe-
rocity following Zachary Taylor's election. When the storm that had been
building since 1846 finally broke in 1850, it tore Georgia Whigs and Democrats from their national party moorings and forever altered the state's party
system.

The short session of Congress that began in December 1848 witnessed an
effort to create John C. Calhoun's desideratum, a united South. Alarmed by
northern antislavery activities in the House, a bipartisan group of Southerners assembled on the evening of 22 December to consider issuing a southern manifesto. Whigs, who still had faith that Zachary Taylor would save
the South, initially cooperated in the movement only, as Robert Toombs
said, to "control and crush it." When a 22 January meeting finally adopted
Calhoun's fiery Southern Address urging sectional unity, only two southern
Whigs signed what had become a southern Democratic document.[1]

After foiling Calhoun's "miserable attempt to form a Southern party,"
southern Whigs endeavored to clear Taylor's path by constructing a gigantic
state of California. Reasoning that California would never be a slave state
and that there was "only the point of honor [avoiding the Wilmot Proviso]
to save," Robert Toombs, William B. Preston of Virginia, and other southern Whigs favored bypassing quarrels over slavery by admitting California
immediately and thus organizing nearly all of the unorganized territory acquired from Mexico. The California statehood solution, Toombs thought,
would lighten Taylor's burdens and "rescue the country from all danger
from agitation." Northern House members, however, promptly tacked an

156

amendment prohibiting slavery onto Preston's California statehood bill, ending the prospects of an early territorial settlement.[2]

While Whigs maneuvered, large numbers of Democrats in Georgia and across the South prepared to scuttle the Jacksonian party system. "The hour is at hand," the *Columbus Times* exclaimed shortly after Taylor's election, "when Mr. Calhoun's long cherished idea of a *Southern party* will be realized, or the Southern States are the degraded satellites and vassals of the North." Outgoing senator Herschel V. Johnson, young radical Henry L. Benning, former Unionist governor Wilson Lumpkin, and a host of other Georgia Democrats seconded the conclusion that national parties were useless when "the whole North is becoming ultra anti-slavery and the whole South ultra pro-slavery." Only a powerful sectional party could present ultimatums to northern states, force a recognition of southern rights, and thwart the enemies of slavery.[3]

Among those resisting the tide rushing toward a southern party were Howell Cobb and John H. Lumpkin. They refused to sign the Southern Address and joined other mountain and upcountry Democrats who retained their faith in the national Democracy. Citing the Southern Address's failure to do justice to sound northern Democrats, Cobb alleged that spiteful Calhounites sought "the dissolution of the democratic party, whether the Union is preserved or not"; John Lumpkin, too, prayed for deliverance from "Calhoun, Calhoun men, and Calhounism."[4]

Even as animosity mounted amount Democrats, Georgia politicians still awaiting decisive signals displayed a dull disinterest in the 1849 campaign. Howell Cobb, Herschel Johnson, and their respective supporters conspired to conceal party divisions at the July Democratic state convention. While adopting resolutions that breathed fire against the Wilmot Proviso, Democrats forbore mentioning the Southern Address, and Hopkins Holsey was dissuaded from offering a resolution of confidence in the northern Democracy. The unanimous nomination of the incumbent governor, George W. B. Towns, who privately promised a cessation of the Southern Address controversy, prevented squabbling over candidates.

Whigs, whose fortunes hinged on what course Zachary Taylor would chart, had little to discuss at their convention. They simply condemned the Wilmot Proviso and expressed confidence in the president. Judge Edward

Y. Hill of Troup County, a second-echelon party figure, claimed the honor of running as Old Rough-and-Ready's surrogate. Many observers commented that they had seldom, if ever, seen a contest so devoid of excitement, and Towns won reelection by almost double his 1847 majority.[5]

Events outside Georgia set the stage for the crisis. Democrats trumpeting sectional rhetoric swept the southern fall elections, and an October 1849 Mississippi convention issued a bipartisan call for southern states to attend a June 1850 meeting in Nashville—the formation of a southern party was the implicit goal. Zachary Taylor, meanwhile, horrified southern Whig politicians by taking his 1848 campaign pledges seriously. Surrounding himself with a nondescript cabinet and antislavery advisers such as New Yorker William H. Seward, Taylor sought to replace the old Whig party and build a personal, bipartisan coalition. He distributed patronage rewards to potential supporters, Free-Soilers and southern Democrats alike, and slighted Whig regulars. Most important, Taylor's decision to promote immediate statehood for California and New Mexico—a plan that would almost certainly make both free soil—devastated southern Whigs; the southern Democratic onslaught drove them to repudiate a proposal they had endorsed only months ago.[6]

On returning to Congress in December 1849, Alexander Stephens discovered that northern Whigs intended "to carry abolition everywhere by the Constitution they can." "With such a party I can not act," Stephens resolved. Devising a test for northern whigs, Stephens and Robert Toombs introduced a resolution at a 1 December Whig caucus that declared the party's opposition to congressional prohibition of slavery in California and New Mexico and to the abolition of slavery in the District of Columbia. When the caucus tabled the resolution, Toombs, Stephens, and Allen F. Owen of Georgia, along with three other southern Whigs, walked out, signaling the approaching end of Georgians' connection with national Whiggery.[7]

As balloting dragged on for weeks in a House of Representatives split between Whigs, southern Whig bolters, Democrats, and Free-Soilers, tempers grew short and sectional tensions crackled. In a memorable philippic delivered on 13 December, Robert Toombs thundered that if Wilmot Provisoists were determined "to fix a national degradation upon half the States of this Confederacy, then "*I am for disunion.*" Howell Cobb's election as Speaker, achieved under a plurality rule on 21 December, finally allowed

Zachary Taylor to send messages to Congress recommending immediate statehood for California and New Mexico. Taylor's policy perhaps had merit as an unambiguous solution for the territorial issue, but it left festering problems over fugitive slave laws and slavery in the District of Columbia unresolved. Most disturbing, it offered Southerners only stark alternatives: resist or accept the rapid exclusion of slavery from the Mexican cession.[8]

Democrats considered the statehood scheme "nothing more or less than the *Wilmot proviso* in disguise." Although they argued plausibly that California, with its extensive boundaries and mixed, transient population, needed extended territorial pupilage before it would be fit for statehood, Democrats' true objections went much deeper. Even if California were initially admitted as a single free state, Herschel Johnson feared that a dozen other states might eventually be carved out of Oregon and California territory. These new states would destroy the sectional equilibrium in the Senate and furnish the North with "the requisite majority in Congress to change the Constitution to suit their purposes." So long as the North insisted on forbidding the extension of slavery, James Gardner contended, "the South should insist that no more Free Soil States shall be admitted into the Union." At a minimum, the minority South had to prevent California's admission, defeat the Wilmot Proviso, and open the Mexican cession to slavery. Perhaps, as many Democrats believed, slavery would never gain a foothold in the Southwest, but northern willingness to give slavery a chance would be a vital gesture toward restoring southern confidence in the future of slavery in the Union.[9]

Georgia Whigs would be practically powerless and badly embarrassed if they abandoned Taylor, their last link to national Whiggery, but electoral survival and southern safety might necessitate sacrificing the president. Some Whigs advised following Taylor and acquiescing in the inevitable. The *Columbus Enquirer* stated flatly that there was no hope of ever establishing slavery in California. Others considered California worth fighting for on principle and incongruously criticized the statehood plan while professing allegiance to Taylor. Still others, among them Senator John Berrien, lost confidence in the president and determined to oppose California's admission regardless of Taylor's wishes.[10]

The faltering Whigs risked falling behind on the march to higher southern ground. George Towns opened the November session of the legislature by observing that a "fell spirit of blind and infuriated fanaticism" on the subject of slavery had seized "a controlling majority of the voters in most, if not all, the non-slaveholding States." In late January 1850, the legislature took up resolutions that recommended calling a state convention to determine the "mode and measure of redress"—meaning anything up to and including disunion—if Congress passed the proviso, abolished slavery in the District of Columbia, or admitted California immediately as a free state, or if northern states persisted in obstructing the recovery of fugitive slaves.[11] Frantic attempts by Charles Jenkins and Andrew Miller to moderate the resolutions and deflect criticism of Taylor failed; most Whigs and almost all Democrats were unwilling to tolerate the outright admission of California. The legislature authorized Towns to call a state convention on certain contingencies, including the admission of California or New Mexico as states; appointed Charles McDonald, Matthew H. McAllister, William Law, and Charles Dougherty as at-large representatives to the Nashville convention; and provided for elections on the first Tuesday in April to select two Nashville delegates from each congressional district.[12]

In the fluid party situation of early February 1850, state leaders stood ready to meet other angry Southerners in Nashville to concert resistance to anticipated wrongs. The prospective admission of California outraged north Georgia and black belt Democrats alike; Howell Cobb's sanguine hymns to the national Democracy swayed fewer and fewer party leaders. Robert Toombs, Alexander Stephens, and John Berrien all distrusted Taylor, and a large number of Whig legislators had helped Democrats define the president's policy as treason against the South. Whigs in Milledgeville talked approvingly of Toombs's and Stephens's caucus bolt and of dissolving ties to the national Whig party.[13]

At this critical juncture, Henry Clay offered to guide the country and Georgia Whigs in finding an avenue of escape. On 29 January, he presented proposals to ease sectional friction in three areas: (1) Congress should admit California as a state and organize New Mexico and Utah as territories without restrictions on slavery; (2) Congress should adjust Texas's boundary and pay an unspecified portion of its public debt; and (3) Congress should end the slave trade in the District of Columbia, but proclaim the abolition of slavery there inexpedient, and pass a more effective fugitive slave law. Debate over Clay's compromise package would consume months, but the emergence of an alternative to Taylor's bald-faced policy almost immediately re-shaped the political landscape.

State politicians either cautiously welcomed or coldly scorned Clay's initiatives. Despite reservations, Robert Toombs and Alexander Stephens expected that Congress could fashion some compromise resembling Clay's and including the admission of California. John Berrien, on the other hand, criticized Clay's proposals and drifted toward the anticompromise camp. The Whig press wishfully suggested that Taylor throw his weight behind compromise. Among Democrats, Howell Cobb aided the procompromise forces in Congress, but Southern Address men remained committed to re-sisting California's admission. James Gardner complained that the "mis-called Compromise resolutions of Mr. Clay, are no compromise at all. They are a palpable naked concession—a total surrender of every thing claimed by the South, and disputed by the North in this controversy." [14]

Most voters did not share Gardner's contempt for Clay's compromise. Leaders typically moved faster than the rank and file, and the southern rights vanguard in 1850 had dangerously outdistanced its supporting col-umns. Four years of sectional discord was more than enough for most Geor-gians, and if Clay's measures preserved the essence of southern rights in the territories, Georgians were not disposed to quibble over California. "We are all sick of the discussion in Congress about California," Athens resident Howell C. Flournoy observed. "We are worn out with it, it has become very stale." "The Slavery question continues to excite the thinking and reading men but the masses are not thinking or talking about it," William Hope Hull wrote to Howell Cobb. All things being equal, Georgians would have pre-ferred to open California to slavery, but other values competed with notions of abstract rights. Skeptical about the chances for transplanting slavery any-way, voters found it difficult to believe that the creation of a free state on the Pacific coast threatened their firesides or justified loose, radical talk. A Dah-lonega man asserted that "a large majority of the people of this section [the mountains] are in favor of the Compromise & opposed to everything like a dissolution of the union" over the admission of California. [15]

The odor of disunion stifled the Nashville convention movement. Nearly all Whig leaders, doubting the motives of the Democrats behind the Nash-ville project, distanced themselves from the convention once Clay had introduced his compromise. Cobbite Democrats such as Hopkins Holsey branded the convention a "revolutionary movement to all intents and purposes." "*It involves the fate of the Union*—and, in our deliberate opinion, will *dissolve* it," Holsey predicted. The widespread public belief that Calhounite conventioneers aimed to foment disunionism prompted much of the Democratic press to defend the convention as a movement designed to "preserve, not to dissolve, the Union" by announcing the South's "inflexible determination" to resist aggression. Although very few convention proponents in Georgia favored disunion, their disclaimers were equivocal and unconvincing. James Gardner declared his devotion to the Union in one breath, and then insisted that Nashville convention delegates should "go with full powers to speak and act for the State of Georgia." "The people of Georgia, and of the South, do not shrink back aghast from disunion," Gardner ominously announced. The *Columbus Times,* not content with warning that "Southern cowardice" was "the deadliest enemy the Union can have," added that if bravery brought "disunion, so be it." [16]

The farcical April elections for the Nashville convention reflected the popular mood. Nominating meetings attracted few delegates, candidates ran unopposed, some actually favored canceling the convention, and most of those chosen to attend never went to Nashville. Slightly more than thirty-seven hundred votes were cast in the fifty-four counties that bothered to open the polls on election day. James Gardner remarked that the pitiful turnout represented "a virtual repudiation by the people of Georgia, of the proposed Southern Convention." The final Nashville delegation of eleven men included five appointed by Governor Towns, who was authorized to fill vacancies. The three Whigs in the group were marginal figures, but Charles McDonald and Walter Colquitt headed the Democratic delegates. [17]

On 8 May, the Senate Committee of Thirteen reported a compromise plan based on Clay's original proposals. The Nashville convention met roughly a month later, repudiated the Senate package, and formulated its own "compromise," which sounded more like an ultimatum. Delegates from nine southern states demanded the extension of the Missouri Compromise line to the Pacific Ocean with an explicit recognition of the right to hold slaves south of that line.

The Nashville platform marked a reversal of field and seemingly superseded previous demands for equal access to all territories. Georgia Democratic legislators had overwhelmingly rejected Missouri Compromise language in January, and much of the Democratic press had pronounced a geographical division of territory undesirable for the South and unobtainable due to northern opposition. Officially recognizing slavery's existence south of 36°30′ required congressional legislation, and while many southern politicians maintained Congress's power to protect but not to prohibit slavery, the call for explicit protection violated the 1848 Democratic platform of congressional nonintervention. Consistency yielded to events as Nashville conventionists strained to counter congressional initiatives.[18]

Critics charged that the attempted resurrection of the moribund Missouri Compromise line proved that agitators wanted secession, not a settlement, and would oppose "any arrangement that Congress will in any human probability adopt." Northerners were mostly unwilling to divide California to extend the 36°30′ line; they would not even consider explicitly sanctioning territorial slavery. Southerner's insistence on the "totally *impracticable*" planks of the Nashville platform, Hopkins Holsey warned, would "DISMEMBER THE UNION." Howell Cobb, John Lumpkin, and many other north Georgia Democrats were convinced that Nashville convention enthusiasts were set on using the Democratic party as a secession vehicle.[19]

Prophecies of an apocalypse if the Nashville demands were not met gave credence to charges of disunionism. Nashville delegate Walter Colquitt told Georgians that the admission of a free California was a prelude to "THE ENTIRE AND FULL ABOLITION OF SLAVERY." Once enough free states had entered the Union, "A Southern Clergyman" predicted, the northern majority would emancipate slaves and make voters of them, in numbers large enough to "elect their own race, and take the whole government of the South into their hands." True compromise meant adjustment, pacification, and safety; the Senate measures instead increased "the strength of the enemy" and acted "as a stimulus to renewed and more determined aggression." The *Columbus Times* asked, "Have the people of the South fallen so low already, that we are driven to the alternative of taking the best terms our masters choose to give us? Are we *already* enslaved?"[20]

Accepting the imperfect, face-saving Senate measures, compromise proponents argued, would forestall a disunion crisis and slay the Wilmot Proviso. California would be free soil in any event, and Georgians could abide the abolition of the slave trade in the District of Columbia. In return, the

Senate proposals opened the rest of the Southwest to slavery and promised a more effective fugitive slave law. Georgia Whigs, in an abrupt volte-face, began touting the doctrine of nonintervention, claiming that congressional noninterference would satisfy the South even though it provided less than the positive protection that was due to slavery in the territories. Procompromise Democrats such as Howell Cobb, of course, also advocated nonintervention as an equitable territorial solution. Like many others, Alexander Stephens supported the Senate package not "as a *compromise,* but simply as a measure to quiet the country." Southerners would gain nothing beyond the bare minimum, but at least "the *proviso* is not in it." [21]

Zachary Taylor's death from acute gastroenteritis on 9 July removed a major obstacle to compromise, and the new president, Millard Fillmore, quickly backed the Senate proposals. Complicated congressional maneuvering made the Compromise of 1850 law by the third week of September, but its success rested more on sectional antagonism than on sectional agreement. Northern majorities opposed a stronger fugitive slave law and the organization of New Mexico and Utah territories without the Wilmot Proviso; southern majorities opposed the admission of California and the abolition of the slave trade in the District of Columbia. Only the cooperation of southern Whigs and a portion of the northern Democracy as a procompromise bloc and the abstentions of some congressmen, chiefly Northerners, on crucial votes allowed the compromise to pass.

The congressional battle scrambled party lines in the Georgia delegation and overturned past positions. Howell Cobb, Robert Toombs, and Alexander Stephens worked together as key procompromise leaders. Stephens and Toombs practically—if not theoretically—abandoned complaints that preexisting Mexican laws barred slavery from the Southwest, sanctioned a Texas–New Mexico bill that forbade New Mexico's territorial legislature to pass laws on slavery, and promoted popular sovereignty. Democratic representatives, on balance, opposed the compromise, although Marshall J. Wellborn voted for the Texas–New Mexico bill. Whig Senator William C. Dawson was a compromise proponent, while John Berrien vacillated so long that he separated himself from both sides. Unable to sanction the compromise because of California, yet unwilling to join the Nashville forces, Berrien occupied a political no-man's-land and watched his influence wane. [22]

Divisions over the compromise shattered the belief that the respective national parties could and would protect slavery and southern rights in the Union. Georgia Whigs cursed their northern counterparts for opposing the compromise; Nashville convention Democrats condemned northern party members for supporting it. Since neither national party offered a haven for its regular Georgia supporters, the traditional hostility between Whigs and Democrats temporarily abated, and party lines abruptly collapsed.

The "future struggle in Georgia," the *Augusta Constitutionalist* predicted in August, would be between the "Clay compromise party" and partisans of the Nashville convention. Former Whig and Democratic enemies forged new alliances at scores of bipartisan summer meetings. Whigs Washington Poe and Samuel T. Chapman joined Democrats John B. Lamar and James A. Nisbet in a Macon meeting that denounced Nashville extremism. Van Leonard and Alfred Iverson, old rivals for the favors of Columbus voters, presided together at a barbecue celebrating the Nashville convention. After years of relying on established party organization, political leaders had to rebuild from the ground up, and Georgia voters had to weigh anew the issues of protecting slavery, the South, and the Union. Governor Towns's call for a state convention, duly issued on California's admission, made the campaign to elect delegates the first battleground for the inchoate crisis parties.[23]

A few of the Nashville conventionists, Southern Address Democrats, and dissatisfied Whigs who collectively called themselves Southern Rights men advocated disunion. "THE GEORGIA CONVENTION. — SECESSION THE REM-EDY," screamed an editorial heading in the *Columbus Times*. The *Columbus Sentinel* saw secession as the only "mode of redress" for the admission of California. The *Macon Georgia Telegraph* asked, "If the territory—the land and property of the South, can be taken by a vote of the majority, why not her slaves?" "For our own part," the editor continued, "we are for secession, for resistance, open, unqualified resistance." A meeting in St. Mary's in coastal Camden County pleaded for action before northern fanatics surrounded the South "with a cordon of free States" and consummated plans for "abolishing the institution of slavery." The South had already yielded too much territory and compromised too often. The formation of a Southern Rights party was necessary "for self-preservation."[24]

Finding that secession was a dangerous—really suicidal—position to occupy, the small contingent of disunionists quickly fell back on mainstream

Southern Rights calls for resistance. Resistance was an attitude, a disposition to protest the compromise, and Southern Rights men deliberately declined to clarify its meaning. John Berrien, for one, broached fanciful plans to eliminate economic intercourse with the North, while others merely contemplated strong state convention resolutions denouncing Congress's action. None of the amorphous plans for resistance short of disunion promised to heal the deepest wound inflicted by the compromise: Georgia blustering would not undo California statehood.[25]

Resistance practically boiled down to the formation of a Southern Rights party. Southern Rights men renounced the party system that had ensnared them. "This cry of party, party, party has bamboozled the South long enough," the *Augusta Constitutionalist* proclaimed. The selfish politicians who had perpetuated the parties could no longer conceal the fact that southern Whigs and Democrats were "not very wide apart." Trifling party arguments meant nothing compared with the "one great issue" of "Resistance or Submission to Anti-slavery." Inveterate abolitionism among northern Whigs and Democrats made the pursuit of national party alliances "blind infatuation and folly." Those who acquiesced in the compromise and opposed a southern party were "submissionists," craven wretches cowering under the lash of northern masters. Submission equaled disunion, Southern Rights men contended; swallowing the compromise would foster aggression and ultimately compel secession to stave off abolition.[26]

The scattered Southern Rights appeals for secession played into the hands of procompromise forces who donned the Unionist mantle. Insisting that the Southern Rights party's disavowals of disunionism were "insincere and dishonest," and that Southern Rights men were only seeking the power to destroy the Republic, Unionists avoided fencing over the compromise measures and relied on patriotic emotions and the public's desire for sectional peace. Unionists reduced complex issues to a simple choice: "If you think this Government should be abandoned as a failure, vote the resistance ticket; if on the other hand you wish it to remain the admiration and praise of the whole earth, and to bless your children as it has blessed you—select a Union ticket."[27]

Submission versus resistance and Union versus disunion were misleading dichotomies quite characteristic of Georgia politics. Few white Georgians desired disunion in 1850; even fewer intended to submit to abolitionism.

But old ideas died harder than old parties, and Georgians retained the assumption that opponents were scoundrels whose triumph would be fatal to the South, the nation, or both. The language of party warfare and the prevailing partisan mindset all but denied the possibility of principled opposition.

The slight but significant difference between the conditional secessionism of Southern Rights men and the conditional Unionism of compromise defenders was enough to keep the new parties at each other's throats throughout the vitriolic convention campaign. Pessimistic Southern Rights men were willing, under protest, to live with a detested compromise they could not change, but they expected future antislavery aggression that would eventually necessitate secession. More optimistic Unionists hoped that the compromise represented a lasting settlement, yet they, too, acknowledged that slavery was endangered and that the compromise did not fully secure southern rights. If the North carried out the compromise measures—especially the fugitive slave law—in good faith and ended antislavery agitation, then Georgia would remain in the Union. But if the North breached the compromise contract, Unionists stressed, the likely result would be secession.

Amidst the furor, a consensus emerged by late October on what course the state convention should and would adopt. The Southern Rights party's failure to arouse voters, who instead responded in overwhelming numbers to the Unionist campaign, forced the abandonment of schemes for immediate resistance. Even John Forsyth, Jr., a Columbus editor who had earlier endorsed secession, seconded Robert Toombs's and Alexander Stephens's suggestions that the Georgia convention set down "the ground of disunion in the *future*" by specifying the conditions under which Georgia would consent to remain in the Union.[28]

The November election results demonstrated the conservative temper of most voters. Unionists elected 243 of the 264 convention delegates; the popular majority for the Union side was 46,963 to 25,253. Unionist candidates ran unopposed in thirteen scattered counties, and the Unionists' regional strength was remarkably uniform; their percentage of the vote ranged from 68.3 percent in the mountains to 62.8 percent along the coast. The low turnout, almost eighteen thousand voters fewer than in the 1849 gubernatorial election, reflected nonvoting by Unionists, who had little incentive to augment already lopsided county majorities, and by Southern Rights men deterred by their likely defeat.[29]

The main body of the Whig party and perhaps one-third of the north Georgia Democracy voted Unionist. Many overwhelmingly Whiggish eastern black belt counties returned huge Unionist majorities, as did most of the Democratic north Georgia counties. The Southern Rights party rested on a Democratic base. Normally Democratic counties in the central black belt formed the single concentrated area of Southern Rights strength, but the party also garnered more than 8,500 votes in north Georgia. Some of the most Democratic mountain counties, such as Union and Rabun, gave roughly one-third of their vote to Southern Rights candidates, and Murray and Campbell Counties elected Southern Rights delegates. The most obvious result of the election, aside from the Unionist landslide, was a schism in the Democratic party. The 1850 crisis separated Howell Cobb, John Lumpkin, and their national Democratic faithful from thousands of other north Georgia Democrats and, most important, from the black belt Southern Rights Democracy.[30]

The five-day state convention that began on 10 December issued the famous Georgia Platform. Nearly all of the preamble and the first three resolutions were drawn from a draft that Charles J. Jenkins prepared before arriving at Milledgeville. The preamble expressed relief that the issues arising from the acquisition of Mexican territory and from northern antislavery aggression had been settled in a "spirit of mutual concession." The compromise had substantially fulfilled the demands issued by the Georgia legislature in early 1850. The admission of California, "in its nature, unsusceptible of repeal," had not injured Georgia's honor or jeopardized its interests so grievously as to justify secession. The state would abide by the flawed compromise "as a permanent adjustment of this sectional controversy." The teeth were in the fourth resolution, framed collectively by the convention. Georgia would "resist, even (*as a last resort*) to a disruption of every tie which binds her to the Union," any act of Congress respecting slavery in the District of Columbia or other federal property inconsistent with the safety of the slave states, any congressional prohibition of the interstate slave trade, any congressional refusal to admit a state because it recognized slavery, any congressional exclusion of slavery from the territories of Utah or New Mexico, and any act repealing or essentially altering the fugitive slave law.

Just nineteen convention delegates opposed the Georgia Platform. Southern Rights dissenters, speaking through W. J. Lawton's alternative resolutions, bewailed the injustice of the compromise, particularly the failure to provide positive congressional protection for territorial slavery; dismissed the new fugitive slave law as a dead letter; and asserted the absolute right of state secession without danger from outside coercion. The dictum on secession, though stated as a general principle, invited concrete application. All understood that South Carolina was contemplating secession, and Lawton wanted to commit Georgia to aiding its neighbor. He further urged Georgians to disdain all connection with national parties as long as Whigs and Democrats violated southern rights. In sum, Lawton's resolutions anticipated future discord and disunion, while the Georgia Platform embodied hopes for enduring sectional peace.[31]

Southern Rights leaders defined the salient issues in 1850 with their appeals for southern unity, their plunge into the Nashville convention, and their talk of secession. National party schisms over the compromise and the perceived Nashville disunionist threat then prompted the formation of the Unionist coalition. Georgia voters, wrenched from their moorings by the sudden, unexpected demolition of the Jacksonian parties, reacted conservatively to the crisis and preferred compromise over extreme measures. Most remained unconvinced that the admission of California violated abstract southern rights, endangered slavery in the South, or thwarted an actual prospect for the expansion of slavery. Once again, as in the nullification era, impatient would-be defenders of the South ran headlong into the roadblock of emotional and practical attachments to the Union. The Georgia Platform struck a balance dear to voters by combining bold assertions of southern rights with devotion to the Union. The issue of southern rights in the Union was and would remain politically potent in Georgia; the issue of southern rights against the Union would not be politically viable for another decade.

The Georgia convention's decision dampened 1851 Southern Rights campaigns in Alabama and Mississippi, where parties reorganized along similar lines; both states returned large Unionist majorities. No large-scale realignments occurred elsewhere, leaving Georgia Unionists and Southern Rights men isolated. Protecting slavery, the Union, or anything else of importance required party allies, and Georgia's crisis parties were barely formed before pressures to rejoin the national party system started pulling them apart.[32]

At the first formal meetings of the Constitutional Union party, held during the state convention, Robert Toombs, Alexander Stephens, and other Union Whigs displayed interest in a national Union party and provided for Georgia representation at a proposed 22 February Union meeting in Washington. Former Whigs badly needed an overhauled party vehicle. The expanding Democratic vote in north Georgia and the erosion of the Whigs' black belt base had made them the state's minority party, and the antislavery proclivities of northern Whigs precluded a comfortable return to their old party fold. Nor were Whigs prepared to bury hostility toward the national Democracy, even if the Democrats were the strongest northern procompromise party. A reconstituted Whig party purged of free-soil elements, operating under the Union label and including enough Union Democratic leaven to give the party national and state power, would best suit Union Whigs.[33]

Having never, in their own minds, left the Democracy, Howell Cobb, John Lamar, and John Lumpkin paid lip service to notions of a national Union party while anticipating "that the union organization would ultimately act in concert with the national democratic party." Since a simple reconstruction of the state Democratic party would leave Union Democrats under the dominion of Southern Rights men, Union Democrats hoped to use their balance-of-power position—neither Southern Rights forces nor Union Whigs alone controlled an electoral majority—to maneuver the Union coalition into the Democratic ranks. To accomplish their goal, William Hope Hull observed, Union Democrats first had to preserve the Union coalition as an independent organization until the eve of the 1852 presidential election. Then, after gaining a commitment from the Union party "to cast their votes for the [presidential] candidate who is most satisfactory, which candidate would of course be Democratic," Howell Cobb and his allies would spring the trap, imprison Union Whigs within the national Democracy, and command an unconquerable host.[34]

Washington politicians obliged Georgia Union Democrats by smothering the national Union party movement; the proposed 22 February gathering never occurred. Congressional leaders long resisted making approval of the compromise an ironclad party test, but northern Democrats campaigning on the compromise in the fall 1850 elections trounced the Whigs in several northern states. Northern Whigs thereafter disingenuously fled toward procompromise ground themselves, rendering the formation of a national Union party irrelevant and impossible.[35]

The Southern Rights party mocked the Unionists' cause and derided their organizational efforts. Denouncing the Georgia Platform "as mere talk, talk, talk," Southern Rights men blamed their defeat on trumped-up charges of disunionism and portrayed the Union party as a "cunning Whig trap to catch gulls." Toombs, Stephens, Cobb, and other Union leaders had "been *forced* together not to save the Union, but to save *themselves.*" Unionism was just "a garb worn by treason in all sections of the country to cloak its selfishness and wickedness." The compromise did not represent a permanent settlement of the slavery question. The conflict between "the Hireling and Slave States" was "irreconcilable," and Southern Rights men intended to meet the issue "at the threshold when the South is strong" rather than to huddle together timidly in Unionist herds.[36]

Fond as they were of the southern party strategy, Southern Rights men recognized the gaping holes in their sectional front. The decision of most southern Democrats to oppose the compromise without resorting to Southern Rights parties consigned Georgians to political limbo. Some Georgia leaders considered cutting their losses and conceding defeat. As "unpalatable and humiliating as acquiescence may be," the *Federal Union* advised in May, continued rebellion against the Georgia Platform would be "madness, the height of folly." A party running on that issue could "not command a corporal's guard in a single county in the State."[37] The stubborn majority of Southern Rights men, however, laughed at the long odds and girded for another sally.

The Southern Rights state convention held on 28 May featured Calhounite Democrats such as James Gardner, Simpson Fouche, John H. Howard, and John Forsyth, Jr. Without mentioning the Georgia Platform, the delegates pledged devotion to the Union under the Constitution—as they understood it—and asserted the right to positive protection for slavery in the territories and the absolute right of state secession. The party nominated its best, the old Jacksonian Charles McDonald. Although McDonald's intimate connection with the Nashville convention made him an easy target for Unionists, he was personally as popular—even in north Georgia—as any Democrat in the state.[38]

The Constitutional Union convention pronounced the Union to be still in peril and promised to save it again. North Georgia Democrats William B. Wofford, Charles Murphey, Hopkins Holsey, and Junius Hillyer sat cheerfully alongside Robert Toombs and a host of other black belt Whigs as the convention reiterated the Georgia Platform and condemned treasonous Southern Rights agitation. To no one's surprise, the Unionists tapped Howell Cobb for governor in the belief that his candidacy would enrapture north Georgia Democrats and counter accusations that Unionism was a "Whig trick."[39]

The 1851 campaign not only replayed the 1850 contest, but also dredged up an issue from 1834, the abstract right of state secession. Seventeen years before, the State Rights party had defended secession as a constitutional right, while Unionists had grounded secession in the natural right of revolution. Since both the crisis parties were of mixed political ancestry, as exemplified by former Unionist Charles McDonald's Southern Rights candidacy, many politicians had to eat their own stale words in trying to explain how the heresies of 1834 had become gospel in 1851, or vice versa.

The Southern Rights party recited an argument for the constitutional right of secession that most voters knew by rote. The Union was a voluntary compact between sovereign states, and states could withdraw their allegiance to the Union at any time for any causes that they deemed sufficient. Neither the federal government nor the other states had the right to coerce seceding states. Southern Rights men contended that acknowledging secession's constitutionality made it a *"peaceable remedy."* Denying the constitutional right of secession, in contrast, would subject seceders to charges of treason and "have this Union dissolved by revolution and drenched in blood." Labeling Howell Cobb "the Civil War Candidate," Southern Rights men warned that federal troops were poised to assault South Carolina, to "burn her cities, rape her women, and hang her men," and vowed that the *"right of Secession will be sustained by arms if necessary."* McDonald's election, however, would mollify South Carolinians and persuade them to forgo secession. The Southern Rights logic of resistance at the threshold produced the conclusions that legitimizing secession would discourage it and that the Unionists' "doctrine of unlimited submission" would "create civil war and dissolve the Union."[40]

The discomfited Unionists dodged the secession question at their state convention, but Howell Cobb explored the issue in a most illogical public letter. A state could not secede without having just cause, Cobb opined, but he admitted "the right of a State to secede for just causes, to be determined solely by her self." In other words, a state could constitutionally secede only if it thought that it had a good reason to do so. Other states, possessing "a corresponding right to judge for themselves," might or might not be justified in using coercion against a seceding state, depending on the justice of their cause and their ability to enforce their decision. The right of coercion existed, then, only if coercion was justified—and succeeded. Cobb promised not to decide grave issues himself as governor; a state convention would determine his course if federal authorities summoned help to coerce South Carolina. By attempting to please everybody yet still distinguish himself from Southern Rights men, Cobb ended up looking foolish.[41]

Following Alexander Stephens's sage advice, most Union leaders, when pressed, treated secession as a right of revolution but kept "the main point prominent, that the only question now is whether we should go into revolution or not." The "contest about the *right* of secession" was "a mere dispute about words, not things," Robert Toombs sensibly remarked. The "political rights of communities in their last analysis are nothing but the blood of the brave." The Union party, after all, was "based upon the idea of preventing secession whether rightfull [*sic*] or not." Orators blared and editors exclaimed that McDonald's election would "demolish the Georgia platform" and force Georgia to "join South Carolina in a crusade against the Union."[42]

Popular patriotism and distrust of South Carolina radicalism propelled Unionists to victory. Cobb collected 59.7 percent of the ballots and trounced McDonald by more than 18,500 votes. Cobb's coalition combined a huge majority of black belt Whigs with nearly half of the mountain Democrats and a third of their upcountry cousins. The Southern Rights party, though, captured most of the old Democratic base and gained considerable ground over the 1850 convention elections. As the crisis dissipated and secession, even by South Carolina, became a more remote possibility, former Democrats started returning like moths to McDonald's flame. McDonald garnered nearly 40 percent of the upcountry vote and almost matched George Towns's 1849 black belt total. Cobb's impressive margin, in sum, was overwhelmingly attributable to the seven thousand or more north Georgia Union Democrats who voted with Union Whigs against Southern Rights Democrats. The Union coalition was unbeatable if it held together.[43]

Two successive drubbings sent Southern Rights leaders scrambling back toward the national Democracy. Herschel Johnson, James Gardner, Walter Colquitt, Hugh Haralson, and others organized a 25 November convention, ostensibly open to all "friends of Democratic principles," though no one expected Union Democrats to attend. Coolly recanting Southern Rights tenets, the convention announced that the Georgia Platform was the true "ground upon which all can rally, for *future action,* without any sacrifice of principle." The national Democracy alone could give the compromise "*efficacy and finality.*" Southern unity was neither possible nor desirable; sectional isolation equaled impotency. Laying their plans with care, Southern Rights leaders disingenuously asked Unionists to join them at a spring gathering to appoint delegates to the Baltimore national convention. The thinly attended Southern Rights version of a Democratic convention duly met on 31 March 1852, an unprecedentedly early date designed to preempt the field, with Union Democrats missing and unmourned. The convention adopted the 1848 national Democratic platform, ignored events of the last three years, and selected national convention delegates to plead the case that Southern Rights men were regular Democrats entitled to represent Georgia.[44]

Howell Cobb and other Union Democratic leaders, faced with becoming tails on a Southern Rights kite, could no longer afford to dawdle in transforming the Union party into a Democratic organization. As a first step, Union Democrats managed to control a January 1852 Union party caucus that passed resolutions tentatively recommending a spring convention to appoint Baltimore delegates. Believing that they had "always been in the National Democratic line," Union Democrats assumed that the national party would aid them by forthrightly endorsing the compromise and excluding Southern Rights men and northern Free-Soilers from party fellowship. Instead, Governor Cobb discovered on a March junket to Washington that congressional Democrats valued every potential vote, whatever its source, and had no intention of establishing a rigid procompromise party test. Georgia Union Democrats would have to fight their own battles.[45]

The apparent impending rapprochement between northern Democrats and Southern Rights men sapped what little confidence Union Whigs had ever had in the national Democracy. Alexander Stephens, along with Georgia Union Whig newspapers, advocated delaying any Union party action until after the national convention season closed, at which time Unionists could either amalgamate with a national Union party—a forlorn hope—or make an informed choice between the major parties. Although some Union Whig politicians, including Stephens, Robert Toombs—just elected to the United States Senate by the Unionist legislature—and Andrew J. Miller, maintained open minds regarding a possible Democratic alliance, the stand-pat strategy involved considerable dissimulation. Instead of bluntly speaking the truth—that most Whigs would never vote for a Democratic presidential candidate—Union Whigs disguised their intentions and only occasionally dropped hints that, one way or another, they planned to have Millard Fillmore as their standard-bearer.[46]

Union Whigs and Democrats parted ways at a 22 April party convention. A committee headed by Charles Jenkins deliberated overnight before recommending that the party take no action regarding the approaching presidential election until after the national party conventions. Debate followed, with Jenkins and former Democrats Thomas W. Thomas and Francis H. Cone arguing against sending delegates to Baltimore, and Howell Cobb's cousin, James Jackson, and veteran Whig Augustus H. Kenan supporting Union party representation. In a Pyrrhic victory for Union Whigs, the convention finally voted 124 to 29 against appointing Baltimore delegates.

Union Democrats and a few Union Whigs, notably John W. H. Underwood and Dr. Homer V. M. Miller from Cherokee Georgia, immediately retired into a "supplemental" meeting. Several of those present had not been delegates to the regular Union convention and had come to Milledgeville solely for preconcerted extramural activities. The gathering affirmed the 1848 national Democratic platform—a ritual betokening Democratic legitimacy that the regular convention could never have performed—and appointed twenty Baltimore delegates, who went with the "distinct understanding" that the national convention would adopt the finality of the compromise "as the only sound and reliable basis of action" for the national Democratic party.[47]

At the Baltimore convention in June, Democrats admitted both the Union and Southern Rights delegations from Georgia and let them act jointly. After a prolonged deadlock over leading contenders James Buchanan, Lewis Cass, and Stephen Douglas, the convention nominated dark horse Franklin Pierce of New Hampshire for president and placed him on a solidly procompromise platform. While Union Democrats welcomed the compromise endorsement, they headed home without the national party's exclusive imprimatur and with an unknown candidate who would be difficult to sell to Union Whigs.[48]

Meanwhile, a portion of the Union Whigs rushed to support Millard Fillmore, a champion of the compromise and the virtually unanimous choice of other southern whigs. Betrayed, they thought, by the supplemental movement, Fillmoreites candidly expressed the long withheld opinion that the "Whig Party of the South" was the "Union Party of the South"—Union Democrats were merely hangers-on. Miller Grieve, James A. Nisbet, Seaton Grantland, and a few other veteran Whigs gathered on 7 June, selected Fillmore delegates for the Whig national convention, and instructed them to insist on an explicit endorsement of the compromise. Unorthodox as the ersatz convention was, it accurately represented the majority of Union Whigs, who preferred Millard Fillmore over all the other candidates.[49]

Georgians instead got "Old Fuss and Feathers," General Winfield Scott, whom William Henry Seward and northern Whigs considered an appropriately malleable figure. Northern Whigs sugared the dose with a procompromise platform that allowed some Southerners to stomach Scott, but dissension nonetheless crippled the party. Several Georgia Union Whig papers had already pronounced Scott anathema, and the *Southern Recorder* commented that his nomination was "received with disapprobation, almost approaching disgust." Alexander Stephens and Robert Toombs instantly repudiated Scott as a cat's-paw of Free-Soilers, and Stephens counseled Unionists to scorn both major candidates and form an independent ticket.[50]

Union Democrats, of course, had other ideas. They first offered to reunite with Southern Rights men, provided that Unionists received spots on a modified electoral slate, but animosities prohibited reconciliation. The Southern Rights faction, smelling Unionist blood, demanded that all good Democrats support their ticket. Unwilling to capitulate, Howell Cobb, John Lamar, James and Henry R. Jackson, and John E. Ward hustled to assemble county delegations to produce a pro-Pierce majority at the 15 July Union party convention.

Waning Whig interest permitted Cobb's forces to capture a hollow shell. An initial committee report recommended dissolving a Union party that could not agree on a presidential candidate. Former Whig Richard R. Cuyler, longtime president of the Central of Georgia Railroad, then presented alternative resolutions that nominated Pierce without a corresponding declaration of allegiance to the national Democracy, a concession necessary to appease the small band of pro-Pierce Whigs. Extended debate culminated in a test motion to strike Pierce's name from Cuyler's resolutions. When that failed by a 61-to-94 vote, most Union Whigs departed to assemble another meeting in the adjoining Senate hall. The remaining members nominated Pierce and selected an electoral ticket evenly split between former Whigs and Democrats. Union Whig bolters rejected both Pierce and Scott, invited all similarly dissatisfied citizens to a 17 August convention in Macon, and tentatively suggested Daniel Webster and Charles Jenkins as independent presidential and vice presidential candidates.

A Union, rather than a Democratic, Pierce ticket availed nothing for Howell Cobb, John Lumpkin, and other leaders who craved recognition by the national Democracy. Dividing the Pierce vote, moreover, might throw the election into the legislature or even defeat Pierce outright. Smarting from Southern Rights accusations of party treason, Cobb, Lumpkin, and John Lamar decided in early August to bury the Union party's remains and seek a truce with their foes. The Union executive committee officially dissolved the party, and Cobb's group asked Southern Rights men to meet them at Atlanta to negotiate a compromise Pierce ticket.[51] In Atlanta on 17 September, the Southern Rights executive committee, headed by James Gardner, rebuffed the Unionists' plea with the dismissive comment that "any change at this time in the Electoral Ticket would weaken rather than strengthen the cause." The indignant Cobbites reconciled themselves to their fate. "We have now to contend with our enemies *in* the organization of the democratic party instead of *out* of it," Howell Cobb ruefully told John Lamar; "*we must bide our time*" and wait for "a brighter day."[52]

This "deep, damning, and infamous" surrender outraged William B. Wofford, Hopkins Holsey, Edward D. Chisholm, Thomas W. Thomas, and thousands of other Union Democrats who worried more about honor than about Howell Cobb's political future. They would not "Return as Slaves" to "Southern Rights Masters." Within a week after the Atlanta meeting, Holsey published a "Tugalo" Pierce ticket—named after a river in north Georgia—in the *Southern Banner* and joined several other north Georgia editors in denouncing Southern Rights arrogance.[53]

The remnants of the Whig party, meanwhile, had gathered in two separate conventions in Macon on 17 and 18 August to perfect their disorganization. When negotiations failed, supporters of Daniel Webster and Winfield Scott clung to their respective candidates and formed different electoral tickets. Both conventions endorsed the finality of the compromise; the principal distinction between the two was that Scott men just deeply distrusted northern Whigs while Webster men disowned them. Alexander Stephens, Robert Toombs, and Charles Jenkins backed Webster; equally stalwart Whigs William C. Dawson, Augustus H. Kenan, and Iverson L. Harris chose Scott. Miller Grieve and Richard H. Orme, who had edited the *Southern Recorder* together for more than two decades, ended their partnership when Orme spurned Scott. To avoid more such painful partings, most Whigs campaigned only listlessly for their candidates and concentrated on preserving enough goodwill to permit a later party reunion.[54]

Richard Orme, reflecting on his thirty-three years as an editor, commented that Georgians had never "manifested so little interest in the Presidential election." Parties that had thrived on presenting choices to voters had dissolved into squabbling factions, each vowing to uphold the finality of the Compromise of 1850. Whether northern Whigs and Democrats—either, neither, or both—would fulfill their procompromise pledges was the sole forward-looking issue; all other discussion involved rehashing the 1850 crisis. Webster Whigs and Tugalo men possessed sound claims to be acting on Union principles, but both tickets represented futile protests. Daniel Webster's death a few days before the election symbolized the demise of Georgia Whiggery. In a fitting climax to a year of conventions, a handful of irreconcilable Southern Rights faithful in Columbus nominated George Troup for president, only to have him announce his support for Pierce.[55]

Election day revealed how little the battle of the tickets mattered to many voters. Turnout declined nearly 35,000 votes from 1851, and the "regular" Democratic slate—the March Southern Rights ticket—carried the state for Pierce with 56.1 percent of the vote. Winfield Scott's 16,636 votes (27.0 percent) placed him second, and the Webster and Tugalo tickets each captured about 5,000 votes (8.5 percent apiece). Scott had a small following throughout the state; his strongest support came from the west-central black belt counties. The Whig stronghold of old middle Georgia, Robert Toombs's and Alexander Stephens's domain, furnished most of the Webster votes. Montgomery and Laurens Counties, ancient Troup–State Rights–Whig pillars, also returned Webster majorities. The Tugalo ticket performed impressively in the northeastern mountains and upcountry. Tugalo forces easily controlled Habersham County, the home of gruff William B. Wofford, and obtained majorities in Jackson, Hall, Union, Gilmer, and Wilkes as well.

The destruction of the Georgia Whig party as a *Whig* party inaugurated an era of unprecedented Democratic ascendancy. Scott and Webster combined polled 25,000 votes less than Zachary Taylor; close to three out of four Whigs refused to vote for Scott, the national party candidate. To be sure, most Whigs refused to vote for Pierce either, but massive abstention was no foundation for a viable party. Franklin Pierce amassed a larger percentage of the vote—64.6 percent, taking all tickets together—than any Whig or Democrat except Andrew Jackson ever had. Pierce carried three quarters of the vote in north Georgia and along the coast, two-thirds of the pine barrens–wiregrass vote, and a previously unthinkable 57.3 percent of the black belt vote. Nationally, Pierce won all but four states; apathy and non-voting afflicted Whigs everywhere in their Waterloo. Robert Toombs summarized the results in biting language: the "nation, with singular unanimity, has determined to take a man without claims or qualifications, surrounded by as dishonest and dirty a lot of political gamesters as ever Cataline assembled, rather than the canting hypocrites who brought out Genl. Scott. The decision was a wise one."[56]

Northern Whigs were incurably antislavery, southern Whigs were on the run in nearly every state, and nobody knew where Georgia Whig refugees might locate a new party residence. The *Southern Recorder* observed that "people can no longer be gulled and deceived by the cry of whig and democrat," terms that conveyed no "distinctive and vital principles, entertained exclusively and uniformly by any particular party." The *Georgia Journal and Messenger* saw "no organization among the Whigs of Georgia," but vaguely hoped that the nucleus of the old party would "act together" in future elections. Whigs found themselves practically back in the 1830s, without a northern party wing or a positive program, driven chiefly by irreconcilable opposition to the Democracy.[57]

Whigs spent 1853 seeking some arrangement and some appellation that would restore the party's old base and attract Union Democrats. Alexander

Stephens orchestrated a June meeting in Taliaferro County at which a strategy for an independent, de-Whigged opposition party grounded on allegiance to the Georgia Platform was outlined. A subsequent 22 June state convention of "Conservative Men" or "Republican Citizens," dominated by Robert Toombs, endorsed the Georgia Platform and added resolutions criticizing government extravagance and Franklin Pierce's appointments of Free-Soilers to patronage posts. In a brilliant, if obvious, move, the convention nominated Charles J. Jenkins for governor. His long and honorable service in the legislature, impeccable integrity, and widely credited authorship of the Georgia Platform made Jenkins one of the state's most respected figures. His candidacy simultaneously revived memories of Whig triumphs and reminded Union Democrats of the 1850 crisis.[58]

The "great bitterness of feeling" between Union and Southern Rights Democrats continued unabated as they competed for Franklin Pierce's favor. Herschel V. Johnson hoped that Pierce would offer no "aid and comfort to the craven submissionists, who under the false clamor of *Union, Union,* have assisted the abolitionists in robbing us of our rights." Johnson, Charles McDonald, and Howell Cobb pulled every string within reach trying to secure cabinet posts, but Pierce excluded them all as he jumbled together a heterogeneous and generally undistinguished collection of advisers. The president's "mongrel programme," as Howell Cobb called it, dashed Unionists' hopes of reward for their consistent procompromise stand.[59]

Merging with the dominant Southern Rights faction wounded Union Democrats' pride, but they had no realistic alternative to letting "the fire eaters have rope, in hopes that they will soon hang themselves." Unionists who balked might be neutralized. Hopkins Holsey had damned Howell Cobb and Southern Rights men equally for months, and he finally had to surrender the *Southern Banner* as a result of political pressure and loss of patronage. Howell Cobb, John Lamar, and their family political allies bought out Holsey and installed James A. Sledge as the new editor. An advocate of political amnesia, Sledge promised to promote Democratic unity "upon the basis of the Baltimore platform of 1852—the doctrines advocated by the Union and Southern Rights wings of the party [being] out of the question altogether."[60]

Democrats performed this reunion script—Southern Rights men directed—at their June state convention. Herschel Johnson led from the outset in the gubernatorial race and won on the fifth ballot. James Gardner's resolutions committee reported the 1852 Baltimore platform as the party's creed. Howell Cobb, John Lumpkin, and other Unionists considered Johnson's nomination a mixed evil. Johnson in 1850 and 1851 had uttered some memorable epithets about cowardly Unionists, but he had more recently been conciliatory—at least in public. Howell Cobb, moreover, wanted Johnson tucked away in the governor's mansion before the 1853 legislature elected a United States senator.[61]

During the campaign, Jenkins and Johnson often traveled and roomed together, indulging in "pleasant conversation, touching on the various strange charges and objections that were urged against us by our respective opponents." Some editors ridiculed Johnson's Swedenborgianism, a religion many Georgians equated with spirit rapping. Democrats howled over Jenkins's connection with the "Algerine law," a measure passed by the 1841 legislature and repealed in 1842 that established a separate board of aldermen for Augusta and gave the board and the city council concurrent control over city finances. Only citizens who owned at least one thousand dollars worth of real estate or paid twenty-five dollars in city taxes could vote for the aldermanic board. Although Charles McDonald and a Democratic legislature had sanctioned the Algerine law, Democrats labeled Jenkins, a co-sponsor of the measure, a lackey of the rich and an oppressor of the poor. Claiming that Jenkins, if elected governor, would disfranchise thousands of white men, Democrats urged every plain farmer who believed in "the true democratic doctrine of universal suffrage, to put the seal of their condemnation upon this damnable [Algerine] heresy."[62]

To meet this rare class issue, Jenkins's supporters stressed Democratic complicity in the Algerine law and rightly emphasized that Augusta's municipal laws had nothing to do with suffrage in the general elections. An Augusta woman calling herself "Justitia" defended Jenkins more boldly, however, charging that Democrats had embraced the "Socialist and Red Republican" spirit of the French Revolution. The Algerine law, in her opinion, was founded on "the plainest justice"—taxpayers had a right to shield their property from confiscation by the improvident mob. "Socialism may do at the North, along with Abolitionism and a thousand other isms," Justitia concluded, "but at the South, let us not belie the boast that we are free from such heresies." Archconservatives, particularly Whigs, had no doubt

entertained thoughts like Justitia's at times over the decades, but, significantly, no male politicians stepped forward to endorse the principle of re-
stricting adult white male suffrage.[63]

The Algerine law and Swedenborgianism aside, the 1853 campaign focused on the fallout from the past three years. Johnson sounded the trumpet
of the national Democracy and chided his de-Whigged opponents. Jenkins
and his band were a "sectional party," the *Milledgeville Federal Union* declared, "having no interest and no principles in common with any party out
of the limits of Georgia." At the same time, Democrats assailed Jenkins as a
Whig and recounted the familiar evils of the northern Whig party. Jenkins
responded that the Democracy was a motley coalition of opposites with no
valid claims to nationality. Voluminous coverage in the Jenkins press created
the impression that President Pierce's northern Free-Soil appointees, not
Herschel Johnson, were running for the Georgia governorship. Most of all,
Jenkins forces maintained that it "would be madness" to elect Johnson, "an
open and avowed secessionist," over the father of the Georgia Platform.[64]

Jenkins's popularity and skillful exploitation of Democratic divisions almost produced a victory. Johnson barely downed Jenkins, 47,638 to 47,145,
but the Democrats gained majorities in both branches of the legislature
and elected six out of eight congressmen. The opposition triumphs came in
old middle Georgia, where Alexander Stephens easily won reelection and
David A. Reese took Robert Toombs's vacated seventh district seat. The
return of black belt Whigs to the polls aided Jenkins most, but he also ran
strongly in north Georgia—despite his Algerine law baggage. Johnson's
identification with the Southern Rights party cost him many Union Democratic ballots. He polled just 58.0 percent of the mountain and 56.1 percent
of the upcountry vote, considerably below traditional Democratic margins.
Still, in this last fight over the 1850 crisis, Southern Rights leaders whose
fortunes had reached a nadir just two years before beat the opposition's best
candidate. Anti-Democratic forces, whether they called themselves Con-
servatives, Republicans, Unionists, or something else, could not dwell forever on bygone questions if they expected to overthrow the imperfectly re-
united Georgia wing of the national Democracy.[65]

A nasty fight between Howell Cobb, Charles McDonald, and Alfred Iverson over William C. Dawson's Senate seat marred the Democrats' celebra-
tions. A Democratic caucus on 16 November nominated McDonald, but

several Union Democrats shortly afterward cooperated with opposition legislators to rescind the senate's resolution to elect a United States senator. As the anger of Southern Rights men welled, James Gardner urged Howell Cobb to have his friends "retrace their steps. Their course is stabbing you." Cobb instead adroitly used the situation to win points toward future rehabilitation while still slaying McDonald. Cobb assumed the comfortable role of conciliator at a 19 December meeting, delivered an impassioned speech on party unity, and denied responsibility for the Unionist insurgence. Then he gleefully watched unrepentant Unionists force Democrats to overturn McDonald's caucus nomination. After the passage of another election resolution, a free-for-all lasting for thirteen ballots resulted in the selection of Southern Rights man Alfred Iverson. Cobb accepted the loss philosophically. The "elements are at work throughout the country reforming and reorganizing parties," he wrote near the end of 1853, and the unfolding realignment would "work out a purification of the national democracy" and put "*national men*" in their true position."[66]

Cobb was a good, if overly optimistic, prophet. Senator Stephen A. Douglas of Illinois was on the verge of introducing a measure that would pose the gravest threat yet to the Democratic party's vaunted nationality. Douglas's proposal to organize the Kansas and Nebraska territories without restrictions on slavery, thereby overturning the slavery prohibition in the Missouri Compromise, would put northern Democrats under siege from an outraged public and provide the spark for the formation of a northern sectional party. The fallout from the fateful Nebraska bill would decimate Cobb's beloved "*national men*" of the northern Democracy and would dominate state and national politics for the remainder of the decade.

# SEVEN

# Kansas, Know-Nothings, and the National Democracy

Lured by the promise of westward expansion and railroad development, Senator Stephen Douglas had struggled unsuccessfully for several years to organize the vast territory west and northwest of Missouri. Renewing his efforts in January 1854, Douglas introduced a bill to carve two territories, Kansas and Nebraska, out of land lying north of the Missouri Compromise line. To secure crucial southern support, Douglas incorporated language that voided the Missouri Compromise restriction and opened Kansas and Nebraska to slavery under the ambiguous doctrine of popular sovereignty. The furor over the Kansas-Nebraska Act and its sequel, "bleeding Kansas," devastated the national Democracy, created a powerful northern Republican party dedicated to antislavery principles, and propelled the nation a long way toward disunion.

No one in Georgia asked for Douglas's measure, but the state's politicians quickly agreed that it embodied the principle that they had been contending for since 1846: the right to take their slaves into the territories without obstruction from Congress. Georgians abstractly considered the Missouri Compromise restriction either unjust or, most commonly, unconstitutional, and they welcomed the repeal of the long-standing ban on slavery extension. Alexander Stephens, Robert Toombs, Howell Cobb, and others echoed Stephen Douglas's disingenuous argument that the Kansas-Nebraska bill simply extended the universal principles of popular sovereignty and congressional nonintervention previously established in the Compromise of 1850. Only a few former Southern Rights men, such as Congressman James L.

Seward, objected to the parallels drawn between the Kansas-Nebraska measure and the once reviled compromise. On 17 February 1854, the Georgia house and senate unanimously resolved "that opposition to the principles of the Nebraska bill, in relation to the subject of slavery, is regarded by the people of Georgia as hostility to the rights of the South."[1]

The United States Senate's large Democratic majority passed the Kansas-Nebraska bill easily, but House opponents managed to bury it beneath a mountain of pending legislation. It took brilliant parliamentary maneuvering, including a masterful endgame by Alexander Stephens, to bring the Kansas-Nebraska bill to a vote on 22 May, when it carried 113 to 100. Most northern Democratic senators and every slave-state senator except two— Democrat Sam Houston of Texas and Whig John Bell of Tennessee— supported the Kansas-Nebraska bill. Southern Democratic representatives voted for it almost unanimously, while the small contingent of slave-state Whigs divided evenly—largely along upper versus lower South lines—on the wisdom of the measure. Forty-four Democratic representatives from the free states sided with Douglas and the Pierce administration; forty-four others opposed them. Not a single northern Whig in either branch of Congress voted for the Kansas-Nebraska bill.[2]

Georgia Democrats expected and could have accepted nothing less than the northern Democratic support that made passage of the Kansas-Nebraska Act possible. As the *Athens Southern Banner* explained, the Union and southern rights could be protected only "through National parties, organized upon National principles," and "the soundness of a National party upon the slavery question" was paramount to "any and all other issues." Declaring that the Whig party was "*thoroughly denationalized*" and that northern Whigs were "devoted to a systematic warfare against" the South, Democrats demanded that southern opposition cease and urged all to assemble under the Democratic banner.[3]

Former Georgia Whigs celebrated the success of the Kansas-Nebraska Act and acknowledged that there could be no further southern connection with northern Whiggery. Instead of gravitating toward the Democratic camp, however, they emphasized the considerable northern Democratic opposition to the Kansas-Nebraska measure and defiantly announced that they would "NEVER UNITE with any party whose bosom has not been purged of the last vestige of abolition." Even Alexander Stephens, who gloated over his role in passing the Kansas-Nebraska Act, disdained the idea of formally joining his de facto Democratic allies. "The truth is the Southern Whigs must strike out a lead for themselves," Stephens wrote. "They can not afford either for their own sake or that of the country to fall into the ranks of either of the great nominal parties as they are now organized and constituted." Stephens talked in 1854, as he had for years, about forming "a sound national organization upon broad—national—republican principles," and neither he nor his Georgia compatriots were yet prepared to concede that the Democratic party was such an organization.[4]

White Georgians valued the "moral effect" of the Kansas-Nebraska Act in securing southern equality in the territories, but in 1854 hardly anyone expected it to promote the actual extension of slavery. Climate and soil would preclude the use of slave labor in Nebraska and probably Kansas as well. Georgians were, accordingly, astonished at the violent northern reactions to the bill. The Kansas-Nebraska Act was no "triumph of the Slave Power," no part of a plot to extend slavery; it was an overdue measure of justice for the aggrieved South. Once the northern public understood that, the *Milledgeville Southern Recorder* predicted, the "threatening and noisy vaporings" of antislavery fanatics would "speedily subside."[5]

The unfolding events of a northern political revolution belied such optimistic forecasts. Two new movements, Know-Nothingism and anti-Nebraska fusion, attracted hundreds of thousands of discontented northern voters in 1854 and badly eroded the bases of the Whig and Democratic parties. The Order of the Star Spangled Banner, whose members were commonly called Know-Nothings because they were instructed to deny all knowledge of it, was a secret organization with elaborate rituals, oaths, and a hierarchical structure of local, state, and national councils. Know-Nothings shared anti-Catholic and nativist prejudices and called for reforms such as stricter naturalization and voting laws. The often interrelated anti-Nebraska fusion efforts mobilized a diverse array of voters in opposition to the Kansas-Nebraska Act and a supposed "slave power" conspiracy involving lordly southern planters and their northern Democratic lackeys. Some Whig organizations weathered the 1854 earthquake, but the party was all but obliterated in several northern states. And, most important for Georgians, northern Whig, Know-Nothing, and anti-Nebraska forces—working together or separately—mauled the northern Democratic party.[6]

The unprecedented overthrow of their northern friends shocked Democrats. Without strong northern allies, Democrats' main claim to support—their ability to use the national party to shield the South from danger—would be fatally compromised. The northern realignment, moreover, indicated the restlessness of northern voters, the attractiveness of issues such as nativism and anti-Catholicism, and the existence of widespread hostility toward the South and the extension of slavery. Fearing the worst, Democrats braced themselves to face a "Northern candidate combining all the Northern *isms*" in the 1856 presidential election—a fair prediction of the ensuing rise of the Republican party.[7]

The same northern developments that worried southern Democrats heartened the opposition and sparked growing interest in Know-Nothingism. The order expanded southward as well as northward in 1854; the organization of Know-Nothing councils in Georgia apparently began in June and proceeded rapidly. Reports of Know-Nothing activity increased throughout the summer, and reputed Know-Nothing candidates scored victories in city elections in Griffin, Milledgeville, Augusta, and elsewhere in late 1854 and early 1855. Without endorsing or actively promoting the order, several old Whig newspapers tacitly supported the Know-Nothings by chronicling their victories and publishing the available details of their creed. The secret political society appealed mainly to former Whigs, but local lodges lured in enough Democrats to cause consternation among Democratic party leaders.[8]

Know-Nothingism, however, failed to create in Georgia anything like the excitement that prevailed in the northern states. There were no state elections for Know-Nothings to contend in 1854, and many of the supposed evils that the secret order sought to remedy scarcely existed in the South. According to the 1850 census, only 6,452 white Georgians, 1.2 percent of the white population, were foreign-born; there were only eight Catholic churches in the state. Most southern Protestants, whether Whigs or Democrats, held generalized prejudices against Catholicism and its adherents, but outside of Louisiana, Maryland, and a few scattered cities, the small foreign-born and Catholic populations posed no credible threat to even the most paranoid southern Know-Nothing. One Democrat aptly prescribed that every Southerner afflicted with Know-Nothingism "ought to apply a copy of the Census-returns to his head, and keep it there for about two hours."[9]

Georgia Know-Nothings, in fact, worried far less about Catholics and foreigners at home than about the impact of the immigrant vote in the free states. The mass of foreign voters in the North, the *Savannah Republican* observed, had become "almost as numerous as are the white men old enough to vote in all the Southern states put together." The *Columbus Enquirer* warned that the yearly addition of "a half million of new recruits" to the antislavery host would enable the North "to wage indiscriminate warfare on our institutions, our social peace, and our political rights." The problem was not, as northern Know-Nothings complained, that immigrants failed to comprehend American conceptions of freedom, but that they embraced dangerous abstract ideas about rights to universal liberty. Foreigners brought "with them a hatred for the tyranny of their fatherlands" that blinded them to the "sensible difference between the slavery of the negro and the white man." They were all too ready to sympathize with the slaves and lend aid to "the enemies of our institutions." Lengthening the naturalization period and eliminating most of immigrant vote that swelled northern majorities would, Americans contended, do more to protect slavery than a dozen Democratic territorial bills.[10]

The most alluring aspect of the Know-Nothing order was its potential for destroying existing party organizations, especially the national Democracy. For that reason, many former Whigs who scorned the order's nativism and secrecy were nonetheless willing to experiment with Know-Nothingism. As one old Whig told Alexander Stephens, "It is enough for me to know, that the present [Democratic] Administration[s], both national and State, are against them, to ensure for them, my sympathies." The veteran Whig editor of the *Augusta Chronicle & Sentinel* defined the "affected dread of Catholic influence and the supremacy of the Pope" as the "veriest humbug ever conjured up by artful, intriguing demagogues," but he remained hopeful that the Know-Nothings could provide an alternative to the hated Democracy.[11]

The antipartyism central to Know-Nothing ideology was second nature to old Whigs reared on the politics of nonpartisanship. The *Macon Georgia Journal and Messenger* thought that Know-Nothingism fed primarily on the "universal distrust among the people of all existing political parties." The *Milledgeville Southern Recorder* echoed the idea that Know-Nothingism arose in reaction to the "two old disordered and corrupt political parties" through which "ambitious demagogues were perseveringly engaged in fomenting and perpetuating sectional strife and ill-blood." Responding to popular discontent, Know-Nothings reiterated timeworn Whig promises to banish officeholding leeches, eliminate party strife, end sectional agitation, and restore the government to the pristine principles of the founding fathers. The long "contest between the People and the professional Politicians" was about to culminate in "an insurrection of the honest masses against the despotism of party and party leaders—a rebellion, like that of our revolutionary sires, against the tyranny and corruption of their rulers." [12]

A Georgia delegation intent on forming "a reliable, conservative, National American party" journeyed to Philadelphia in June 1855 to attend the meeting of the Know-Nothing national council. At the start of the gathering, most northern Know-Nothings, despite their antislavery leanings and their contempt for the Kansas-Nebraska Act, wanted to find a modus vivendi that would make a national American party possible. But sharp sectional antagonism soon disrupted the proceedings. A large majority of Northerners opposed the so-called twelfth section of the proposed platform, which deprecated sectional agitation and pledged to uphold existing laws regarding slavery. This implied endorsement of the Kansas-Nebraska Act, insisted on by Southerners, led to a bolt by many northern delegates that split the fledgling American party. [13]

Making the best of a bad setback, Georgia Americans optimistically emphasized the ultimate adoption of the twelfth section and opined that the northern walkout had pruned away the "rank fungus of abolitionism" and left the rest of the party "stronger than it was before." [14] "Stronger," of course, meant sounder on slavery. Americans viewed the national party project as a means to one primary end: the protection of the South and slavery within the Union. Their attachment to anti-Catholic, nativist, and antiparty ideas was decidedly secondary to their overriding goal of creating a powerful, non-Democratic national party that would defend southern interests.

The American party was just one of the political options that oppositionists explored in early 1855. Many former Whigs first looked to Charles Jenkins as a gubernatorial candidate and advocated running him independently, without a nomination from Know-Nothings or any other group. Jenkins, however, scotched these plans by repudiating Know-Nothingism and refusing to reprise his 1853 candidacy.

Old Whigs then considered joining the Columbus movement. In a late

May meeting in Temperance Hall in Columbus, Georgia, John H. Howard, Hines Holt, Van Leonard, Seaborn Jones, and several other ex–Southern Rights men and Calhounites laid plans for a southern sectional party. Convinced that the downfall of the northern Democracy had destroyed all hopes for effective national party alliances, the Columbus actors hoped to draw Know-Nothings, unattached Whigs, and, eventually, the bulk of the Democrats into a single state party. Some Columbus men, such as editor James N. Bethune of the *Columbus Corner Stone,* were disunionists per se who viewed the movement as a prelude to secession. Although supportive Whig editors blindly professed to see no extremism in the Columbus movement, virtually every Democratic leader denounced the Columbus call for southern unity. Support for the Columbus movement, never strong, collapsed quickly once the Know-Nothings forged ahead with their own party organization.[15]

The chance, however remote, that the power of northern Know-Nothingism could still be harnessed in a national party alliance gave American party members a decisive edge in organizing the scattered opposition. Garnett Andrews, a former Union Democrat from Wilkes County, received the American gubernatorial nomination in late June at a semisecret convention—Americans would not fully abandon the secrecy and trappings of Know-Nothingism until later in the summer. The party's platform included several nativist and anti-Catholic tenets, but, more important, it also contained slavery planks crafted strictly for home consumption. The Americans essentially repeated the legislature's 1854 decree that opposition to the Kansas-Nebraska Act was "hostility to the constitutional rights of [the] South" and declared that all persons holding such opinions—including, as it turned out, nearly the whole northern Know-Nothing order—were "unfit to be recognized as members of the American party."[16]

Although the American party attracted most of the oppositionists, the state temperance organization rallied a few thousand supporters behind former Whig Basil H. Overby's bid for the governorship. Unlike northern Maine Law advocates, who concentrated on prohibition, temperance forces in Georgia aimed only at repealing license laws and eliminating the sale of liquor by the drink. Overby and his followers combined moral and religious objections to drinking with an emphasis on the violence, drunkenness, and improvidence fostered by groggeries. Lowlier taverns also illicitly served slaves and free blacks, a dangerous practice that most white Georgians favored eradicating. While ardent defenders of excessive tippling and cross-roads doggeries were few, the lack of a committed, evangelical, perfectionist constituency—the backbone of northern Maine Law drives—prevented reformers from moving effectively from moral suasion to legal coercion. Temperance reform was, moreover, associated in the public mind with abolitionism and other northern "isms." Even many prominent temperance leaders, such as Joseph Henry Lumpkin, opposed mixing temperance and politics and contended that temperance laws were unenforceable in Georgia's rural society. Twenty years of intermittent reform efforts had already demonstrated the feebleness of temperance as a political issue, and Overby's 1855 campaign was a sidelight to the Democratic-American contest.[17]

Almost from the moment that the first Know-Nothing lodge appeared in Georgia, Democrats attacked "the new Secret, Oath-bound Order" as a more sinister version of "the Whig party under a new name." Brushing aside the "affected alarm for the Protestant religion" as "too hypocritical to need much comment," the *Augusta Constitutionalist* characterized Georgia Know-Nothingism as "essentially and emphatically a whig movement" and dismissed the pretended national organization as nothing more than the "mere fusion of all the anti-Democratic elements in each State."[18]

Most Democrats, and many old Whigs as well, saw the Know-Nothings' midnight meetings, passwords, rituals, and proposed proscription of Catholics and foreigners as disturbing assaults on American freedom. Leading southern Methodist divine Augustus Baldwin Longstreet and Primitive Baptist preacher and politician William Moseley, among other ministers, denounced the Know-Nothings for setting up religious tests in politics. Moseley expressed a common view when he stressed that the government's only role in religious matters was to let worshippers have "their Bibles, and let them alone." "Half the work of the [American] Revolution would be undone, or go for naught, if the principle of religious toleration is to be trampled under foot," the *Augusta Constitutionalist* contended. "All secret political societies are anti-Republican—anti-American." To the anger of many old Whig compatriots, Alexander Stephens and Robert Toombs likewise repudiated Know-Nothingism and emphasized the threat that political secrecy posed to a nation founded on the ideal of a free and enlightened citizenry. In a republic, Stephens observed, "every man should wear his principles inscribed on his forehead."[19]

Moving beyond general objections to Know-Nothing secrecy and bigotry, Stephens, Toombs, and nearly all other critics of Know-Nothingism focused on the order's bearing on the institution of slavery. James Gardner viewed the incoming "flood" of "ignorant and rowdy foreigners, paupers and convicts" as a "vast evil," but a northern one. The few immigrants who came to the South became valuable citizens. The rest, the rabble who clustered in northern cities, had no place in southern society. The servile work that northern immigrants performed was done in the South by slaves, and this "exemption from the evil of a turbulent and vicious foreign population" was one of the great blessings of the institution of slavery. Alexander Stephens thought that Know-Nothingism revealed the longings of the New England "Cod Fish aristocracy" for a northern form of slavery. The Know-Nothings' proposed extension of the naturalization period would eliminate immigrant voting and produce "some millions of people of our own race amongst us who would be neither *citizens* or *Slaves.*" The idea of blurring the fundamental distinction between white citizens and black slaves repelled Stephens; he wanted "no *degraded* class of people of our own race as an element in our society."[20]

Many white men viewed the northern Know-Nothing party as a gigantic abolition society spawned by "that loathesome old prostitute, Massachusetts." Democrat and former governor Charles McDonald sorrowfully observed that hostility toward the Democratic party had driven southern Know-Nothings—hopefully unwittingly—into an alliance "with open and avowed abolitionists at the North." McDonald reminded Know-Nothings that the Constitution, the bulwark of southern rights, was "not a midnight production" and would not be defended by the enemies of slavery scheming in northern lodges. Even more ominously, the *Milledgeville Federal Union* warned that white Southerners ought to be the last people on earth to encourage secret societies. Northern Know-Nothings could use midnight conclaves to "introduce Abolition principles into the Southern States. We all know that there are bitter Abolitionists among us, but these men dare not come out openly in defiance of public opinion. To protect these men in their treason, by the machinery of a secret society, is a great Abolition stride in advance." The rights of free Southerners, Democrats stressed, could be protected only by conducting politics in the open, where public-spirited citizens could detect, and instantly suppress, any criticism of the institution of slavery.[21]

Native northern Protestants, not immigrants, were the real enemies of the South. "The adopted Irish citizens form the strongest pillar of our power in the free States," one Democrat declared. "Disfranchise them and the Abolitionists would sweep the North like a desolating blast." An Augusta man who proclaimed himself a "Native Whig" thanked God for sending the Irish to Boston to overwhelm the abolitionist Yankees, who had "abjured the precepts of the blessed Saviour, and made unto themselves a God, with a black skin, wooly hair, and blubber lips, whose very stench is sweet perfume in the nostrils of their fair maidens." "One would seek in vain elsewhere, short of Hell," he continued, "for worse Christians than these same freesoil protestants" who "in place of prayers, mutter curses and revilings upon the white citizens of the South." Many Protestant ministers relished slandering the South, James Gardner concluded, but no abolitionist sermons were delivered "from Catholic pulpits."[22]

Convinced that Know-Nothingism was "the political chloroform employed to" prepare the South for "the keen blade of the Black Republican surgeons," increasing numbers of Democrats considered all Northerners outside the Democratic party to be abolitionists and viewed the ascendancy of the national Democracy as a prerequisite for the continuance of the Union. Former governor Howell Cobb, Governor Herschel V. Johnson, and other leading Democrats repeatedly emphasized that the Union rested on the power of the national Democratic party to protect the South from all menaces, foreign and domestic. "When Northern Whigs and Abolitionists annihilate the Democratic party in the Northern States, then, and probably not till then," James Gardner predicted, "will there be a necessity for the dissolution of the Union." The stakes in the contest against Know-Nothingism and general northern fanaticism were incredibly high, and if the Democrats lost, many men were prepared to quit the game.[23]

Even as the debate over Know-Nothingism raged, public attention in 1855 turned inexorably to the developing struggle on the Kansas plains. The race to control the fate of slavery in Kansas began before the Kansas-Nebraska Act cleared Congress. Northern emigrant aid societies sponsored settlers as missionaries for freedom, while proslavery Missourians organized to repel what they saw as an abolitionist invasion. The proslavery forces took advantage of their proximity and initially held a majority in the territory. To make doubly sure, though, thousands of Missourians crossed the border to vote in the 30 March 1855 territorial election. The proslavery legislature elected partly by these fraudulent votes promptly passed draconian laws protecting slavery. Similar political ploys punctuated by occasional episodes of bloodshed kept Kansas in turmoil for the next several years. The course of events simultaneously outraged northern public opinion, hastened the development of the Republican party, and enticed Southerners with the prospect of making Kansas a slave state.

When the settlement of Kansas became a trial of sectional strength, Georgia politicians forgot their previous free-state forecasts and recast the Kansas question in apocalyptic terms. Winning the territory for slavery, the ideal outcome, would demonstrate the vitality of southern institutions and equalize sectional representation in the Senate. But even if slavery ultimately failed the Kansas test, Georgia leaders insisted that Kansans be given the opportunity to decide the slavery question themselves, without interference from Congress. Any antislavery meddling would violate the popular sovereignty principle of the Kansas-Nebraska Act and infringe on southern rights in the territories. Mincing no words, the June state Democratic convention, which renominated Herschel V. Johnson for the governorship, declared that Kansas's "rejection by Congress, on account of slavery, would be a just cause for the disruption of all the ties that bind the State of Georgia to the Union."[24]

The American party also readily embraced the Kansas issue. What American candidate Garnett Andrews called his "main appeal to Georgians" was nothing other than a plan to succeed where he alleged the national Democracy had failed. The South needed allies to carry proslavery measures through Congress, Andrews reasoned, and the recent defeat of the northern Democracy meant that Southerners had to strike a bargain with conservative northern Know-Nothings. If Southerners acted in concert, they could use the "matter of Catholics and foreigners," so obviously important to northern voters, as a lever to secure concessions on slavery issues. Andrews phrased his calculations baldly: "As we expect to get help for the South by the popularity of some issue in which the North is interested, ought not the South to support the side or issue in which the North is interested?" "Is it not policy then," Andrews continued, "to ally ourselves with the American party? It is an increasing party, and our only hope is increase of votes."[25] Georgians had to "try new issues, new attractions, new powers of cohesion," anything to induce Northerners to drop their antislavery fixation.[26]

With both parties offering identical promises to protect slavery and southern rights, the 1855 campaign boiled down to interminable arguments over which party was best able to honor such pledges. The American party operated under severe handicaps. Anti-Catholicism and nativism attracted few voters who were not already anti-Democratic and repelled many old Whigs. Heading the list of defectors were Alexander Stephens and Robert Toombs, who became de facto Democratic converts. The loss of former Whigs who decided to back Overby further weakened Americans. Most of all, Americans suffered from a credibility gap. As halfway members of an inchoate national party who themselves distrusted their northern allies, Americans were unable to offer convincing assurances that they could provide national political strength for the South.[27]

Herschel Johnson won reelection comfortably, if not overwhelmingly, with 54,136 votes (52.2 percent), followed by Andrews with 43,358 (41.8 percent), and Overby with 6,294 (6.1 percent). Johnson improved on his 1853 total in every region of the state, while Andrews's vote fell nearly 3,800 votes short of Charles Jenkins's 1853 total. Robert Toombs and Alexander Stephens refused to campaign for Johnson, but their assault on Know-Nothingism badly damaged the American party. In Stephens's eighth congressional district, which he carried by more than 2,700 votes, Johnson's share of the gubernatorial vote leaped from 33.3 percent in 1853 to 50.6 percent in 1855. Elbert, Oglethorpe, Taliaferro, and Warren Counties, which altogether had returned just one Democratic majority since 1835, all gave majorities to Johnson. Overby garnered significant support (above 5 percent of the vote) only in a dozen counties in the eastern black belt and a handful of western upcountry counties. Large majorities in both branches of the legislature and victories in six of eight congressional races capped the Democratic triumph.

The American party's defeat in Georgia was part of a larger southern disaster. The Americans lost every southern gubernatorial election held in 1855, and the Democrats won majorities in every state legislature except that of Tennessee. Unable to overcome the basic weakness on slavery issues—the lack of a sound northern party wing—that had killed southern Whiggery, southern Americans were a stranded minority. They would have to find other issues to revive their fortunes in the 1856 presidential election.[28]

The presidential campaign unfolded against the backdrop of turmoil in Congress and Kansas. Alexander Stephens and Robert Toombs, who belatedly acknowledged reality and formally joined the Democratic party in November 1855, returned to a Congress transformed by the northern party realignment. Sectional warfare began with a two-month contest for the House Speakership in which Republicans and northern Know-Nothings failed to unite on a candidate, and southern Americans doggedly refused to support the Democratic nominees. Northern votes cast under the plurality rule finally elected Republican Nathaniel Banks on 2 February, giving that party its first major national victory. Alarmed southern Democrats and Americans failed to act together even against the Republicans, and each blamed the other for Banks's triumph.

While Congress argued, Kansas bled. By early 1856 the territory was divided into two hostile camps: proslavery men who backed the Lecompton legislature and free-staters who had established a shadow government in Topeka. With the spring thaw came violence and disorder. On 21 May, a proslavery posse invaded the town of Lawrence and terrorized free-state residents. Immediately afterward, John Brown, a self-proclaimed holy warrior against slavery, led a small party composed mainly of his sons in a brutal raid down Pottawottamie Creek and slaughtered five men loosely connected to the proslavery forces. These events convinced many Kansans that civil war was at hand, and disorganized citizen armies ranged over the territory. Killings and lootings were frequent enough to sustain a climate of fear in Kansas and a sense of outrage elsewhere in the country.[29]

Southerners, with a few exceptions, maintained that the Lecompton government was the sole legal authority in Kansas, that it represented a majority of the bona fide residents, and that any move toward statehood had to be made under its auspices. Alexander Stephens, among many others, deemed complaints about invading Missourians, election frauds, and political violence irrelevant to the central issue of legality; free-staters were simply "lawless, insubordinate, and insurrectionary." Republicans and northern Know-Nothings scoffed at the Lecompton government's claim to legitimacy and accused Southerners of trying to shackle slavery on Kansas against the will of the free-state majority. Sectionalism and partisanship combined to kill all moderate solutions. Robert Toombs's Senate bill called for a new registration of Kansas voters followed by a carefully supervised election for constitutional convention delegates, who would then draft a document under which Kansas would be admitted as a state. After easily passing the Senate, Toombs's bill died at the hands of northern House members. Republicans wanted grievances and discord for electioneering purposes, Toombs bitterly concluded, not a viable settlement.[30]

Georgia Americans, too, glimpsed possibilities for political gain in the Kansas impasse. At their December 1855 state convention, Americans put themselves in fighting trim for an all-out sectional campaign by sundering their always tenuous and increasingly burdensome ties to northern Know-Nothings. Americans did not overtly repudiate their northern namesakes; they simply declined to send delegates to the American party's scheduled February 1856 national convention and advocated holding a different gathering, one composed of "all national men," in early May. By this roundabout method of boycotting one national convention and suggesting another that would never be held, the Americans assumed the status of an independent state party.[31]

As the Georgia Americans had obviously expected, northern and southern Americans divided once again, and finally, over slavery issues at their national convention. The defeat of a plank calling for the restoration of the Missouri Compromise line, the adoption of a vague prosouthern platform, and the nomination of ex-president Millard Fillmore drove scores of northern delegates out of the convention. The northern American bolters subsequently abandoned their separate organization and fused with the Republicans. The union of Republicans and a large body of northern Know-Nothings behind the Republican candidate, John C. Frémont, left Millard Fillmore with only a small remnant of conservative old Whig supporters in the free states.[32]

Georgia Americans had long planned to run Fillmore, and they offered him *their* nomination at a July state convention. Fillmore, in graciously accepting the endorsement, quizzically noted that he was already the national American candidate, but his Georgia backers adamantly refused to regard him as such. Fillmore was only "nominally the candidate of a party"; he was really "the candidate of the *people*." The Fillmore movement was "an insurrection of the honest masses against the despotism of party and party leaders." The "proud and independent" Georgia Americans rejoiced that they and their candidate were untrammeled by platforms "framed in Northern latitudes." Determined to mold Fillmore in their own image, Americans created a proslavery, prosouthern Unionist who deplored partisanship but nonetheless loathed the national Democracy.[33]

The Democratic nominee in 1856 was James Buchanan of Pennsylvania, a cautious, crafty politician who seldom took a step that others had not taken first. Although many Southerners, including Georgians, had preferred President Franklin Pierce, Buchanan's record as a conservative national man with marked southern sympathies made him acceptable to nearly all southern Democrats.

The divided 1856 contest isolated the Georgia parties from their Republican enemies. Both Americans and Democrats recognized that Frémont's election would endanger the South and the Union; cries that only Fillmore, or only Buchanan, could defeat the Republicans resounded throughout the campaign. Instead of drawing Georgians together, however, the grave Republican threat drove the parties to attack each other with histrionic, hysterical charges. Fillmore and Buchanan were personally as conservative on slavery issues as northern politicians of any consequence could be, but the heat of the canvass transformed them into surrogate "Black" Republicans. The sole campaign strategy for each side in 1856 was to hammer away on slavery issues "to prove the unsoundness" of the opposition's northern allies.[34]

The American party's belated discovery of squatter sovereignty in the Kansas–Nebraska Act best exemplifies the search for a winning slavery issue. Americans had repeatedly declared that the principles of congressional nonintervention and popular sovereignty contained in the Kansas–Nebraska Act were identical with those found in the territorial measures of the revered Compromise of 1850. They had also maintained that defending the Kansas–Nebraska Act against northern assaults was essential to preserving southern rights in the territories. Yet, in late 1855 and early 1856, Americans reversed themselves and condemned the Kansas–Nebraska Act as a "stupendous electioneering fraud, by which the South was to lose *every thing in territory and gain nothing in principle.*"[35]

Americans disingenuously insisted that they had been duped. Although every citizen mildly conversant with political affairs had known since 1848 that northern Democrats believed that territorial legislatures could bar slavery, Americans professed to be astonished that popular sovereignty had a "Northern face." They had naively considered only the southern understanding of popular sovereignty: that territories could not make decisions on slavery until they applied for statehood. This principle was what Americans had championed and endorsed; this protection for southern rights was what had made the Kansas-Nebraska Act valuable. The revelation that popular sovereignty could be construed differently suggested that sinister motives lay behind what had first appeared to be a southern victory. Northern Democrats had supported the Kansas-Nebraska Act as a Free-Soil measure designed to let northern squatters rob Southerners of their rights in the territories! This devious, heretofore concealed scheme, Americans thought, made the Kansas-Nebraska Act "more odious than the Wilmot Proviso." [36]

Northern Democrats' professions of friendship for Southerners were just soothing words spoken to gull intended victims. Northern Democrats lived by bidding for antislavery votes; they were "so thoroughly *freesoil,* that the keeping up of the Black Republican organization is entirely a work of supererogation." The umbrella of the national Democratic party sheltered two antithetical sectional wings mutually devoted to hoodwinking the American people. The national Democratic platform framed at Cincinnati was "a miserable, cowardly *dodge,*" deliberately worded to allow northern and southern Democrats to interpret popular sovereignty however they pleased. "Silence was the only hope of continued union," Americans charged, and traitorous southern Democrats had willingly participated in a ruse that compromised the "dignity, rights and equality of their own section." More unscrupulous than a gang of pirates, more dangerous to the South than any band of Black Republicans, the Democrats had piled lies upon lies in a desperate attempt to preserve their party's ascendancy. [37]

Although the Democrats were the immediate targets, Americans' attacks on the popular sovereignty swindle amounted to a rejection of the compromises on slavery necessary to maintain national parties. Janus-faced campaigns, in which the parties appeared as proslavery in the South and antislavery in the North, had been routine since the mid-1840s. The Whigs had used this very strategy to elect Zachary Taylor, and the existence of the national Democratic party depended on preserving the mostly unspoken agreement to disagree over the precise meaning of popular sovereignty. By denying the legitimacy of ambiguity, Americans hoped to hector southern Democrats into taking an unequivocal, unyielding stand on popular sovereignty that would rupture the national Democracy.

Democrats did not, yet, rise to the bait—a party showdown over territorial policy was still four years away. But the Georgia party was sensitive about the charge that the only thing truly national about the principle of popular sovereignty was that Democrats everywhere supported the doctrine as they understood it. Some party editors overcame the difficulty by lying about the opinions of northern Democrats and proclaiming that the southern version of popular sovereignty was national party dogma. With skillful effort, even James Buchanan's vague acceptance letter, in which he broadly hinted that he thought territorial legislatures could prohibit slavery before statehood, could be interpreted as a forceful restatement of the southern construction of the Kansas-Nebraska Act.[38]

Other Democrats more forthrightly and realistically discussed the territorial controversy. Alexander Stephens, who privately believed that the Supreme Court would uphold the constitutionality of the Wilmot Proviso, tried to move beyond abstract debate over Congress's constitutional power over slavery in the territories. In a January 1856 quarrel with American Congressman Felix Zollicoffer of Tennessee, Stephens refused to state flatly that congressional prohibition of slavery was unconstitutional, observing only that "it would be unjust and a great wrong for Congress to exercise any such power." He further maintained that territorial settlers had no "rightful power to exclude slavery so long as they remained in a territorial condition." Having said that, however, Stephens announced that he was willing to countenance squatter sovereignty, willing to let territorial residents make decisions on slavery during the territorial stage. Given the balance of power in Congress and in the country, he believed that the practical options in territorial policy had been narrowed down to two: the intolerable Republican program of congressional exclusion of slavery and the merely unpalatable solution of squatter sovereignty. He preferred to allow territorial residents to settle slavery questions in their own way rather than to create agitation that might aid the Republican cause.[39]

Many Democrats considered quibbling over different interpretations of popular sovereignty a futile exercise. "If the majority of the people of a Territory have the right to fix the character of their domestic institutions," the *Milledgeville Federal Union* asked, "what *practical difference* will it make either to the North or to the South whether the will of the majority is expressed through a Territorial Legislature or a [state constitutional] Convention; will not the results in both cases be the same?" Union Democrat and former congressman Junius Hillyer considered it "a waste of time for us to be splitting hairs, and drawing legal distinctions, for slavery will exist in Kansas just as the legislature of the territory may be in favor of it or opposed to it." To exist anywhere, the *Athens Southern Banner* declared, the institution of slavery needed "laws to protect it." If the people of a territory opposed slavery, their legislature could easily exclude it by refusing to enact the necessary laws to protect slave property.[40]

Northern Democrats, whatever their failings, had at least provided Southerners with a chance to plant slavery in Kansas. "If the Kansas bill contain[s] squatter sovereignty," the *Augusta Constitutionalist* observed, "a pro-slavery Legislature and pro-slavery laws are its legitimate fruits. The South has no reason to complain of the product." Southerners need only stand behind the national Democratic party and elect James Buchanan to take advantage of the "probability that Kansas will become permanently a slaveholding country, and be admitted as a slaveholding State into the Union."[41]

Democrats thus made a crucial distinction between what southern rights were and what rights it was practicable to demand. Most Democrats believed—for varying reasons—that all American territory was slave territory and that no power on earth could rightfully exclude slavery until a territory applied for statehood. Over the years, Alexander Stephens, Robert Toombs, and many others had even asserted the theoretical right of positive congressional protection for slavery in the territories. But they had always recognized that Northerners would never sanction a congressional slave code for the territories and that insisting on one would destroy all national party alliances. Democrats knew that they would be stuck with the ambiguity of popular sovereignty for as long as they valued maintaining the national Democracy.[42]

Democrats contrasted their situation with that of the American party, which was "weak alike in numbers and policy" and had "nothing to propose for the peace of the country" or "the settlement of this vexed question of slavery." The perpetuation of party divisions among Southerners, Democrats stressed, only aided the Republicans and the American party's abolitionist allies in the North. Millard Fillmore was a hopeless cause; he could not carry a single northern state. His few northern supporters were, in any case, but a step away from being "Black Republicans."[43]

Americans were, in fact, critics without solutions, moderate men who lacked the means to practice moderation. Of sincere grievances they had plenty: the Kansas–Nebraska Act had brought territorial warfare rather than sectional peace, and the rise of the Republican party posed the greatest threat yet to southern safety. Americans were entitled to complain about these disasters, which had happened on the Democratic watch, but their efforts to crucify northern Democrats and destroy the national Democratic party offered not the slightest realistic hope of remedying existing evils. Driven by their anti-Democratic convictions, the proslavery imperatives of Georgia politics, and their isolated position as a state party, Americans tried to conquer the prosouthern high ground by demanding a nationwide recognition of southern rights in the territories as Southerners interpreted them. Georgia Americans did not factor northern political realities into their equations because they had no northern allies. They were free to make demands that neither they nor Georgia Democrats could possibly obtain. While they tirelessly admonished others to cease agitating over slavery, Americans' immediate program for resolving sectional difficulties amounted to harping on slavery issues to undermine southern confidence in the national Democracy.

The extravagant rhetoric employed on behalf of Millard Fillmore equated Democrats and Republicans. The Frémont and Buchanan forces were all "rabid spoilsmen" and "deadly foes to the Union" who were "blinded with insane fury." A Fillmore victory was "the only possible means of enabling Southern institutions to flourish in Kansas. The success of BUCHANAN and Squatter Sovereignty are as fatal to the South as FREMONT and Black Republicanism." The northern Democracy had already "*abolitionized itself*" in trying to conquer the Republicans, and the South could expect nothing from Democratic "victories but chains and degradation."[44]

Democrats were, paradoxically, also too southern and sectional for Americans' taste. The contest between Buchanan and Frémont, the figureheads of fanatical factions in the South and the North, was "dangerous in all its tendencies, and is obliged to result, at least, in permanent sectional estrangement." Fillmore was the true national candidate in the race, a man who viewed "sectionalism as the stepping-stone to disunion" and flung "it from him as he would dishonor." Despite all evidence to the contrary, Americans insisted throughout the canvass that Fillmore and Frémont were the only viable candidates, and that a groundswell of conservative northern support—coming, oddly enough, from defecting Democrats—would carry Fillmore to victory.[45]

Charles J. Jenkins was one of many old Whig leaders who announced their support for Buchanan and derided the American party's empty promises. Alexander C. Walker, a planter, devoted Whig, and longtime state legislator from Richmond County, concluded that Fillmore had not a "ghost of a chance of election"; there were but two parties in the field, "the Black Republicans against us, the Democrats for us." "Is it to be supposed that I am such a fanatic fool," Walker asked, "as to give up my rights, and my negroes, because none but Democrats will defend them for me?" Iverson L. Harris, John Berrien's former political lieutenant in Milledgeville, gratefully accepted a spot on the Buchanan electoral ticket as a compliment to old Whigs. Fillmore's northern friends were "hollow men" in Harris's judgment; there was no difference between Fillmore and Frémont on slavery. Respected lawyer, former congressman, and leading Know-Nothing Eugenius A. Nisbet took it as a "fact that the American Party is without nationality," "without power to control the State of the North," and "in a minority in all the Southern States." To avert a Republican victory, which Nisbet predicted would spark civil war, Southerners had to place their faith in James Buchanan.[46]

Both parties campaigned as Unionists, but disunion loomed like a thunderstorm on the horizon. Although Democrats remained confident that Buchanan would carry enough northern states to stave off disaster, many party leaders declared that Frémont's election would rend the Union. The antislavery furor in the North had destroyed nearly all fraternity between sections, John B. Lamar lamented. If the Republicans captured the government, "the condition of the Southern States in the Union would be like that of Ireland toward Great Britain—a conquered province." Regardless of the immediate outcome, James Gardner believed "the virus of Abolition fanaticism" to be so pervasive in the North that disunion was "ultimately inevitable." "Sentinel" likewise warned that the coming generation of northern politicians and voters, who had "sucked in Abolition opinions with their mother's milk," would never rest until they had destroyed slavery or driven the South out of the Union.[47]

Americans denounced disunionism while sharing many of these forebodings. The "reckless BUCHANAN demagogues," Americans alleged, were determined to ruin the nation if they could not rule it. Democratic leaders had already hatched plans for hasty secession in the event of a Republican triumph—another good reason to vote for Fillmore and the Union. But even as they tried to tar Democrats with a disunionist brush, Americans acknowledged that the "rabid hordes of incendiaries" in the North might soon compel the South to secede. If Frémont were elected under his "sixteen-starred banner, utterly ignoring the rights of half of the country," the South would flee the Union. In an ultimatum that perfectly reflected the militantly pro-southern Unionism of the American party, the *Savannah Republican* proclaimed: "This slavery agitation *must* cease. The South has borne it as long as she will. No future discriminations must be made against her on account of that institution. . . . She came with it, as an equal, into the great family of republican States. She will remain in it *only as an equal.*"[48]

James Buchanan won 57.1 percent of the vote and carried 89 of the 118 counties (the subdivision of older counties had created 25 new ones since 1849). Buchanan's impressive majorities, even in the traditionally Whiggish black belt, proved that most voters believed the message that the national Democracy alone remained to protect the South, slavery, and the Union. The American party, though, retained scattered strongholds, and some 40 percent of the electorate was and would remain staunchly anti-Democratic.

The national results demonstrate the dramatic sectionalization of politics that had occurred in the wake of the Kansas-Nebraska Act. Buchanan carried all of the slave states except Maryland—Fillmore won his only electoral votes there—and five free states; Frémont took the rest. Fillmore attracted a paltry 14 percent of the vote in the North, but he received more than 40 percent of the vote in ten southern states. Although southern Democrats and Americans alike sighed in relief over Frémont's narrow defeat, they realized that the Republican party had been scotched, but not killed.[49]

On Democrats fell the responsibility of making James Buchanan's victory a meaningful step toward sectional peace. Although the distinction had sometimes become blurred, the Georgia Democratic party had not promised to make Kansas a slave state, only to ensure that Kansans would have a fair chance to choose slavery. Northern Democrats had campaigned on assurances that popular sovereignty would make Kansas free, and Georgia Democrats professed some willingness to acquiesce in that outcome to "relieve" Buchanan "from the Kansas difficulty." But they intended to insist that Buchanan unstintingly support the Lecompton government and give proslavery forces the benefit of every doubt. Only if Buchanan satisfied these conditions would Georgia Democrats assent to the admission of a free Kansas. Such standards of "fairness," in fact, practically required a proslavery triumph in Kansas and drove Georgians inexorably toward conflict with the Buchanan administration and northern Democrats.[50]

James Buchanan assembled a Unionist cabinet that included the decrepit Lewis Cass as a figurehead secretary of state and Howell Cobb as secretary of the treasury. Cobb's vindication, along with the immediate rise of Stephens and Toombs to Democratic party leadership, vexed Charles McDonald, Herschel Johnson, and a host of other old Southern Rights leaders. Cobb, moreover, was widely and rightly understood to have presidential ambitions, and he used his position as Buchanan's most influential cabinet adviser to promote the interests of himself and his allies. Before the president had even begun to deal with the troubles in Kansas, long-standing animosities predisposed Southern Rights Democrats to expect that Buchanan and his Unionists would betray southern rights.

The Supreme Court's decision in the *Dred Scott* case stiffened—if possible—Georgians' determination to see their version of justice done in Kansas. Chief Justice Roger B. Taney's rabidly proslavery opinion, composed with a singular disregard for historical facts and legal precedents, wrote Calhounite dogma into constitutional law. Taney denied that persons of African descent—free or slave—could be citizens of the United States and declared the Missouri Compromise restriction on slavery unconstitutional. In the process of asserting that Congress lacked the power to prohibit slavery in the territories, Taney implied that territorial legislatures, mere creatures of Congress, were also powerless to act against slavery. Thus, in one stroke Taney undercut both the Republican platform of congressional exclusion of slavery and the northern Democratic interpretation of popular sovereignty. The Supreme Court, the *Macon Georgia Telegraph* exulted, had confirmed "as law and right all [Southerners] have contended for, and outlaws every doctrinal position of the North upon these sectional questions." Under the succinct heading "The Dred Scott Case—The Nationality of Slavery," James Gardner observed that the South occupied a "vantage-ground upon the subject of slavery, since this decision was rendered, which it never had before."[51]

Through such lenses did Georgians view the penultimate phase of the Kansas struggle. Thousands of settlers poured into Kansas during 1857, continually augmenting the free-state majority. Panicky Lecompton legislators met in mid-February and adopted a constitutional convention bill that provided for early registration of voters to bar many free-state newcomers from participating in the June election for convention delegates. The legislature kept the election process in proslavery hands and omitted any plan for popular ratification of the constitution—minority rule was the last hope for making Kansas a slave state.

To straighten out this mess, James Buchanan appointed Robert J. Walker, a volatile northern-born Mississippian who had been Polk's secretary of the treasury, as the new territorial governor. Buchanan's and Walker's plan was simple: persuade free-staters to take control of Kansas by participating in the convention elections. As a backup in case that strategy failed, Buchanan and Walker agreed that the finished constitution would have to be submitted to a popular vote. Walker, in his inaugural address on 27 May, assured free-state voters that the upcoming elections would be fairly conducted, urged them to cast ballots, and warned Lecompton officials that Congress would reject any constitution not ratified by the people. He also imprudently opined that natural laws of climate and soil had destined Kansas for freedom. The free-state forces, totaling perhaps seventeen thousand potential voters, ignored Walker's advice and boycotted the election. Fewer than two thousand voters elected sixty delegates to draft a proslavery constitution in defiance of the free-state majority; popular sovereignty in Kansas was a sham.[52]

Walker failed to thwart proslavery Kansans yet succeeded in alienating large portions of the southern Democracy. "*We are betrayed,*" exclaimed Thomas W. Thomas on reading Walker's inaugural address. Buchanan had "turned traitor" and had encouraged Walker to ally "himself in thought, feeling, and hope with our enemies." James Gardner believed that Walker's intervention irreparably violated the principles of the Kansas-Nebraska Act by preventing territorial residents from making their own decisions on slavery in their own way. Southern Democrats, to salvage even a semblance of southern rights, had to oppose democracy in Kansas; they had to resist "at all hazards and to the last extremity" Walker's demand for a popular vote on the constitution, a vote that would "make Kansas a free State." [53]

Not all Democrats were enraged by Walker's conduct. Some editors dismissed the idea that Walker's remarks could decide the Kansas outcome, defended the propriety of popular ratification, and cautioned against blaming the president for his subordinate's indiscretions. Howell Cobb, nettled by the criticism, privately informed Alexander Stephens that Buchanan and his cabinet had indeed approved the idea of popular submission—not, Cobb stressed, because Buchanan and the cabinet favored the free-staters, but because they "believed that without such submission we could not justify and carry through the admission [of Kansas]." Democrats at home should keep quiet, Cobb advised, and not foolishly injure him, Buchanan, and the southern cause in Kansas. [54]

The June Democratic state convention denounced Walker and recommended his removal, yet stopped short of implicating Buchanan in Walker's treachery. The convention also rejected all attempts to commit the party to a specific future course on Kansas. Such hedging indicated how fearful Democrats were of the Kansas issue. Pro-Buchanan Unionists, headed by Howell Cobb, viewed the resolution condemning Walker as a needless, damaging stab at the administration. Alexander and Linton Stephens, Robert Toombs, and others, however, believed that Buchanan and Walker had to be made to respect the principle of nonintervention. Everyone knew that the dispute involved much more than the welfare of the Democratic party. If Congress refused to admit Kansas as a slave state on the grounds that its constitution had not been popularly ratified, the hallowed Georgia Platform pointed toward the appropriate response: secession. [55]

The fight for the gubernatorial nomination exposed further, more longstanding, divisions. Unionist John H. Lumpkin, the chief of the Cherokee Democracy, faced off against Southern Rights aspirants James Gardner and Henry G. Lamar. Support for the candidates was unprecedentedly geographical in character; north Georgians solidly favored Lumpkin, and the black belt counties split between Gardner and Lamar. The two-thirds rule and firm commitments to the various candidates produced a deadlock. After twenty fruitless ballots, William Hope Hull, one of Howell Cobb's Athens friends, suggested the formation of a special committee to break the impasse. The committee, goaded by Linton Stephens, chose Joseph E. Brown, a Southern Rights veteran from Cherokee Georgia, as a compromise candidate; the convention nominated him unanimously.

The eldest son of a yeoman family, Brown was born in 1821 in South Carolina and raised in the mountains near Dahlonega. After a childhood of doing farm chores, fidgeting in country schools, and absorbing Baptist sermons, Brown attended various academies and then taught school himself. He passed the bar in 1845 and briefly studied at Yale law school, but left before graduation. On returning to Georgia, he opened a law practice and in 1847 married Elizabeth Grisham, the pious daughter of a Baptist minister and substantial landowner. Brown had a knack for business; by the 1850s he owned extensive tracts in north Georgia, mining interests, and several slaves. While serving in the state senate in 1849–50, Brown took a strong Southern Rights stand and earned a spot as an elector for Franklin Pierce on the Southern Rights ticket—Brown even named a son after the president. As judge of the Blue Ridge circuit beginning in 1855, Brown impressed observers with his common sense and his rigid—some thought fanatical— insistence on proper courtroom decorum. Brown's nomination for governor surprised him as much as anyone: he received the news at the end of a long day of harvesting wheat. His politically useful image as a man of the soil would, indeed, endure long after the reality faded. Ever calculating, Brown was serious about life in general and three things in particular: his religion, his money, and his political advancement.[56]

Benjamin Harvey Hill, the best man the Americans had and perhaps the best stump speaker in Georgia, received his party's unanimous gubernatorial nomination. Born to a Jasper County slaveholding family, Hill was a graduate of Franklin College and an accomplished lawyer who lived in LaGrange, in Troup County. Just thirty-four years old in 1857, Hill had entered politics in 1850 as a Unionist and had quickly risen to the head of the state opposition. Hill's slashing wit and dashing demeanor had so vexed Alexander Stephens in their 1856 debates that Stephens had demanded a duel to avenge his honor. In contemptuously dismissing the challenge, Hill had explained his moral and religious opposition to dueling and raised the practical objection that killing Stephens would prove "a great annoyance to me ever afterward."[57]

Hill and other American campaigners insisted that the Democrats were unfit to govern either Kansas or Georgia. The South, the *Macon Georgia Journal and Messenger* charged, has "more to dread from democratic presses and leaders" than from all the "free-soil and abolition hordes" in the North. If Georgians chose to endorse Walker by electing Brown governor, they should "prepare themselves for submission to any and every outrage free-soilism in the name of democracy may inflict upon them." "Shall the election of Judge Brown be considered as an endorsement of Buchanan and his man Walker?" the *Milledgeville Southern Recorder* asked. Or would a victory for Hill "speak in thunder tones the indignation of the people of Georgia for the violation of the Kansas Act, as understood and maintained by them?" [58]

The strongest arguments Americans had were that they were not Democrats, they were not responsible for Walker, and they were not to blame for the "disturbed condition of the country." [59] One editor concisely summarized the familiar American indictment of the national Democracy:

> Re-opening heedlessly and needlessly the exciting issues that were finally disposed of by the great adjustment measures of 1850, this mixed and mongrel party has again brought the Republic to the brink of disruption and overthrow. By reckless and lavish expenditure of the public money, and the public domain, it has corrupted legislation, debauched and cheated the South; and now, in the plethora of its insolent arrogance, it again calls upon Southern Americans and freemen to sign the bill of their sale and degradation, and to fly to the democratic ark—filled as it is, with all manner of creeping things, reeking in corruption—as their only safety. [60]

Democratic arguments were likewise familiar and still unmatched in popular appeal. James Buchanan would fire Walker soon, Democrats predicted, and uphold southern rights in Kansas. American humbug about squatter sovereignty notwithstanding, Kansas already had a proslavery government, and the South's friends were poised to draft a slave-state constitution. The Republicans would not admit a slave Kansas; the impotent Americans could not; only the national Democracy had the power and the will to add another slave-state star to the broad blue field. [61]

Joseph Brown fared better than Herschel Johnson had in 1855, worse than Buchanan had in 1856, and well enough to win by nearly 11,000 votes and carry 55.2 percent of the ballots. Hill gained some 3,500 votes over Millard Fillmore's showing in the black belt and upcountry regions and managed to recapture the black belt with 50.9 percent of that region's vote. The core of

American party support remained, but the Democrats still carried nearly three quarters of the state's counties. As they had in 1855, the Democrats won six of the eight congressional races, and they increased their majorities to better than two-thirds in both branches of the legislature. Alexander Stephens's reelection race was his closest ever, almost solely because he ran as a Democrat. In a November sequel, Robert Toombs overcame token opposition from Charles McDonald and easily won another Senate term.[62]

As the public campaign moved from start to finish, Howell Cobb worked privately to try to reconcile Georgia leaders to probable defeat in Kansas. Cobb, Buchanan, and nearly every northern Democrat considered a popular vote and a fair verdict on the Kansas constitution—in short, an ultimate free-state outcome—indispensable to preserving the party in the free states. If the Lecompton convention resisted pressure and refused to submit its work to the voters, Cobb confessed to Alexander Stephens, the administration would be left without a program and the country would be plunged into the "most dangerous crisis" yet.[63]

The Lecompton convention worked sporadically from September through early November to draft a slave-state constitution. The delegates, after much deliberation, submitted the slavery section alone to a popular vote, offering Kansans a misleading choice between the Lecompton constitution with slavery or without slavery. Neither option, in reality, promised to exclude slavery from Kansas. A December vote, controlled by proslavery officials and boycotted by free-state men, ratified the constitution with slavery. A comparison of the December results with those of the October territorial election, in which free-staters had participated, conclusively demonstrated that a free-state majority existed in Kansas.

Panicky northern Democrats implored James Buchanan to repudiate the Kansas swindle, but the president instead convinced himself that the bogus referendum satisfied his demand for popular ratification and reluctantly embraced the Lecompton constitution. In return for sacrificing the feelings and political interests of northern Democrats, Buchanan won only contingent support from Southerners, whose continuing goodwill depended on the admission of Kansas. Seldom had a president made a worse bargain. When Congress convened in December, Stephen Douglas denounced the Lecompton constitution as a base fraud and led a determined group of northern Democrats in a desperate fight for political survival. Although the

Democrats had rebounded in the North in 1856 and 1857 and controlled both branches of Congress, the party schism made the defeat of the Lecompton constitution exceedingly likely.

Georgia Democrats agreed on the principle involved in the controversy. A November state Democratic convention unanimously declared that if a state applied for admission "with a constitution republican in form," Congress was obligated to welcome it into the Union. Any congressional inquiries into the "*matter* or the *manner*" of a constitution's adoption were "unconstitutional and dangerous to the rights of the States."[64]

Left unanswered in these resolutions was the question of what Kansas was worth. Thomas R. R. Cobb stated the problem precisely: "Now if Lecompton came untainted by any suspicion that it does not speak the will of the majority, and was rejected purely because of its Slavery clause, the people of the South would be a unit; but the undoubted fact, that notwithstanding its perfect regularity, it is *not* the *will* of a majority, gives the coloring of excuse to its opponents." Georgia voters were not prepared to "make war upon an abstraction," and hollow threats of secession would not alter the reality that Kansas was destined to be a free state. Peterson Thweatt, a state official and observer of politics, likewise assumed that Kansas was "*really* a free state" and doubted whether "*much fire* can be *raised up* in Georgia upon this subject." Neither politicians nor voters were willing, after all, to base a revolution on such a dubious cause.[65]

The Democrats still fought tenaciously for what they now admitted would be a hollow victory. Howell Cobb damned Stephen Douglas and joined the rest of the Buchanan administration in a clumsy campaign designed to suppress northern Democratic dissent. Alexander Stephens, who attributed the Lecompton mess mainly to Buchanan's bungling rather than to Douglas's apostasy, employed sophistry and parliamentary skill in trying to drive the constitution through the House of Representatives. The backbiting and blame casting that the struggle occasioned made Cherokee Democrat John W. H. Underwood fear that the state party would "be split to atoms." And Richard Arnold rightly observed that the Lecompton debacle dealt "a severe, if not fatal blow," to the integrity of the national Democracy.[66]

Americans half desired a humiliating Democratic defeat, yet they refused to repudiate the Lecompton constitution, as upper South oppositionists such as Senators John Bell of Tennessee and John Crittenden of Kentucky did. American Congressmen Robert Trippe and Joshua Hill argued that Kansas's admission under the Lecompton constitution would quiet agitation and that Kansas would become a free state in any event—precisely James Buchanan's thinking. On Lecompton as on other issues, Americans occupied prosouthern ground while remaining poised to launch a Unionist crusade if Democrats overreacted to congressional rejection of Kansas.

Four years of agitation ended with a curious compromise in which Congress tried to pretend that the Lecompton struggle had nothing to do with slavery. The deadlock between a pro-Lecompton Senate and an anti-Lecompton House was finally broken by the adoption of the so-called English bill, a face-saving measure that sent the constitution back to Kansas for ratification. Kansans were not asked to decide the status of slavery, but instead whether they would accept a smaller public land grant than the one claimed under the Lecompton constitution. The overwhelming rejection of the constitution by territorial voters finished the business—Kansas would not enter the Union until after Georgia had left it.[67]

Depending on which Democratic press one read, the English bill settlement was either "an insult to the intelligence of the Southern people," a "humiliating abandonment" of southern rights, an "insidious and intentional swindle," or "a triumph of the administration and the South." The most perceptive, if partisan, postmortem on Kansas came from an American party editor, who alleged that Georgia politicians had always realized that Kansas would become a free state. The unnecessary and "angry contest" over Kansas had raised up a northern Republican party, "placed the government in great peril," and "weakened the bonds of the Union more than any question that has ever been presented." The editor drew a moral: "Slavery agitation must stop or our government cannot stand."[68]

# EIGHT

# *A White Men's Revolution*

Near the end of December 1860, President-elect Abraham Lincoln assured his old Whig compatriot, Alexander Stephens, that Southerners need have no "fears that a Republican administration would, *directly*, or *indirectly*, interfere with" slavery in the existing slave states. "I suppose, however," Lincoln continued, "this does not meet the case. You think slavery is *right* and ought to be extended; while we think it is *wrong* and ought to be restricted. That I suppose is the rub. It certainly is the only substantial difference between us." "We at the South do think African slavery, as it exists with us, both morally and politically right," Stephens replied. "This opinion is founded upon the inferiority of the black race. You, however, and perhaps a majority of the North, think it wrong." Instead of tolerating southern opinions and respecting southern rights, Stephens complained, "the leading [Republican] object seems to be simply, and wantonly, if you please, to put the institutions of nearly half the States under the ban of public opinion and national condemnation."[1]

Shortly after Lincoln and Stephens exchanged notes, the perceived Republican threat to slavery drove Georgia out of the Union. Secession, which few had ever desired and most had desperately sought to avoid, sacrificed the Union to save an institution that made masters of all white men. Augustus Baldwin Longstreet had long ago explained the governing logic. "Slavery is the main thing, but it is not every thing," Longstreet wrote. "If we must give up that, or every thing else, why let every thing else go; but if we can secure that and many things that we desire besides, why all the better for us." White men who could no longer have "many things" acted in 1861 to preserve the "main thing."[2]

The first battle of Governor Joseph Brown's administration, though, involved banks rather than slavery. Prosperity, with its feverish railroad construction, expanding cotton production, and rising land and slave values, had led the Georgia legislature to charter thirty-three new banks between 1850 and 1857; nineteen were created in 1856 alone. Many of these new institutions operated out of Savannah and other principal cities, but most were country banks, located in growing places like Albany, Griffin, Dalton, and Rome. Men everywhere seemed starved for capital, credit, and paper money, and Democratic legislators shook off any lingering inhibitions and bounteously fed the public hunger.

The panic of 1857 rekindled the people's smoldering hostility toward banks. Georgia banks, following northern institutions, suspended specie payments shortly before the legislative session opened in November, once again putting their charters at risk by violating state laws. The legislature responded as it had in the 1840 crisis and passed a bill that effectively legalized the bank suspension. Governor Brown, however, returned the bill along with a veto message that echoed vintage Jacksonian warnings about rapacious, monopolistic banks that devoured the substance of the common people. Many legislators wavered, but the pleadings of Senator John E. Ward, national Democrat and spokesman for the Savannah banking interests, helped persuade the house and senate to override Brown's veto. American-Opposition legislators strongly, though not unanimously, supported legalizing the bank suspension. Democrats were divided: nearly half supported the original bank bill, and more than half voted to override the veto. Mass abstentions on the part of fearful or irresolute members influenced the outcome of both votes.[3]

The clash between a Democratic governor and a Democratic legislature reflected an underlying public ambivalence evident since the 1830s: Georgians wanted booms without busts, credit without risk, and public punishment of banks without public pain. Several Democratic newspapers, most of them located in north Georgia or in smaller towns, applauded Joseph Brown's stand and argued that only the gradual abolition of banks and paper currency would permanently break the cycle of panics. At a typical pro-Brown meeting in Macon, prominent citizens of both parties denounced banks as faithless monsters that turned broken promises into profits at the expense of honest note holders, and they called on the next session of the legislature to repeal the act legalizing bank suspensions. Experience had proven, the Macon gathering concluded, that "nothing but gold and silver can furnish" a sound currency, and that substituting "Linen Rags" for hard money "must result as it ever has resulted in a cheat and swindle of the people." Other newspapers and other meetings, however, condemned such sentiments, excused the bank suspension, and blessed the legislature's action. Those who defended the banks, like those who upheld Joseph Brown, came from both parties and all regions. The Democratic *Albany Patriot* acknowledged the evils associated with banks, but nonetheless proclaimed that "the money affairs of the people are so interwoven and complicated with the banks" that any effort to destroy banks would destroy the economy—a conclusion reached in every banking crisis in antebellum Georgia.[4]

Like a passing comet, Brown's bank war flared briefly and stirred excitement, but it left the political universe unchanged—banks resumed specie payments in May 1858. Only in rare instances had state issues figured largely in Georgia politics; never in three decades had they provided the basis for party divisions. The same Monroe County citizens who declared the banking system "dangerous to the rights and liberties of the people" also carefully explained that "it is neither our wish or intention to connect this matter with the political principles of either of the dividing parties of our State." The *Macon Georgia Telegraph* favored abolishing banks, but it did not "wish to see a party organized on that point" or to see the state's economy damaged by "mere party strifes." The parties would live or die by national questions; most white men wanted it that way.[5]

The struggle that transfixed Georgia's Democratic leadership during 1858 took place far to the north. While Stephen Douglas confronted Abraham Lincoln on the stump in Illinois, Howell Cobb masterminded the Buchanan administration's drive to destroy the Little Giant. Buchanan, Cobb, and most southern Democrats believed that allowing Douglas to escape unscathed after his crusade against the Lecompton constitution would demoralize sound northern Democrats, undermine party discipline, and possibly destroy the national Democracy's ability and willingness to protect the South.

Ostracizing Douglas would also, not coincidentally, further Howell Cobb's long-shot bid for the 1860 presidential nomination, a quest destined to splinter the Georgia Democracy. As John H. Lumpkin, John E. Ward, and other faithful Cobbites labored through 1859 to consolidate home-state support for their favorite, they became ever more jealous and suspicious of Alexander Stephens, whom they feared both as an open rival and as a potential stalking-horse for Stephen Douglas. Stephens's incidental endorsement of Douglas in the Illinois senatorial race, made during a trip to Chicago to have portraits painted, drew howls of protest from southern Democrats and fueled rumors that Stephens and Douglas had a secret understanding about the presidential contest.

After months of anxious correspondence and conversation, the June 1859 Democratic state convention passed off relatively harmoniously. Assiduous efforts by Howell Cobb's forces produced a much desired, if distressingly vague, resolution expressing confidence in the Buchanan administration, and the delegates enthusiastically nominated Joseph Brown for a second term. Avoiding all discussion of the Douglas imbroglio, Democrats took advantage of Brown's popularity and centered their campaign on the bank-bashing Baptist yeoman who doubled as an astute manager of the lucrative Western & Atlantic Railroad.[6]

Not that Democrats needed much of a campaign. The American party, short of willing candidates and convinced that Brown was unbeatable, initially contemplated conceding the election. The party disbanded in early June, then reorganized as the Opposition party in a July convention held in Macon. Finally, at an August meeting in Atlanta, the party thrust the gubernatorial burden on Warren Akin, a little-known old Whig lawyer from Cass County. Akin's poor health prevented him from conducting an active canvass in a hopeless cause.[7]

Oppositionists desperate for an issue officially embraced the controversial idea of congressional protection for slavery in the territories. The resolutions of the Macon convention asserted that the right to hold slaves as property existed "independently of the Constitution," and that Congress could not "legislate on the subject of slavery, *except for its protection.*" During the campaign, Benjamin Harvey Hill and other Oppositionists continually goaded Democrats to "get off double-meaning Kansas bills and all treacherous party platforms, and step on the *law.*" Oppositionists wanted southern Democrats to disavow squatter sovereignty, repudiate Stephen Douglas, insist on a strict enforcement of the *Dred Scott* decision, and demand all necessary congressional protection for territorial slavery—in other words, sacrifice the national Democratic party on the altar of southern rights.[8]

The decline of Georgia anti-Democratic forces contrasted sharply with the resilience of their counterparts in upper South states such as Tennessee, Virginia, and North Carolina, where Whiggish Unionists still competed effectively with the Democracy. The greater salience of slavery issues in Georgia, a Deep South cotton state in which more than four out of every ten people were slaves, prevented Oppositionists from rallying around state concerns or from issuing moderate appeals to attract conservative support, as upper South anti-Democrats did. The Georgia Democracy skillfully occupied both the prosouthern and Unionist grounds, and the collapse of the American party all but forced Georgia Oppositionists into a proslavery shouting match that they simply could not win. The lack of northern allies freed Oppositionists to speak their minds on southern rights in the territories, but resolutions were no substitute for political power.[9]

Brown slaughtered Akin, amassing 63,806 votes (60.3 percent) and carrying every region. Akin ran markedly worse than Benjamin Harvey Hill had in 1857, but he nearly matched Millard Fillmore's total in the 1856 presidential contest. The Democrats, however, had added thousands of supporters over the years, as younger voters who came of age during Democratic ascendancy flocked into the party. Dramatic population growth in north Georgia and the erosion of old Whig black belt strength had made continuing Democratic triumphs inevitable—if the party held together.

Democrats dissatisfied with the status quo posed the only real threat to state party supremacy. In a July 1859 speech in Griffin, Senator Alfred Iverson outlined the course that events would follow in the months ahead. Slavery united all white men, from the wealthy planter to the laborer who had only the "dignity of his color and race," Iverson intoned. *"Slavery must be maintained—in the Union, if possible—out of it if necessary—peaceably if we may—forcibly if we must."* Congress had a duty to "pass laws for the protection and regulation of slavery, wherever it exists or may exist upon the common soil." That demands for such protection would destroy the national Democracy, or at least Stephen Douglas, Iverson thought probable, and he did not care. Iverson, Jefferson Davis of Mississippi, William Lowndes Yancey of Alabama, and other prominent southern Democrats planned to build a platform that Douglas could never stand on, slay the Little Giant, and bring the northern wing of the party to heel.[10]

John Brown's October 1859 raid on Harper's Ferry strengthened the hand of the hotspurs. Brown's bungled attempt to incite a general slave insurrection horrified and terrified white Southerners. Rumors of revolts persisted throughout 1860, long after Brown had swung from the gallows, as panicky whites uncovered plots—a few perhaps real, most imaginary—and retaliated brutally against supposed conspirators. Scattered but significant northern expressions of sympathy for Brown deepened the shock. Brown's treason seemed part of a Republican malignancy destined to devour slavery unless the South separated from the diseased Union. White Southerners never again looked at slaves or the North in quite the same way after John Brown's excursion.[11]

By late 1859, all the combustible elements were in place to produce a grand Democratic explosion over the presidential question. Democratic legislators, moved by months of covert campaigning by Howell Cobb's lieutenants, disregarded the party executive committee's plans for a March convention and hastily called an 8 December 1859 meeting to appoint delegates to the Charleston national convention. The December gathering resolved to "yield nothing" on southern "rights *for the sake of harmony*"; appointed a pro-Cobb slate of national convention delegates who were instructed to oppose all candidates—especially Stephen Douglas—who failed to proclaim their "firm, strict and *unqualified*" adherence to the *Dred Scott* decision; and recommended that Howell Cobb be the nominee of the national Democracy.[12]

Although the December convention followed precedent (November-December conventions of legislators had usually chosen national convention delegates), Cobb's assorted enemies immediately challenged its actions. Many of Cobb's old Southern Rights foes instantly wheeled into action to overturn the December nomination. The Democratic state executive committee, including David C. Campbell, a former editor of the *Milledgeville Federal Union* who had despised Cobb for years, forged ahead with plans for the March convention. Alexander Stephens's prospective candidacy served as a rallying point for recently converted black belt Democrats of Whiggish antecedents—"new lights"—who still resented Cobb's 1852 flight from the Union party. Stephens's quiet, ineffectual protestations that he was not a candidate more encouraged than slowed the movement. Even Joseph Brown, whom Cobbites had wooed for months, privately backed the March convention.[13]

Recognizing that the tainted victory already obtained might prove as fatal to his interests as "an out and out defeat," Howell Cobb reluctantly bowed to demands for another convention. Working mainly in north Georgia, always Cobb's primary base of support, John H. Lumpkin, James Spullock, and others urged county politicians to appoint March delegates pledged to sustain the December decision. The struggle for control of the March convention largely replicated past battles for party dominance between north Georgia and black belt Democrats, although the involvement of Alexander Stephens and his friends complicated alignments, and both pro- and anti-Cobb men shared the goal of stopping Stephen Douglas.[14]

The Cobb December convention forces maneuvered adeptly to capture the convention presidency at the 14 March gathering, but then squandered their advantage through delays and indecision. Former Southern Rights men, led by Solomon Cohen of Savannah, formed the core of Cobb's opposition. Joseph Brown also influenced some delegates to abandon Cobb, and Alexander Stephens's friends kept rumors and options alive by withholding a letter—written to be read at the convention—in which Stephens renounced any interest in the presidency. Near midnight, after a day of acrimonious debate, the convention voted 192 to 146 to reorganize the Charleston delegation.

The next morning, the convention doubled the size of the party's national convention contingent by keeping the December appointees and choosing an equal number of additional delegates. The revamped delegation still contained a pro-Cobb majority, which, under the unit rule, could silence dissenters and cast the state's entire vote. Cobb supporters, not satisfied with this half loaf, foolishly pushed for the readoption of the December convention resolutions, including the one naming Cobb for the presidency. What had been an admonition then became an open repudiation. The convention rejected the December resolutions by a 174 to 162 vote and sent the delegation to Charleston uninstructed. Once again, north Georgia Democrats, outvoted by their black belt brethren, felt cheated. Within a week, an exasperated Howell Cobb publicly withdrew his name from presidential consideration.[15]

Accretions during the 1850s had turned the Georgia Democratic party into a conglomerated, contentious mass. Leaders were angry at each other and at northern Democrats, and all felt the pressure of the Republican threat. Odd bedfellows such as Alfred Iverson and Howell Cobb were prepared to wield the weapon of congressional protection for slavery in the territories in the war against Stephen Douglas, but the March rejection of the defiant December resolutions indicated that most Democrats desired some accommodation that would preserve the national Democracy. Robert Toombs, for example, wanted Douglas to be defeated at the Charleston convention, but he did not want northern Democrats to be "crippled or driven off" by new platform tests. A group centered on Alexander Stephens and James Gardner was even willing to accept Douglas as the nominee rather than split the party. A small but growing contingent, however, shared Alfred Iverson's sentiments and had all but given up hope on the national Democratic party and the Union. Heading into the Charleston convention, most Georgia Democrats would have settled for a southern candidate, possibly Alexander Stephens or Senator Robert M. T. Hunter of Virginia, and a reiteration of the 1856 Cincinnati platform, perhaps with a general endorsement of the *Dred Scott* decision added to it. But the situation was fluid, and the momentum of events would quickly carry Georgians, somewhat against their will, into revolt.[16]

Once Democrats convened in Charleston on 23 April, the course of other Southerners largely controlled that of the Georgia delegation. Amidst all the details and complications, one essential fact was well known: the northern pro-Douglas majority was strong enough to write the platform, but not strong enough to nominate Douglas under the two-thirds rule. The convention, against the wishes of the Georgia delegation, chose to fight the platform battle first. Southerners managed to control the platform committee, in which each state had one vote, and offered a platform that endorsed congressional protection for slavery in the territories; most of the divided Georgia delegation backed this demand. Douglasites countered with the 1856 Cincinnati platform, along with additional resolutions leaving the precise powers of Congress and territorial legislatures over slavery open to further judicial interpretation.

After a week of wrangling, the full convention adopted the Douglas platform, whereupon the whole lower South, except Georgia, promptly withdrew from the convention; parts of the Delaware and Arkansas delegations also exited. The Georgia delegation deliberated overnight before narrowly voting to join the bolters. The bulk of the Georgia delegates, led by Henry R. Jackson with his contingent of Cobbites, afterward participated in a separate meeting that laid plans for an 11 June convention in Richmond. A motley group, however, including old Unionist Hiram Warner, editor Henry Cleveland of the *Augusta Constitutionalist,* and Southern Rights veterans Solomon Cohen and James L. Seward, stayed in the regular convention, although a procedural decision prevented them from casting Georgia's vote. With the cotton South gone, Douglasites could not obtain the two-thirds majority of all delegates (including bolters) deemed necessary for a nomination. They finally gave up trying on 3 May, and the weary conventioneers adjourned to meet again on 18 June at Baltimore.[17]

Regardless of their opinions beforehand, most Georgia Democratic leaders defended the Charleston bolt once it had occurred. Backing the bolters became a matter of honor and a test of will; many vowed to master northern Douglasites or quit the party. As Howell Cobb explained in a *Milledgeville Federal Union* editorial, Douglas's candidacy was the main obstacle to party harmony. Northern Democrats had insisted on "not only an unsatisfactory platform but *an unsound candidate.* The *platform and candidate proposed,* must be considered together, for the plain and simple reason, that the platform proposed was satisfactory enough *with the proper construction put upon it.*" To preserve the national party, Northerners would have to abandon Douglas and allow the South to dictate the candidate—the traditional southern Democratic definition of compromise on disputes involving slavery. A Southerner need not be chosen; Cobb was prepared "to take a northern man—any of them will be acceptable after we get clear of Douglas."[18]

Robert Toombs, who opined that the "real difficulty at Charleston" had been that many southern Democrats "had committed themselves so far against Douglas that they were lost if he was nominated, and they therefore preferred ruining the party with themselves than ruining themselves without the party," nonetheless advised against shrinking or turning back. Douglas had to either withdraw or consent to be placed on a platform endorsing congressional protection for territorial slavery. Toombs's blood had been up since early in the year; in January, he had called for disunion in the event of a Republican victory. Hotheaded and touchy on matters that he believed involved principle and the safety of the South, Toombs argued that Douglasites were attempting to roll back southern victories on the territorial question and commit the Democratic party to squatter sovereignty. In a spirit of defiance typical of most Georgia Democratic leaders, Toombs insisted that the time had come for northern and southern Democrats to "understand one another" on slavery questions, even if that understanding destroyed the party.[19]

Here Toombs and Alexander Stephens finally came to a parting of political ways. Stephens considered the southern demand for a platform that recognized the right of congressional protection for slavery in the territories an act of bad faith, an abandonment of a pledge to stand by congressional nonintervention. He and a number of other prominent figures, including Herschel Johnson, Hiram Warner, and Joseph Brown, argued that congressional nonintervention was the settled policy of the South and the national Democracy and that the destruction of the Democratic party meant disunion. The "personal ambition of a few leaders and their individual animosity toward each other" had, according to Joseph Brown, caused the Charleston break, and greater prudence exercised at Baltimore could yet close the rift. Eugenius Nisbet curtly lectured his elders in Democracy on the basics of national party strategy. To "split hairs," to "break down the leaders of the party at the North" by quarreling over abstractions, was to deliver the South into the hands of Republicans. The dispute was over policy as much as principle: both Toombs and Stephens had long contended that the South had a right to congressional protection, yet they differed crucially now over the propriety and expediency of demanding that the national Democracy write that right into its platform.[20]

Irreconcilable views clashed at the 4 June Democratic state convention. The overwhelming majority of delegates, led by Howell Cobb and several of the Charleston bolters, approved the platform of congressional protection and gave the old Charleston contingent—minus a few dissenters—instructions to travel to Baltimore by way of the Richmond convention. Northern Democrats had yielded before, and perhaps would again, but Georgians' intransigence invited a replay of Charleston and a permanent party schism. The majority, at bottom, preferred to split the national Democracy rather than accept Douglas or any Douglasite candidate. Like Robert Toombs, they viewed the national party as not worth saving unless it could be placed firmly under southern control.

After the majority acted, seventy or so self-proclaimed national Democrats—including Hiram Warner, Herschel Johnson, James Gardner, and James L. Seward—organized a separate convention, appointed their own delegation to go directly to Baltimore, and framed a platform that explicitly repudiated all appeals for congressional protection. Most of these men, like Hiram Warner, were Unionist veterans, but Johnson, Gardner, and others had marched near the front of Southern Rights ranks in 1850. The onetime radicals had since grown grayer and perhaps wiser, and they had developed remarkable attachments to the national party. Countless times through the 1850s they had declared that the national Democracy was the only organization that could protect slavery and the Union. They had said it so often that they had convinced themselves of its truth, and they were reluctant to desert the party so long as any hope for honorable reconciliation remained. National Democrats, whatever their personal political antecedents, were willing to support any decent candidate, including Stephen Douglas, capable of uniting the party against the Republicans. The heart of their strength lay in a cluster of counties near Augusta, in and around Alexander Stephens's old congressional district, and in a few scattered north Georgia counties—old Unionist areas from 1850 for the most part.

Neither Georgia delegation, in the end, was seated at Baltimore. The credentials committee recommended splitting the state's vote between the rival delegations, but the rest of the committee report rendered that point irrelevant. When the convention majority decided to seat alternative, national Democratic delegations from Alabama and Louisiana, the mass of southern delegates withdrew to organize a separate convention. Bolters from nineteen states then nominated John C. Breckinridge of Kentucky for president on a congressional protection platform. The remaining, chiefly northern, states in the regular convention nominated Stephen Douglas on the nonintervention platform previously adopted at Charleston. When the original vice presidential nominee, Benjamin Fitzpatrick of Alabama, declined, Herschel Johnson reluctantly accepted the second spot on the Douglas ticket. Subsequent Georgia state conventions formalized the division between Douglas and Breckinridge Democrats; the national and state Democratic parties had split.[21]

The labors of Oppositionists helped to produce "this consummation so devoutly wished"; their prodding contributed to, although it certainly did not cause, Georgia Democrats' break with the national party. The Oppositionists knew from the beginning of the 1860 campaign that a party "composed only of the existing American, Whig or Opposition party of the South, and the anti-Republican Opposition of the North" had no chance for success. They needed new recruits, especially from the national Democracy. The Opposition accordingly goaded southern Democrats on the congressional protection issue throughout early 1860 while simultaneously praying that northern Democrats would cling to Stephen Douglas. The 2 May Opposition state convention, which donned a new mantle as the Constitutional Union party, substantially adopted the rejected congressional protection platform from Charleston. Oppositionists praised the Charleston bolters as men of principle, urged them to stand firm, and issued invitations for a new party alliance. The *Augusta Chronicle & Sentinel,* long the most conservative and the most implacably anti-Democratic paper in Georgia, averred in May that the congressional protection question could not "be dodged or evaded, *and a denial of the right* is worth the government itself"—or at least worth the life of the national Democracy.[22]

Once their fire-eating talk had achieved its purpose at Baltimore, the Oppositionists executed a planned retreat into the national Constitutional Union party, an impromptu coalition based on the premises that politicians had created the sectional controversy and that the proper way to resolve slavery issues was to stop discussing them. A May national convention attended by a Georgia delegation nominated old Whig John Bell of Tennessee for president on a platform that promised nothing more specific than devotion to the Union, the Constitution, and the enforcement of the laws. Although Oppositionists had earlier warned themselves against joining such a "shifting, halting, ambiguous, delphic concern," Constitutional Unionism represented the only marginally viable non-Democratic option: any hopes that Democratic bolters might coalesce with Constitutional Unionists collapsed with Breckinridge's nomination. After years of lecturing Democrats about southern rights, Georgia Opposition leaders embraced an uncommitted candidate on a platitudinous platform; they would soon dismiss the idea of congressional protection for slavery in the territories as a pernicious abstraction. By resuming national party ties, weak as that national party was,

Oppositionists necessarily committed themselves to moderating their sectional appeals—appeals that had not, in any case, improved their political position. Oppositionists were, in their own way, principled and consistent; they adopted the stance that, at a given moment, seemed most likely to undermine the national Democracy, a party they always identified as the main source of the evils afflicting the country.[23]

The North again was the decisive battleground. There the race pitted Abraham Lincoln against Stephen Douglas, although Bell and Breckinridge men in Georgia insisted that their candidates had large free-state followings. Most southern Democrats backed Breckinridge; Douglas attracted a small minority; the various opposition parties adopted the Constitutional Union name and supported Bell. Furious competition to "be the most Southern and the most sectional" continued, but Breckinridge men, Douglasites, and Bell enthusiasts also each vowed that they, and only they, could save the Union. The tension between devotion to southern rights and attachment to the Union, always evident in antebellum Georgia politics, was never more evident than in the 1860 campaign.[24]

Broken faith and blind injustice were the major themes of the Douglasites, who seethed with bitterness over the destruction of the national party. James Gardner, Alexander Stephens, Herschel Johnson, and others blamed southern Democrats for dishonoring the national Democracy's long commitment to congressional nonintervention and for pursuing a senseless vendetta against Stephen Douglas, the one candidate who stood a remote chance of defeating the Republicans. Douglasites believed that Breckinridge Democrats had been plotting for months to produce a Republican victory that would destroy the Union. The congressional protection issue had been trumped up solely to split the Democracy; John Breckinridge was no sounder on slavery than Stephen Douglas or thousands of other northern Democrats. Radicals North and South, Douglasites concluded, had manufactured a crisis that threatened to overturn all the victories of the national Democracy and plunge the country into civil war.[25]

Douglasites knew they had no chance of carrying Georgia; most Democrats had already repudiated Douglas, and the Constitutional Unionists had long loathed the Little Giant. Despair, regrets over valiant efforts wasted and glorious strength dissipated, pervaded the Douglas camp. James Gardner's *Augusta Constitutionalist*, the only substantial Douglas organ, dwelt on the past and spoke with foreboding of the future. Alexander Stephens's defeatism, combined with a nasty fall from his front steps, kept him at home through much of the campaign. Herschel Johnson faced untold abuse as Douglas's running mate; his hanging effigies greeted him on the campaign trail. "Everything it seems to me is tending, or rather rapidly rushing to national disruption and general anarchy," Alexander Stephens wrote. "There is not political virtue enough in the land to save it." Considering themselves sane men in a country gone mad, Douglas Democrats felt surrounded by traitors and overwhelmed by catastrophe.[26]

Constitutional Unionists likewise attributed the crisis to "insane *party spirit, sectional animosity,* reckless *political charlatanry,* and popular ignorance." Democrats, who had spawned the Kansas-Nebraska Act and were responsible for its tragic aftermath, had played politics with slavery and "deceitfully lured" the South and the country down the path "to sectionalism, to hatred, to geographical parties, and possibly to the destruction of our constitutional rights and the overthrow of the Union." Corrupt Breckinridge partisans, interested in stirring up "*artificial excitements,*" refused to tell the people that the slavery question had been "settled *conclusively,* and settled *satisfactorily* to the South, on every foot of soil" belonging to the United States. Instead, they held out the "gilded bait" of congressional protection for slavery in the territories, "a humbug, a cheat, and a swindle" devised to justify horrific misdeeds and cloak their selfish motives. Constitutional Unionists wanted no mistake made: "If LINCOLN be elected the fault will rest with the BRECKINRIDGE leaders."[27]

The Breckinridge Democracy was, Constitutional Unionists warned, "essentially a disunion party." Lincoln's election coupled with a Breckinridge majority in Georgia would furnish the pretext for raising "the blood-red flag of revolution." Tyrannical conspirators planned to ram a secession ordinance through the legislature, confiscate the property of dissenters, and use the funds to equip an army. In plain words, a vote for Breckinridge was a vote for disunion, anarchy, and bloodshed. "Patriotism and love of quiet, and freedom from internal strife," the *Milledgeville Southern Recorder* argued, "demands the election of Mr. Bell by a majority in all the Southern States." Bell might somehow—improbable scenarios abounded in the Bell press—defeat Lincoln in the electoral college or in the House of Representatives. But even "if LINCOLN *must* be elected, if disunion *must* come," the *Augusta Chronicle & Sentinel* urged, "it is of the utmost importance that the *movement* be in the hands of *moderate men.*" The "dissolution of the Union and the establishment of a Southern Confederacy" would not be "child's play"; Breckinridge Democrats who had ruined one government were surely incompetent to found another.[28]

Breckinridge men presented their party as the true national Democracy; questioned their opponents' soundness on slavery; touted their devotion to southern rights, including congressional protection for slavery in the territories; and promised that Breckinridge's election would preserve the Union. The sectional conflict, they stressed, was not of their making; they had simply done their duty in defending the South against northern aggression. To make such arguments was simply to restate dogma; the secession question, however, required thought and delicate handling. On the one hand, much of the Breckinridge leadership, from Alfred Iverson, Robert Toombs, and Howell Cobb on down, had publicly acknowledged that they favored disunion in the event of a Republican triumph, and they did intend to move quickly if Abraham Lincoln became president-elect. On the other hand, to say as much, at least very often, risked belittling Breckinridge's prospects, validating the charges leveled by the Bell and Douglas forces, and alienating voters who expected an earnest effort at victory. Breckinridge commanders therefore discussed contingencies infrequently and reluctantly, preferring to concentrate on the immediate election rather than on the momentous choices that loomed ahead.[29]

The campaign tapered off in mid-October, after northern state election results made a Republican victory appear certain. Some Georgians even paused to express regrets over their state's intractable party divisions. "We are divided upon questions of material policy but not material interest," the pro-Breckinridge editor of the *Columbus Daily Times* observed. "The same loyalty to the Constitution and protection to home and slavery, beats alike in the bosom of every Southern man—no matter what may be his party proclivities." The *Augusta Chronicle & Sentinel* believed that the parties disagreed "somewhat in principle" on the problem of slavery in the territories and "*vastly*" over matters of party strategy, but that there was no essential difference between them that "should alienate them from one another in view of a common cause and a common danger." Despite all that had been said and done, the truth was that Bell and Breckinridge men were both fighting for southern rights and southern safety in a desperate struggle against Douglas Democrats and Republicans. "It is time this unnatural contest was ended," the editor concluded. "This deplorable bitterness should cease."[30]

But it did not cease. Benjamin Hill, Herschel Johnson, James Gardner, and other Bell and Douglas leaders intermittently discussed fusion, but a late October effort to unite the three parties behind a common electoral ticket collapsed when confident Breckinridge forces spurned the movement. Each party wanted fusion only on its own terms and only behind its own candidates. Party passions created by decades of strife over dozens of issues still persisted, and all the parties—even Breckinridge Democrats at this point—still paid more homage to the Jacksonian goal of using national party alliances to protect the South than to John C. Calhoun's dream of a united southern front. No matter that these alliances had been shattered by conflict over slavery. Each party still believed that its northern allies, however few or great in number, were the soundest, and that it alone truly represented southern interests. To say, as many Georgians did on reflection, that white men differed over means but not ends, was to say that they differed over more than enough to sustain party conflict.[31]

The arguments of the 1860 campaign revealed the fundamentals of Georgia politics. Promises to protect the South and slavery within the Union and to safeguard the liberty of white men echoed pledges that all parties had made in every election for the past thirty years. When all the other issues—banks, tariffs, and the like—had been stripped away, as they had been by 1860, the defense of white men's mastery and black slavery remained the ideological core of state politics. The dramatic language, the hyperbolic assaults on opponents, the contempt for unscrupulous politicians, the demonization of outside assailants, and the paeans to the Union were all characteristic of state political culture—were, indeed, largely variations of national political culture. White Georgians, then, conducted the 1860 campaign as they had dozens of others, only they cared more than ever about the potential consequences.

The enduring patterns of Georgia politics emerged clearly in the election returns. John Breckinridge led with 52,172 votes (48.8 percent), followed by John Bell with 43,069 (40.3 percent), and Stephen Douglas with 11,629

(10.9 percent). Bell carried just twenty-three counties, and his vote barely exceeded Millard Fillmore's 1856 total. All but two of the Bell counties were located in the black belt, mostly in formerly Whiggish areas in western Georgia. Montgomery and Laurens, counties that had voted overwhelmingly anti-Democratic since Andrew Jackson's second administration, gave Bell his largest majorities. The combined Democratic vote for Breckinridge and Douglas fell only 5 votes short of Joseph Brown's 1859 total. The Constitutional Union party, then, was as weak as the feeblest incarnations of the Georgia opposition.

Breckinridge, billed as the true nominee of the national Democracy, captured majorities in seventy-eight counties, carried every region except the black belt, and garnered most of the traditional Democratic vote. Breckinridge drew much of his strength from predominantly white counties in north Georgia and the pine barrens–wiregrass region, and he also won by large margins in every coastal county. The twenty-two counties that gave at least 70 percent of their vote to Breckinridge had slave populations ranging from 2.5 percent (Gilmer) to 76.4 percent (Camden). Breckinridge partisans in the mountains and the upcountry primarily cast Democratic votes, following patterns of county allegiance that dated back decades. Along the coast and in the black belt, especially in counties where Democratic majorities were of a very recent vintage, many of the votes for Breckinridge expressed secessionist sentiment.

Douglas made a modest showing (10–15 percent of the vote) in several north Georgia counties, but nearly half of his total vote came from a small area in the eastern black belt near the homes of Alexander Stephens and Herschel Johnson—the four counties that Douglas carried were located there. Voters in old middle Georgia, formerly the heartland of Whiggery, were among the newest Democratic converts, yet they furnished the most support for a northern Democratic candidate who ran poorly almost everywhere else. As was evident throughout the campaign, Douglasites loathed Breckinridge Democrats, valued national parties as bulwarks of the Union, and considered Douglas the only opponent capable of challenging Abraham Lincoln.

Lincoln's election to the presidency with less than 40 percent of the popular vote and without a single electoral vote from the slave states shocked, confused, and angered white Southerners. Immediate calls for resistance raised divisive questions regarding what forms it should take. Unionists or conditional Unionists, who dominated in the upper South, tended to favor vigilance and remonstrances; at most, they wanted a convention of the southern states to issue ultimatums looking toward Republican concessions. A large segment of the lower South desired immediate secession. South Carolina led the rush to call state conventions, followed quickly by Alabama, Florida, and Mississippi. The Georgia legislature, after considering and wisely rejecting proposals that it move toward a declaration of secession, set 2 January 1861 as the election date for a 16 January state convention—Louisiana and Texas conventions would meet after Georgia decided.[32]

Despite initial pleas for unity, white men rapidly divided into opposing camps over the selection of state convention delegates. Those who favored immediate and separate state secession, led by Howell Cobb, Thomas R. R. Cobb, Henry Jackson, Robert Toombs, and other Breckinridge stalwarts, had a clear plan of action and the support of the overwhelming majority of Democratic newspapers. Against them stood cooperationists led by Alexander Stephens, Herschel Johnson, and Benjamin Harvey Hill and backed by the Constitutional Union party press. Cooperationists' renunciation of the much more familiar Unionist label indicated the complexities and ambiguities of their purposes. Hoping for redress of southern grievances within the Union, yet doubting that conciliation was possible, they advanced various blueprints for vindicating Georgia's rights, for promoting southern unity, and, ultimately, for coordinating the secession of Georgia with that of other states. All the cooperationists' schemes involved greater or lesser delay; indeed, cooperationists proved far more dedicated to staving off immediate secession than to preventing secession per se.[33]

The Georgia contest differed crucially from debates under way simultaneously in the upper South. Although some individual Unionists could be found, especially in the mountains, the militant Unionism that frustrated immediate secessionists in the upper South did not exist as a political force in Georgia in late 1860 and early 1861. The Constitutional Union party had carried Virginia, Kentucky, and Tennessee in the presidential election, and potent opposition parties provided nuclei for organizing opposition to immediate secession. Unionist coalitions controlled the upper South in the months after Lincoln's election and decisively defeated early efforts at secession. Most opponents of immediate secession in Virginia, North Carolina, and Tennessee were not, to be sure, unconditional Unionists, but they were far more staunchly Unionist and far more powerful than were Georgia co-operationists. Conflict among white Georgians during the secession crisis, in short, paled in comparison with the doubts, divided loyalties, and turmoil that troubled the upper South.[34]

Whatever else the Georgia secession debate was, it was not a debate over white men's allegiance to slavery. Immediatists and cooperationists agreed that the threat posed by Republican and northern hostility to slavery was the sole compelling reason for contemplating secession, and they further agreed that agitation over slavery had to cease or the Union would be dissolved. Disputes over policy and timing, over how to move and when to move to protect slavery, had been constants in state politics and were not miraculously resolved during the secession crisis. But the immediatists and the cooperationists who engaged each other in 1860–61 unhesitatingly accepted the defense of slavery and white men's democracy as paramount goals; assumed overwhelming, if not quite universal, white loyalty to slavery; and identified Northerners, not each other, as the enemies of slavery.

The resolutions passed by county meetings all over Georgia voiced similar grievances. According to the common interpretation, northern violations of southern rights had already effectively broken the constitutional compact. Most obnoxious were the personal liberty laws of northern states, which aimed at subverting acts of Congress designed to protect Southerners' clear constitutional right to the rendition of fugitive slaves. Some northern states, in what seemed like a calculated insult, allowed free blacks to vote in a white men's government. (Many even believed that free black votes had elected Lincoln and that Hannibal Hamlin, the vice president–elect, was black.) Northern efforts to exclude slavery from the territories and to abolish slavery in the District of Columbia unjustly discriminated against southern institutions. Finally, northern toleration of abolitionists and their emissaries—John Brown, for example—threatened the lives and property of all southern whites.[35]

To preserve a society based on fundamental distinctions between races and sexes, the planters, yeomen, mechanics, and laborers of Georgia believed that they had to be the equals of all other white men. The equality of free white men and the equality of the states were the cardinal principles of republicanism. "Equality in the Union, or equality and independence out of it," Troup County cooperationists resolved, "is the only true ground for Southern men to occupy." The election of Lincoln, Lowndes County residents contended, had "finally reduced the Southern members of the Confederacy to a state of inequality and dependence." Republicans had declared "the institution upon which rests the prosperity and happiness of the Southern people, a damning sin, a foul blot upon our National honor," Carroll County immediatists warned. If white men remained in the Union, their position would be "one of inequality, degradation, and absolute submission to Black Republican domination and misrule."[36]

Black, a word associated with evil and with Africa in Western culture, seemed an apt adjective to describe a Republican party dedicated—as white Georgians understood it—to the proposition "that the negro is by nature the equal of the white man and ought by law to enjoy equal civil, political and social rights." Republicans, wedded to "the principles of abolition fanaticism," had vowed "that the last slave-holder is born, and that negroes shall be the equals of the white race." Republicans intended to prosecute their unnatural war against slavery and the white race until freed blacks could take their former masters' places at the polls, in jury boxes, and in marriage beds. Mountain cooperationists in White County called Lincoln's election "a climax upon those injuries which have already despoiled us of our property, invaded our homes, and sought the ruin of our happiness, by inciting murder and insurrection in our midst." While they loved the Union and hoped to maintain it, they readily identified the ongoing northern effort to equalize the races as the "only cause which can lead to its overthrow." Clay County immediate secessionists alleged that the exclusion of slavery from the territories was the first step in a grand Republican design "to free our slaves, and make them incendiaries to destroy us by fire, and monsters to immolate our wives and daughters at the shrine of their only god on earth—Abolitionism." "This Government is and ought to be, the Government of the WHITE PEOPLE," the freemen resolved; they would never submit "to a NEGRO Government."[37]

That unchecked Republican rule would lead to the end of slavery appeared axiomatic. Since the rise of immediate abolitionism in the early 1830s, white Georgians had virtually outlawed criticism of slavery in their midst and had repeatedly called on their northern political allies to silence antislavery zealots. Slavery might survive for a time, but not for long, with an "incendiary Abolitionist" in the White House and John Browns stalking through southern woods. The Union under the Constitution was "a pro-slavery government, in fact, and by necessity." To live indefinitely under Republican tyrants who spoke of an "irrepressible conflict" between slavery and free labor was unthinkable. Ardent cooperationists in black belt Marion County warned that the "permanent ascendancy of the Black Republican party" meant "the eventual destruction of the institution of slavery" and called on the southern states "to prepare for a final and total dissolution of the Union."[38]

Immediate secessionists stressed exactly this: Lincoln's election was a final verdict against the South. Howell Cobb emphasized that the process of "educating the hearts of the people to hate the institution of slavery" had proceeded too far to be reversed; ever increasing northern majorities would only battle ever more fanatically to exterminate slavery. John H. Howard believed that Northerners were "resolutely determined upon the extinguishment of slavery, and if all their present leaders were dead and buried, the conflict would be unabated because the people are wrong." Even if, as cooperationists often said, Abraham Lincoln was comparatively conservative and would "not allow ultra-fanaticism to dictate his policy," Republicans would elect someone in 1864—William Seward, Horace Greeley, Charles Sumner, even William Lloyd Garrison himself—who more closely mirrored the party's true nature. "It is the conviction that this growing power must inevitably overshadow the South if she remains in the Union," the *Augusta Constitutionalist* concluded, that "renders our people anxious to dissolve the political band now uniting them with the Abolition States."[39]

Immediatists, like their oft-cited Republican adversaries, also saw an "irrepressible conflict" between the labor systems of the North and the South. There could "be no peace between the sections from this very antagonism of social systems." While an advancing southern civilization built on the bedrock of slavery enjoyed order and stability, the North faced the tensions—exemplified by the shoemakers' strike around Lynn, Massachusetts, in 1860—of a free labor society that could end only in a ruinous war of the poor against the rich. The great flaw in the social organization of the free states was that the mass of laborers, the "mudsill" class who were slaves in the South, were "permitted and persuaded to vote." Cunning northern politicians had directed the wrath of "the lowest dregs of their populace" at the

South to relieve the pressures within their own society, but if the South fell, the northern masses would turn on their own leaders. The South should withdraw now to save itself, immediatists urged, and leave the North's free-labor system to collapse under the weight of its contradictions.[40]

Immediate secessionists had shed their emotional attachments to the Union. The northern "people hate us, annoy us, and would have us assassinated by our slaves if they dared," Thomas R. R. Cobb wrote. "They are a *different* people from us, whether better or worse, and *there is no love* between us." James Barrow, the son of planter and Breckinridge leader David C. Barrow, told his father that the South could not stand a "rail-splitter for president and a negro for vice president, both declaired enimies [*sic*] to her interests." Secession would only reify politically a separation that had long ago occurred in feeling.[41]

Many cooperationists, in contrast, remained uncertain whether the northern antislavery tide was irreversible and sectional conflict inevitable. State opposition forces had long insisted that a conservative northern majority lay waiting to be mobilized, that slavery agitation should and could be kept out of politics, and that demagogic politicians, not the people, were responsible for sectional conflict. "Party influence and party machinery" had produced "the ills and evils of which we complain," the *Columbus Sun* explained, and had "put Mr. Lincoln in the position he now occupies." Incessant "harping, blustering and ranting about our rights through party leaders and party conventions," the *Milledgeville Southern Recorder* contended, had divided the South and alienated erstwhile northern friends. Constitutional Unionists believed that Democrats had deliberately manipulated slavery issues for party gain, and Alexander Stephens and many other Douglas Democrats considered the vendetta against Stephen Douglas a major cause of Lincoln's election. Wiser leaders, cooperationists hoped, could yet heal the country's wounds.[42]

Perhaps Lincoln's election was a dreadful fluke attributable more to hatred of Democracy than to hatred of slavery. Cooperationists certainly felt that a Republican victory *alone* was insufficient reason to rush into revolution. Lincoln would not assume power until 4 March; even after that, he would be restrained by a Democratic Congress and a pro-South Supreme Court. Cooperationists wanted a united South to take time to determine whether Northerners seriously intended to support the Republican party

and its antislavery principles. Only if Northerners rejected southern ultimatums would cooperationists concede that it was impossible to save the
Union.[43]

Benjamin Harvey Hill's 15 November speech in Milledgeville outlined
the basic cooperationist position. Immediate secessionists, Hill began,
thought that "innate anti-slavery fanaticism" had elected Lincoln, and that
"such fanaticism is never convinced—is never satisfied—never ends but in
victory or blood." The Republicans were unquestionably "a party seeking
to administer the Government on principles which must destroy the Government." But cooperationists still hoped that the Republicans might back
down, that Northerners might come to their senses. Immediate secession
was unnecessary and rash, but white men could "not let this crisis pass without a settlement" that would "end the agitation of slavery forever." "The
only ground of difference now is," Hill concluded, "some of us think we can
get redress in the Union, and others think we cannot." [44]

The settlement that cooperationists sought entailed nothing less than the
renunciation of the Republican platform. Foremost among the required concessions was an ironclad guarantee that the right to hold slaves in the territories would not be restricted or impaired. The *Rome Courier* wanted the
repeal of all personal liberty bills in the northern states and Northerners'
pledge never to "interfere with the constitutional rights of slavery anywhere." Failure to grant these terms by 4 March would compel the southern
states to "proceed at once to a dissolution of the Union." The *Savannah
Republican* comprehensively declared that white Southerners could never
agree to live under a Republican government without "an authoritative
guaranty from the northern States of the Union, that every cause that has
made the idea of such dominion objectionable and odious shall be effectually
removed. This alone can preserve the union and give peace to its parts." To
ask Republicans to forfeit their victory and the North to accede to guarantees, legislation, or constitutional amendments that conceded every point at
issue in the sectional controversy was to ask for the impossible, a fact that
made cooperationism fundamentally an alternative mode of secession.[45]

A few cooperationists, most notably Alexander Stephens, adopted a
quasi-Unionist stance, arguing that Georgia and the other southern states
should shun secession unless Lincoln clearly violated the Constitution or
the northern states categorically refused to repeal their personal liberty laws.

Like other cooperationists, Stephens and his circle retained a love for the Union and sincerely desired to save it, if it could be saved without sacrificing southern safety and honor. But other motives also moved them. Alexander and Linton Stephens, Herschel Johnson, and others fixated on—almost became obsessed with—the idea that southern politicians had brought evil on themselves. Stephens sulked during the crucial weeks of the convention campaign, bemoaning the follies of lesser mortals and ruminating, as he often did, on the inevitable decay and death of all bodies, corporeal and political. Treating the sectional conflict as real, and not the creation of contemptible demagogues, would have forced Stephens to confront devastating questions about his own career. No other Georgian had invested so much in the doctrines of nonintervention and popular sovereignty. From the Compromise of 1850 through the Kansas-Nebraska Act and beyond, Stephens had proclaimed each apparent southern success a personal triumph. In his own mind, he had saved the South a hundred times through wise and skillful leadership. If Lincoln's election amounted to a decisive northern repudiation of that work, then Stephens had been wrong—and the victories he had celebrated had mattered naught. Unable to live with such a conclusion, Stephens found fault with others—with those who had betrayed both him and the South, the immediate secessionists of the Breckinridge Democracy.[46]

Cooperationists longed to achieve the elusive ideal of southern unity. They knew that the South was not and had never been solid: slavery had been withering away for decades in some of the border states, and party divisions had long prevented concerted action. It became apparent soon after Lincoln's victory that Virginia, Kentucky, Tennessee, and other upper South states would not leave the Union quickly, if at all. Hence, cooperationists such as Charles J. Jenkins pushed for a southern convention to secure "that which probably can be secured in no other way—*united action* of the South." The cotton states, Jenkins argued, could well afford to wait a few months to gain the crucial allegiance of Virginia, Maryland, Kentucky, and Tennessee, which "are, and of necessity must be, our impregnable break-water, against which the surging billows of Abolitionism dash." Cooperation might allow the South to obtain its rights in the Union; failing that, it would lay the groundwork for the "simultaneous secession of all the Southern States." Seceding without the upper South, the *Columbus Enquirer* observed, would "separate a dependent section of planters from the

Southern states that supply the live stock and provisions necessary to the economical prosecution of their business." To "separate slave-selling Virginia from slave-buying Alabama and Mississippi" would "subject the former to an aggravated crusade against frontier slavery, which must greatly hasten its extermination there." Cooperationists' desire for consultation in advance of action reflected their conviction that, in the Union or out, in peace or war, the cotton states had to have the upper South on their side to have a chance of prevailing against the North.[47]

The *Augusta Chronicle & Sentinel* expressed a common cooperationist opinion when it predicted, "Separate secession is war." Separate secession would alienate the upper South and encourage the Republicans to attack isolated states. Only cooperation, the *Columbus Enquirer* contended, would enable the South "to present such a *retiring front* that neither the North nor the Federal Government will venture to try coercion." Cooperationists rightly regarded South Carolina as a potential flash point, and their jaundiced view of their neighbors gave them little confidence that the prudence of South Carolinians could be relied on to minimize possibilities for armed collisions. Cooperationists themselves were committed to defending South Carolina against federal assault, and they assumed that the other cotton states, at least, would also rush to South Carolina's defense, ending chances for reconciliation or redress within the Union.[48]

General apprehensions of "commotions, convulsions, servile insurrections, conflagrations, murders, civil war, ruin, anarchy, despotism and destruction" plagued cooperationists. Men witnessing the disintegration of the world's "best government," framed by "the wisest and purest men that ever lived," anxiously wondered how their generation could possibly improve on the founders' handiwork. No cooperationist spied any budding Washingtons or Jeffersons among the immediate secessionists. Could the South, under such leaders, fashion a separate republic that would protect white liberty and black slavery, or would the collapse of the old Union bring on a state of anarchy leading to despotism? "To tear down and build up again are very different things," Alexander Stephens cautioned, "and before tearing down even a bad Government we should first see a good prospect for building up a better."[49]

Cooperationists, then, hoped to unite the southern states in a convention that would present ultimatums to the Republicans and the North. Perhaps

organized pressure would secure Union-saving concessions. If not, cooperationists reasoned that exhausting other options before resorting to secession
would cement an alliance between the border and cotton states and convince
even the most reluctant white Southerners that disunion was unavoidable.
Cooperationists, finally, intended to control the entire process. They considered the South safe in their hands and no others, and their distrust of Breckinridge Democrats accounted for a substantial part of their opposition to
immediate secession.

Cooperationists had powerful sentiments—love for the Union and fear
of change—to draw on, and a considerable majority of white men embraced
variations of cooperationism at the outset of the state convention campaign.
But irresolution and accumulating contradictions dissipated that strength.
Cooperationists' antipathy for outright Unionism exceeded their opposition
to immediate secession, and their every argument about the proper timing
and mode for southern resistance conceded that unmitigated Republican
rule was intolerable and that disunion was the appropriate final remedy.
Plans for cooperation with other southern states accordingly remained hazy,
never came close to fruition, and were outmoded by events.

South Carolina, Alabama, Mississippi, and Florida seceded before the
Georgia convention even met, further undermining the logic of cooperationists' arguments and compelling some to admit that "in order to *act* with
them we must go with them." The departure of neighboring states and the
dismal electoral experience of the Georgia opposition strongly suggested
that cooperationism was an irrelevant and lost cause. If the rest of the Deep
South seceded and the upper South remained in the Union, who, exactly,
did Georgia's cooperative secessionists propose to cooperate with? Would
cooperationism in fact isolate Georgia and expose the state to the very dangers that cooperationists feared? Alexander Stephens and Herschel Johnson
were only the most prominent among many cooperationist leaders who, unable satisfactorily to answer such questions for themselves or others, con-
fined their campaign activities largely to the exchange of gloomy notes. Cooperationists who lacked the "heart to dwell upon the discouraging prospect
before" them unsurprisingly failed to match the energy and will of their
adversaries.[50]

Instead of concentrating on refuting cooperationist arguments, immediate secessionists tried to override them with passionate appeals for the pro-

tection of slavery, white men's honor and equality, and racial supremacy. Like patriots of the Revolutionary War era, immediatists emphasized that temporizing in the face of tyranny would end in the loss of all liberty. White men had to strike for independence before Lincoln's inauguration or become "slaves the moment we are compelled to obey rulers in whose election we had no voice." Just as Southern Rights men had applied the "submissionist" label to Unionists in 1850, immediate secessionists denounced "Union-shriekers" whose "cowardly" policy of postponing resistance until after the Republicans had actually applied the lash was "not only disgraceful to a Southerner, but TREASON to the soil of his nativity." The *Columbus Times* admonished, "Let us not be worshippers of a Union, whose spirit, whose life, whose vitality has departed. Let us act like men. Let us be equals." [51]

The dichotomy of immediate secession versus submission caricatured the cooperationist position, but subtle delineation of issues had never been a hallmark of Georgia campaigns. Regardless of which side they had been on in 1850, Robert Toombs, Joseph Brown, Howell Cobb, and other leading secessionists knew from experience that bold words and determined action would be necessary to overcome the ingrained conservatism of most voters. Secessionists, Henry R. Jackson told Howell Cobb, should rally the "brave men and the enthusiastic; and cow, as they ought to be cowed, the cowards." Anything less than immediate secession would betray "a want of confidence, a fear of danger, which will encourage aggression abroad, and play the D——l at home." [52]

Immediatists counted on South Carolina's secession to embolden the hesitant. Once South Carolina went out, immediatists argued, other states, including those in the upper South, would be bound to follow. When South Carolina seceded alone on 20 December, Athens secessionists fired cannons and marched in a torchlight parade under banners bearing mottoes such as "Protect Our Homes" and "Resistance to Abolition Is Obedience to God." In the battle against abolition and "Negro Equality," Congressman Martin J. Crawford blared, "THE CAUSE OF SOUTH CAROLINA IS THE CAUSE OF ALL." [53]

Some immediatists' exhortations, most notoriously those of Thomas R. R. Cobb in his early November speech in Milledgeville, betrayed distrust of their fellow white men. Cobb, convinced that Lincoln's election was unconstitutional and that the northern threat to slavery was permanent, urged

state legislators to take Georgia immediately out of the Union without waiting for "the grog-shops and cross-roads" to "send up a discordant voice
from a divided people." One postponement might lead to another and then
to another, until men would grow accustomed to wearing the Republican
yoke and courage would give way to cowardice. Delay also risked pitting
neighbor against neighbor. Some "zealous, warm spirits" might prefer to
"grace a traitor's gallows than to wear the badge of a slave" and would reject
a popular verdict against secession. Or a clash between Lincoln's government and a seceding state might force Georgians to choose their enemies.
Once the "dogs of war" lapped "the blood of freemen," the "gory head" of
civil war might cast its shadow over Georgia. Strong leadership could avert
such calamities, Cobb concluded, could rally the "great heart of this great
people" before timid counsel and public trepidation produced disaster.[54]

Although the legislature spurned Cobb's secession proposal, the questions he raised about the fragility of white unity lingered. Particularly worri-
some was the prospect that the corrupting power of patronage could be used
to create a southern Republican party. Republican rule, Joseph Brown observed, meant either that some Southerners "must if possible, be bribed into
treachery to their own section, by the allurements of office; or a hungry
swarm of abolition emissaries must be imported among us as office-holders,
to eat out our substance, insult us with their arrogance [and] corrupt our
slaves." "Sentinel" had no doubt that Republicans intended "to build up in
the South under the name of a Union party—first, a party for submission,
and gradually through its instrumentality an antislavery party." The "effects
of patronage and the blindness of party zeal" would spread the "anti-slavery
virus" first in the border states, and then Republicans would endeavor to
"stir up class jealousies" in the Deep South and set nonslaveholders against
slaveholders.[55]

The concern was not so much that antislavery sentiment existed in Georgia (the doubtful loyalty of some white men in the upper South was another
matter), but that it *could be made to exist* under certain conditions. Experience had taught that even the best men could be seduced by the lure of
office, and it would be leaders, not common white men, whom Republicans
would tempt. Only if influential politicians turned traitor would there be a
danger of the masses embracing Republicanism. If it were built at all, in
other words, a southern Republican party would be built from the top

down, like other political organizations. Cooperationists, in fact, charged that Robert Toombs and other "fat and oily" Breckinridge Democrats would be quickest to feed off Republican pap. While cooperationists indignantly denied that there ever had been or ever could be a Free-Soil party in Georgia, immediate secessionists hoped that quick action would prevent assaults by northern abolitionist officeholders and immunize the South against any possibility of antislavery contagion.[56]

North Georgia yeomen, who had long supported a national Democratic party devoted to preserving the Union, posed the greatest obstacle to the success of immediate secessionists. Despite the "perfect blaze" of enthusiasm for John Breckinridge in the presidential campaign, the mostly slaveless mountain counties bordering Tennessee—a state still staunchly Unionist in early 1861—remained the region of strongest Union feeling. Howell Cobb, who sensed trouble in the mountains early on, rushed out on a speaking tour and disconcertingly "found the Union or submission sentiment, *overwhelming.*"[57]

Unlimbering their heaviest ideological artillery, immediate secessionists reminded North Georgia nonslaveholders of fundamentals. The *Athens Southern Banner* printed an advertisement, purportedly taken from a Rochester, New York, newspaper, in which a black family sought to employ a white servant boy. "It tells a great deal of the practical working of the abolition of slavery," editor James Sledge commented sadly. "We trust the time never will come when the children of any poor white man in Georgia shall be thus humbled and abased." Abolition would cost slaveholders their property, Sledge further observed, "but the poor white man *would lose much more*, and what is all in all to him and to every man, viz.: *the consciousness of political and social superiority.*"[58] Joseph Brown likewise underscored that in a slave society the "poor white laborer" was "respected as an equal" and belonged "to the only true aristocracy, the race of *white men.*" If slavery fell, renegade blacks would soon be "plundering and stealing, robbing and killing, in all the lovely vallies [*sic*] of the mountains." Blacks would step forward to "claim social equality with" white men, to "ask the hands of their children in marriage." As a child of north Georgia, Brown could not believe that honest yeomen there would submit to such degradation or consent to "take the negro's place."[59]

Brown did not misjudge his constituency. White men in north Georgia supported slavery; they would die by the thousands in the service of the Confederacy. Brown's appeals moved some, but the problem for him and his allies was that the choice between cooperation and immediate secession in north Georgia or anywhere else in the state did not hinge on degrees of loyalty to slavery. Mountain and upcountry oppositionists had fought for decades against the likes of Brown and Howell Cobb. North Georgia Democrats, of course, had followed Howell Cobb in several crusades against black belt politicians and black belt dictation. They had rejected impulsive radicalism and Calhounite fervor in 1833, 1843, and 1850, to cite only major instances, and many north Georgia Democrats were understandably reluctant to concede what they had never conceded before: that devotion to the South, slavery, and white men's democracy was incompatible with devotion to the Union.

The convention election was a contest to select county delegates whom voters could trust to formulate a policy to safeguard black slavery and white liberty. A vote for immediate secession was relatively unambiguous, but a ballot cast for cooperation could signify support for anything from outright Unionism—in rare cases—to secession within a few weeks. The difference between cooperation and immediate secession was widest in extreme north Georgia and narrowed unevenly as one moved into the upcountry and the black belt. The argument in many black belt counties was primarily over who could best execute secession, since even cooperationists did not plan to tarry past 4 March, if that long, unless Republican concessions were forthcoming. The vast majority of coastal voters embraced immediate secession; citizens in the pine barrens–wiregrass were much divided in sentiment.[60]

The second of January was a miserable, rainy day; many voters stayed home. Immediate secessionists eked out a bare majority at best, with 44,152 votes (around 51.5 percent) to 41,632 for cooperationists. Delegates running as cooperationists may actually have carried a slight majority of the statewide vote (table 14).[61] More than 21,000 fewer votes (20 percent) were cast than in the November election; the decline was greatest along the coast and least in the mountains and pine barrens–wiregrass. Most counties heavily favored one side or the other, and lopsided contests decreased turnout. No contest took place in fifteen counties (ten immediatist and five cooperationist), and three quarters of the counties gave at least 60 percent of their votes to either immediatists or cooperationists.[62] Given the low turnout, the complexity of

*Table 14. Voting by Regions in the Convention Election of 2 January 1861*

| | Immedi-atist Votes | Coopera-tionist Votes | Immedi-atist % | Coopera-tionist % | % of Total Immedi-atist Vote | % of Total Coopera-tionist Vote |
|---|---|---|---|---|---|---|
| Mountains | 4,479 | 8,375 | 34.8 | 65.2 | 10.1 | 20.1 |
| Upcountry | 12,370 | 11,846 | 51.1 | 48.9 | 28.0 | 28.5 |
| Black belt | 22,230 | 18,387 | 54.7 | 45.3 | 50.4 | 44.2 |
| Pine barrens– | | | | | | |
| wiregrass | 2,722 | 2,790 | 49.4 | 50.6 | 6.2 | 6.7 |
| Coast | 2,341 | 234 | 90.9 | 9.1 | 5.3 | 0.6 |
| Total | 44,142 | 41,632 | 51.5 | 48.5 | 100 | 100.1 |

*Source:* Michael P. Johnson, "A New Look at the Popular Vote for Delegates to the Georgia Secession Convention," *Georgia Historical Quarterly* (Summer 1972): 259–75.

the issues, the confusing nature of many county races, and the closeness of the outcome, the results yield a very imprecise index to the attitudes of a divided electorate.

Regional voting patterns are clear only at the extremes. Just 35 percent of mountain voters and only one mountain county favored immediate secession, while all of the coastal counties and 90 percent of the voters in them endorsed immediate secession. Mountain voters furnished 20 percent of the statewide cooperationist vote and 10 percent of the immediatist ballots. The overwhelming coastal vote comprised only 5 percent of the total immediatist vote. Immediate secessionists gained a slight majority in the upcountry and a larger but still slim majority in the black belt. More than half of immediatist voters and 44 percent of cooperationists lived in the black belt, the center of population. Cooperationists carried the pine barrens–wiregrass by the tiny margin of sixty-eight votes.

Despite the obvious division between the mostly black coastal region and the overwhelmingly white mountain counties, the votes show no strong, positive relationship between levels of slave population and support for immediate secession (table 15).[63] A division of counties into quartiles based on

*Table 15. Counties Ranked in Quartiles by Slave Population Percentages, with Levels of Support for Immediate Secession in the Convention Election of 2 January 1861*

| Quartile | Immedi-atist Counties | Coopera-tionist Counties | Median Slave % | Median Immediatist % | Total Immediatist % |
|---|---|---|---|---|---|
| First | 21 | 12 | 66.0 | 62.5 | 50.5 |
| Second | 21 | 12 | 47.5 | 61.7 | 59.9 |
| Third | 17 | 16 | 29.1 | 50.8 | 54.0 |
| Fourth | 13 | 20 | 12.4 | 43.3 | 41.8 |
| Total | 72 | 60 | 45.0 | 57.9 | 51.5 |

*Sources:* Michael P. Johnson, "A New Look at the Popular Vote for Delegates to the Georgia Secession Convention," *Georgia Historical Quarterly* (Summer 1972): 259–75; *Eighth Census of the United States, 1860.*

the percentage of slaves in the county population reveals that a slight majority of all voters in counties in the top three quartiles favored immediate secession, and that levels of slave population did not vary consistently with levels of support for immediate secession. Counties in the bottom quartile, with a median slave population percentage of just 12.4, still gave 42 percent of their ballots to immediate secessionists. In the pine barrens–wiregrass, nine of the ten counties with the lowest slave populations—ranging from 8 to 23 percent—yielded large majorities for immediate secession.

A county's vote for John C. Breckinridge in the presidential election was a somewhat better predictor of voting in the convention races (tables 16 and 17).[64] Counties that had favored Breckinridge tended to give larger shares of their vote to immediate secessionists, while counties that had opposed Breckinridge usually offered greater support to cooperationists. Exceptions to this pattern, however, abounded. Fifty-five counties returned majorities for both Breckinridge and immediate secession, but Breckinridge also carried twenty-four counties that voted against immediate secession. Pro-Breckinridge, cooperationist counties had an average slave population of 18 percent; seventeen of them were in north Georgia. At least four thousand voters in the mountains and the upcountry backed Breckinridge but

Table 16. Counties Ranked in Quartiles by Percentage of Breckinridge Vote, with Levels of Support for Immediate Secession in the Convention Election of 2 January 1861

| Quartile | Immediatist Counties | Cooperationist Counties | Median Breckinridge % | Median Immediatist % | Total Immediatist % |
|----------|------|------|------|------|------|
| First | 23 | 10 | 75.8 | 61.4 | 60.8 |
| Second | 22 | 11 | 58.5 | 60.8 | 54.2 |
| Third | 16 | 17 | 48.1 | 49.2 | 52.8 |
| Fourth | 11 | 22 | 29.5 | 34.0 | 40.7 |
| Total | 72 | 60 | 53.4 | 57.9 | 51.5 |

*Sources:* Michael P. Johnson, "A New Look at the Popular Vote for Delegates to the Georgia Secession Convention," *Georgia Historical Quarterly* (Summer 1972): 259–75; Walter Dean Burnham, *Presidential Ballots, 1836–1892* (Baltimore: Johns Hopkins University Press, 1955).

Table 17. County Support for Breckinridge and Position on Secession in the Convention Election of 2 January 1861

| | Pro-Breckinridge, Immediatist | Anti-Breckinridge, Immediatist | Pro-Breckinridge, Cooperationist | Anti-Breckinridge, Cooperationist | Total Counties |
|---|------|------|------|------|------|
| Mountains | 0 | 1 | 12 | 4 | 17 |
| Upcountry | 11 | 2 | 5 | 6 | 24 |
| Eastern black belt | 10 | 10 | 1 | 15 | 36 |
| Western black belt | 16 | 4 | 2 | 7 | 29 |
| Pine barrens– wiregrass | 12 | 0 | 4 | 4 | 20 |
| Coast | 6 | 0 | 0 | 0 | 6 |
| Total | 55 | 17 | 24 | 36 | 132 |

*Sources:* Michael P. Johnson, "A New Look at the Popular Vote for Delegates to the Georgia Secession Convention," *Georgia Historical Quarterly* (Summer 1972): 259–75; Walter Dean Burnham, *Presidential Ballots, 1836–1892* (Baltimore: Johns Hopkins University Press, 1955).

rejected immediate secession.[65] The thirty-six anti-Breckinridge, cooperationist counties were proportionally balanced by region and had large (average, 45 percent) slave populations. Finally, nearly all of the seventeen anti-
Breckinridge counties that favored immediate secession were located in the
black belt and had an average slave population of 49 percent. To summarize
in refined terms, pro-Breckinridge counties outside the mountains strongly
tended to vote for immediate secession, but most of the largely white, pro-
Breckinridge counties in north Georgia were cooperationist. There was no
meaningful difference between slave population levels in anti-Breckinridge
immediatist and anti-Breckinridge cooperationist counties.

Considered alone, the past party allegiance of counties was a poor predictor of voting in the convention election (table 18).[66] The top quartile of most
strongly Democratic counties—including many in north Georgia—and the
bottom quartile of most strongly Whiggish counties—nearly all in the black
belt—voted very similarly in the convention election. The second quartile

Table 18. *Counties Ranked in Quartiles by Past Democratic Percentage,*
*with Levels of Support for Immediate Secession in the Convention Election of*
*2 January 1861*

| Quartile | Immedi- atist Counties | Coopera- tionist Counties | Median Past Democratic %[a] | Median Immediatist % | Average Immediatist % |
|---|---|---|---|---|---|
| First | 18 | 15 | 75.8 | 50.9 | 52.1 |
| Second | 17 | 16 | 60.4 | 50.7 | 56.9 |
| Third | 21 | 12 | 51.6 | 60.8 | 60.6 |
| Fourth | 16 | 17 | 42.0 | 47.4 | 45.5 |
| Total | 72 | 60 | 57.7 | 57.9 | 53.8 |

*Sources:* Michael P. Johnson, "A New Look at the Popular Vote for Delegates to the Georgia Secession
Convention," *Georgia Historical Quarterly* (Summer 1972): 259–75; Walter Dean Burnham, *Presidential
Ballots, 1836–1892* (Baltimore: Johns Hopkins University Press, 1955); *Macon Georgia Messenger,* 16 Nov.
1837; *Milledgeville Southern Recorder,* 14 Nov. 1837, 9 Nov. 1841, 17 Oct. 1843, 21 Oct. 1845, 12 Oct.
1847, 25 Oct. 1853, 16 Oct., 4 Dec. 1855, 20 Oct. 1857; *Milledgeville Federal Union,* 31 Oct. 1835, 23 Oct.
1838, 16 Oct. 1849, 29 Nov. 1853, 25 Oct. 1859; *Augusta Chronicle & Sentinel,* 14 Nov. 1851.
[a] Median past Democratic percentage is the median of Democratic percentages in statewide elections from
1835 to 1859, excluding the 1851 election.

of counties was a mixed group in terms of regional location and slightly favored immediate secessionists. The third quartile of counties, which most strongly supported immediate secession, consisted mostly of narrowly Democratic black belt counties.

Rather than any single factor, a combination of regional, social, political, and historical factors best explains the convention election voting patterns. The Democratic mountain counties, which had a strong Jacksonian Unionist tradition, low slave populations, and bordered on Unionist Tennessee, voted solidly—but hardly unanimously—against immediate secession. Coastal counties, regardless of past party allegiances, overwhelmingly supported immediate secession. White planters, enormously outnumbered by their slaves on rice and sea island cotton plantations, had the most to fear and the most to lose if Republicans attacked slavery.[67] Traditionally close commercial ties, particularly between Charleston and Savannah, also pushed coastal Georgians toward secession once the surrounding states had left the Union. In the pine barrens–wiregrass, all but one of the dozen immediate secessionist counties had been strongly Democratic and had polled majorities for John Breckinridge. Pine barrens–wiregrass Democrats, unlike their mountain brethren, had lent support to southern rights causes in 1850 and at other times in the past; several counties had a notable history of active southern rights leadership. Conversely, Montgomery and Tattnall Counties, ancient Whig bastions, overwhelmingly opposed immediate secession.

The upcountry races were generally closer than those in the rest of the state, and the county voting patterns defy a general explanation. Three of the four upcountry counties with the highest slave populations were cooperationist, and three of the four counties with the lowest slave populations favored immediate secession. Paulding and Harris Counties, which were each only 8 percent slave, cast nearly two-thirds of their votes for immediate secession. Upcountry counties that backed immediate secession were usually more strongly Democratic and more pro-Breckinridge than cooperationist counties, but several counties contradicted this pattern. Franklin County, for example, gave 84 percent of its vote to Breckinridge and had a historical Democratic majority exceeding 75 percent, but voters favored cooperation by better than a two-to-one margin. Upcountry voting, in sum, depended on factors of local sentiment and leadership not reducible to any formula.[68]

Voting patterns in the black belt most clearly displayed the power of past

*Table 19. Voting of Eastern and Western Black Belt Region
in the Convention Election of 2 January 1861*

|          | Immediatist % | % Black Belt Immediatist | % Black Belt Cooperationist |
|----------|---------------|--------------------------|------------------------------|
| Eastern  | 52.6          | 56.6                     | 61.7                         |
| Western  | 57.8          | 43.4                     | 38.3                         |
| Total    | 54.7          | 100                      | 100                          |

*Source:* Michael P. Johnson, "A New Look at the Popular Vote for Delegates to the Georgia Secession Convention," *Georgia Historical Quarterly* (Summer 1972): 259–75.

political influences (table 19). Twenty-four of the twenty-nine counties (83 percent) that had regularly yielded Democratic majorities supported immediate secession. Nearly all were located either in the traditional Democratic belt in central Georgia or in the southwestern cotton belt. Many of them, such as Scriven, Butts, and Muscogee Counties, had for decades been strongholds of the Calhounite, Southern Rights Democracy. A strong Bell-opposition presence in these counties limited Breckinridge to 53 percent of the total vote, but Democrats carried many Bell voters with them in returning larger majorities for immediate secession. Except for the coastal counties, Democratic black belt counties collectively produced the biggest majorities for immediate secession.

The choice between immediatism and cooperationism split Whig-opposition black belt counties significantly, though far from perfectly, along east-west lines. The western black belt had always been less Whiggish than the whole eastern part, and much less Whiggish than old middle Georgia. Although the eastern black belt as a whole gave a slight majority of its total vote to immediate secessionists, the historically Whiggish counties there gave 54 percent of their total vote to cooperationists, and fourteen of the twenty-two Whiggish counties were cooperationist. Almost two-thirds of the black belt cooperationist voters lived in the eastern section, and they elected the single largest bloc of cooperationist state convention delegates. Whiggish counties in the western black belt were fewer and much more likely to back immediate secession; they gave a bare majority of their total

vote to immediatists, and eight of fourteen Whiggish counties elected secessionist delegates. The western black belt altogether—including many
Democratic, immediatist counties—overwhelmingly elected delegates that
favored immediate secession.[69]

The strongest bloc of cooperationist counties in the black belt lay in old
middle Georgia, including Taliaferro and Jefferson, the home counties of
Alexander Stephens and Herschel V. Johnson, along with Hancock, Washington, and Columbia. To be sure, some old middle Georgia counties—such
as Elbert, Richmond, and Wilkes, where Robert Toombs resided—gave
large majorities to immediate secessionists. But in general, where Whiggery
had been strongest in the black belt, cooperationism was strongest as well.
Troup County, which anti-Democratic voters had dominated for three decades, unanimously elected a cooperationist delegation headed by Benjamin H. Hill. The cardinal tenets of oppositionists, their seeming radicalism
on slavery issues in the 1850s notwithstanding, had long been conservatism,
Unionism, and hatred of the Democracy. Despite the predominance of
slaveholders, the huge slave population, and the acknowledged Republican
threat that might necessitate secession, most voters in old middle Georgia
rejected what they viewed as a hasty secession movement engineered by
Breckinridge Democrats.

Because delegates were elected by counties, even a closely divided statewide vote could, and did, translate into a controlling convention majority
for immediate secession. The state convention was an august assemblage,
including Alexander Stephens, Robert Toombs, Eugenius A. Nisbet, Herschel Johnson, and Benjamin H. Hill. The crucial vote occurred on 18 January 1861, when Eugenius Nisbet offered resolutions for immediate secession
and Herschel Johnson countered with a proposal for a convention of the
southern states. Johnson's plan embodied the cooperationist formula of seeking redress for grievances in the Union while reserving secession as the ultimate remedy. Georgia's conditions for remaining in the Union, as outlined
by Johnson, included constitutional amendments opening all territories to
slavery and providing for the unrestricted admission of new slave states,
along with the repeal of personal liberty laws in the northern states. After
debate, the convention passed Nisbet's resolutions by a 166-to-130 vote.
The next day, 19 January, the delegates voted 208 to 89 to adopt an ordinance
of secession—Georgia was out of the Union.[70]

The history of the antebellum Georgia parties began in a sectional crisis over nullification and ended in another that dissolved the Union. Secession was simultaneously the culmination of the parties' long quest to protect slavery and white men's liberty, and the final, decisive failure of their quest to secure that protection in the Union. The parties had contested many issues in three decades, but in the end, during the 1850s and in January 1861, preserving slavery mattered most. Many of the partisan tendencies and regional divisions that had characterized state politics for decades continued on through the secession crisis and, indeed, eventually plagued the government of the new southern Confederacy.[71]

After years of defining themselves politically by their opposition to the northern men and measures that they hated most, white men discovered even deeper reasons to hate the Yankees on the battlefields of Manassas and Chancellorsville, Vicksburg and Gettysburg, and Atlanta and Appomattox. The four years of war that followed a revolution to save slavery ultimately destroyed the peculiar institution that had formed the foundation for a white men's democracy. As the work of white men took the state quietly out of the Union in January 1861, all Georgians—men and women, white and black, free and slave—embarked on an unforeseen journey toward a different world.

# NOTES

## Abbreviations Used in the Notes

DU      Special Collections, Duke University Library, Durham, North Carolina

EU      Special Collections, Emory University Library, Atlanta, Georgia

GDAH      Georgia Department of Archives and History, Atlanta, Georgia

LC      Library of Congress, Washington, D.C.

MCSH      Manhattanville College of the Sacred Heart, Purchase, New York

SHC      Southern Historical Collection, University of North Carolina, Chapel Hill

TSC      "The Correspondence of Robert Toombs, Alexander H. Stephens, and Howell Cobb," in *Annual Report of the American Historical Association,* ed. Ulrich B. Phillips, 2 vols., 1911. Washington, D.C.: Government Printing Office, 1913.

UGA      Special Collections, University of Georgia Library, Athens, Georgia

## Preface

1. Charles B. Dew, "The Slavery Experience," and Jacquelyn Dowd Hall and Anne Firor Scott, "Women in the South," in John B. Boles and Evelyn Thomas Nolen, eds., *Interpreting Southern History: Essays in Honor of Sanford W. Higginbotham* (Baton Rouge: Louisiana State University Press, 1987), 120–61, 454–509; Stephanie McCurry, "The Two Faces of Republicanism: Gender and Proslavery Politics in Antebellum South Carolina," *Journal of American History* 78 (March 1992): 1245–64; and McCurry, *Masters of Small Worlds: Yeoman Households, Gender Relations, and the Political Culture of the Antebellum South Carolina Low Country* (New York: Oxford University Press, 1995): Elizabeth Fox-Genovese, *Within the*

*Plantation Household: Black and White Women in the Old South* (Chapel Hill: University of North Carolina Press, 1988).

2. Daniel Feller, "Politics and Society: Toward a Jacksonian Synthesis," *Journal of the Early Republic* 10 (Summer 1990): 135–61; Edward Pessen, *Jacksonian America: Society, Personality, and Politics,* 2d rev. ed. (Homewood, Ill.: Dorsey Press, 1978), 149–323; Joel Silbey, "'The Salt of the Nation': Political Parties in Antebellum America," in *The Partisan Imperative: The Dynamics of American Politics before the Civil War* (New York: Oxford University Press, 1985), 50–68; Silbey, *The American Political Nation, 1838–1893* (Stanford: Stanford University Press, 1991); Lawrence Frederick Kohl, *The Politics of Individualism: Parties and the American Character in the Jacksonian Era* (New York: Oxford University Press, 1989); John Ashworth, *"Agrarians" and "Aristocrats": Party Political Ideology in the United States, 1837–1846* (Cambridge: Cambridge University Press, 1983).

3. Ronald Formisano, "The Invention of the Ethnocultural Interpretation," *American Historical Review* 99 (April 1994): 453–77, reviews the work of the "ethnocultural school" and its critics and disputes the accuracy of that and related labels. Harry Watson's excellent synthesis, *Liberty and Power: The Politics of Jacksonian America* (New York: Noonday Press, 1990), relies mainly on the market economy and republicanism to explain political behavior, reflecting current wisdom. Watson does concede something to diversity in scattered qualifications and in a chapter on state politics. The impact of the market economy explains nearly everything in Charles Sellers, *The Market Revolution: Jacksonian America, 1815–1846* (New York: Oxford University Press, 1991); Sellers claims, for example, that "every popular cultural or political movement in the early republic arose originally against the market" (208). I might agree with the assertion of Feller ("Politics and Society," 156) that scholars "can now say with some confidence not only who was a Whig and who was a Democrat, but why," depending upon how much confidence "some" is. Historians unsurprisingly find it easier to account for extremes than to explain the behavior of the broad middle. Ethnocultural explanations, for obvious reasons, do not apply very well to the South; few scholars have even attempted to apply them. And market economy explanations can cut many different ways. Marc Kruman, *Parties and Politics in North Carolina, 1836–1865* (Baton Rouge: Louisiana State University Press, 1983), 3–28, contends that eastern planters embedded in the market still feared it and supported the Democrats, while western backcountry farmers hungered for the opportunities that internal improvements and markets would bring and voted Whig. Steven Hahn, *The Roots of Southern Populism: Yeoman Farmers and the Transformation of the Georgia Upcountry, 1850–1890* (New York: Oxford University Press, 1983), 99–105, reverses this logic in explaining why market-oriented black belt residents backed Whiggery and market-shy upcountry yeomen favored the Democrats. Actually, I think that both of these explanations make considerable

sense if not stretched too far, and illustrate that general forces like the market operated in different ways in different places.

4. Daniel T. Rodgers, "Republicanism: The Career of a Concept," *Journal of
American History* 79 (June 1992): 11–38; Robert Shalhope, "Republicanism and
Early American Historiography," *William & Mary Quarterly* 39 (1982): 334–56;
J. William Harris, *Plain Folk and Gentry in a Slave Society: White Liberty and Black
Slavery in Augusta's Hinterlands* (Middletown, Conn.: Wesleyan University Press,
1985); J. Mills Thornton III, *Politics and Power in a Slave Society: Alabama, 1800–
1860* (Baton Rouge: Louisiana State University Press, 1978); Lacy K. Ford, Jr.,
*Origins of Southern Radicalism: The South Carolina Upcountry, 1800–1860* (New
York: Oxford University Press, 1988).

5. For two places rather different from rural Georgia, see Ronald P. Formisano,
*The Transformation of Political Culture: Massachusetts Parties, 1790s–1840s* (New
York: Oxford University Press, 1983); and Sean Wilentz, *Chants Democratic: New
York City & the Rise of the American Working Class, 1788–1850* (New York: Oxford
University Press, 1984).

6. William J. Cooper, Jr., *The South and the Politics of Slavery, 1828–1856* (Baton
Rouge: Louisiana State University Press, 1978); Ford, *Origins of Southern Radical-
ism;* Thornton, *Politics and Power;* Eric Foner, *Free Soil, Free Labor, Free Men: The
Ideology of the Republican Party before the Civil War* (New York: Oxford University
Press, 1970; William E. Gienapp, *The Origins of the Republican Party, 1852–1856*
(New York: Oxford University Press, 1987).

7. George M. Fredrickson, *The Black Image in the White Mind: The Debate on
Afro-American Character and Destiny, 1817–1914* (New York: Harper & Row, 1971),
1–96; Fox-Genovese, *Within the Plantation Household,* 55; Eugene D. Genovese,
*The Political Economy of Slavery: Studies in the Economy and Society of the Slave
South* (New York: Pantheon Books, 1965); Genovese, *The World the Slaveholders
Made: Two Essays in Interpretation* (New York: Pantheon Books, 1969); Genovese,
*Roll, Jordan, Roll: The World the Slaves Made* (New York: Pantheon Books, 1974);
Genovese, "Yeomen Farmers in a Slaveholders' Democracy," in Elizabeth Fox-
Genovese and Eugene D. Genovese, *Fruits of Merchant Capital: Slavery and Bour-
geois Property in the Rise and Expansion of Capitalism* (New York: Oxford University
Press, 1983), 249–64; James Oakes, *The Ruling Race: A History of American Slave-
holders* (New York: Alfred A. Knopf, 1982); Oakes, *Slavery and Freedom: An Inter-
pretation of the Old South* (New York: Alfred A. Knopf, 1990).

8. Hahn, *Roots of Southern Populism,* 15–133; David F. Wieman, "The Economic
Emancipation of the Non-Slaveholding Class: Upcountry Farmers in the Georgia
Cotton Economy," *Journal of Economic History* 45 (March 1985): 71–93. On pages
40–49, for example, Hahn hangs large arguments on slight changes in property
distribution between 1850 and 1860 and simultaneously minimizes the significance

of the expansion of cotton cultivation in the upcountry after 1850 to fit the evidence into his market resistance thesis. In remarks on politics, Hahn confidently asserts that Georgia "partisan divisions reflected deeper cleavages between those social groups and locales participating extensively in the market economy and those on the periphery or virtually isolated from it" (100). He supports this claim with a brief discussion of banking issues and overdrawn contrasts between black belt and up-country voting patterns. He does not tackle contradictory evidence or attempt to utilize his market participation model to explain politics *within* the upcountry. The two counties Hahn focuses on, Jackson and Carroll, actually differed considerably politically, a fact that Hahn does not explore. Jackson was only mildly Democratic, no more so than many black belt counties, while Carroll returned large Democratic majorities. Hahn, indeed, seems to be caught in a bit of an interpretative bind. The Whigs received about 40 percent of the upcountry vote. To attribute upcountry Whiggery to an embrace of the market economy undermines the idea of yeoman resistance to market intrusions; to attribute it to anything else undermines the claim that voters' relationships to the market economy formed the basis of partisan allegiance.

9. Ulrich B. Phillips, *Georgia and State Rights* (Washington, D.C.: Government Printing Office, 1902; reprint ed., Yellow Springs, Ohio: Antioch Press, 1968); Horace Montgomery, *Cracker Parties* (Baton Rouge: Louisiana State University Press, 1959); Richard H. Shryock, *Georgia and the Union in 1850* (Durham: Duke University Press, 1926).

10. Donald A. DeBats, "Elites and Masses: Political Structure, Communication, and Behavior in Antebellum Georgia" (Ph.D. diss., University of Wisconsin, Madison, 1973); DeBats, *Elites and Masses: Political Structure, Communication, and Behavior in Ante-Bellum Georgia* (New York: Garland Press, 1990), especially 423–41.

11. Ibid., 237, 433.

12. Michael P. Johnson, *Toward a Patriarchal Republic: The Secession of Georgia* (Baton Rouge: Louisiana State University Press, 1977).

13. In addition to the state studies cited above, see John C. Inscoe, *Mountain Masters, Slavery, and the Sectional Crisis in Western North Carolina* (Knoxville: University of Tennessee Press, 1989); Thomas E. Jeffrey, *State Parties and National Politics: North Carolina, 1815–1861* (Athens: University of Georgia Press, 1989).

## *1. Surveying a White Men's Democracy*

1. Roland M. Harper, "Development of Agriculture in Lower Georgia from 1850–1880," *Georgia Historical Quarterly* 6 (June 1922): 107–8; James C. Bonner,

*A History of Georgia Agriculture, 1732–1860* (Athens: University of Georgia Press, 1964), 48; Julia Floyd Smith, *Slavery and Rice Culture in Low Country Georgia 1750–1860* (Knoxville: University of Tennessee Press, 1985).

2. *Milledgeville Federal Union,* 26 January 1832; Harper, "Agriculture in Lower Georgia," 103–7; Bonner, *Georgia Agriculture,* 42–43.

3. Bonner, *Georgia Agriculture,* 46, 54–59, 61–72; Ralph B. Flanders, *Plantation Slavery in Georgia* (Chapel Hill: University of North Carolina Press, 1933), 75–78; Helen I. Greene, "Politics in Georgia, 1830–1854," (Ph.D. diss., University of Chicago, 1945), 2; F. N. Boney, "Part Three: 1820–1865," in Kenneth Coleman, gen. ed., *A History of Georgia* (Athens: University of Georgia Press, 1977), 162–63; Roland M. Harper, "Development of Agriculture in Upper Georgia from 1850–1880," *Georgia Historical Quarterly* 6 (March 1922): 9–11; Joseph P. Reidy, *From Slavery to Agrarian Capitalism in the Cotton Plantation South: Central Georgia, 1800–1880* (Chapel Hill: University of North Carolina Press, 1992); Steven Hahn, *The Roots of Southern Populism: Yeoman Farmers and the Transformation of the Georgia Upcountry, 1850–1890* (New York: Oxford University Press, 1983), 29; J. William Harris, *Plain Folk and Gentry in a Slave Society: White Liberty and Black Slavery in Augusta's Hinterlands* (Middletown, Conn.: Wesleyan University Press, 1985).

4. Ulrich B. Phillips, *Georgia and State Rights* (Washington, D.C.: Government Printing Office, 1902; reprint ed., Yellow Springs, Ohio: Antioch Press, 1968), 62–65, 68–86.

5. Questionnaire of Andrew Jackson Gass, in Colleen Morse Elliott and Louise Armstrong Moxley, eds., *The Tennessee Civil War Veterans Questionnaires,* 5 vols. (Easley, S.C.: Southern Historical Press, 1985), 3:889; Harper, "Agriculture in Upper Georgia," 8–9; Bonner, *Georgia Agriculture,* 45–46.

6. E. Merton Coulter, *Georgia: A Short History,* 3d ed. (Chapel Hill: University of North Carolina Press, 1960), 219–20; Milton S. Heath, *Constructive Liberalism: The Role of the State in Economic Development in Georgia to 1860* (Cambridge: Harvard University Press, 1954), 143–48; Hahn, *Roots of Southern Populism,* 15–28; Harris, *Plain Folk and Gentry,* 21–26.

7. Stephanie McCurry, "The Two Faces of Republicanism: Gender and Proslavery Politics in Antebellum South Carolina," *Journal of American History* 78 (March 1992): 1245–64; McCurry, *Masters of Small Worlds: Yeoman Households, Gender Relations, and the Political Culture of the Antebellum South Carolina Low Country* (New York: Oxford University Press, 1995); Elizabeth Fox-Genovese, *Within the Plantation Household: Black and White Women in the Old South* (Chapel Hill: University of North Carolina Press, 1988), 37–99.

8. *Seventh Census of the United States, 1850,* xxxvi, 366, 376; Boney, "Part Three: 1820–1865," 152–73; Fox-Genovese, *Within the Plantation Household,* 70–99. Like

Fox-Genovese, I see the rural nature of the South as fundamental, not incidental—as the product of a social commitment to preserving an agricultural world centered on the institution of slavery.

9. Hahn, *Roots of Southern Populism,* 20–28, 40–44; Harris, *Plain Folk and Gentry,* 20–40, 77–90; Bill Cecil-Fronsman, *Common Whites: Class and Culture in Antebellum North Carolina* (Lexington: University Press of Kentucky, 1992); Charles C. Bolton, *Poor Whites of the Antebellum South: Tenants and Laborers in Central North Carolina and Northeast Mississippi* (Durham: Duke University Press, 1994); Frederick A. Bode and Donald E. Ginter, *Farm Tenancy and the Census in Antebellum Georgia* (Athens: University of Georgia Press, 1986), 1–146, carefully discusses the immensely complex subject of antebellum tenancy.

10. Questionnaires of Joe Free and Charles D. Beasley, in Morse and Moxley, eds., *Tennessee Civil War Veterans Questionnaires,* 2:857, 1:302–3; Hahn, *Roots of Southern Populism,* 15–49; Lacy K. Ford, Jr., *Origins of Southern Radicalism: The South Carolina Upcountry, 1800–1860* (New York: Oxford University Press, 1988); Frank L. Owsley, *Plain Folk of the Old South* (Baton Rouge: Louisiana State University Press, 1949); Bertram Wyatt-Brown, *Southern Honor: Ethics and Behavior in the Old South* (New York: Oxford University Press, 1982); Elliott J. Gorn, "'Gouge and Bite, Pull Hair and Scratch': The Social Significance of Fighting in the Southern Backcountry," *American Historical Review* 90 (February 1985): 18–43.

11. Questionnaire of James Haynes, in Morse and Moxley, eds., *Tennessee Civil War Veterans Questionnaires,* 3:1061–62; Ralph A. Wooster, *The People in Power: Courthouse and Statehouse in the Lower South, 1850–1860* (Knoxville: University of Tennessee Press, 1969); James Oakes, *The Ruling Race: A History of American Slaveholders* (New York: Alfred A. Knopf, 1982); Eugene D. Genovese, *The Political Economy of Slavery: Studies in the Economy and Society of the Slave South* (New York: Pantheon Books, 1965); Genovese, *The World the Slaveholders Made: Two Essays in Interpretation* (New York: Pantheon Books, 1969); Genovese, *Roll, Jordan, Roll: The World the Slaves Made* (New York: Pantheon Books, 1974); Genovese, "Yeomen Farmers in a Slaveholders' Democracy," in Elizabeth Fox-Genovese and Eugene D. Genovese, *Fruits of Merchant Capital: Slavery and Bourgeois Property in the Rise and Expansion of Capitalism* (New York: Oxford University Press, 1983), 249–64; George M. Fredrickson, *The Black Image in the White Mind: The Debate on Afro-American Character and Destiny, 1817–1914* (New York: Harper & Row, 1971), 64–96. I obviously lean toward Genovese on questions of planter power, and I believe that paternalistic ideas were widespread, especially among planters but also among white male heads of households generally. And, like Genovese, I emphasize at many points the vital distinctions between societies based on free labor, such as the antebellum North, and those based on slave labor, like the Old South. However,

following Fredrickson, I would argue that the ideology of "herrenvolk democracy," though contradicted by real inequalities of wealth and status, governed relations among white men, especially in the realm of party politics. I see no necessary inconsistency in believing simultaneously that the planter class exerted great political and economic power, that other white men nonetheless benefited from the peculiar construction of southern society and enjoyed a considerable voice in government, and that white men could appreciate paternalism as heads of households—particularly in a slave society—and value racial distinctions that separated all whites from all blacks.

12. Sources for and further discussion of county voting can be found in chapter 5.

13. Folks Huxford, *Pioneers of Wiregrass Georgia: A Biographical Account of Some of the Early Settlers of That Portion of Wiregrass Georgia Embraced in the Original Counties of Irwin, Appling, Wayne, Camden, and Glynn,* 7 vols. (Adel, Ga.: Patten Publishing, 1951–75), 1:112–13; 2:130, 164; 3:290, 370–71; 4:124–25, 158–59; 5:232–33; McCurry, *Masters of Small Worlds,* 239–76; Christopher Morris, *Becoming Southern: The Evolution of a Way of Life, Warren County and Vicksburg, Mississippi, 1770–1860* (New York: Oxford University Press, 1995), 132–55; Robert C. Kenzer, *Kinship and Neighborhood in a Southern Community: Orange County, North Carolina, 1849–1881* (Knoxville: University of Tennessee Press, 1987), 52–70; Daniel W. Crofts, *Old Southampton: Politics and Society in a Virginia County, 1834–1869* (Charlottesville: University Press of Virginia, 1992), 126–31.

14. Hahn, *Roots of Southern Populism,* 50–85; Harris, *Plain Folk and Gentry,* 64–122; Genovese, "Yeomen Farmers in a Slaveholders' Democracy," 249–64; John T. Schlotterbeck, "The 'Social Economy' of an Upper South Community: Orange and Greene Counties, Virginia, 1815–1860," in Orville Vernon Burton and Robert C. McMath, Jr., eds., *Class, Conflict, and Consensus: Antebellum Southern Community Studies* (Westport, Conn.: Greenwood Press, 1982), 3–28. One would not want to overstress the idea of cooperation, but I do think that class and community relations differed significantly in this regard from those in the developing antebellum Northeast and from the far more exploitative conditions that developed in the New South.

15. Bernard Bailyn, *The Ideological Origins of the American Revolution* (Cambridge: Harvard University Press, 1967); Gordon S. Wood, *The Creation of the American Republic, 1776–1787* (Chapel Hill: University of North Carolina Press, 1969). Robert Shalhope, "Republicanism and Early American Historiography," *William & Mary Quarterly* 39 (1982): 334–56; and Daniel T. Rodgers, "Republicanism: The Career of a Concept," *Journal of American History* 79 (June 1992): 11–38, discuss the rest of the vast, oft-cited, and controversial literature on republicanism. I call antebellum Georgia a "white men's democracy" yet suggest the continuing importance of some republican strains, while being cognizant that republicanism

and democracy are not the same. The prevailing ideas of white male egalitarianism and the enthusiastic embrace of political party competition, particularly, seem to me rather more democratic than republican.

16. David P. Hillhouse to Oliver H. Prince, 29 October 1828, Oliver H. Prince Papers, UGA.

17. Harris, *Plain Folk and Gentry;* Ford, *Origins of Southern Radicalism;* Harry Watson, *Liberty and Power: The Politics of Jacksonian America* (New York: Noonday Press, 1990); J. Mills Thornton III, *Politics and Power in a Slave Society: Alabama, 1800–1860* (Baton Rouge: Louisiana State University Press, 1978); Carl J. Vipperman, *William Lowndes and the Transition of Southern Politics, 1782–1822* (Chapel Hill: University of North Carolina Press, 1989).

18. *Congressional Globe Appendix*, 34th Cong., 1st sess., 1855–56, 728–29.

19. Genovese, *World the Slaveholders Made;* Drew Gilpin Faust, *The Ideology of Slavery: Proslavery Thought in the Antebellum South, 1830–1860* (Baton Rouge: Louisiana State University Press, 1981); John C. Miller, *The Wolf by the Ears: Thomas Jefferson and Slavery* (New York: Free Press, 1977); Larry E. Tise, *Proslavery: A History of the Defense of Slavery in America, 1701–1840* (Athens: University of Georgia Press, 1987); William S. Jenkins, *Pro-Slavery Thought in the Old South* (Chapel Hill: University of North Carolina Press, 1935).

20. *Augusta Chronicle & Sentinel*, 30 March, 15 June 1860, 1 March 1860.

21. *Augusta Chronicle*, 18 April 1835; *Augusta Constitutionalist*, 29 June 1853; Joseph Henry Lumpkin to Howell Cobb, 11 June 1850, Howell Cobb Papers, UGA; Nisbet's opinion is in Flanders, *Plantation Slavery*, 247; for Stephens's address at Augusta on 2 July 1859, see Henry Cleveland, *Alexander H. Stephens, in Public and Private, with Letters and Speeches, before, during, and since the War* (Philadelphia: National Publishing, 1866), 647–50.

22. *Eighth Census of the United States, 1860, Agriculture*, 22–29; Hahn, *Roots of Southern Populism*, 15–85; Harris, *Plain Folk and Gentry*, 20–40, 64–104; David F. Wieman, "The Economic Emancipation of the Non-Slaveholding Class: Upcountry Farmers in the Georgia Cotton Economy," *Journal of Economic History* 45 (March 1985): 71–93; James C. Bonner, "Profile of a Late Ante-Bellum Community," *American Historical Review* 49 (July 1944): 663–80. These authors differ not so much over the direction of change as over the interpretative meaning and significance of it. George B. Crawford, in "Cotton, Land, and Sustenance: Toward the Limits of Abundance in Late Antebellum Georgia," *Georgia Historical Quarterly* (Summer 1988): 215–47; and "Preface to Revolution: Agriculture, Society and Crisis in Georgia, 1840–1860" (Ph.D. diss., Claremont Graduate School, 1988), labors to develop the thesis that an agricultural subsistence crisis existed in antebellum Georgia, and that this crisis somehow helped impel the state toward secession.

23. *Seventh Census, 1850*, 366; *Eighth Census, 1860, Manufactures*, 80–82, and

*Population,* 74. The increase in town population was in the 3 percent range, but the definite underreporting of town population in 1850 makes exact comparisons impossible.

24. J. Henly Smith to Alexander H. Stephens, 3 April 1860, Alexander H. Stephens Papers, LC (microfilm, UGA); "Novissemus," in the *Augusta Constitutionalist,* 10 September 1856; *Augusta Constitutionalist,* 28 February 1857; *Savannah Republican,* 1 October 1852.

## 2. *"Animosities Which Neither Time nor Reflection Ever Healed": The Formation of Georgia's Jacksonian Parties*

1. George Gilmer, *Sketches of Some of the First Settlers of Upper Georgia, of the Cherokees, and the Author* (New York: D. Appleton, 1854), 561.

2. Ibid., 201; Ulrich B. Phillips, *Georgia and State Rights* (Washington, D.C.: Government Printing Office, 1902; reprint ed., Yellow Springs, Ohio: Antioch Press, 1968), 16–32; James H. Broussard, *The Southern Federalists 1800–1816* (Baton Rouge: Louisiana State University Press, 1978), 247–56, 273, 296, 364, 373, 377, 381–82; Chase C. Mooney, *William H. Crawford, 1772–1834* (Lexington: University Press of Kentucky, 1974), 1–16; Edward J. Harden, *The Life of George M. Troup* (Savannah: E. J. Purse, 1859), 1–13; William O. Foster, Sr., *James Jackson: Duelist and Militant Statesman* (Athens: University of Georgia Press, 1960); George R. Lamplugh, *Politics on the Periphery: Factions and Parties in Georgia, 1783–1806* (Newark: University of Delaware Press, 1986).

3. Gilmer, *Sketches,* 1–176, 259; Milton S. Heath, *Constructive Liberalism: The Role of the State in Economic Development in Georgia to 1860* (Cambridge: Harvard University Press, 1954), 71; Lamplugh, *Politics on the Periphery,* 144–202; J. E. D. Shipp, *Giant Days, or the Life and Times of William H. Crawford* (Americus, Ga.: Southern Printers, 1909), 44–76; W. H. Sparks, *The Memories of Fifty Years,* 3d ed. (Philadelphia: Claxton, Remsen, & Heffelfinger, 1872), 19–27.

4. Francis N. Thorpe, comp., *The Federal and State Constitutions, Colonial Charters, and Other Organic Laws of the States, Territories, and Colonies, Now or Heretofore Forming the United States of America,* 5 vols. (Washington, D.C.: Government Printing Office, 1909), 2:791–809. The constitution could be altered by a state convention or by the passage of an amendment in two successive sessions of the legislature. Property qualifications were five hundred acres of land and at least $4,000 in property for the governor, a freehold estate worth $500 or $1,000 in other property for senators, and a freehold estate worth $250 or $500 in other property for representatives. Property qualifications for legislators were eliminated in 1835. Gubernatorial elections were held in odd years, congressional elections in even years. The state

experimented with biennial legislative sessions and elections between 1843 and 1857 and with the election of senators by districts from 1845 through 1851 before returning to former modes and schedules in the last antebellum years.

5. Phillips, *State Rights,* 95–112; Mooney, *Crawford,* 213–321; Richard P. McCormick, *The Second American Party System: Party Formation in the Jacksonian Era* (Chapel Hill: University of North Carolina Press, 1966), 238–39; Jack N. Averitt, "The Democratic Party in Georgia, 1824–1837" (Ph.D. diss., University of North Carolina, Chapel Hill, 1957), 11–14, 22–30, 158–88; Donald A. DeBats, *Elites and Masses: Political Structure, Communication, and Behavior in Ante-Bellum Georgia* (New York: Garland Press, 1990), 25–30.

6. Sparks, *Memories of Fifty Years,* 130.

7. Gilmer, *Sketches,* 499; McCormick, *Second Party System,* 239–41; Phillips, *State Rights,* 52–59, 68–86, 102–8; Averitt, "Democratic Party," 30–32, 51–59, 63–67, 196–215; Alvin L. Duckett, *John Forsyth: Political Tactician* (Athens: University of Georgia Press, 1962), 1–41, 81–104; James C. Chase, *Emergence of the Presidential Nominating Convention, 1789–1832* (Urbana: University of Illinois Press, 1973), 94–118; William J. Cooper, Jr., *The South and the Politics of Slavery, 1828–1856* (Baton Rouge: Louisiana State University Press, 1978), 5–15; Robert V. Remini, *The Election of Andrew Jackson* (Philadelphia: J. B. Lippincott, 1963); John W. Ward, *Andrew Jackson: Symbol for an Age* (New York: Oxford University Press, 1955); Ronald N. Satz, *American Indian Policy in the Jacksonian Era* (Lincoln: University of Nebraska Press, 1975), 44–51, 99–101; Thomas P. Govan, "John M. Berrien and the Administration of Andrew Jackson," *Journal of Southern History* 5 (November 1939): 447–49.

8. Royce C. McCrary, "John MacPherson Berrien (1781–1856): A Political Biography" (Ph.D. diss., University of Georgia, 1971), 1–103.

9. George M. Troup to William C. Daniell, 27 March 1829, William and Nell Harden Collection, UGA; George R. Gilmer to Tomlinson Fort, 27 August 1829, Tomlinson Fort to John C. Calhoun, 29 January 1830, Tomlinson Fort Papers, EU; William H. Crawford to Samuel Smith, October 1828, William H. Crawford Papers, DU; William T. Williams to John M. Berrien, 19 July 1831, John MacPherson Berrien Papers, SHC; Richard W. Habersham to John M. Berrien, 3 August 1831, in Thomas P. Govan, "Banking and Credit System in Georgia 1810–1860" (Ph.D. diss., Vanderbilt University, 1937), 77; Gilmer, *Sketches,* 306–17; Duckett, *Forsyth,* 128–49; Averitt, "Democratic Party," 76–85, 118–30; McCrary, "Berrien," 32–91; Govan, "Berrien and Andrew Jackson," 449–51, 457–60; E. Merton Coulter, "The Nullification Movement in Georgia," *Georgia Historical Quarterly* 5 (March 1921): 1–5; William W. Freehling, *Prelude to Civil War: The Nullification Controversy in South Carolina 1816–1836* (New York: Harper & Row, 1965), 89–153, 219–

27; John Niven, *Martin Van Buren: The Romantic Age of American Politics* (New York: Oxford University Press, 1983), 182–83; Donald B. Cole, *Martin Van Buren and the American Political System* (Princeton: Princeton University Press, 1984), 203–20; John Niven, *John Calhoun and the Price of Union: A Biography* (Baton Rouge: Louisiana State University Press, 1988), 158–62, 174–76.

10. Tomlinson Fort to John C. Calhoun, 15 July 1831, Fort Papers, EU; George M. Troup to William C. Daniell, 23 May 1831, 9 September 1831, Harden Collection, UGA; Charles J. McDonald to John C. Calhoun, 30 May 1831, Charles J. McDonald Papers, SHC; Iverson L. Harris to John M. Berrien, 30 September 1831, Berrien Papers, SHC; Coulter, "Nullification," 5–6.

11. *Milledgeville Federal Union*, 7 April 1831; Tomlinson Fort to John C. Calhoun, 15 July 1831, Fort Papers, EU.

12. Phillips, *State Rights*, 124–28; Averitt, "Democratic Party," 285–302; Govan, "Berrien and Andrew Jackson," 451–56, 460–63; Paul Murray, *The Whig Party in Georgia, 1825–1853*, James Sprunt Studies in History and Political Science 29 (Chapel Hill: University of North Carolina Press, 1948), 20–25; Wilson Lumpkin, *The Removal of the Cherokee Indians from Georgia*, 2 vols. (New York: Dodd, Mead, 1907), 1:9–48.

13. *Columbus Enquirer*, 28 April 1832; Augustin S. Clayton to Edward Harden, 26 January 1832, James Hamilton, Jr., to Edward Harden, 31 August 1832, Edward Harden Papers, DU; George M. Troup to William C. Daniell, 12 March 1832, Harden Collection, UGA; *Milledgeville Southern Recorder*, 18 August 1831; *Milledgeville Georgia Journal*, 21 June 1832; Coulter, "Nullification," 11–12.

14. *Macon Georgia Messenger*, 10 March 1832; *Milledgeville Southern Recorder*, 1 September 1831; *Milledgeville Georgia Journal*, 13, 20, 27 September 1832.

15. George M. Troup to William C. Daniell, 29 August 1832, Harden Collection, UGA; George M. Troup to Edward Harden, 20 September 1832, Harden Papers, DU; *Milledgeville Georgia Journal*, 9, 23 August 1832; *Milledgeville Southern Recorder*, 9, 30 August 1832; Coulter, "Nullification," 14–24; McCrary, "Berrien," 196–203; Richard D. Ellis, *The Union at Risk: Jacksonian Democracy, States' Rights, and the Nullification Crisis* (New York: Oxford University Press, 1987), 106–7; Porter L. Fortune, Jr., "George M. Troup: Leading State Rights Advocate" (Ph.D. diss., University of North Carolina, Chapel Hill, 1949), 288–92.

16. *Milledgeville Federal Union*, 26 January 1832; *Milledgeville Georgia Journal*, 26 July 1832; George M. Troup to William C. Daniell, 29 August 1832, Harden Collection, UGA; *Macon Georgia Messenger*, 19 July 1832; *Milledgeville Southern Recorder*, 26 July 1832; Heath, *Constructive Liberalism*, 173–75; Averitt, "Democratic Party," 346–50; Govan, "Berrien and Andrew Jackson," 465–66; Edward L. Tucker, *Richard Henry Wilde: His Life and Selected Poems* (Athens: University of

Georgia Press, 1966), 1–42; Robert V. Remini, *Andrew Jackson and the Bank War* (New York: W. W. Norton, 1967), 78.

17. *Milledgeville Federal Union,* 7 June 1832, 7 April 1831, 1, 15 March, 5 July 1832; *Augusta Chronicle,* 2 June, 20 October 1832; Chase, *Presidential Nominating Convention,* 185–263; Cooper, *Politics of Slavery,* 15–22; Averitt, "Democratic Party," 329–46, 373–76.

18. *Augusta Chronicle,* 12, 26 September, 3 November 1832; Gilmer, *Sketches,* 461–63; Averitt, "Democratic Party," 369–76; Alexander A. Lawrence, *James Moore Wayne: Southern Unionist* (Chapel Hill: University of North Carolina Press, 1943), 3–52.

19. Stephen F. Miller, *The Bench and Bar of Georgia: Memoirs and Sketches. With an Appendix, Containing a Court Roll from 1790 to 1857, etc.,* 2 vols. (Philadelphia: J. B. Lippincott, 1858), 1:34–39, 60–63; 2:30–34; Ellis, *Union at Risk,* 107–9; Duckett, *Forsyth,* 150–66; Averitt, "Democratic Party," 359–62; McCrary, "Berrien," 203–6; Coulter, "Nullification," 26–29. About 130 delegates from sixty-one counties attended the convention; the delegates remaining after the Forsyth-led bolt represented fewer than half of Georgia's counties. Both the Berrien and Forsyth groups contained delegates from counties scattered all across the state.

20. James D. Richardson, comp., *A Compilation of the Messages and Papers of the Presidents, 1789–1897,* 10 vols. (Washington, D.C.: Government Printing Office, 1896–99), 2:643, 648.

21. *Milledgeville Southern Recorder,* 20 December 1832; *Augusta Chronicle,* 25 December 1832; *Macon Georgia Messenger,* 20 December 1832.

22. *Milledgeville Federal Union,* 22 March 1832; *Milledgeville Southern Recorder,* 15 March 1832; *Macon Georgia Messenger,* 17 March 1832, 24 January 1833; *Augusta Chronicle,* 26 May 1832; Coulter, "Nullification," 9–10; Ellis, *Union at Risk,* 29–32, 112–20.

23. *Macon Georgia Messenger,* 14 March 1833; *Milledgeville Georgia Journal,* 27 December 1832; *Columbus Enquirer,* 16 March 1833; *Milledgeville Southern Recorder,* 27 February, 17 April, 26 June 1833; Ellis, *Union at Risk,* 160–77; Freehling, *Prelude to Civil War,* 295–97; Merrill D. Peterson, *The Great Triumvirate: Webster, Clay, and Calhoun* (New York: Oxford University Press, 1987), 212–33.

24. *Augusta Chronicle,* 25 May 1833; *Athens Southern Banner,* 22 June, 27 July, 17 August 1833; *Milledgeville Southern Recorder,* 31 July, 18 September 1833; *Macon Georgia Messenger,* 16 May, 15 August 1833; *Milledgeville Federal Union,* 16 May 1833; Lawrence, *Wayne,* 53–68; Murray, *Whig Party,* 53–54; Averitt, "Democratic Party," 404–6.

25. *Milledgeville Southern Recorder,* 20 November 1833, 1 January 1834; *Milledgeville Federal Union,* 27 November, 18 December 1833; *Athens Southern Banner,*

30 November 1833; Miller, *Bench and Bar,* 1:27–30; Averitt, "Democratic Party," 414–17.

26. Richardson, comp., *Messages and Papers,* 3:5–19, 30–32; Remini, *Bank War,* 111–53; Bray Hammond, *Banks and Politics in America: From the Revolution to the Civil War* (Princeton: Princeton University Press, 1957), 411–39.

27. *Columbus Enquirer,* 22 February 1834, 14 December 1833; diary entry for 8 May 1834, in James Z. Rabun, ed., "Alexander H. Stephens's Diary, 1834–1837," *Georgia Historical Quarterly* 26 (March 1952): 82; *Savannah Republican,* 2, 6 January, 9 April 1834; *Macon Georgia Messenger,* 16 January 1834; *Milledgeville Southern Recorder,* 8 January 1834; Thomas Brown, *Politics and Statesmanship: Essays on the American Whig Party* (New York: Columbia University Press, 1985), 157–58.

28. *Milledgeville Southern Recorder,* 16 July 1834; address to the friends of State Rights in Georgia, in the *Macon Georgia Messenger,* 2 January 1834; *Macon Georgia Messenger,* 17 July, 25 September 1834; *Augusta Chronicle,* 1 February 1834; *Milledgeville Southern Recorder,* 6 February 1833, 5 March, 4, 18, 26 June, 9 July, 6 August, 3 September 1834.

29. *Milledgeville Federal Union,* 15 October 1833, 22 January, 12 February, 16, 30 July 1834, 14 January 1835; *Athens Southern Banner,* 21 December 1833, 22 February, 7 June 1834; *Milledgeville Southern Recorder,* 22 October 1834; McCormick, *Second Party System,* 242; Averitt, "Democratic Party," 420–28; DeBats, *Elites and Masses,* 51–52.

30. "Cato," in the *Milledgeville Federal Union,* 5 May 1835; *Athens Southern Banner,* 19 March, 9, 16 April 1835; *Macon Georgia Messenger,* 7 May 1835; Averitt, "Democratic Party," 441–48; Richard P. McCormick, "Was There a 'Whig Strategy' in 1836?" *Journal of the Early Republic* 4 (Spring 1984): 47–70; Thomas Brown, "From Old Hickory to Sly Fox: The Routinization of Charisma in the Early Democratic Party," *Journal of the Early Republic* 11 (Fall 1991): 339–69; Jonathan M. Atkins, "The Presidential Candidacy of Hugh Lawson White in Tennessee, 1832–1836," *Journal of Southern History* 58 (February 1992): 27–56.

31. *Milledgeville Federal Union,* 19 May, 18 July 1835; *Macon Georgia Telegraph,* 24 March 1836; Richard Hofstadter, *The Idea of a Party System: The Rise of Legitimate Opposition in the United States, 1780–1840* (Berkeley: University of California Press, 1969).

32. *Milledgeville Federal Union,* 16 June 1835; *Athens Southern Banner,* 27 August 1835; Richard Brown, "The Missouri Crisis, Slavery, and the Politics of Jacksonianism," *South Atlantic Quarterly* 65 (Winter 1966): 55–72; Richard P. McCormick, "The Jacksonian Strategy," *Journal of the Early Republic* 10 (Spring 1990): 1–17.

33. *Columbus Enquirer,* 24 April 1835; *Milledgeville Southern Recorder,* 6 January 1835; *Augusta Chronicle,* 24 January 1835; *Savannah Republican,* 2 February 1835.

34. *Milledgeville Southern Recorder,* 23 June 1835; *Milledgeville Federal Union,* 4 July 1835; *Athens Southern Banner,* 20 May, 9 July 1935; *Macon Georgia Messenger,* 27 August 1835; *Savannah Republican,* 31 July 1835; Averitt, "Democratic Party," 449–50.

35. *Milledgeville Southern Recorder,* 21 July 1835; *Athens Southern Banner,* 30 July, 17 September 1835; *Columbus Enquirer,* 31 July 1835; *Macon Georgia Messenger,* 3 September 1835; Averitt, "Democratic Party," 451–59.

36. *Milledgeville Southern Recorder,* 6 October 1835; *Macon Georgia Messenger,* 6 August 1835; letter from Robert A. Beall, 14 September 1835, in the *Macon Georgia Messenger,* 17 September 1835; Leonard L. Richards, *"Gentlemen of Property and Standing": Anti-Abolition Mobs in Jacksonian America* (New York: Oxford University Press, 1970); Glyndon G. Van Deusen, *The Jacksonian Era, 1828–1848* (New York: Harper & Row, 1959), 107–9; William W. Freehling, *The Road to Disunion: Secessionists at Bay, 1776–1854* (New York: Oxford University Press, 1990), 289–352; Cooper, *Politics of Slavery,* 58–59.

37. *Columbus Enquirer,* 22 April 1836, 16 July 1835; *Milledgeville Southern Recorder,* 10 May 1836; Nisbet's letter, in the *Milledgeville Southern Recorder,* 20 September 1836; Black's letter, in the *Savannah Republican,* 26 September 1836; *Columbus Enquirer,* 3 November 1836.

38. *Milledgeville Federal Union,* 11 October 1836; *Cassville Standard of the Union,* in the *Milledgeville Federal Union,* 27 September 1836; *Augusta Constitutionalist,* 8 March, 12 April 1836; *Macon Georgia Telegraph,* 7 April 1836; *Milledgeville Federal Union,* 8, 14, 21 April, 20, 27 September, 3, 18 October 1836.

39. Hiram Warner to Arthur A. Morgan, 7 June 1836, Arthur A. Morgan Papers, DU; *Augusta Chronicle,* 7 May 1835; *Columbus Enquirer,* 20 May 1836; *Savannah Republican,* 19 September 1836; *Milledgeville Southern Recorder,* 13, 20 October 1836; *Milledgeville Federal Union,* 25 October 1836; Averitt, "Democratic Party," 474–79. The above and all subsequent voting statistics for the period from 1835 to 1860, unless otherwise noted, are derived from my analysis of state electoral returns found in newspapers—typically the mid-October issues—and presidential election data contained in Walter Dean Burnham, *Presidential Ballots, 1836–1892* (Baltimore: Johns Hopkins University Press, 1955). Estimates of voter turnout are based on linear interpolation of census returns. The Pearson's correlation between the 1835 gubernatorial and 1836 presidential election was .89, indicating substantial continuity in voting patterns despite the shifts that caused Van Buren's defeat.

40. For discussion of the power of so-called valence issues, see Joel Silbey, *A Respectable Minority: The Democratic Party in the Civil War Era, 1860–1868* (New York: W. W. Norton, 1977), 165.

41. *Milledgeville Federal Union,* 25 April 1837; John B. Lamar to Howell Cobb, 31 December 1837, Cobb Papers, UGA.

42. Heath, *Constructive Liberalism,* 160–204; Govan, "Banking and Credit System," 10–13, 119–28; Van Deusen, *Jacksonian Era,* 104–6, 116–17; Peter Temin, *The Jacksonian Economy* (New York: W. W. Norton, 1969), 22–23, 77–78, 91–112, 118–28, 136–47, 165–71; Larry Schweikart, *Banking in the American South from the Age of Jackson to Reconstruction* (Baton Rouge: Louisiana State University Press, 1987), 112–13, 258, 261.

43. *Macon Georgia Messenger,* 7 December 1835; *Milledgeville Southern Recorder,* 14 November 1837.

44. *Macon Georgia Telegraph,* 4 December 1838; *Augusta Constitutionalist,* 10 January 1837; Harold D. Woodman, *King Cotton & His Retainers: Financing & Marketing the Cotton Crop of the South, 1800–1925* (Lexington: University of Kentucky Press, 1968), 5–195.

45. *Macon Georgia Messenger,* 9 June 1836; *Milledgeville Southern Recorder,* 17 November 1835; *Milledgeville Federal Union,* 14 July 1831, 13 November 1835, 9, 16, 23 June, 2 August, 8 November 1836, 2 May 1837.

46. Richardson, comp., *Messages and Papers,* 3:324–26; Van Deusen, *Jacksonian Era,* 121–28; James C. Curtis, *The Fox at Bay: Martin Van Buren and the Presidency, 1837–1841* (Lexington: University Press of Kentucky, 1970), 96–110.

47. *Augusta Chronicle & Sentinel,* 30 September 1837; *Macon Georgia Telegraph,* 23 October 1837; *Milledgeville Federal Union,* 27 June 1837; *Macon Georgia Messenger,* 18 May 1837; *Athens Southern Banner,* 30 September 1837; Ansley B. Barton, "The Political Career of George Rockingham Gilmer, 1829–1839" (M.A. thesis, Emory University, 1963), 12–16.

48. *Milledgeville Federal Union,* 3 July 1838; *Macon Georgia Telegraph,* 29 August 1837, 18 September 1838.

49. *Athens Southern Banner,* 26 January 1839; *Macon Georgia Telegraph,* 11 December 1837, 2 December 1837; *Augusta Constitutionalist,* 19 January 1837; *Milledgeville Federal Union,* 22 September 1840; Lee Benson, *The Concept of Jacksonian Democracy: New York as a Test Case* (Princeton: Princeton University Press, 1961), 94–97; Arthur Schlesinger, Jr., *The Age of Jackson* (Boston: Little, Brown, 1945); Sean Wilentz, *Chants Democratic: New York City & the Rise of the American Working Class, 1788–1850* (New York: Oxford University Press, 1984).

50. *Augusta Constitutionalist,* 29 August 1837; *Milledgeville Federal Union,* 31 March 1840, 31 July 1838.

51. John M. Berrien to Colonel Hunter, 17 May 1836, Berrien Papers, UGA (photostatic copy of the original in the Simon Gratz Collection, Historical Society of Pennsylvania Library, Philadelphia); Ambrose Baber to Mary Baber, 14 March 1838, Baber-Blackshear Collection, UGA; "Baldwin," in the *Augusta Chronicle & Sentinel,* 2, 9 November 1837; *Milledgeville Southern Recorder,* 24 July, 11, 25 September 1838; *Macon Georgia Messenger,* 11 May 1837, 26 April, 22 June, 12, 19 July,

2, 16 August, 20 September 1838; *Augusta Chronicle & Sentinel* (triweekly), 8, 27 March, 11 September 1838; *Savannah Republican*, 30 December 1839.

52. *Savannah Republican*, 24 August 1838; *Milledgeville Federal Union*, 25 September, 23 October 1838; *Augusta Chronicle & Sentinel* (triweekly), 20 March 1838; *Macon Georgia Messenger*, 9 August 1838; *Milledgeville Southern Recorder*, 16, 30 October 1838.

53. *Athens Southern Banner*, 1 December 1838; *Augusta Constitutionalist*, 22 November 1838, 9 February 1839; *Columbus Enquirer*, 2 January 1839; *Macon Georgia Messenger*, 31 January 1839; *Milledgeville Federal Union*, 22 January, 2 April, 29 October 1839, 25 February 1840; *Macon Georgia Telegraph*, 3 December 1839; Heath, *Constructive Liberalism*, 206–7; Schweikart, *Banking in the South*, 113; Temin, *Jacksonian Economy*, 152–55; Govan, "Banking and Credit System," 15–21.

54. *Macon Georgia Messenger*, 3 October 1839; *Augusta Chronicle & Sentinel* (triweekly), 20 April, 25 July 1839; *Athens Southern Banner*, 20, 27 September 1839; *Milledgeville Federal Union*, 30 July, 10 September, 1 October 1839; Kenneth Coleman and Charles Stephen Gurr, eds., *Dictionary of Georgia Biography*, 2 vols. (Athens: University of Georgia Press, 1983), 2:657–58.

55. *Macon Georgia Messenger*, 19 December 1839; *Milledgeville Federal Union*, 3, 10 December 1839, 7 January, 4 February 1840; Heath, *Constructive Liberalism*, 211–14; Murray, *Whig Party*, 75–77, 85–86; Govan, "Banking and Credit," 135–37.

56. *Milledgeville Federal Union*, 25 December 1838; Cooper, *Politics of Slavery*, 119–29; William N. Chambers, "Election of 1840," in Arthur Schlesinger, Jr., et al., eds., *History of American Presidential Elections, 1789–1968*, 4 vols. (New York: Chelsea House, 1971), 1:656–67, 688.

57. Ford, *Origins of Southern Radicalism*, 143–44, 173–74; Marc Kruman, *Parties and Politics in North Carolina, 1836–1865* (Baton Rouge: Louisiana State University Press, 1983), 3–28; Thomas E. Jeffrey, *State Parties and National Politics: North Carolina, 1815–1861* (Athens: University of Georgia Press, 1989), 46–48, 68–90; J. Mills Thornton III, *Politics and Power in a Slave Society: Alabama, 1800–1860* (Baton Rouge: Louisiana State University Press, 1978), 20–58. In general, anti-Democratic parties in the upper South were more akin to northern Whigs than those in the lower South, and they formed earlier party ties to northern Whigs.

58. *Macon Georgia Messenger*, 7 June 1838; *Savannah Republican*, 27 December 1839; *Milledgeville Southern Recorder*, 30 July 1839, 17 March 1840.

59. *Savannah Republican*, 13 December 1839, 28 November 1839; Richard W. Habersham to John M. Berrien, 28 December 1839, William C. Dawson to John M. Berrien, 20 February 1840, Berrien Papers, SHC.

60. Cooper's circular, in the *Milledgeville Southern Recorder*, 7 April 1840; James S. Calhoun to Thomas Butler King, 27 November 1839, Thomas Butler King Pa-

pers, SHC; William C. Dawson to Edward Harden, 29 December 1839, Harden Papers, DU; William C. Dawson to John M. Berrien, 20 February 1840, Berrien Papers, SHC; John C. Calhoun to John R. Mathewes, 24 February, 30 October 1838, John C. Calhoun to William C. Daniell, 26 October 1838, in W. Edwin Hemphill, Robert L. Meriwether, and Clyde Wilson, eds., *The Papers of John C. Calhoun,* 21 vols. to date (Columbia: University of South Carolina Press, 1959–93), 14:158–59, 444–49, 452–54; *Macon Georgia Messenger,* 20 February 1840; *Milledgeville Southern Recorder,* 25 February 1840; *Augusta Chronicle & Sentinel,* 7 February 1840; Cooper, *Politics of Slavery,* 103–18.

61. *Augusta Chronicle & Sentinel,* 31 March 1840; William C. Dawson to Edward Harden, 8, 22 April 1840, Harden Papers, DU; John M. Berrien to Ambrose Baber, 20 April 1840, 26 May 1840, Baber-Blackshear Collection, UGA; John M. Berrien to Thomas Butler King, 11 May 1840, John T. Sharpe to Thomas Butler King, 16 May 1840, King Papers, SHC; Absalom H. Chappell to John M. Berrien, 24 May 1840, Berrien Papers, SHC; entry for 1840, in "Recollections of Iverson L. Harris, 1826–1861," Charles Haynes Andrews Papers, SHC; John M. Berrien to Joseph H. Lumpkin, 27 April 1840, Joseph Henry Lumpkin Papers, UGA; Alexander H. Stephens to John L. Stephens, 17 May 1840, Alexander H. Stephens Papers, DU; *Macon Georgia Messenger,* 16 April, 11 June 1840; *Milledgeville Southern Recorder,* 21 April, 5 May 1840.

62. Henry L. Benning to Howell Cobb, 18 May 1840, Thomas Glascock to Howell Cobb, 5 June 1840, James Jackson to Howell Cobb, 7 June 1840, Cobb Papers, UGA; Edward J. Black to James McLaws, [?] May 1840, Lafayette McLaws Papers, SHC; Thomas Glascock to William A. Turner, 17 June 1840, William A. Turner Papers, DU; *Milledgeville Federal Union,* 26 May, 16 June, 7 July 1840; *Athens Southern Banner,* 10 July 1840; Cooper, *Politics of Slavery,* 113–17.

63. *Macon Georgia Messenger,* 20 August 1840; Thomas Butler King to Henry King, 4 June 1840, King Papers, SHC; P. M. Kollock to George J. Kollock, 29 July 1840, in Edith D. Johnston, ed., "The Kollock Letters, 1799–1850. Part VII," *Georgia Historical Quarterly* 32 (March 1948): 43; *Milledgeville Southern Recorder,* 18 August 1840; *Macon Georgia Telegraph,* 21 April 1840.

64. *Milledgeville Southern Recorder,* 18 August 1840; *Savannah Republican,* 26 June 1840.

65. *Milledgeville Southern Recorder,* 8 September 1840, 26 May, 25 August, 15 September 1840; *Savannah Republican,* 15 September 1840.

66. *Milledgeville Federal Union,* 22 September 1840; *Augusta Constitutionalist,* 13 February 1840; *Athens Southern Banner,* 16 October 1840.

67. Forsyth's address, in the *Augusta Chronicle & Sentinel,* 15 September 1840.

68. George M. Troup to Edward Harden, 4 August 1840, Harden Papers, DU;

*Milledgeville Southern Recorder,* 30 June 1840; letter of Walter T. Colquitt, in the *Milledgeville Federal Union,* 26 May 1840; *Athens Southern Banner,* 7 August 1840.

    69. Charles J. Jenkins to John M. Berrien, 25 October 1840, Berrien Papers, SHC.

## 3. From Tyler to Texas: Jacksonian Parties at Their Zenith

    1. References to the Whig party in Georgia were fairly frequent by mid-1841, but the names Harrison and State Rights also appeared often. Although the name Whig only gradually superseded alternative party names in the early 1840s, State Rights men will, for simplicity's sake, hereafter be referred to as Whigs.

    2. *Journal of the House of Representatives of the State of Georgia,* 1840, 10–11, 27–28, 51–54, 342–43; *Journal of the Senate of the State of Georgia,* 1840, 182–87; *Acts of the General Assembly of the State of Georgia,* 1840, 26–27; Alexander H. Stephens to John L. Stephens, 23 November 1840, Alexander H. Stephens Papers, EU; *Augusta Chronicle & Sentinel,* 24 November 1840; *Macon Georgia Telegraph,* 15 December 1840; *Augusta Constitutionalist,* 14 November, 5 December 1840; Milton S. Heath, *Constructive Liberalism: The Role of the State in Economic Development in Georgia to 1860* (Cambridge: Harvard University Press, 1954), 196–201, 211–14; Peter Wallenstein, *From Slave South to New South: Public Policy in Nineteenth-Century Georgia* (Chapel Hill: University of North Carolina Press, 1987), 28–30; Thomas P. Govan, "Banking and Credit System in Georgia 1810–1860" (Ph.D. diss., Vanderbilt University, 1937), 21–24. The vote on the resumption bill was 75 to 5 in the Senate and 144 to 33 in the House.

    3. *Columbus Enquirer,* 1 January 1840; *Georgia House Journal,* 1840, 12, 252; see also 190–93, 249–51.

    4. *Georgia House Journal,* 1840, 425–26, 333–35, 344, 359–61, 505; *Georgia Senate Journal,* 1840, 369; *Acts of the General Assembly,* 1840, 22–23; *Augusta Chronicle & Sentinel,* 28 December 1840; Milton S. Heath, *Constructive Liberalism,* 215–16.

    5. *Milledgeville Southern Recorder,* 29 June 1841; *Augusta Chronicle & Sentinel,* 8 April 1841; *Augusta Constitutionalist,* in the *Savannah Republican,* 24 November 1841; *Savannah Republican,* 2 December 1841; *Macon Georgia Messenger,* 25 March 1841; Heath, *Constructive Liberalism,* 216; Govan, "Banking and Credit System," 21–24. Near the end of 1841, the fourteen specie-paying banks had a circulation of $802,029 against specie reserves of $624,547. Five of the non-specie-paying banks, including the Central Bank, had more than $2 million in bills in circulation and specie reserves of only $110,777.

    6. *Cassville Standard of the Union,* in the *Milledgeville Federal Union,* 1 June 1841; *Milledgeville Federal Union,* 12 January 1841.

7. *Milledgeville Federal Union,* 3 August 1841, 22 December 1840, 12 January 1841.

8. Thomas Butler King to Henry King, 21 June 1841, Thomas Butler King Papers, SHC; Eugenius A. Nisbet to Amanda Nisbet, 8 August 1841, Eugenius A. Nisbet Letters, UGA; Henry Clay to John M. Berrien, 20 April 1841, in Lowry Axley, ed., "Letters of Henry Clay to John MacPherson Berrien," *Georgia Historical Quarterly* 29 (March 1945): 25; *Columbus Enquirer,* 5 May 1841; *Macon Georgia Messenger,* 26 August 1841; *Savannah Republican,* 29 June, 24 August 1841; *Augusta Chronicle & Sentinel,* 3 April, 23 August, 8, 15 September 1841; William J. Cooper, Jr., *The South and the Politics of Slavery, 1828–1856* (Baton Rouge: Louisiana State University Press, 1978), 149–53; Govan, "Banking and Credit System," 89; Royce C. McCrary, "John MacPherson Berrien (1781–1856): A Political Biography," (Ph.D. diss., University of Georgia, 1971), 245–56; Norma Lois Peterson, *The Presidencies of William Henry Harrison & John Tyler* (Lawrence: University of Kansas Press, 1989), 31–93; George R. Poage, *Henry Clay and the Whig Party* (Chapel Hill: University of North Carolina Press, 1936), 38–72, 85, 91.

9. *Augusta Constitutionalist,* 31 July 1841; *Milledgeville Federal Union,* 27 July 1841; *Columbus Enquirer,* 13 October 1841; *Augusta Chronicle & Sentinel,* 23 September, 8 October, 11 November 1841; *Milledgeville Southern Recorder,* 1, 22 June, 5 October 1841; *Macon Georgia Messenger,* 9 September, 14 October 1841; *Macon Georgia Telegraph,* 28 September 1841; *Athens Southern Banner,* 19 March, 30 July, 17 September 1841; Paul Murray, *The Whig Party in Georgia, 1825–1853,* James Sprunt Studies in History and Political Science, 29 (Chapel Hill: University of North Carolina Press, 1948), 96–99. Turnout in the election was nearly equal to that in 1840, and the Democratic relief campaign generated gains in every region, including 7.3 percent in the mountains, 7.5 percent in the upcountry, and 8.2 percent (amounting to a nearly eight-thousand-vote shift) in the black belt.

10. *Georgia House Journal,* 1841, 16–18; *Acts of the General Assembly,* 1841, 24–25, 29–30; *Athens Southern Banner,* 15 October, 12 November, 31 December 1841; Heath, *Constructive Liberalism,* 216; Govan, "Banking and Credit System," 145–46. The legislature's bill allowed Governor McDonald to arrest judicial proceedings against suspended private banks (effectively legalizing past suspensions) and gave these banks until 1 January 1842 to begin making specie payments.

11. Proceedings of a Jefferson County meeting, in the *Augusta Chronicle & Sentinel,* 16 May 1842; Henry Clay to John M. Berrien, 4 September 1842, in Axley, ed., "Letters of Clay to Berrien," 29; Thomas Butler King to Henry King, 21 June 1841, King Papers, SHC; Eugenius A. Nisbet to Amanda Nisbet, 8 August 1841, Nisbet Letters, UGA; *Columbus Enquirer,* 5 May 1841; *Macon Georgia Messenger,* 26 August 1841, 26 May 1842; *Savannah Republican,* 29 June, 24 August 1841, 7,

17 June 1842; *Augusta Chronicle & Sentinel*, 3 April, 23 August, 8, 15 September 1841, 13, 16, 30 May 1842; *Milledgeville Southern Recorder*, 16 June 1842; McCrary, "Berrien," 245–56.

12. John B. Lamar to Howell Cobb, 17 May 1842, Howell Cobb Papers, UGA; letter from James M. Kelly, 4 May 1842, in the *Augusta Chronicle & Sentinel*, 13 May 1842; *Milledgeville Southern Recorder*, 4 January 1842; *Milledgeville Federal Union*, 22 March 1842.

13. *Congressional Globe Appendix*, 27th Cong., 2d sess., 1841–42, 531, 111–23.

14. Ibid., 847, 852.

15. Ibid., 680, 760.

16. *Congressional Globe*, 27th Cong., 2d sess., 1841–42, 926, 960; *Savannah Republican*, 13 September 1842; Peterson, *Presidencies of Harrison & Tyler*, 98–108.

17. *Macon Georgia Messenger*, 23 June, 9 September 1841, *Milledgeville Southern Recorder*, 21 June 1842; *Savannah Republican*, 6 October, 29 November 1842.

18. *Macon Georgia Messenger*, 19 August 1842.

19. *Milledgeville Southern Recorder*, 2 April 1844; *Macon Georgia Messenger*, 14 July 1842; *Augusta Chronicle & Sentinel*, 28 June 1842; *Washington News*, in the *Augusta Chronicle & Sentinel*, 15 July 1843.

20. *Milledgeville Federal Union*, 9 May 1843; *Athens Southern Banner*, 16 September 1842; *Augusta Constitutionalist* (triweekly), 22 March 1842.

21. Proceedings of the 1842 Democratic state convention, in the *Athens Southern Banner*, 22 July 1842; *Augusta Constitutionalist* (triweekly), 16 January 1844.

22. *Savannah Republican*, 18 February 1842; *Columbus Times*, 26 March 1845, in John R. Detreville, "The Little New South: Origins of Industry in Georgia's Fall-Line Cities, 1840–1865" (Ph.D. diss., University of North Carolina, Chapel Hill, 1986), 59; *Milledgeville Federal Union*, 9 May 1843.

23. *Macon Georgia Messenger*, 7 April 1842; *Milledgeville Southern Recorder*, 5 April 1842. The issue of southern manufacturing development, or the lack of it, remains controversial, but many of the points made in Eugene D. Genovese, *The Political Economy of Slavery: Studies in the Economy and Society of the Slave South* (New York: Pantheon Books, 1965), still seem persuasive. While disagreeing with Genovese on many factual and interpretative matters, Fred Bateman and Thomas Weiss, in *A Deplorable Scarcity: The Failure of Industrialization in the Slave Economy* (Chapel Hill: University of North Carolina Press, 1981), 160, conclude that limitations on southern industrialization stemmed from the "entrepreneurial attitudes and decisions" of the planter class. The argument that the Whig party's strength in the market-oriented black belt made Whigs more receptive to protariff arguments has a long history. In a famous article titled "Who Were the Southern Whigs?" *American Historical Review* 59 (January 1954): 335–46, Charles Sellers stresses that commercial elements predominated over states' rights forces in southern Whiggery.

In Georgia, at least, the planters who founded the State Rights party in the early 1830s desired low tariffs and high cotton prices, and they still did a decade later. Regardless of their market orientation, it is difficult to see how cotton planters had any direct economic interest in promoting higher tariffs to encourage—mainly northern—manufacturing development. Georgia Whigs were Whigs in spite of the national party's protective tariff bias, not because of it.

24. Many historians have recognized aspects of this dialectic of party competition. William J. Cooper, in *Politics of Slavery*, perceptively analyzes how southern politicians demonized Northerners and struggled to convince their constituents that only their party could be trusted to protect slavery and southern rights. Rather than calling this competition a unique "politics of slavery," however, I would suggest that the same basic partisan process, adapted to differing circumstances and issues, operated continuously in South and North. The tactics of the politics of slavery, in other words, were fundamental to Jacksonian politics generally. Michael F. Holt, *The Political Crisis of the 1850s* (New York: John Wiley & Sons, 1978), 30–37, discusses the flexibility of the federal system and politicians' conscious drive to form party dichotomies. John Ashworth, in *"Agrarians" & "Aristocrats": Party Political Ideology in the United States, 1837–1846* (Cambridge: Cambridge University Press, 1983), 125–31, acknowledges that the gulf separating "radical Democrats" from "conservative Whigs" served to define party lines, yet he proceeds to argue that this extreme dichotomy accurately reflected party differences. In heavily emphasizing the economic basis of the party system, Ashworth focuses only on the years immediately following the panic of 1837 and draws most of his evidence from the North, particularly the Northeast. Thomas E. Jeffrey, *State Parties and National Politics: North Carolina, 1815–1861* (Athens: University of Georgia Press, 1989), 135–37, presents the tariff debate in North Carolina as a heated rhetorical battle over negligible state party differences.

25. "To the People of Georgia" from the 1842 Whig and State Rights convention, in the *Milledgeville Southern Recorder*, 21 June 1842; Democratic address to the people of Georgia, in the *Macon Georgia Telegraph*, 19 July 1842; *Augusta Chronicle & Sentinel*, 27 September 1842.

26. Kenneth Coleman and Charles Stephen Gurr, eds., *Dictionary of Georgia Biography*, 2 vols. (Athens: University of Georgia Press, 1983), 2:594–95; John E. Simpson, *Howell Cobb: The Politics of Ambition* (Chicago: Adams Press, 1973), 1–28.

27. *Georgia House Journal*, 1842, 9–14, 324–25, 418–19, 450–51; ibid., 1843, 15–16; *Acts of the General Assembly*, 1842, 27–28, 32, 172–73; ibid., 1843, 144; Alexander H. Stephens to Linton Stephens, 8 December 1842, Alexander H. Stephens Papers, EU; A. B. Reid to John M. Berrien, 19 December 1842, John MacPherson Berrien Papers, SHC; *Milledgeville Southern Recorder*, 20, 27 December

1842; *Macon Georgia Messenger,* 26 January 1843; *Savannah Republican,* 27 December 1842; Murray, *Whig Party,* 114–15; Wallenstein, *Slave South to New South,* 52–53; Heath, *Constructive Liberalism,* 216–17; Govan, "Banking and Credit System," 151–54. Gradual improvement in the economy and the rapid liquidation of the Central Bank left subsequent legislatures with little to do on banking matters. The Central Bank took in and burned some $837,000 in bills during 1843; public confidence in the prospects for future bill redemption raised its note value to nearly par with the bills of specie-paying banks. The 1843 session marked the beginning of biennial legislatures—the next meeting would be in 1845.

28. For further discussion, see chapter 5.

29. On Calhounites and southern radicals generally, see Cooper, *Politics of Slavery,* 166–71; William W. Freehling, *The Road to Disunion: Secessionists at Bay, 1776–1854* (New York: Oxford University Press, 1990); Lacy K. Ford, Jr., *Origins of Southern Radicalism: The South Carolina Upcountry, 1800–1860* (New York: Oxford University Press, 1988); and Eric Walther, *The Fire-Eaters* (Baton Rouge: Louisiana State University Press, 1992).

30. George M. Troup to William C. Daniell, 16 May 1843, William and Nell Harden Collection, UGA; Wilson Lumpkin to John C. Calhoun, 13, 26 October, 15 November 1841, John H. Howard to John C. Calhoun, 27 October, 13 November 1841, John R. Mathewes to John C. Calhoun, [?] November 1841, Ker Boyce to John C. Calhoun, 21 October, 2 November 1842, Curtis Humphreys to John C. Calhoun, 18 November 1842, James Hamilton, Jr., to John C. Calhoun, 4 June 1843, John C. Calhoun to Wilson Lumpkin, 26 December 1841, 4 February 1842, John C. Calhoun to John R. Mathewes, 2 January 1842, in W. Edwin Hemphill, Robert L. Meriwether, and Clyde Wilson, eds., *The Papers of John C. Calhoun,* 21 vols. to date (Columbia: University of South Carolina Press, 1959–93), 15:792–93, 796–800, 805–7, 810–16; 16:19–20, 30–31, 108–9, 501, 521–22, 551–52; 17:233–35; *Milledgeville Federal Union,* 6 December 1842, 25 April 1843. Each county was entitled to as many votes in the Democratic convention as that county had members in the legislature. Large black belt counties with proportionately fewer Democrats thus had more weight in the convention than did the more Democratic upcountry and mountain regions. Black belt Calhounites were able to amass great convention strength without having a significant popular base.

31. *Athens Southern Banner,* 12 May 1843; *Milledgeville Federal Union,* 13 June 1843; Marco Bozarres to John B. Lamar, 25 May 1843, Cobb Papers, UGA; Tomlinson Fort to John C. Calhoun, 17 June 1843, Edward J. Black to John C. Calhoun, 1 September 1843, in Wilson et al., eds., *Calhoun Papers,* 17:246–47, 389–91; William C. Daniell to John C. Calhoun, 2 April 1846, in Chauncey S. Boucher and Robert P. Brooks, eds., "Correspondence Addressed to John C. Calhoun, 1837–

1849," in *Annual Report of the American Historical Association,* 1929 (Washington, D.C.: Government Printing Office, 1930), 338–40; "A Spectator," in the *Macon Georgia Telegraph,* 13 June 1843; *Milledgeville Southern Recorder,* 13 June 1843. More than eighty delegates from black belt counties that the Whigs had carried in the 1841 election attended the convention, compared with only fifty-two delegates from the mountains and the upcountry, the regions most opposed to the Calhounite wing of the party.

32. James P. Simmons to Howell Cobb, 14 June 1843, William C. Daniell to Howell Cobb, 7 July 1843, Cobb Papers, UGA.

33. John M. Berrien to Thomas Butler King, 12 May 1843, Andrew J. Miller to Thomas Butler King, 29 May 1843, William C. Dawson to Thomas Butler King, 8 August 1843, King Papers, SHC; Robert Toombs to John M. Berrien, 6 June 1843, Berrien Papers, SHC; Henry Clay to John M. Berrien, 17 July 1843, in Axley, ed., "Letters of Clay to Berrien," 31–33; *Milledgeville Southern Recorder,* 27 June 1843; Len G. Cleveland, "George W. Crawford of Georgia, 1798–1872" (Ph.D. diss., University of Georgia, 1974), 2–67.

34. James Z. Rabun, ed., "Alexander H. Stephens's Diary, 1834–1837," *Georgia Historical Quarterly* 26 (March 1952): 78–87; Richard M. Johnston and William M. Browne, *Life of Alexander H. Stephens* (Philadelphia: J. B. Lippincott, 1878), 125–30, 138–39, 156–67; Thomas E. Schott, *Alexander H. Stephens of Georgia: A Biography* (Baton Rouge: Louisiana State University Press, 1988), 1–47; Ulrich B. Phillips, *The Life of Robert Toombs* (New York: Macmillan, 1913), 3–34; William Y. Thompson, *Robert Toombs of Georgia* (Baton Rouge: Louisiana State University Press, 1966), 3–25. Stephens was running for the seat in Congress that would be left vacant by Mark A. Cooper's expected resignation.

35. *Milledgeville Southern Recorder,* 22 August 1843; *Savannah Republican,* 22 May, 21 August, 2 September 1843.

36. *Milledgeville Federal Union,* 19 December 1843; Albon Chase to Howell Cobb, 15 December 1843, Cobb Papers, UGA; James Hamilton, Jr., to John C. Calhoun, 15 October, 21 November 1843, Francis W. Pickens to John C. Calhoun, 22 October 1843, in Wilson et al., eds., *Calhoun Papers,* 17:507–9, 517–18, 554–58; *Macon Georgia Telegraph,* 10 October 1843; *Athens Southern Banner,* 12 October 1843. Calhoun's candidacy was faltering badly everywhere; only Georgia and his native state had ever officially endorsed him.

37. James M. Kelly to Howell Cobb, 8 February 1844, Milledge H. Gathright to Howell Cobb, 11 February 1844, William C. Daniell to Howell Cobb, 19 March 1844, Cobb Papers, UGA; Wilson Lumpkin to John C. Calhoun, 22 December 1843, 6 February 1844, Edward J. Black to John C. Calhoun, 8 January 1844, in Wilson et al., eds., *Calhoun Papers,* 17:637–38, 679–82, 769–70; Edward J. Black to the

editor of the *Athens Southern Banner*, [?] January 1844, in the *Augusta Constitutionalist*, 15 February 1844; *Augusta Constitutionalist* (triweekly), 11, 16, 20, 30 January 1844.

38. George W. Crawford to John M. Berrien, 13 February 1844, George W. Crawford to John M. Berrien, 2 January, 6 March 1844, Robert A. Toombs to John M. Berrien, 28 January 1844, Berrien Papers, SHC; William M. Reese to Alexander H. Stephens, 28 December 1843, Stephens Papers, EU; George W. Crawford to Alexander H. Stephens, 10 March 1844, Alexander H. Stephens Papers, LC (microfilm, UGA); Henry Clay to John M. Berrien, 7 July, 4, 22 September 1843, in Axley, ed., "Letters of Clay to Berrien," 31–35; *Savannah Republican*, 25 March 1844; James C. Bonner, *Milledgeville: Georgia's Antebellum Capital* (Athens: University of Georgia Press, 1978), 78–79.

39. T. R. R. Cobb to Howell Cobb, 10 April [1844], Thomas Reade Rootes Cobb Papers, UGA; John B. Lamar to Howell Cobb, 16 April 1844, John H. Lumpkin to Howell Cobb, 18 April 1844, Cobb Papers, UGA; *Macon Georgia Telegraph*, 2 April 1844; *Milledgeville Federal Union*, 2 April 1844; *Athens Southern Banner*, 18 April 1844; James D. Richardson, comp., *A Compilation of the Messages and Papers of the Presidents, 1789–1897*, 10 vols. (Washington, D.C.: Government Printing Office, 1896–99), 3:307–13; Cooper, *Politics of Slavery*, 176–99; Peterson, *Presidencies of Harrison & Tyler*, 185–218; Freehling, *Road to Disunion*, 355–425; Frederick Merk, *Slavery and the Annexation of Texas* (New York: Alfred A. Knopf, 1972).

40. *Milledgeville Federal Union*, 23 April 1844.

41. *Milledgeville Southern Recorder*, 30 April 1844, 9, 16 April 1844; *Savannah Republican*, 30 April 1844.

42. Cooper, *Politics of Slavery*, 199–201; Charles Sellers, "Election of 1844," in Arthur Schlesinger, Jr., et al., eds., *History of American Presidential Elections, 1789–1968*, 4 vols. (New York: Chelsea House, 1971), 1:761–65, 814–17, 822–28.

43. *Athens Southern Banner*, 16 May 1844; Albon Chase to Howell Cobb, 5 May 1844, Cobb Papers, UGA.

44. *Macon Georgia Telegraph*, 7 May 1844; William C. Daniell to Howell Cobb, 11 May 1844, William L. Mitchell to Howell Cobb, 21 May 1844, James Jackson to Howell Cobb, 7 May 1844, Charles J. McDonald to Howell Cobb, 8, 29 May 1844, Albon Chase to Howell Cobb, 27 May 1844, Cobb Papers, UGA.

45. *Milledgeville Federal Union*, 11 June 1844; Sellers, "Election of 1844," in Schlesinger et al., ed., *American Presidential Elections*, 1:765–73, 829–52.

46. *Milledgeville Southern Recorder*, 7 May 1844; Miller Grieve and Richard H. Orme to John M. Berrien, 30 June 1844, Berrien Papers, SHC; *Milledgeville Southern Recorder*, 2 July 1844; Grieve and Orme to Berrien, 30 June 1844, Berrien Papers, SHC; Alexander H. Stephens to Linton Stephens, 22 April 1844, Alexander H. Stephens Papers, MCSH (microfilm, EU); Alexander H. Stephens to

John L. Stephens, 30 April 1844, Stephens Papers, EU; Alexander H. Stephens to James Thomas, 17 May 1844, Stephens Papers, LC; Henry Clay to John M. Berrien, 9 December 1843, in Axley, ed., "Letters of Clay to Berrien," 36–37.

47. "Old Thirteen," in the *Savannah Republican*, 9 May 1844; Michael A. Morrison, "Westward the Curse of Empire: Texas Annexation and the American Whig Party," *Journal of the Early Republic* 10 (Summer 1990): 221–49, offers a fine analysis of Whig reactions to the Texas issue, although Morrison overstates national party unity and southern Whig opposition to annexation.

48. *Savannah Republican*, 22 May 1844. In a couple of highly exceptional cases, the *Milledgeville Southern Recorder*, 30 April 1844; and the *Milledgeville Federal Union*, 13 February, 14 May 1844, suggested that Texas annexation would draw superfluous slaves from the eastern states and gradually eliminate their slave populations, clearing the way for free white farmers.

49. *Congressional Globe Appendix*, 28th Cong., 1st sess., 1843–44, 701–4; Merk, *Slavery and the Annexation of Texas*, 81.

50. *Macon Georgia Telegraph*, 16 April 1844; "Jacinto," in the *Augusta Constitutionalist*, 4 July 1844; *Athens Southern Banner*, 25 July 1844; *Augusta Constitutionalist* (triweekly), 23 April, 7, 18, 21, 30 May, 27 June 1844.

51. Letter from Matthew H. McAllister, 14 May 1844, in the *Augusta Constitutionalist* (triweekly), 23 May 1844; Edward J. Black to John C. Calhoun, 7 March 1844, Wilson Lumpkin to John C. Calhoun, 23 March 1844, in Wilson et al., eds., *Calhoun Papers*, 1843–44, 17:831, 885; John R. Mathewes to John C. Calhoun, [?] April, 12 May 1844, John H. Howard to John C. Calhoun, 2 May 1844, John C. Calhoun to John R. Mathewes, 9 May 1844, Wilson Lumpkin to John C. Calhoun, 23 September 1844, in ibid., 1844, 18:373–80, 404–5, 467–68, 494–96, 832–35.

52. Sellers, "Election of 1844," in Schlesinger et al., eds., *American Presidential Elections*, 1:853; *Macon Georgia Messenger*, 1 August 1844; *Augusta Constitutionalist* (triweekly), 13 July, 10 August, 3, 5 September 1844.

53. *Augusta Constitutionalist* (triweekly), 30 May 1844; Alexander H. Stephens to James Thomas, 16 July 1844, in TSC, 59–60; *Savannah Republican*, 10 May, 20 September 1844; *Athens Southern Banner*, 11 July, 22 August 1844; *Milledgeville Southern Recorder*, 6 August, 24 September 1844; *Milledgeville Federal Union*, 13 August 1844; *Macon Georgia Messenger*, 8 August 1844.

54. *Macon Georgia Messenger*, 31 October 1844; "Observer," in the *Augusta Constitutionalist* (triweekly), 12 September 1844; *Augusta Constitutionalist* (triweekly), 17 September 1844; *Macon Georgia Telegraph*, 29 October 1844; *Savannah Republican*, 17 October 1844.

55. Sellers, "Election of 1844," in Schlesinger et al., eds., *American Presidential Elections*, 1:861; Cooper, *Politics of Slavery*, 218–19.

56. *Savannah Republican*, 25 November 1844; John M. Berrien to George W.

Crawford, 25 November 1844, Berrien Papers, UGA (photostatic copy of the original in the John M. Berrien Papers, LC).

## 4. Detours Around the Territorial Impasse, 1844–1848

1. George W. Crawford to John M. Berrien, 1 January 1845, John MacPherson Berrien Papers, SHC.

2. *Congressional Globe Appendix*, 28th Cong., 2d sess., 1844–45, 193, 314, 383–87; Alexander H. Stephens to Linton Stephens, 3, 5 January 1845, Alexander H. Stephens Papers, MCSH (microfilm, EU); Alexander H. Stephens to John L. Bird, 10 January 1845, Alexander H. Stephens to John L. Stephens, 14 January 1845, Alexander H. Stephens Papers, EU; John M. Berrien to Ambrose Baber, 12 March 1845, Baber-Blackshear Collection, UGA; Charles J. Jenkins to John M. Berrien, 3 February 1845, Berrien Papers, SHC; Thomas E. Schott, *Alexander H. Stephens of Georgia: A Biography* (Baton Rouge: Louisiana State University Press, 1988), 60–61; William J. Cooper, Jr., *The South and the Politics of Slavery, 1828–1856* (Baton Rouge: Louisiana State University Press, 1978), 223. All six Georgia Democrats supported the joint resolution; nine Southern Whigs voted for it and seven against it.

3. Robert Toombs to John M. Berrien, 13 February 1845, N. C. Barnett to John M. Berrien, 18 February 1845, Berrien Papers, SHC; Robert S. Burch to Alexander H. Stephens, 8 February 1845, W. M. Reese to Alexander H. Stephens, 13 February 1845, Gabriel T. Spearman to Alexander H. Stephens, 4 March 1845, Stephens Papers, MCSH; Samuel T. Chapman to Alexander H. Stephens, 4 February 1845, David S. Anderson to Alexander H. Stephens, 11 February 1845, Alexander H. Stephens Papers, LC (microfilm, UGA); Robert Toombs to Alexander H. Stephens, 16 February 1845, Stephens Papers, EU; Robert Toombs to Alexander H. Stephens, 24 January 1845, in TSC, 61–62.

4. Charles J. Jenkins to John M. Berrien, 3 May 1845, Christopher B. Strong to John M. Berrien, 25 April, 10 June 1845, Charles J. Jenkins to John M. Berrien, 5 June 1845, Berrien Papers, SHC; *Congressional Globe*, 28th Cong., 2d sess., 1844–45, 362, 372; Samuel T. Chapman to Alexander H. Stephens, 4 February 1845, Stephens Papers, LC; James E. Harvey to Thomas Butler King, 22 October 1844, Thomas Butler King Papers, SHC; *Milledgeville Southern Recorder*, 5 November 1844; *Milledgeville Federal Union*, 11 December 1845; Royce C. McCrary, "John MacPherson Berrien (1781–1856): A Political Biography" (Ph.D. diss., University of Georgia, 1971), 286–91; Frederick Merk, *Slavery and the Annexation of Texas* (New York: Alfred A. Knopf, 1972), 152–58, 289–90. The Senate passed the

amended joint resolution by 27 to 25 on 27 February 1845. The House concurred, and John Tyler dispatched a courier to offer Texans the terms of annexation.

5. James A. Meriwether to John M. Berrien, 10 May 1845, George W. Crawford to John M. Berrien, 1 January 1845, James A. Meriwether to John M. Berrien, 21 April 1845, Charles J. Jenkins to John M. Berrien, 22 April, 5 June 1845, Christopher B. Strong to John M. Berrien, 25 April, 9 May 1845, Francis J. Bartow to John M. Berrien, 3 August 1845, Berrien Papers, SHC; John M. Berrien to Ambrose Baber, 14 July, 12, 29 August 1845, Ambrose Baber to John M. Berrien, 25 August 1845, Baber-Blackshear Collection, UGA; Samuel T. Chapman to Alexander H. Stephens, 4 February 1845, Stephens Papers, LC; Alexander H. Stephens to Linton Stephens, 8 July, 23 August 1845, Stephens Papers, MCSH; Alexander H. Stephens to John L. Stephens, 9 July 1845, Stephens Papers, EU; Robert Toombs to Alexander H. Stephens, 24 January 1845, in TSC, 60–61; *Macon Georgia Messenger,* 2 January, 27 February, 24 April 1845; *Savannah Republican,* 8 February, 19, 26 April, 10 June 1845; *Milledgeville Southern Recorder,* 6 July 1845; *Milledgeville Federal Union,* 24 June 1845; Len G. Cleveland, "George W. Crawford of Georgia, 1798–1872" (Ph.D. diss., University of Georgia, 1974), 108–19.

6. *Athens Southern Whig,* 28 August 1845; Francis S. Bartow to John M. Berrien, 30 July 1845, Berrien Papers, SHC; Alexander H. Stephens to Linton Stephens, 10 July, 4 September 1845, Stephens Papers, MCSH; Joseph Henry Lumpkin to Alexander H. Stephens, 26 June 1845, Ralph E. Wager Papers, EU; *Athens Southern Banner,* 5 June, 14 August 1845; *Milledgeville Federal Union,* 5 August, 2 September 1845; *Milledgeville Southern Recorder,* 27 May, 26 August, 9 September 1845; *Savannah Republican,* 28 August, 6 September 1845; *Macon Georgia Messenger,* 7, 21 August 1845; *Augusta Chronicle & Sentinel;* 7 August, 4 September 1845; *Savannah Republican,* 20 September 1845; McCrary, "Berrien," 298–303.

7. Alexander H. Stephens to Linton Stephens, 10 October 1845, Stephens Papers, MCSH. The Democratic share of the vote dropped slightly in every region, ranging from a 4.0 percent loss in the mountains to a 0.8 percent loss along the coast. By the mid-1840s the parties had stabilized at such a highly competitive point that only unusual circumstances—such as Mark Cooper's candidacy in 1843—had any dramatic effect on overall results.

8. *Journal of the Senate of the State of Georgia . . . ,* 1845, 32–33, 44, 48, 54, 58; George W. Crawford to John M. Berrien, 17 October 1845, John M. Berrien to George W. Crawford et al., 13 November 1845 (copy), George W. Crawford et al. to John M. Berrien, 14 November 1845, Allen F. Owen et al. to John M. Berrien, 14 November 1845, Charles J. Jenkins to John M. Berrien, 25 November 1845, Berrien Papers, SHC; Alexander H. Stephens to Linton Stephens, 7, 10, 17 November 1845, Stephens Papers, MCSH; *Savannah Republican,* 11, 18 November 1845;

*Macon Georgia Messenger,* 13 November 1845; *Athens Southern Whig,* 20, 27 November 1845; *Milledgeville Federal Union,* 11 December 1845; McCrary, "Berrien," 304–7; Brian G. Walton, "Georgia's Biennial Legislatures, 1840–1860, and Their Elections to the U.S. Senate," *Georgia Historical Quarterly* 61 (Summer 1977): 142–45.

9. Robert Toombs to George W. Crawford, 6 February 1846, in TSC, 74; James D. Richardson, comp., *A Compilation of the Messages and Papers of the Presidents, 1789–1897,* 10 vols. (Washington, D.C.: Government Printing Office, 1896–99), 3:392–98; Alexander H. Stephens to John L. Stephens, 4 January, 11 June 1846, Stephens Papers, EU; Alexander H. Stephens to Linton Stephens, 8 February 1846, Stephens Papers, MCSH; Robert Toombs to John Milledge, Jr., 17 February 1846, John Milledge, Jr., Papers, DU (microfilm, GDAH); Alexander H. Stephens to George W. Crawford, 3 February 1846, Howell Cobb to John B. Lamar, 2 January 1846, John B. Lamar to Howell Cobb, 5 January 1846, Albon Chase to Howell Cobb, 17 January 1846, James Jackson to Howell Cobb, 19 January, 22 March 1846, William Hope Hull to Howell Cobb, 1 May 1846, Cobb Papers, UGA; William Hope Hull to Howell Cobb, 22 May 1848, Howell Cobb to Mary Ann Lamar Cobb, 14 June 1846, in TSC, 73–74, 79, 81–82; John H. Howard to John C. Calhoun, 16 January 1846, Edward J. Black to John C. Calhoun, 22 February 1846, in Chauncey S. Boucher and Robert P. Brooks, eds., "Correspondence Addressed to John C. Calhoun, 1837–1849," in *Annual Report of the American Historical Association,* 1929 (Washington, D.C.: Government Printing Office, 1930), 319–20, 325–26; *Milledgeville Southern Recorder,* 24 February 1846; *Milledgeville Federal Union,* 20 January 1846; David M. Pletcher, *The Diplomacy of Annexation: Texas, Oregon, and the Mexican War* (Columbia: University of Missouri Press, 1973), 312–51.

10. Richardson, comp., *Messages and Papers,* 3:442; John H. Schroeder, *Mr. Polk's War: American Opposition and Dissent, 1846–1848* (Madison: University of Wisconsin Press, 1973), 3–19; Royce C. McCrary, "Georgia Politics and the Mexican War," *Georgia Historical Quarterly* 60 (Fall 1976): 212–13.

11. *Macon Georgia Messenger,* 5 February 1846; Alexander H. Stephens to Linton Stephens, 13 July 1846, Stephens Papers, MCSH; John P. King to Howell Cobb, 7 May 1846, Howell Cobb to Mary Ann Lamar Cobb, 10 May 1846, Thomas R. R. Cobb to Howell Cobb, 12 May 1846, in TSC, 75–77; John H. Howard to John C. Calhoun, 12 May 1846, Wilson Lumpkin to John C. Calhoun, 20 May 1846, in Boucher and Brooks, eds., "Calhoun Correspondence," 344–47; *Athens Southern Whig,* 21 May 1846; Robert W. Johannsen, *To the Hall of the Montezumas: The Mexican War in the American Imagination* (New York: Oxford University Press, 1985).

12. *Congressional Globe Appendix,* 29th Cong., 1st sess., 1845–46, 946–50; *Augusta Chronicle & Sentinel,* 11 June, 31 July 1846; *Milledgeville Southern Recorder,* 16 June 1846, Schroeder, *Polk's War,* 26–31.

13. John B. Lamar to Howell Cobb, 24 June 1846, Albon Chase to Howell Cobb, 20 May 1846, William Hope Hull to Howell Cobb, 22 May 1846, Howell Cobb to Mary Ann Lamar Cobb, 4 June 1846, in TSC, 82, 78–80; Howell Cobb to Thomas R. R. Cobb, 12 May 1846, Thomas R. R. Cobb to Howell Cobb, 21 May 1846, Cobb Papers, UGA; Edward J. Black to John C. Calhoun, 22 February 1846, William C. Daniell to John C. Calhoun, 2 April 1846, in Boucher and Brooks, eds., "Calhoun Correspondence," 325–26, 338–40; *Milledgeville Federal Union*, 26 May, 10 November, 29 December 1846; *Augusta Constitutionalist*, 5 August 1846, 17 January 1846.

14. *Congressional Globe Appendix*, 29th Cong., 1st sess., 1845–46, 1030–35; George D. Phillips to Howell Cobb, 9 July 1846, Cobb Papers, UGA; John H. Lumpkin to Howell Cobb, 13 November 1846, in TSC, 86–87; *Augusta Constitutionalist*, 10, 24 July, 9, 21 October 1846; *Milledgeville Federal Union*, 11 August 1846; *Savannah Republican*, 5, 13 August, 25 September 1846; *Milledgeville Southern Recorder*, 28 April, 11 August 1846; *Macon Georgia Messenger*, 16 July 1846; Joel H. Silbey, *The Shrine of Party: Congressional Voting Behavior 1841–1852* (Pittsburgh: University of Pittsburgh Press, 1967), 71–76, 173; David M. Potter, *The Impending Crisis 1848–1861*, completed and edited by Don E. Fehrenbacher (New York: Harper & Row, 1976), 18–27.

15. *Milledgeville Southern Recorder*, 20 October 1846; *Augusta Constitutionalist*, 26 August 1846; *Athens Southern Whig*, 9 July 1846; *Macon Georgia Messenger*, 8 October 1846; McCrary, "Mexican War," 216–17; Schott, *Stephens*, 73–74.

16. Potter, *Impending Crisis*, 51–62; Don E. Fehrenbacher, *The Dred Scott Case: Its Significance in American Law and Politics* (New York: Oxford University Press, 1978), 11–147.

17. *Congressional Globe Appendix*, 29th Cong., 2d sess., 1846–47, 363; *Milledgeville Southern Recorder*, 11 July, 24 October 1848; Cooper, *Politics of Slavery*, 238–43; Bertram Wyatt-Brown, *Southern Honor: Ethics and Behavior in the Old South* (New York: Oxford University Press, 1982), 25–87.

18. George Gilmer, *Sketches of Some of the First Settlers of Upper Georgia, of the Cherokees, and the Author* (New York: D. Appleton, 1854), 519; Richard D. Arnold to Rev. E. L. Bascom, n.d. [1837?], Richard D. Arnold to Rev. Chandler Robbins, 15 August 1837, in Richard H. Shryock, ed., "Letters of Richard D. Arnold, M.D. 1808–1876," *Papers of the Trinity College Historical Society*, double series 18–19 (1929), 17, 14.

19. Elihu S. Barclay to Howell Cobb, 4 January 1848, Cobb Papers, UGA; William H. Underwood to John M. Berrien, 19 December 1847, Berrien Papers, SHC; Henry L. Benning to Howell Cobb, 23 February 1848, in TSC, 97–103; *Milledgeville Federal Union*, 31 December 1844; *Augusta Chronicle & Sentinel*, 26 January, 13 July 1848; *Savannah Republican*, 2 February 1848; *Macon Georgia Journal and*

*Messenger,* 27 September 1848; *Augusta Constitutionalist,* 19 December 1848. White men in Georgia concentrated on *how* to oppose the Wilmot Proviso; the reasons for opposing it seemed too obvious to bother belaboring. My sense is that, through the 1840s and 1850s, most party leaders considered actual slavery expansion—first in the Southwest and California, then in Kansas—unlikely.

20. *Congressional Globe,* 29th Cong., 2d sess., 1846–47, 240; *Congressional Globe Appendix,* 29th Cong., 2d sess., 1846–47, 351–54, 296–302; Robert Toombs to John C. Calhoun, 30 April 1847, in Boucher and Brooks, eds., "Calhoun Correspondence," 373–74; *Milledgeville Southern Recorder,* 16 February 1847; William Y. Thompson, *Robert Toombs of Georgia* (Baton Rouge: Louisiana State University Press, 1966), 41–43.

21. *Congressional Globe,* 29th Cong., 2d sess., 1846–47, 187, 198, 360–62, 424–25; Charles J. McDonald to Howell Cobb, 29 January 1847, Cobb Papers, UGA; *Athens Southern Banner,* 5 January 1847; *Milledgeville Federal Union,* 16 February 1847; Potter, *Impending Crisis,* 64–67.

22. Iverson L. Harris to John M. Berrien, 9 May 1847, Berrien Papers, SHC; K. Jack Bauer, *Zachary Taylor: Soldier, Planter, Statesman of the Old Southwest* (Baton Rouge: Louisiana State University Press, 1985).

23. *Macon Georgia Journal and Messenger,* 15 April 1847; *Milledgeville Southern Recorder,* 13 April, 25 May 1847; *Macon Georgia Journal and Messenger,* 20 October 1847, 15 April 1847; *Savannah Republican,* 8, 20, 28 April, 12, 14 July 1847.

24. *Augusta Constitutionalist,* 16 May 1847; Howell Cobb to Thomas D. Harris, 17 May 1847, Thomas DeKalb Harris Family Papers, GDAH; John H. Lumpkin to Howell Cobb, 16 May, 18 June 1847, Cobb Papers, UGA; *Augusta Constitutionalist,* 16, 25 April, 27 May, 3, 16 June 1847; *Athens Southern Banner,* 11 May, 22 June 1847; *Milledgeville Federal Union,* 20, 27 April, 25 May, 15 June 1847.

25. Edward J. Black to John C. Calhoun [June–December?] 1847, in Boucher and Brooks, eds., "Calhoun Correspondence," 380–82; *Milledgeville Federal Union,* 6 July 1847; *Augusta Constitutionalist,* 1, 4 July 1847; *Macon Georgia Journal and Messenger,* 30 June, 14 July 1847.

26. *Milledgeville Southern Recorder,* 6 July 1847; Rembert W. Patrick, *Aristocrat in Uniform: General Duncan L. Clinch* (Gainesville: University of Florida Press, 1963).

27. *Augusta Constitutionalist,* 29 September 1847; Alexander H. Stephens to John L. Stephens, 22 September 1847, Stephens Papers, EU; Francis S. Bartow to John M. Berrien, 27 September 1847, Iverson L. Harris to John M. Berrien, 8 August 1847, Berrien Papers, SHC; Wilson Lumpkin to John C. Calhoun, 27 August 1847, in Boucher and Brooks, eds., "Calhoun Correspondence," 398; *Augusta Constitutionalist,* 17 August, 11 September 1847; *Savannah Republican,* 25 May 1847; *Macon Georgia Journal and Messenger,* 8 September 1847; *Milledgeville Fed-*

*eral Union,* 3, 10, 31 August, 21 September 1847; *Milledgeville Southern Recorder,* 17 August 1847.

28. The 3,959 additional votes cast in north Georgia over the 1845 vote translated into a net Democratic gain of 1,705 votes. The Pearson's correlation between the 1845 and 1847 votes is .98.

29. *Georgia Senate Journal,* 1847, 122—53, 428—30; Iverson L. Harris to John M. Berrien, 8 March, 9 May, 8 August, 10 September 1847, William C. Dawson to John M. Berrien, 8 July 1847, Berrien Papers, SHC; James Jackson to Howell Cobb, 2 November 1847, 11 January 1848, Elihu S. Barclay to Howell Cobb, 3 December 1847, Cobb Papers, UGA; Alexander H. Stephens to Linton Stephens, 12 November 1847, Stephens Papers, MCSH; Luther J. Glenn to Howell Cobb, 1 December 1847, in TSC, 89; *Augusta Constitutionalist,* 12 November 1847; *Milledgeville Federal Union,* 16 November 1847; *Macon Georgia Journal and Messenger,* 17 November 1847. The resolutions renouncing past party issues and nominating Taylor passed on straight party votes. The vote on Glenn's resolution to endorse the Missouri Compromise line found seventeen Democrats and three Whigs in favor, twenty-one Whigs and five Democrats opposed.

30. *Milledgeville Federal Union,* 28 December 1847. In hindsight, of course, the action of the December convention appears extraordinary and ironic. Democrats would soon denounce the doctrine promulgated at their December 1847 convention as "squatter sovereignty," and their outrage over northern Democrats' adherence to squatter sovereignty would cause them to bolt the Charleston national convention in 1860.

31. Hopkins Holsey to Howell Cobb, 31 December 1847, in TSC, 92; Luther J. Glenn to Howell Cobb, 16 December 1847, Elihu S. Barclay to Howell Cobb, 24 December 1847, Cobb Papers, UGA.

32. Holman Hamilton, "Election of 1848," in Arthur Schlesinger, Jr., et al., eds., *History of American Presidential Elections, 1789—1968,* 4 vols. (New York: Chelsea House, 1971), 2:909; Chaplain W. Morrison, *Democratic Politics and Sectionalism: The Wilmot Proviso Controversy* (Chapel Hill: University of North Carolina Press, 1967), 86—92; Willard Carl Klunder, "Lewis Cass and Slavery Expansion: 'The Father of Popular Sovereignty' and Ideological Infanticide," *Civil War History* 32 (December 1986): 293—317. Morrison is mistaken when he says (110) that the December 1847 Georgia Democratic convention took no position on popular sovereignty.

33. *Milledgeville Southern Recorder,* 1, 8 February 1848, 25 January 1848; for the convention proceedings, see ibid., 24 December 1847.

34. Robert Toombs to James Thomas, 16 April 1848, in TSC, 104; Joseph L. Locke to Thomas Butler King, 22 May 1848, King Papers, SHC; Iverson L. Harris

to John M. Berrien, 25 March 1848, Charles J. Jenkins to John M. Berrien, 13 December 1847, Berrien Papers, SHC.

35. *Augusta Chronicle & Sentinel,* 27 January, 26 April, 3, 10 May 1848; Thomas Butler King, Jr., to Thomas Butler King, 10 January 1848, R. R. Cuyler to Thomas Butler King, 26 March 1848, William B. Hodgson to Thomas Butler King, 15 May 1848, Joseph L. Locke to Thomas Butler King, 24 May 1848, Thomas Bomke to Thomas Butler King, 24 May 1848, W. W. Paine to Thomas Butler King, 6 June 1848, King Papers, SHC; Alexander H. Stephens to Linton Stephens, 16 December 1847, 11, 18, 29 January, 22, 24 March 1848, Stephens Papers, MCSH; letters of Toombs and Stephens, in the *Milledgeville Southern Recorder,* 21 March 1848; Robert Toombs to Andrew J. Miller, 13 April 1848, in ibid., 2 May 1848; *Milledgeville Southern Recorder,* 15 February, 7 March, 4, 25 April, 9 May 1848; *Athens Southern Whig,* 6 May 1847, 30 March 1848; *Savannah Republican,* 11 February, 21 March, 8, 14, 28 April, 9 May 1848; *Macon Georgia Journal and Messenger,* 9, 16, 23 February, 12, 19 April 1848.

36. Taylor's Allison letter, in the *Macon Georgia Journal and Messenger,* 3 May 1848; *Milledgeville Southern Recorder,* 9 May 1848; *Macon Georgia Journal and Messenger,* 10 May 1848; *Savannah Republican,* 10 May 1848.

37. Hopkins Holsey to Howell Cobb, 16 May 1848, Cobb Papers, UGA; Joseph G. Rayback, *Free Soil: The Election of 1848* (Lexington: University Press of Kentucky, 1970), 131–200.

38. Alexander H. Stephens to Linton Stephens, 18 January 1848, Stephens Papers, EU; *Milledgeville Southern Recorder,* 26 October 1847, 11 January 1848; *Savannah Republican,* 3 February, 4 September 1847; *Milledgeville Federal Union,* 3 August 1847; *Augusta Constitutionalist,* 11 October 1846, 5 February, 12 October 1847, 6 January, 25 August 1848.

39. *Augusta Constitutionalist,* 11 January, 29 February, 17 May, 1, 8 July 1848; Hopkins Holsey to Howell Cobb, 16 May 1848, Cobb Papers, UGA; *Athens Southern Banner,* 8 June 1848; for proceedings of the Democratic state convention, see *Milledgeville Federal Union,* 27 June 1848.

40. *Congressional Globe Appendix,* 30th Cong., 1st sess., 1847–48, 887–93 (quotation on 893). Johnson had been appointed to fill Walter Colquitt's seat on the latter's resignation.

41. Ibid., 843, 845.

42. Ibid., 775, 778.

43. *Congressional Globe,* 30th Cong., 1st sess., 1847–48, 1002–7, 1061–63; *Congressional Globe Appendix,* 30th Cong., 1st sess., 1847–48, 844–45, 1103–7, 1188–91; John M. Berrien to Iverson L. Harris, 2 October 1848, Berrien Papers, UGA (photostatic copy of the original in the Berrien Papers, LC); Alexander H. Stephens

to the editor of the *Federal Union*, 30 August 1848, in TSC, 117–24; *Augusta Constitutionalist*, 15 August 1848; *Athens Southern Banner*, 24 August 1848; *Milledgeville Federal Union*, 8 August, 12, 26 September 1848; *Milledgeville Southern Recorder*, 15, 22, 29 August 1848; Schott, *Stephens*, 87–91; Potter, *Impending Crisis*, 73–75. Robert Toombs had earlier adopted the same theoretical position as Stephens, but Toombs voted against tabling the Clayton Compromise.

44. *Augusta Chronicle & Sentinel*, 7 November 1848, 28 October 1848; *Savannah Republican*, 7 August 1848.

45. *Augusta Chronicle & Sentinel*, 10 July 1848, 22 June 1848; *Savannah Republican*, 26 July 1848.

46. Iverson L. Harris to John M. Berrien, 14 July 1848, Berrien Papers, SHC; *Macon Georgia Journal and Messenger*, 28 June, 5 July 1848; John T. Thweatt to Thomas Butler King, 13 June 1848, King Papers, SHC; William H. Underwood to John M. Berrien, 22 July 1848, Berrien Papers, SHC; *Savannah Republican*, 17 August, 13 September 1848; *Milledgeville Southern Recorder*, 11 July, 29 August, 19 September, 3 October 1848; *Macon Georgia Journal and Messenger*, 19 July, 2, 30 August 1848; *Augusta Chronicle & Sentinel*, 6, 19 July, 14 September 1848.

47. *Savannah Republican*, 4 November 1848; *Athens Southern Whig*, 6 July 1848.

48. Alexander H. Stephens to J. W. Harris, 4 July 1848, Stephens Papers, LC; *Augusta Chronicle & Sentinel*, 21 September 1848; *Savannah Republican*, 12 June, 21 August 1848; *Milledgeville Southern Recorder*, 26 September, 3 October, 7 November 1848.

49. *Athens Southern Banner*, 19 August 1848; Hiram Warner to Howell Cobb, 17 July 1848, Cobb Papers, UGA; *Augusta Constitutionalist*, 5 November 1848.

50. *Milledgeville Federal Union*, 31 October 1848; *Athens Southern Banner*, 5 October 1848.

51. *Augusta Constitutionalist*, 27 July 1848, 8 February, 14, 17, 22 June, 26 July, 29 October 1848; *Athens Southern Banner*, 16 March, 25 May, 15 June, 28 September 1848; *Milledgeville Federal Union*, 27 June, 21 October 1848.

52. James F. Cooper to Howell Cobb, 11 November 1848, in TSC, 137.

53. John B. Lamar to Howell Cobb, 12 July 1848, in TSC, 116; *Athens Southern Banner*, 16 November 1848.


*5. "In Politics, We Are* Party *Men": Voting Patterns, the Legislature, and Party Organization*


1. *Macon Georgia Telegraph*, 27 November 1837; Jean H. Baker, *Affairs of Party: The Political Culture of Northern Democrats in the Mid-Nineteenth Century* (Ithaca:

Cornell University Press, 1983); Joel H. Silbey, *The American Political Nation, 1838–1893* (Stanford: Stanford University Press, 1991), 1–214.

2. Linton Stephens to Alexander H. Stephens, 20 May 1856, Alexander H. Stephens Papers, MCSH (microfilm, EU); Robert A. Toombs to John M. Berrien, 7 January 1843, John MacPherson Berrien Papers, SHC.

3. *Milledgeville Southern Recorder,* 25 October 1842; Joseph H. Lumpkin to Howell Cobb, 19 December 1843, Howell Cobb Papers, UGA.

4. A. Reid to John M. Berrien, 13 June 1845, Berrien Papers, SHC; *Columbus Enquirer,* 5 August 1840; "Peter Q. C. Smith," in the *Augusta Chronicle & Sentinel,* 3 August 1856; *Athens Southern Banner,* 14 April 1836.

5. *Milledgeville Federal Union,* 30 March 1847.

6. As in earlier chapters, all of the election statistics are based on the presidential election figures taken from Walter Dean Burnham, *Presidential Ballots, 1836–1892* (Baltimore: Johns Hopkins University Press, 1955); and state election results found in newspapers. The population figures are taken from the *Fifth Census of the United States, 1830; Sixth Census of the United States, 1840; Seventh Census of the United States, 1850;* and *Eighth Census of the United States, 1860.*

7. Ralph B. Flanders, *Plantation Slavery in Georgia* (Chapel Hill: University of North Carolina Press, 1933), 70, 73–75, 79; Ulrich Bonnell Phillips, "The Origin and Growth of the Southern Black Belts," *American Historical Review* 11 (July 1906): 99, 109–10; J. William Harris, *Plain Folk and Gentry in a Slave Society: White Liberty and Black Slavery in Augusta's Hinterlands* (Middletown, Conn.: Wesleyan University Press, 1985), 40. Drawing on poll books from Prince Edward County, Virginia, Paul F. Bourke and Donald A. DeBats, in "Identifiable Voting in Nineteenth-Century America: Toward a Comparison of Britain and United States Before the Secret Ballot," *Perspectives in American History* 11 (1977–78): 259–88; and William G. Shade, in "Society and Politics in Antebellum Virginia's Southside," *Journal of Southern History* 53 (May 1987): 163–93, come to sometimes conflicting conclusions about the social bases of the parties. A main conclusion that I draw from both articles is that an enormous majority of voters were slaveholders, and I find Bourke and DeBats's points about the importance of neighborhoods and leadership persuasive.

8. On county "political style," the politics of neighborhoods, and the importance of local leaders, see J. Mills Thornton III, *Politics and Power in a Slave Society: Alabama, 1800–1860* (Baton Rouge: Louisiana State University Press, 1978), 153–60; Christopher Morris, *Becoming Southern: The Evolution of a Way of Life, Warren County and Vicksburg, Mississippi, 1770–1860* (New York: Oxford University Press, 1995), 132–55; Robert C. Kenzer, *Kinship and Neighborhood in a Southern Community: Orange County, North Carolina, 1849–1881* (Knoxville: University of Tennes-

see Press, 1987), 52–70; Stephanie McCurry, *Masters of Small Words: Yeoman Households, Gender Relations, and the Political Culture of the Antebellum South Carolina Low Country* (New York: Oxford University Press, 1995), 239–76; Daniel W. Crofts, *Old Southampton: Politics and Society in a Virginia County, 1834–1869* (Charlottesville: University Press of Virginia, 1992), 126–40.

9. Donald A. DeBats, *Elites and Masses: Political Structure, Communication, and Behavior in Ante-Bellum Georgia* (New York: Garland Press, 1990), 428–29, provides a detailed regression analysis. DeBats found that black:white population ratios and taxes paid in a county (measures of the economic basis, racial composition, and wealth) explained 10 percent of voting behavior between 1827 and 1835, 16 percent between 1837 and 1844, and 13 percent between 1846 and 1853. The large number of anomalous counties made level of slave population (or any other social variable) a poor predictor of individual county voting behavior. Past political behavior—that is, the previous voting results in a county—was normally a far better predictor of voting behavior in any given election than were all other social and economic variables combined. DeBats found that the correlation between county voting and his combined social and economic variables explained, on average, just 26 percent of voting behavior in elections in the 1827–60 period. DeBats considers many variables at length on pages 305–457, and concludes, among other things, that region was a significant factor in determining voting behavior—a point clearly revealed by my own work.

10. Richard D. Arnold to his wife, 6 December 1837, in Richard H. Shryock ed., "Letters of Richard D. Arnold, M.D. 1808–1876," *Papers of the Trinity College Historical Society,* double series 18–19 (1929): 16–17; *Seventh Census, 1850,* 366; James C. Bonner, *Milledgeville: Georgia's Antebellum Capital* (Athens: University of Georgia Press, 1978), 17–47, 66, 93–110, 127–37.

11. Donald A. DeBats, "An Uncertain Arena: The Georgia House of Representatives, 1808–1861," *Journal of Southern History* 56 (August 1990): 428–37. DeBats's excellent article parallels my own research (although I also consider the Georgia senate), and our conclusions on most points are similar. My calculations put the average length of service in the house from 1833 to 1849 at 1.68 terms; senators elected from counties between 1836 and 1843 (before the change to a district system) had an average tenure of 1.85 terms. I arrived at the averages by dividing the total number of terms available by the number of different men elected to serve those terms. All statistics regarding legislators, unless otherwise noted, are based on my database of several thousand Georgia legislators elected to the house and senate between 1836 and 1861. I compiled a basic list of legislators from the county-by-county listings in the *Georgia Official* and *Statistical Register, 1977–1978* (Atlanta: Perry Communications, 1978), and then checked it against membership lists in the

legislative journals. I obtained party designations for legislators from the October postelection issues of Georgia newspapers, chiefly from the *Milledgeville Southern Recorder* and the *Milledgeville Federal Union*. The resulting information on membership and party affiliation, though extremely accurate, is not perfect. My database has 19 incomplete or missing cases (party designation uncertain or name of legislator missing) out of 3,901 total cases. DeBats used the same sources and presents compatible data, but he seems to have more incomplete and missing cases. He also appears to include some legislators—late-arriving replacements for men who died or resigned during sessions—that I excluded from my calculations. In compiling my database, I was primarily interested in producing comparable party and county totals over time, and the inclusion of more than one legislator per seat per session—although I knew that more than one had served—would have defeated the purpose. DeBats, in contrast, focuses mainly on roll-call analysis, and thus properly includes the legislators actually serving at the moment when the roll call occurred—as I do also when performing roll-call analysis. In any event, the differences between DeBats's house data and mine amount to a few cases out of many hundreds; both sets of figures show the same patterns and trends.

12. My list of veteran legislators includes all the men who served four or more terms in the house (1836–49) and senate (1836–43) combined, except for a couple of legislators who were excluded because their party designations were contradictory. Eighty-six of the veteran legislators were Democrats; sixty-two were Whigs. The mountains and the pine barrens–wiregrass particularly tended to elect the same men year after year; veteran legislators served more than one-third of the terms in those regions. My argument about veteran legislators somewhat contradicts the general point made in DeBats, "Uncertain Arena," about the inexperience of legislators and the legislature's institutional weakness. The disagreement is conceptual rather than statistical and involves a difference of opinion regarding how many experienced leaders the legislature and the parties needed to function effectively.

13. Kenneth Coleman and Charles Stephen Gurr, eds., *Dictionary of Georgia Biography*, 2 vols. (Athens: University of Georgia Press, 1983), 1:529–53; 2:715–17; Olive H. Shadgett, "Charles Jones Jenkins, Jr.," in Horace Montgomery, ed., *Georgians in Profile: Historical Essays in Honor of Ellis Merton Coulter* (Athens: University of Georgia Press, 1958), 220–44.

14. "One of the People," in the *Macon Georgia Telegraph*, 2 April 1839.

15. *Journal of a General Convention of the State of Georgia, to Reduce the Members of the General Assembly. Begun and Held at Milledgeville, the Seat of Government, in May 1833* (Milledgeville: Federal Union Office, 1833); *Milledgeville Southern Recorder*, 22 March, 10 May, 7, 14 June 1832; Jack N. Averitt, "The Democratic Party in Georgia, 1824–1837" (Ph.D. diss., University of North Carolina, Chapel Hill,

1957), 385–404; Paul Murray, *The Whig Party in Georgia, 1825–1853,* James Sprunt Studies in History and Political Science 29 (Chapel Hill: University of North Carolina Press, 1948), 38–44. The Troupite, Clarkite, and neutral party designations for counties are adapted from a map in Ulrich B. Phillips, *Georgia and State Rights* (Washington, D.C.: Government Printing Office, 1902; reprint ed., Yellow Springs, Ohio: Antioch Press, 1968), facing 126. Black belt delegates from Troupite counties supported the federal basis by a vote of 57 to 4; those from Clarkite counties opposed it 14 to 34. The motion to retain the federal ratio failed by a vote of 122 to 126. Under the actual apportionment in place in 1833, the black belt, for example, held 63.1 percent of the house seats. Had voters approved the 1833 convention plan, the black belt would have had 61.5 percent of the house seats.

16. *Athens Southern Banner,* 1 June 1833; *Milledgeville Federal Union,* 8 August 1833, 6 June 1833; *Milledgeville Southern Recorder,* 7 August 1833; *Macon Georgia Messenger,* 1 August, 3 October 1833.

17. *Journal of the Convention, to Reduce and Equalize the Representation of the General Assembly of the State of Georgia, Assembled in Milledgeville, on the 6th day of May, Eighteen Hundred and Thirty-nine* (Milledgeville: P. L. Robinson, State Printer, 1839); *Milledgeville Federal Union,* 26 March, 21 May, 18 June 1839; *Augusta Constitutionalist,* 26, 28 February, 20 April, 21 May 1839; *Columbus Enquirer,* 22 May 1839; *Macon Georgia Messenger,* 23 May 1839; *Macon Georgia Telegraph,* 16 April 1839; *Milledgeville Southern Recorder,* 4 June 1839; *Savannah Republican,* 23 May 1839; Murray, *Whig Party,* 81–84. County party designations are based on results of the 1835–37 elections. The black belt vote to sustain the federal ratio was 157 to 17; the total recorded vote was 197 to 83.

18. *Journal of the House of Representatives of the State of Georgia,* 1841, 21; ibid., 1843, 31; *Acts of the General Assembly of the State of Georgia,* 1840, 33–34; ibid., 1841, 60–61; ibid., 1842, 56–57; ibid., 1843, 15–16, 54–56. The 1843 amendment gave two house seats to the twenty-seven counties with the largest population under the federal ratio; all other counties had one seat.

19. Ralph A. Wooster, *The People in Power: Courthouse and Statehouse in the Lower South, 1850–1860* (Knoxville: University of Tennessee Press, 1969), 29, 37, 43, 129–34. A more complete investigation by Peter Wallenstein, *From Slave South to New South: Public Policy in Nineteenth-Century Georgia* (Chapel Hill: University of North Carolina Press, 1987), 21, indicates that Wooster's figures understate the slaveholdings of Georgia legislators in 1850, and that more than 80 percent of legislators in that year were slaveholders. Either set of figures demonstrates that slaveholders, especially planters, dominated the Georgia legislature out of all proportion to their numbers in the state as a whole.

20. Folks Huxford, *Pioneers of Wiregrass Georgia: A Biographical Account of Some*

*of the Early Settlers of That Portion of Wiregrass Georgia Embraced in the Original Counties of Irwin, Appling, Wayne, Camden, and Glynn,* 7 vols. (Adel, Ga.: Patten Publishing, 1951–75), 1:86–88, 205–6; 2:64–66, 221; 3:132–34, 369, 372; 4:343, 367; 5:73–74, 205–6; Dorothy Brannen, *Life in Old Bulloch: The Story of a Wiregrass County in Georgia* (Gainesville, Ga.: Magnolia Press, 1987), 41, includes a list of county officers in an unnumbered appendix. The individuals mentioned represent only a fraction of those I identified by matching my database of Georgia legislators with Huxford's genealogical research.

21. John B. Lamar to Howell Cobb, 27 July 1837, Cobb Papers, UGA; "Backwoods' Candidate," in the *Augusta Constitutionalist,* 8 September 1847.

22. John Hughes to Thomas Butler King, 28 September 1844, Thomas Butler King Papers, SHC. Major Bacon may have been Edwin H. Bacon, a former state senator from adjoining Liberty County.

23. Stephen F. Miller, *The Bench and Bar of Georgia: Memoirs and Sketches. With an Appendix, Containing a Court Roll from 1790 to 1857, etc.,* 2 vols. (Philadelphia: J. B. Lippincott, 1858), 2:154–55.

24. William Tappan Thompson, *Major Jones's Courtship: Detailed, with Other Scenes, Incidents, and Adventures, in a Series of Letters by Himself* (Philadelphia, 1840; rev. ed., New York, 1872; reprint ed., Atlanta: Cherokee Publishing, 1973). On Thompson, see Coleman and Gurr, eds., *Dictionary of Georgia Biography,* 2:974–76.

25. Thompson, *Major Jones's Courtship,* 25–30 (quotation on 25).

26. Ibid., 30–31.

27. Ibid., 32.

28. Coleman and Gurr, eds., *Dictionary of Georgia Biography,* 2:981–82.

29. Entry of 8 August 1847, Nelson Tift Diary, GDAH; see also *Albany Patriot,* 16 June, 4, 18, 25 August 1847.

30. Entry of 14 September 1847, Tift Diary, GDAH; see also *Albany Patriot,* 8, 22 September 1847.

31. *Albany Patriot,* 29 September 1847.

32. Entry of 7 October 1847, Tift Diary, GDAH; see also *Albany Patriot,* 6, 13 October 1847.

33. *Savannah Republican,* 22 November 1842; Oliver H. Prince to William Schley, 21 March 1836, Telamon Cuyler Collection, UGA; Ambrose Baber to Mary Baber, 15 November 1838, Baber-Blackshear Papers, UGA; entries of 9 and 15 November 1841, Tift Diary, GDAH; Francis S. Bartow to Howell Cobb, 18 December 1841, Cobb Papers, UGA; *Augusta Chronicle & Sentinel,* 19 November 1840; *Milledgeville Federal Union,* 8 January 1850; *Athens Southern Banner,* 23 February 1854; *Macon Georgia Journal and Messenger,* 8 March 1854.

34. Charles J. McDonald to Howell Cobb, 17 October 1841, Cobb Papers, UGA; entry of 2 November 1841, Tift Diary, GDAH; *Macon Georgia Telegraph*, 20 November 1849; DeBats, "Uncertain Arena," 441–48.

35. Wallenstein, *Slave South to New South*, 23–26. I borrow heavily here and below from Peter Wallenstein's excellent analysis, but he places much greater emphasis than I do on taxation's significance as an issue in Georgia politics. Peter has graciously shared information and observations with me over several years.

36. Ibid., 40–41, 58.

37. George W. Crawford to John M. Berrien, 13 February 1844, Berrien Papers, SHC; Peter Wallenstein, "'More Unequally Taxed than any People in the Civilized World': The Origins of Georgia's Ad Valorem Tax System," *Georgia Historical Quarterly* 69 (Winter 1985): 459–87. Virtually all of Wallenstein's evidence on taxation issues comes from official documents such as governors' messages and legislative journals, rather than from stump speeches or newspaper discussions. The reason is simple: little recorded public discussion of taxation issues occurred outside Milledgeville.

38. *Georgia House Journal*, 1851, 453–54; *Journal of the Senate of the State of Georgia*, 1851, 377–78.

39. Wallenstein, *Slave South to New South*, 56–59. The comparison of Georgia with other states is based on tables in the *Eighth Census of the United States, Mortality, Property, etc., 1860*, 339, 511. I excluded Delaware from my computations because of incomplete returns for taxation. Levels of taxation for the southern states generally were quite low, especially compared with the Northeast.

40. *Macon Georgia Messenger*, 22 January 1846; *Rome Courier*, in the *Savannah Republican*, 10 June 1843; Milton S. Heath, *Constructive Liberalism: The Role of the State in Economic Development in Georgia to 1860* (Cambridge: Harvard University Press, 1954), 231–53, 260–61.

41. Heath, *Constructive Liberalism*, 262–69; Averitt, "Democratic Party," 434–37; Ulrich B. Phillips, *A History of Transportation in the Eastern Cotton Belt to 1860* (New York: Columbia University Press, 1908), 221–64; Jefferson M. Dixon, "The Central Railroad of Georgia, 1833–1892" (Ph.D. diss., George Peabody College for Teachers, 1953), 35–49; William T. Jenkins, "Antebellum Macon and Bibb County, Georgia" (Ph.D. diss., University of Georgia, 1966), 141–47. Newspapers of both parties consistently supported the idea of state aid for railroad projects, including the W&A, despite numerous disagreements over details. See *Columbus Enquirer*, 20 January 1837; *Macon Georgia Messenger*, 29 November 1838; *Milledgeville Federal Union*, 17 January, 7 November 1837, 30 October, 6 November 1838, 5 November 1839; *Milledgeville Southern Recorder*, 23 October 1838; *Macon Georgia Telegraph*, 25 December 1837, 22 January 1838.

42. *Georgia House Journal,* 1841, 279; ibid., 1843, 446–47; ibid., 1847, 257–58; *Georgia Senate Journal,* 1841, 183–185, 255; ibid., 1843, 276-77; ibid., 1847, 320; George W. Crawford to Alexander H. Stephens, 31 October, 7 December 1843, Alexander H. Stephens Papers, LC (microfilm, UGA); Robert A. Toombs to Alexander H. Stephens, 1 January 1844, in TSC, 53; Cleveland, "Crawford," 95–108, 145–56; Heath, *Constructive Liberalism,* 270–71. The 1841 bill to suspend work passed quickly, without a roll-call vote in either branch of the legislature. Eighty-seven percent of house Whigs and 95.3 percent of senate Whigs supported the 1843 bill; only 22.9 percent of house Democrats and 17.8 percent of senate Democrats favored it. In 1847, 83.9 percent of house Whigs and 90.9 percent of senate Whigs voted for the appropriation; 25.9 percent of house Democrats and 38.1 percent of senate Democrats voted for it.

43. *Georgia House Journal,* 1851, 479; *Georgia Senate Journal,* 1851, 443–44; Heath, *Constructive Liberalism,* 271–72. Analyzing the house vote is difficult; the number of absentee members, fifty-nine, exceeded the number of votes for the bill. Strong support from north Georgia saved the appropriation bill in the senate by a 21 to 20 vote. Several counties in the southwestern black belt inexplicably had senators who supported the bill and representatives who opposed it.

44. Heath, *Constructive Liberalism,* 273–81, 286–91; Wallenstein, *Slave South to New South,* 38–39; Steven Hahn, *The Roots of Southern Populism: Yeoman Farmers and the Transformation of the Georgia Upcountry, 1850–1890* (New York: Oxford University Press, 1983), 34–38. Hahn makes some sound remarks on railroad issues, but if north Georgia's long-standing support for the W&A is any indication, he considerably overstates the upcountry folk's economic and ideological opposition to railroads.

45. *Eighth Census, 1860,* 328; "Autobiography of Herschel V. Johnson," 96–97, Herschel V. Johnson Papers, DU; John H. Lumpkin to Howell Cobb, 17 March 1854, Cobb Papers, UGA; Joseph E. Brown to A. V. Brown, 19 August 1858, Cuyler Collection, UGA; Peterson Thweatt to Alexander H. Stephens, 15 December 1858, Stephens Papers, LC; *Augusta Constitutionalist,* 22 December 1852, 9 March 1855, 16 December 1857; *Augusta Chronicle & Sentinel,* 8, 26 August, 28 October, 18 November 1855; *Macon Georgia Journal and Messenger,* 14 March 1855; *Milledgeville Federal Union,* 13, 20 December 1853, 17 January 1854, 5 February 1856; "Baldwin" and "Crawford," in ibid., 11 December 1856; *Milledgeville Southern Recorder,* 4 December 1855, 18 December 1855, 4 March 1856, 18 August 1857; *Macon Georgia Telegraph,* 23 October 1855, 10 May 1859; Heath, *Constructive Liberalism,* 276–92; Wallenstein, *Slave South to New South,* 59–60, 63–68; Joseph H. Parks, *Joseph E. Brown of Georgia* (Baton Rouge: Louisiana State University Press, 1977),

53–65; Bruce W. Collins, "Governor Joseph E. Brown, Economic Issues, and Georgia's Road to Secession, 1857–1859," *Georgia Historical Quarterly* (Summer 1987): 216–18; James M. Russell, *Atlanta 1847–1890: City Building in the Old South and the New* (Baton Rouge: Louisiana State University Press, 1988), 53–57; Dorothy Orr, *A History of Education in Georgia* (Chapel Hill: University of North Carolina Press, 1950), 169–77.

46. *Milledgeville Southern Recorder,* 29 June 1847; Cornelius R. Hanleiter to John M. Berrien, 27 December 1847, Charles J. Jenkins to John M. Berrien, 29 June 1847, Berrien Papers, SHC.

47. James F. Cooper to Howell Cobb, 19 February 1848, Cobb Papers, UGA; *Augusta Chronicle & Sentinel,* 18 June 1849; "A Warren Delegate," in ibid., 18 September 1849; *Macon Georgia Telegraph,* 16 August 1853; *Athens Southern Banner,* 15 May 1851.

48. Richard D. Arnold to Howell Cobb, 13 July 1857, Cobb Papers, UGA; Richard H. Haunton, "Savannah in the 1850s" (Ph.D. diss., Emory University, 1968), 197–205, 211–14; Wooster, *People in Power,* 157–59. Harris, *Plain Folk and Gentry,* 113–14, stresses that local leaders were a mixed group in terms of personal wealth.

49. Alexander H. Stephens to John L. Stephens, 20 April 1840, Alexander H. Stephens Papers, EU; Alexander H. Stephens to Linton Stephens, 5 September 1845, Alexander H. Stephens to Linton Stephens, 12 September 1839, 23 August 1845, Alexander H. Stephens Papers, MCSH; *Milledgeville Southern Recorder,* 21 October 1845.

50. *Milledgeville Southern Recorder,* 25 June 1844; *Milledgeville Federal Union,* 30 July 1844; *Augusta Constitutionalist,* 19 August 1846.

51. Samuel T. Chapman to Thomas Butler King, 13 January 1846, Joseph S. Fay to Thomas Butler King, 15 May 1846, Edward T. Sheftall to Thomas Butler King, 15 May 1848, King Papers, SHC; *Savannah Republican,* 12 May 1846.

52. M. H. Gathright to Howell Cobb, 4 June 1846, Howell Cobb to Mary Ann Lamar Cobb, 13 September 1846, Cobb Papers, UGA; Albon Chase to Howell Cobb, 20 May 1846, William Hope Hull to Howell Cobb, 22 May 1846, James F. Cooper to Howell Cobb, 8 July 1846, in TSC, 77–79, 85–86.

53. *Milledgeville Federal Union,* 25 June 1844.

54. Thomas C. Livesay to William Ephraim Smith, 15 September 1849, William Ephraim Smith Papers, DU; *Athens Southern Banner,* 6 March 1845; *Milledgeville Federal Union,* 15 June 1847; Gabriel T. Spearman to Alexander H. Stephens, 4 March 1845, Stephens Papers, MCSH; Alexander H. Stephens to John L. Stephens, 16 July 1843, Stephens Papers, EU.

55. *Milledgeville Southern Recorder,* 22 December 1840, 27 June 1843.

56. *Macon Georgia Messenger,* 11 June 1840; *Milledgeville Southern Recorder,* 16 June 1842; *Milledgeville Federal Union,* 27 December 1836, 25 December 1838, 29 December 1840.

57. *Milledgeville Federal Union,* 13 June, 19 December 1843; "An Old Union Man" and "Democracy," in ibid., 4, 23 April 1843.

58. *Seventh Census, 1850,* 384.

59. *Rome Courier,* 26 February 1852; *Macon Georgia Telegraph,* 15 February 1859; *Columbus Enquirer,* 8 March 1834; *Athens Southern Banner,* 22 September 1853.

60. Alexander H. Stephens to Linton Stephens, 17 December 1853, Stephens Papers, MCSH; A. S. Burnett to Alexander H. Stephens, 7 December 1844, Stephens Papers, EU.

61. Charles J. Jenkins to John M. Berrien, 25 November 1845, Berrien Papers, SHC; *Augusta Chronicle,* 2 February 1833; *Columbus Enquirer,* 1 January, 25 March, 6 May, 3 June 1840.

62. Francis S. Bartow to John M. Berrien, 30 July 1845, Berrien Papers, SHC; Edward C. Councell to Thomas Butler King, 20 March 1848, King Papers, SHC; S. A. Lamar to Mary Ann Cobb, 9 October 1840, James Sledge to Howell Cobb, 1 September 1857, Cobb Papers, UGA; "A Democrat," in the *Macon Georgia Telegraph,* 27 December 1859; *Augusta Chronicle & Sentinel,* 20 September 1841; *Milledgeville Federal Union,* 22 October 1844; *Rome Courier,* 25 September 1851. On campaign editions, see, as one of a hundred possible examples, an advertisement for the "Reformer," a paper boosting William Henry Harrison, in the *Augusta Chronicle & Sentinel,* 9 May 1840 (the *Chronicle* itself issued the "Reformer"). Both direct evidence and the consistency of party voting totals for state and national offices strongly suggest that the vast majority of voters used party ballots. The *Milledgeville Southern Recorder,* 16 October 1860, took the unusual step of printing electoral tickets for John Bell and Edward Everett in the paper itself, in ten small boxes down the side of one page. The editor urged party men to cut these out and distribute them at the polls, commenting, "There are many voters who are ignorant of the mode of voting; thinking that to vote simply for the Presidential candidates, as they would for Governor, is sufficient, not thinking the names of the electors necessary to be upon the ticket."

63. Alexander H. Stephens to Linton Stephens, 14 August 1845, Alexander H. Stephens to Herschel V. Johnson, 19, 20 August 1846, Stephens Papers, MCSH; Alexander H. Stephens to John L. Stephens, 25 August 1846, Stephens Papers, EU; Thomas E. Schott, *Alexander H. Stephens of Georgia: A Biography* (Baton Rouge: Louisiana State University Press, 1988), 73–74.

64. *Macon Georgia Telegraph,* 18 September 1855 (quotes); *Macon Georgia Citizen,* 15, 22 September 1855. I basically accept Tracy's account of the affair.

65. S. A. Williams to John M. Berrien, 25 February 1850, Berrien Papers, SHC; James F. Cooper to Howell Cobb, 9 January 1849, Cobb Papers, UGA; J. A. L. Lee to John M. Berrien, 30 May 1849, Berrien Papers, SHC; *Milledgeville Southern Recorder,* 4 January 1842. As a rough gauge of the interest in patronage, perhaps half of the enormous collection of Howell Cobb's papers at the University of Georgia consists of letters from office seekers, their supporters, and their detractors.

66. John M. Berrien to Ambrose Baber, 17 March 1841, Baber-Blackshear Papers, UGA.

67. J. G. McWhorter to Howell Cobb, 20 November 1844, Lewis Kennon to Howell Cobb, 10 December 1844, John Phinizy, Jr., to Howell Cobb, 21 December 1844, Cobb Papers, UGA; *Augusta Constitutionalist,* 10 December 1844; James G. McWhorter to the Democratic party of Richmond County, in ibid., 26 November 1844.

68. A copy of the resolutions is enclosed in John Phinizy, Jr., to Howell Cobb, 21 December 1844, Cobb Papers, UGA. Glascock was ultimately dismissed.

69. George Gilmer, *Sketches of Some of the First Settlers of Upper Georgia, of the Cherokees, and the Author* (New York: D. Appleton, 1854), 518; letter from Eugenius A. Nisbet, 12 October 1841, in the *Augusta Chronicle & Sentinel,* 21 October 1841.

70. Alfred Iverson to Howell Cobb, 17 October 1848, James F. Cooper to Howell Cobb, 20 October 1848, in TSC, 130–31; Harris, *Plain Folk and Gentry,* 94–95.

71. Thomas W. Thomas to Howell Cobb, 20 August 1846, Cobb Papers, UGA; Alexander H. Stephens to John L. Stephens, 4 September 1843, Stephens Papers, EU, relates the incidents of one campaign trip to north Georgia. Charles McDonald carried 242 votes in Elbert County in the 1841 election, compared with just 79 votes in 1839.

72. Alexander H. Stephens to Linton Stephens, 2 June 1841, in Richard M. Johnston and William M. Browne, *Life of Alexander H. Stephens* (Philadelphia: J. B. Lippincott, 1878), 153.

73. James S. Buckingham, *The Slave States of America,* 2 vols. (London: Fisher, Son, 1842), 2:147; Robert Toombs to Alexander Stephens, 3 September 1856, in TSC, 380.

74. Howell Cobb to Thomas D. Harris, 29 September 1848, Thomas DeKalb Harris Family Papers, GDAH.

75. Alexander H. Stephens to John L. Stephens, 6 July 1852, Stephens Papers, EU; Thomas Butler King to John M. Berrien, 18 July 1843, Berrien Papers, SHC; Milledge H. Gathright to Howell Cobb, 4 January 1844, Elihu S. Barclay to Howell Cobb, 11 January 1844, Howell Cobb to Mary Ann Lamar Cobb, 16 December 1846, Cobb Papers, UGA; Allen F. Owen to John M. Berrien, 2 December 1847,

Berrien Papers, SHC; Alexander H. Stephens to Linton Stephens, 1 September 1856, Alexander H. Stephens Papers, MCSH; Robert Toombs to Alexander H. Stephens, 3 August 1857, in TSC, 408.

76. George W. Lamar to Howell Cobb, 1 September 1853, John B. Lamar to Howell Cobb, 9 May 1853, William Hope Hull to Howell Cobb, 16 May 1853, Cobb Papers, UGA; Richard D. Arnold to R. M. Goodwin, 19 March 1857, in Shryock, ed., "Arnold Letters," 81–82.

77. Francis S. Bartow to Howell Cobb, 20 September 1841, Cobb Papers, UGA; Thomas W. Thomas to Alexander H. Stephens, 12 January 1857, in TSC, 391; Richard D. Arnold to [?], 8 November 1844, in Shryock, ed., "Arnold Letters," 24–25; *Athens Southern Banner*, 26 September 1844; *Macon Georgia Messenger*, 6 January 1842; *Augusta Chronicle & Sentinel*, 5 June 1845, 26 October 1856; "Justice," in the *Augusta Chronicle & Sentinel* (weekly), 21 October 1857; Jenkins, "Antebellum Macon and Bibb County," 291–92.

78. S. A. Lamar to Mary Ann Lamar Cobb, 9 October 1840, Cobb Papers, UGA; *Macon Georgia Telegraph*, 16 December 1856.

79. *Macon Georgia Journal and Messenger*, 28 October 1857.

## 6. *Slavery and the Union, 1849–1853*

1. Robert Toombs to John J. Crittenden, 3 January 1849, in TSC, 139; *Milledgeville Southern Recorder*, 6 February 1849; *Columbus Enquirer*, 6 February 1849; *Savannah Republican*, 15 February 1849; Royce C. McCrary, "John MacPherson Berrien (1781–1856): A Political Biography" (Ph.D. diss., University of Georgia, 1971), 343–48; Charles M. Wiltse, *John C. Calhoun, Sectionalist: 1840–1850* (Indianapolis: Bobbs-Merrill, 1951), 375–88.

2. Robert Toombs to John J. Crittenden, 22 January 1849, in TSC, 141; William J. Cooper, Jr., *The South and the Politics of Slavery, 1828–1856* (Baton Rouge: Louisiana State University Press, 1978), 272–73, 377–78.

3. *Columbus Times*, 14 November 1848; Henry L. Benning to Howell Cobb, 1 July 1849, in TSC, 169; Wilson Lumpkin to John C. Calhoun, 3 January 1849, Herschel V. Johnson to John C. Calhoun, 28 June 1849, in Chauncey S. Boucher and Robert P. Brooks, eds., "Correspondence Addressed to John C. Calhoun, 1837–1849," in *Annual Report of the American Historical Association*, 1929 (Washington, D.C.: Government Printing Office, 1930), 492, 513; Herschel V. Johnson to Robert A. L. Atkinson, 29 June, 5 July 1849, in Percy S. Flippin, ed., "Herschel V. Johnson Correspondence," *North Carolina Historical Review* 4 (April 1927): 184, 190; *Macon*

*Georgia Telegraph,* 13 February, 20 March 1849; *Milledgeville Federal Union,* 14, 28 August 1849.

4. Howell Cobb to John B. Lamar, 24 January 1849, Howell Cobb Papers, UGA; John H. Lumpkin to Howell Cobb, 12 March 1849, in TSC, 157; Howell Cobb, Linn Boyd, Beverly L. Clarke, and John H. Lumpkin to their constituents, in Robert P. Brooks, ed., "Howell Cobb Papers," *Georgia Historical Quarterly* 5 (June 1921): 39–52; *Cassville Standard of the Union,* in the *Augusta Chronicle & Sentinel,* 28 March 1849.

5. Charles J. Jenkins to John M. Berrien, 16 July 1849, Iverson L. Harris to John M. Berrien, 17 August, 6 October 1849, John MacPherson Berrien Papers, SHC; John B. Lamar to Howell Cobb, 9 April, 18 May 1849, Cobb Papers, UGA; Thomas W. Thomas to Howell Cobb, 16 February 1849, John W. Burke to Howell Cobb, 22 March 1849, Howell Cobb to James Buchanan, 2, 17 June 1849, John H. Lumpkin to Howell Cobb, 6, 13 June 1849, in TSC, 152, 157–64; Herschel V. Johnson to John C. Calhoun, 20 July 1849, Herschel V. Johnson to Sampson W. Harris, 22 July 1849, in Flippin, ed., "Johnson Correspondence," 191–93; J. Raven Mathews to John C. Calhoun, 7 October 1849, in Boucher and Brooks, eds., "Calhoun Correspondence," 529–30; *Milledgeville Southern Recorder,* 26 June, 31 July 1849; *Athens Southern Banner,* 17 May, 14 June, 26 July, 6 September 1849; *Augusta Chronicle & Sentinel,* 11 April 1849; *Columbus Enquirer,* 3, 10 July, 21 August, 18, 25 September, 9, 16 October 1849; *Macon Georgia Journal and Messenger,* 25 July, 15 August, 12, 26 September 1849; *Milledgeville Federal Union,* 17 July, 14, 28 August, 25 September 1849; *Savannah Republican,* 5 April, 26 July, 19 September 1849.

6. Lacy K. Ford, Jr., *Origins of Southern Radicalism: The South Carolina Upcountry, 1800–1860* (New York: Oxford University Press, 1988), 187–88; Wiltse, *Calhoun, Sectionalist,* 398–400, 406–8; Michael F. Holt, *The Political Crisis of the 1850s* (New York: John Wiley & Sons, 1978), 69–79; Cooper, *Politics of Slavery,* 273–82, 291–92; William W. Freehling, *Prelude to Civil War: The Nullification Controversy in South Carolina 1816–1836* (New York: Harper & Row, 1965), 477–81; Holman Hamilton, *Zachary Taylor: Soldier in the White House* (Indianapolis: Bobbs-Merrill, 1951), 149–83, 203–18, 229–42; Edward M. Steel, Jr., *T. Butler King of Georgia* (Athens: University of Georgia Press, 1964), 68–83.

7. Alexander H. Stephens to Linton Stephens, 3 December 1849, 2, 5 December 1849, 15 April 1850, Alexander H. Stephens Papers, MCSH (microfilm, EU); Robert Toombs to John J. Crittenden, 25 April 1850, in Mrs. Chapman Coleman, ed., *The Life of John J. Crittenden, with Selections from His Correspondence and Speeches,* 2 vols. (Philadelphia: J. B. Lippincott, 1871; reprint ed., New York: Da Capo Press, 1970), 1:365–66; William Y. Thompson, *Robert Toombs of Georgia* (Baton Rouge: Louisiana State University Press, 1966), 55–57; Thomas E. Schott, *Alexander H.*

*Stephens of Georgia: A Biography* (Baton Rouge: Louisiana State University Press, 1988), 105–7.

8. *Congressional Globe,* 31st Cong., 1st sess., 1849–50, 27–28; James D. Richardson, comp., *A Compilation of the Messages and Papers of the Presidents, 1789–1897,* 10 vols. (Washington, D.C.: Government Printing Office, 1896–99), 5:18–19, 26–30; Howell Cobb to Mary Ann Lamar Cobb, 8 December 1849, Howell Cobb to Thomas R. R. Cobb, 10 December 1849, Cobb Papers, UGA; Howell Cobb to Mary Ann Lamar Cobb, 20 December 1849, in TSC, 179; John E. Simpson, *Howell Cobb: The Politics of Ambition* (Chicago: Adams Press, 1973), 59–60.

9. *Columbus Times,* 12 February 1850; Herschel V. Johnson to John C. Calhoun, 19 January 1850, in Flippin, ed., "Johnson Correspondence," 201; *Augusta Constitutionalist,* 8 January 1850; Herschel V. Johnson to John C. Calhoun, 20 July, 25 August 1849, Herschel V. Johnson to Henry S. Foote, 19 January 1850, in Flippin, ed., "Johnson Correspondence," 191–92, 197, 199; Herschel V. Johnson to John C. Calhoun, 4 July 1849, in J. Franklin Jameson, ed., "Correspondence of John C. Calhoun," in *Annual Report of the American Historical Association,* vol. 2 (Washington, D.C.: Government Printing Office, 1899), 1199; *Athens Southern Banner,* 9 August 1849; *Milledgeville Federal Union,* 21 August 1849; *Macon Georgia Telegraph,* 15 January 1850.

10. *Columbus Enquirer,* 7 August 1849; Iverson L. Harris to John M. Berrien, 17 August 1849, Charles J. Jenkins to John M. Berrien, [n.d., late November–early December 1849], John M. Berrien to Charles J. Jenkins, 10 December 1849, Berrien Papers, SHC; *Savannah Republican,* 27 February 1850; *Macon Georgia Journal and Messenger,* 2 January 1850; *Athens Southern Whig,* 16 May 1850; *Augusta Chronicle & Sentinel,* 14 February, 13 November 1849, 6 January 1850.

11. *Journal of the House of Representatives of the State of Georgia,* 1849, 34, 37, 484–85.

12. *Journal of the Senate of the State of Georgia,* 1849, 478, 486, 493; *Georgia House Journal,* 1849, 487–88, 503–4, 515–20, 546–48; Luther J. Glenn to Howell Cobb, 15 January 1850, Cobb Papers, UGA; John M. Berrien to Charles J. Jenkins, 10 December 1849, Charles J. Jenkins to John M. Berrien, [n.d., late November–early December 1849], Andrew J. Miller to John M. Berrien, 5 January 1850, John M. Berrien to Charles J. Jenkins, 7 January 1850, Berrien Papers, SHC; letters from Andrew J. Miller and Charles J. Jenkins, in the *Augusta Constitutionalist,* 11 April 1850; *Savannah Republican,* 29 January 1850; *Columbus Times,* 5 February 1850; *Athens Southern Banner,* 7, 21 February 1850; *Milledgeville Federal Union,* 12 February 1850; Richard H. Shryock, *Georgia and the Union in 1850* (Durham: Duke University Press, 1926), 219–30.

13. Iverson L. Harris to John M. Berrien, 7, 24 December 1849, Berrien Papers,

SHC; Miller Grieve to Joseph H. Lumpkin, 13 December 1849, Howell Cobb to Joseph H. Lumpkin, 11 January 1850, Joseph Henry Lumpkin Papers, UGA; Alexander H. Stephens to Linton Stephens, 21 January 1850, Stephens Papers, MCSH; *Augusta Chronicle & Sentinel,* 12 December 1849.

14. *Augusta Constitutionalist,* 5 February 1850; *Congressional Globe Appendix,* 31st Cong., 1st sess., 1849–50, 202–11; Alexander H. Stephens to John L. Stephens, 10 February 1850, Alexander H. Stephens Papers, EU; Alexander H. Stephens to Linton Stephens, 24 February 1850, Stephens Papers, MCSH; Robert Toombs to Linton Stephens, 22 March 1850, in TSC, 188; *Columbus Enquirer,* 5 February 1850; *Augusta Chronicle & Sentinel,* 5 February 1850; *Milledgeville Federal Union,* 5 February 1850; *Macon Georgia Telegraph,* 19 February 1850; Holman Hamilton, *Prologue to Conflict: The Crisis and Compromise of 1850* (Lexington: University of Kentucky Press, 1964), 52–62.

15. William Woods to Howell Cobb, 10 March 1850, Howell C. Flournoy to Howell Cobb, 7 April 1850, William Hope Hull to Howell Cobb, 7 March 1850, Cobb Papers, UGA; Amos T. Akerman to John M. Berrien, 5 January 1850, Iverson L. Harris to John M. Berrien, 25 April 1850, Berrien Papers, SHC.

16. *Athens Southern Banner,* 14 February 1850; *Augusta Constitutionalist,* 31 January 1850; *Milledgeville Federal Union,* 5 March 1850; *Augusta Constitutionalist,* 31 January 1850; *Columbus Times,* 26 March 1850, 29 January 1850; Alexander H. Stephens to Linton Stephens, 19 March 1850, Stephens Papers, MCSH; *Savannah Republican,* 22 March 1850; *Augusta Chronicle & Sentinel,* 22 March 1850; *Columbus Enquirer,* 23 April 1850.

17. *Augusta Constitutionalist,* 6 April 1850, 9, 24 March, 3 May 1850; John H. Lumpkin to Howell Cobb, 21 March 1850, Cobb Papers, UGA; *Columbus Times,* 12 March, 9 April 1850; Thelma Jennings, *The Nashville Convention: Southern Movement for Unity, 1848–1851* (Memphis: Memphis State University Press, 1980), 116–20, 216.

18. Charles J. McDonald to Farish Carter, 10 June 1850, Farish Carter Papers, SHC; *Augusta Constitutionalist,* 18 January, 16, 26 February, 29 May, 21, 28 June 4, 9 July 1850; *Milledgeville Federal Union,* 5 March, 9 July 1850; *Macon Georgia Telegraph,* 4 July 1850; *Columbus Times,* 2 July 1850; Jennings, *Nashville Convention,* 146–54; Hamilton, *Prologue to Conflict,* 95–97.

19. *Columbus Enquirer,* 14 May 1850; *Athens Southern Banner,* 18 July 1850; William B. Wofford to Howell Cobb, 20 February 1850, Howell Cobb to John B. Lamar, 26 June 1850, John H. Lumpkin to Howell Cobb, 21 July, 3 August 1850, Cobb Papers, UGA; George D. Phillips to Howell Cobb, 10 March 1850, Hiram Warner to Howell Cobb, 17 March 1850, Williams Rutherford, Jr., to Howell Cobb, 16 April 1850, in TSC, 185–90.

20. Walter T. Colquitt to John H. Howard et al., 14 May 1850, in *Macon Georgia Telegraph,* 28 May 1850; "A Southern Clergyman," in the *Augusta Constitutionalist,* 13 September 1850; *Milledgeville Federal Union,* 21 May 1850; *Columbus Times,* 18 June 1850.

21. Alexander H. Stephens to Linton Stephens, 10 May 1850, Stephens Papers, MCSH; Charles J. Jenkins to John M. Berrien, 15, 29 May 1850, Francis S. Bartow to John M. Berrien, 21 May 1850, Iverson L. Harris to John M. Berrien, 14 June 1850, Berrien Papers, SHC; James Jackson to Howell Cobb, 14 June 1850, Howell Cobb to John B. Lamar, 26 June 1850, Cobb Papers, UGA; Thomas R. R. Cobb to Howell Cobb, 7 May 1850, James A. Meriwether to Howell Cobb, 24 August 1850, Howell Cobb to William Hope Hull, 17 July 1850, in TSC, 191, 196–206, 211; *Athens Southern Banner,* 8 March 1850; *Milledgeville Southern Recorder,* 28 May, 11 June, 23 July 1850; *Savannah Republican,* 8 June, 22, 26 July 1850; *Augusta Chronicle & Sentinel,* 7 June, 10 July 1850; *Columbus Enquirer* 21 May, 11 June 1850; *Macon Georgia Journal and Messenger,* 22 May, 3 July 1850.

22. *Congressional Globe,* 31st Cong., 1st sess., 1849–50, 1774–75, 1188–89, 1193–94, 1199–1200, 1216, 1219; *Congressional Globe Appendix,* 31st Cong., 1st sess., 1849–50, 202–11, 668–69, 725–28, 1065–68, 1080–84; John M. Berrien to Iverson L. Harris, 19 July 1850, Berrien Papers, UGA (photostatic copy of the original in the John MacPherson Berrien Papers, LC); Hamilton, *Prologue to Conflict,* 84–165, 191–200; Hamilton, *Soldier in the White House,* 372–400; David M. Potter, *The Impending Crisis 1848–1861,* completed and edited by Don E. Fehrenbacher (New York: Harper & Row, 1976), 106–20; Robert W. Johannsen, *Stephen A. Douglas* (New York: Oxford University Press, 1973), 262–98; Ulrich B. Phillips, *The Life of Robert Toombs* (New York: Macmillan, 1913), 57–88; Thompson, *Toombs,* 61–71; Schott, *Stephens,* 111–21; McCrary, "Berrien," 255–372; John T. Hubbell, "Three Georgia Unionists and the Compromise of 1850," *Georgia Historical Quarterly* 51 (September 1967): 310–18; Mark J. Stegmaier, "Zachary Taylor versus the South," *Civil War History* 33 (September 1987): 219–41. The divisions within the Georgia delegation emerged more through publicly announced opposition to or support for the compromise than through voting patterns. Alexander Stephens and Howell Cobb missed nearly all the final votes on the compromise measures but were recognized as key proponents of conciliation. The recorded key votes of William Dawson and John Berrien were identical, but their attitudes were very different. For voting records, see Hamilton, *Prologue to Conflict,* 191–200.

23. *Augusta Constitutionalist,* 2 August 1850, 6, 9, 10, 28 July 1850; Howell Cobb to John B. Lamar, 26 June 1850, Cobb Papers, UGA; John B. Lamar to Howell Cobb, 3 July 1850, William H. Morton to Howell Cobb, 10 July 1850, John H. Lumpkin to Howell Cobb, 21, 29 July 1850, in TSC, 191–92, 194–95, 206–9;

*Columbus Times,* 23 July, 8 October 1850; *Columbus Enquirer,* 21 May, 23 July 1850; *Macon Georgia Journal and Messenger,* 10 July 1850; *Macon Georgia Telegraph,* 30 July 1850.

24. *Columbus Times,* 10 September 1850; *Columbus Sentinel,* in the *Milledgeville Southern Recorder,* 10 September 1850; *Macon Georgia Telegraph,* 17 September 1850; *Augusta Constitutionalist,* 5 September 1850.

25. Alfred Iverson to John M. Berrien, 23 October 1850, Berrien Papers, SHC; "A Practical Conservative," in the *Augusta Constitutionalist,* 8 October 1850; *Rome Southerner,* in the *Augusta Constitutionalist,* 20 October 1850; *Augusta Constitutionalist,* 21 September, 19, 31 October 1850; *Columbus Times,* 29 October 1850; *Macon Georgia Telegraph,* 29 October 1850; McCrary, "Berrien," 372–78.

26. *Augusta Constitutionalist,* 18 September, 15 November 1850; *Milledgeville Federal Union,* 24 September, 1, 8 October 1850; *Macon Georgia Telegraph,* 1 October, 19 November 1850.

27. *Rome Courier,* 17 October, 14 November 1850; William Hope Hull to Howell Cobb, 20 August 1850, Cobb Papers, UGA; Charles J. Jenkins to John M. Berrien, 14 September 1850, Berrien Papers, SHC; *Augusta Chronicle & Sentinel,* 21 August, 19 September, 16 October 1850; *Milledgeville Southern Recorder,* 24 September 1850; *Savannah Republican,* 23, 24 November 1850; *Columbus Enquirer,* 16 July, 10 September, 22 October, 2 November 1850.

28. *Columbus Times,* 22 October 1850; letter of Elijah R. Young and James L. Seward, 18 October 1850, in the *Macon Georgia Telegraph,* 29 October 1850; Robert Toombs's address "To the Voters of the Eighth Congressional District," in the *Milledgeville Southern Recorder,* 15 October 1850; Marshall J. Wellborn's address "To the Voters of the Second Congressional District," in the *Milledgeville Southern Recorder,* 22, 29 October 1850; *Augusta Constitutionalist,* 22 October, 8, 9, 12, 13, November 1850; *Savannah Republican,* 9 September, 22 October 1850; *Macon Georgia Journal and Messenger,* 23 October, 20 November 1850; *Augusta Chronicle & Sentinel,* 15 November 1850; *Milledgeville Southern Recorder,* 5 November 1850; *Milledgeville Federal Union,* 24 September 1850; Schott, *Stephens,* 123–28; Thompson, *Toombs,* 72–75. The most widely noticed early version of the Georgia Platform was the resolutions passed at the October 22 "Union and Southern Rights" meeting in Savannah; see *Savannah Republican,* 24 October 1850.

29. Two major problems complicate the analysis of voting results. First, the contest was between county slates of candidates, and local and personal factors influenced outcomes. The vote for individual candidates, even those on the same ticket, varied, sometimes widely. The total vote figures given here were calculated using the *highest* vote given for any Union or Southern Rights candidate in each county; they represent the *maximum* vote for the two parties in each county and statewide.

Although Appling County sent delegates to the convention, voting figures from that county are missing. Second, since neither crisis party had an official platform or established leadership, there is some doubt—as there was in 1850—about which party some candidates represented. I have relied on the party designations from the *Milledgeville Southern Recorder*, 10 December 1850, because they seemed to me the most accurate. The *Milledgeville Federal Union*, 10 December 1850, however, included forty-two Southern Rights men in its list of elected delegates—exactly double the number reported in the *Southern Recorder*.

30. Of the counties that gave more than 40 percent of their vote to Southern Rights candidates, twenty-four had returned a Democratic majority in 1849, and ten had returned a Whig majority. Comparing 1849 and 1850 election results, it appears that roughly a third of north Georgia Democrats voted Unionist, a third voted Southern Rights, and a third did not vote. In the black belt, the Whigs had carried 27,604 votes in 1849; the Unionists totaled 25,460 votes in 1850. The Southern Rights party, in contrast, fell 8,436 votes short of the Democratic total in 1849. The overall drop in black belt turnout of 10,580 votes suggests that many black belt Democrats either voted Unionist or did not vote.

31. *Journal of the State Convention, Held in Milledgeville, in December, 1850* (Milledgeville: R. H. Orme, State Printer, 1850), 3–19, 24–26, 31–33 (quotations on 12, 14, 18–19); Francis S. Bartow to John M. Berrien, 16 December 1850, Charles J. Jenkins to John M. Berrien, 12 March 1851, Berrien Papers, SHC; Royce C. McCrary, ed., "The Authorship of the Georgia Platform of 1850: A Letter by Charles J. Jenkins," *Georgia Historical Quarterly* (Winter 1970): 585–90. The provision regarding the District of Columbia and federal property occasioned debate over whether abolition in these areas, if sanctioned by the states or individual slaveholders immediately affected, should be made grounds for resistance by Georgia. The resolution as finally worded left this point vague.

32. J. Mills Thornton III, *Politics and Power in a Slave Society: Alabama, 1800–1860* (Baton Rouge: Louisiana State University Press, 1978), 184–95; Holt, *Political Crisis*, 91–92; Ford, *Origins of Southern Radicalism*, 193–95; Arthur C. Cole, *The Whig Party in the South* (Washington, D.C.: American Historical Association, 1914), 184–88.

33. *Milledgeville Southern Recorder*, 17, 24 December 1850; *Savannah Republican*, 22 October 1850; *Augusta Chronicle & Sentinel*, 4 April 1851; *Rome Courier*, 19 December 1850, 13 February 1851; *Macon Georgia Journal and Messenger*, 8 January, 19 February 1851.

34. John H. Lumpkin to Howell Cobb, 23 March 1851, William Hope Hull to Howell Cobb, 3 February 1851, John H. Lumpkin to Howell Cobb, 6 December 1850, Robert W. Flournoy to Howell Cobb, 9 April 1951, Luther J. Glenn to Howell

Cobb, 21 April 1851, Cobb Papers, UGA; John H. Lumpkin to Howell Cobb, 16 February 1851, James F. Cooper to Howell Cobb, 5 May 1851, Andrew Jackson Donelson to Howell Cobb, 15 July 1851, in TSC, 229–30, 233–34, 244–45; Richard D. Arnold to John W. Forney, 17 June 1851, in Richard H. Shryock, ed., "Letters of Richard D. Arnold, M.D. 1808–1876," *Papers of the Trinity College Historical Society,* double series 18–19 (1929): 50–51; *Athens Southern Banner,* 16 January, 13 March, 17 April 1851. Letters in the pamphlet *Union Celebration, in Macon, Georgia, on the Anniversary of Washington's Birthday, February 22, 1851* (Macon: Georgia Journal and Messenger Office, 1851) provide an index to the divergent attitudes of Union Whigs and Democrats.

35. Robert Toombs to Howell Cobb, 2 January 1851, in TSC, 218–20; Holt, *Political Crisis,* 89–91, 94–96.

36. *Augusta Constitutionalist,* 18 December 1850, 10 December 1850; *Milledgeville Federal Union,* 27 May 1951; *Columbus Times,* 24 June 1851.

37. *Milledgeville Federal Union,* 6 May 1851.

38. Ibid., 3 June 1851.

39. James A. Nisbet to Howell Cobb, 7 February 1851, Howell Cobb to Mary Ann Cobb, 25 February 1851, Cobb Papers, UGA; Thomas W. Thomas to Howell Cobb, 14 April 1851, in TSC, 230–32; *Athens Southern Banner,* 3 April 1851; *Milledgeville Southern Recorder,* 3 June 1851.

40. *Macon Georgia Telegraph,* 15 July 1851; *Columbus Times,* 8 July 1851; *Macon Georgia Telegraph,* 20 May, 30 September 1851; John H. Howard to Judge Nicoll, 20 July 1851, in the *Columbus Times,* 5 August 1851; *Milledgeville Federal Union,* 24 June, 22 July, 16, 30 September 1851.

41. Howell Cobb to John Rutherford and others, 12 August 1851, in TSC, 249–59 (quotations on 257). For logic's sake, Cobb needed to declare flatly that secession, whatever the cause, was extraconstitutional. Once he conceded that secession was in some cases a constitutional right, it became impossible theoretically to distinguish between better or worse causes for exercising the right. For Unionist attempts to hedge on the secession issue, Samuel T. Chapman to Howell Cobb, 11 June 1851, in TSC, 236; *Athens Southern Banner,* 26 June 1851; *Augusta Chronicle & Sentinel,* 30 August 1851. The *Savannah Republican,* 3 July 1851, made a logical case for secession as solely a right of revolution.

42. Alexander Stephens to Howell Cobb, 23 June 1851, in TSC, 238; Robert Toombs to Howell Cobb, 9 June 1851, Cobb Papers, UGA; *Rome Courier,* 14 August 1851.

43. The assumption, as all the evidence indicates, that Whigs overwhelmingly supported the Union party permits estimates of the Democratic Unionist vote. Despite an increase in turnout of 3,159 votes in north Georgia from 1849, McDonald's

vote fell off 7,111 votes (35.4 percent) from Towns's 1849 vote, indicating an approximate minimum number of Democratic Unionists. The Southern Rights mountain vote (3,383) amounted to only 52.5 percent of the 1849 Democratic vote (6,438). In the black belt, both county results and overall figures suggest that at most a few thousand Democrats voted Unionist. McDonald's and Towns's totals were very similar, and the Union party gained just 3,058 votes over the 1849 Whig black belt total, almost matching the increased black belt turnout of 2,590 votes.

44. *Athens Southern Banner,* 27 November 1851; *Milledgeville Federal Union,* 2 December 1851, 4 November 1851, 27 January, 6 April 1851; *Columbus Times,* 28 October, 18 November, 2, 9 December 1851; *Macon Georgia Telegraph,* 13, 27 January, 17, 24 February, 2 March 1852. The November convention did not actually accept all of the Georgia Platform. The first three platform resolutions, which tacitly or explicitly endorsed the compromise, were omitted.

45. *Athens Southern Banner,* 25 March 1852, 25 December 1851, 18 March, 15 April 1852; Howell Cobb to Alexander H. Stephens, 22 December 1851, John H. Lumpkin to Alexander Stephens, 28 January 1852, Alexander H. Stephens Papers, LC (microfilm, UGA); Junius Hillyer to Howell Cobb, 18 December 1851, William Hope Hull to Howell Cobb, 25 December 1851, Phillip Clayton to Howell Cobb, 30 December 1851, John H. Lumpkin to Howell Cobb, 29 February 1852, Howell Cobb to Mary Ann Lamar Cobb, 2, 6 March 1852, Isham S. Fannin to Howell Cobb, 11 April 1852, Cobb Papers, UGA; Thomas D. Harris to Howell Cobb, 2 February, 7 April 1852, Howell Cobb to C. W. Denison, 3 February 1852, Hopkins Holsey to Howell Cobb, 6 February 1852, John B. Lamar to Howell Cobb, 8 March 1852, in TSC, 277–80, 287–89; *Augusta Chronicle & Sentinel,* 16, 23 January 1852.

46. Alexander Stephens to Howell Cobb, 5 December 1851, Robert Toombs to Howell Cobb, 27 May 1852, in TSC, 268, 297–98; Robert Toombs to Joseph H. Lumpkin, 30 April 1852, Joseph H. Lumpkin Papers, UGA; Alexander Stephens to Howell Cobb, 26 January 1852, Andrew J. Miller to Howell Cobb, 3 April 1852, Cobb Papers, UGA; letter from Stephens, in the *Milledgeville Southern Recorder,* 24 February 1852; *Milledgeville Southern Recorder,* 2 March 1852; *Augusta Chronicle & Sentinel,* 17 October 1851, 18, 24, 25 January 1852; *Macon Georgia Journal and Messenger,* 11, 25 February, 7 April 1852; *Rome Courier,* 19 February, 25 March, 8 April 1852.

47. *Milledgeville Southern Recorder,* 27 April 1852; James Jackson to Howell Cobb, 7 February 1852, Elijah W. Chastain to Howell Cobb, 8 February 1852, Isham S. Fannin to Howell Cobb, 11 April 1852, Cobb Papers, UGA; John Milledge to Howell Cobb, 17 April 1852, in TSC, 291–93; *Milledgeville Federal Union,* 27 April 1852.

48. Robert Toombs to Howell Cobb, 8 April 1852, John H. Lumpkin to Howell

Cobb, 19 May 1852, Solomon Cohen to Howell Cobb, 29 April 1852, Cobb Papers, UGA; Thomas D. Harris to Howell Cobb, 28 May 1852, John H. Lumpkin to Howell Cobb, 6 June 1852, James Jackson to Howell Cobb, 8 June 1852, in TSC, 298–301; Richard D. Arnold to Ellen Arnold, [?] June 1852, in Shryock, ed., "Arnold Letters," 60–61; "A Delegate," in the *Macon Georgia Telegraph,* 6 July 1852; Roy F. Nichols, *Franklin Pierce: Young Hickory of the Granite Hills,* 2d ed., rev. (Philadelphia: University of Pennsylvania Press, 1958), 64–204; Roy Nichols and Jeannette Nichols, "Election of 1852," in Arthur Schlesinger, Jr., et al., eds. *History of American Presidential Elections, 1789–1968,* 4 vols. (New York: Chelsea House, 1971), 3: 936–42, 951–53.

49. *Macon Georgia Journal and Messenger,* 9 June 1852, 19 May, 2 June 1852; *Milledgeville Southern Recorder,* 18 May, 8 June 1852.

50. *Milledgeville Southern Recorder,* 6 July 1852; *Macon Georgia Journal and Messenger,* 30 June 1852; *Augusta Chronicle & Sentinel,* 29 May, 23 June 1852; Alexander H. Stephens to the editor of the *Chronicle & Sentinel,* 28 June 1852, in TSC, 304–6; Thompson, *Toombs,* 85–87; Cooper, *Politics of Slavery,* 322–31. In mid-June, Robert Toombs was still broadly hinting to Howell Cobb that he expected Union Whigs to support Franklin Pierce; see Robert Toombs to Howell Cobb, 10 June 1852, Cobb Papers, UGA.

51. John Milledge to Howell Cobb, 21 June 1852, Henry R. Jackson to Howell Cobb, 26 June 1852, John H. Lumpkin to Howell Cobb, 23 July 1852, Garnett Andrews to Howell Cobb, 4 August 1852, James Jackson to John B. Lamar, 6 August 1852, William Hope Hull to Howell Cobb, 25 August 1852, James Jackson to Howell Cobb, 17 September 1852, Cobb Papers, UGA; George S. Owens to George W. Owens, 13 July 1852, Wallace-Owens Family Papers, SHC; John B. Lamar to Howell Cobb, 1 July, 10 August 1852, John H. Lumpkin to Howell Cobb, 11 July 1852, Howell Cobb to Orion Stroud, 4 August 1852, Henry R. Jackson to Howell Cobb, 7 August 1852, in TSC, 307–16; *Marietta Union,* in the *Rome Courier,* 17 June 1852; *Rome Courier,* 10 June 1852; *Macon Georgia Telegraph,* 6, 13 July 1852; *Milledgeville Federal Union,* 15, 22 June, 20 July, 31 August 1852; *Athens Southern Banner,* 24 June, 1, 22 July 1852; *Milledgeville Southern Recorder,* 20, 27 July 1852; *Macon Georgia Journal and Messenger,* 21 July 1852.

52. *Atlanta Intelligencer,* in the *Milledgeville Federal Union,* 28 September 1852; Howell Cobb to John B. Lamar, 18 September 1852, Howell Cobb to Mary Ann Lamar Cobb, 27 August 1852, Henry L. Benning to Howell Cobb, 2 September 1852, George D. Phillips to Howell Cobb, 15 September 1852, in TSC, 318–20; Alexander C. Morton to Howell Cobb, 19 July 1852, Solomon Cohen to Howell Cobb, 28 July 1852, Hopkins Holsey to Howell Cobb, 16 September 1852, Cobb Papers, UGA; Herschel V. Johnson to A. K. Patton, 25 September 1852, Herschel V.

Johnson to S. W. Burney, 25 September 1852, Herschel V. Johnson to R. J. Cowart, 25 September 1852, Herschel V. Johnson to Joseph E. Brown, 25 September 1852, Herschel V. Johnson to James Gardner, Jr., 28 September 1852, in "Letterpress Book 1849–1868," Herschel V. Johnson Papers, DU; John H. Howard and Samuel T. Bailey to R. B. Hilton, 9 September 1852, in *Macon Georgia Telegraph,* 21 September 1852; *Milledgeville Federal Union,* 27 July, 14, 21 September, 5 October 1852.

53. *Marietta Union,* in the *Augusta Chronicle & Sentinel,* 25 September 1852; *Athens Southern Banner,* 23 September, 14, 21 October 1852; *Dahlonega Mountain Signal* and *Cassville Standard of the Union,* in the *Athens Southern Banner,* 7 October 1852; *Cassville Standard of the Union,* in the *Augusta Chronicle & Sentinel,* 20, 23 October 1852; *Rome Courier,* 8, 16 September 1852.

54. Alexander H. Stephens to John L. Stephens, 8 September 1852, Alexander H. Stephens Papers, DU; *Augusta Chronicle & Sentinel,* 2 July, 20, 24 August 1852; *Macon Georgia Journal and Messenger,* 28 July 1852; *Milledgeville Southern Recorder,* 20, 27 July, 24 August, 7 September, 12, 19 October 1852.

55. *Milledgeville Southern Recorder,* 19 October 1852; "Green," in the *Milledgeville Southern Recorder,* 17 August, 28 September 1852; *Augusta Chronicle & Sentinel,* 20 July, 2 November 1852; *Milledgeville Federal Union,* 28 September 1852; *Macon Georgia Journal and Messenger,* 29 September, 6, 27 October 1852; *Rome Courier,* 23 September 1852.

56. Robert Toombs to John J. Crittenden, 15 December 1852, in TSC, 322; Holt, *Political Crisis,* 119–30; William E. Gienapp, *The Origins of the Republican Party, 1852–1856* (New York: Oxford University Press, 1987), 13–35.

57. *Milledgeville Southern Recorder,* 24 May 1853; *Macon Georgia Journal and Messenger,* 27 April 1853.

58. *Milledgeville Southern Recorder* 29 March, 15 April, 17, 24 May, 7, 28 June 1853; *Augusta Chronicle & Sentinel,* 8 June 1853.

59. Howell Cobb to Alexander Stephens, 2 February 1853, Stephens Papers, LC; Herschel V. Johnson to Robert M. T. Hunter, 8 November 1852, in Charles H. Ambler, ed., "Correspondence of Robert M. T. Hunter," in *Annual Report of the American Historical Association,* vol. 2 (Washington, D.C.: Government Printing Office, 1918), 51; Howell Cobb to Alexander H. Stephens, 2 February 1853, Stephens Papers, LC; Herschel V. Johnson to David J. Bailey, 14 December 1852, Herschel V. Johnson to Robert M. T. Hunter, 15 December 1852, in "Letterpress Book, 1849–1868," Johnson Papers, DU; Charles J. McDonald to Robert Tyler, 14 November 1852, Keith Read Collection, UGA; Howell Cobb to John B. Lamar, 6 November 1852, John H. Lumpkin to Howell Cobb, 17 November 1852, Junius Hillyer to Howell Cobb, 11 January 1853, Howell Cobb to John B. Lamar, 12 January 1853,

Thomas D. Harris to Howell Cobb, 24 January 1853, Howell Cobb to William L. Marcy, 2 June 1853, John E. Ward to Howell Cobb, 23 June 1853, Howell Cobb to Mary Ann Lamar Cobb, 3 August 1853, Cobb Papers, UGA; Lewis Cass to Howell Cobb, 18 December 1852, John B. Lamar to Howell Cobb, 12 January 1853, George W. Jones to Howell Cobb, 11 February 1853, in TSC, 322–24; *Macon Georgia Telegraph,* 9 November, 7 December 1852; Nichols, *Pierce,* 247–58; Larry Gara, *The Presidency of Franklin Pierce* (Lawrence: University Press of Kansas, 1991), 43–52.

60. William Hope Hull to Howell Cobb, 7 April 1853, Cobb Papers, UGA; *Athens Southern Banner,* 2 June 1853, 2 December 1852, 27 January, 17 March, 14 April, 12, 26 May 1853; John H. Lumpkin to Howell Cobb, 6 November 1852, Junius Hillyer to Howell Cobb, 6 December 1852, Charles Murphey to Howell Cobb, 28 January 1853, John B. Lamar to Howell Cobb, 9 May 1853, James A. Sledge to Howell Cobb, 10 June 1853, Cobb Papers, UGA; Richard D. Arnold to John W. Forney, 15 May 1853, in Shryock, ed., "Arnold Letters," 63–64; William Hope Hull to the editor of the *Constitutionalist* [March–April 1853], Howell Cobb to Thomas Morris, 21 March 1853, in Robert P. Brooks, ed., "Howell Cobb Papers," *Georgia Historical Quarterly* 6 (March 1922): 37–47.

61. James Jackson to Howell Cobb, 21 March 1853, John H. Lumpkin to Howell Cobb, 7 June 1853, Howell Cobb to John B. Lamar, 25 June 1853, Cobb Papers, UGA; John H. Lumpkin to Howell Cobb, 2 July 1853, in TSC, 329–30; Herschel V. Johnson to A. E. Cochran et al., 18 June 1853, in the *Milledgeville Southern Recorder,* 28 June 1853; *Milledgeville Federal Union,* 19 April, 21 June 1853.

62. Herschel V. Johnson Autobiography, 77–79, Johnson Papers, DU; *Athens Southern Banner,* 22 September 1853; *Augusta Chronicle & Sentinel,* 13 July 1853; *Milledgeville Federal Union,* 19 July, 6 September 1853; *Macon Georgia Telegraph,* 5 July, 20 September 1853. Jenkins and Andrew J. Miller had guided the Algerine law through the legislature, basing their actions on a memorial from interested Augusta citizens.

63. "Justitia," in the *Augusta Chronicle & Sentinel,* 27 August 1853.

64. *Milledgeville Federal Union,* 23 March 1853; *Milledgeville Southern Recorder,* 16 August 1853, 9 August, 6, 13 September 1853; Charles J. Jenkins to John M. Berrien, 17 August 1853, Berrien Papers, SHC; *Augusta Chronicle & Sentinel,* 30 July, 10 August, 15, 21, 23, 29 September, 2 October 1853; *Macon Georgia Journal and Messenger,* 7, 14 September 1853; *Athens Southern Banner,* 15 September 1853.

65. Charles J. Jenkins to John M. Berrien, 22 October 1853, Berrien Papers, SHC; *Athens Southern Banner,* 13 October 1853; *Milledgeville Southern Recorder,* 25 October 1853.

66. James Gardner, Jr., to Howell Cobb, 18 November 1853, Howell Cobb to John B. Lamar, 4 December 1853, Henry L. Benning to Howell Cobb, 21 April

1853, John T. Grant to Howell Cobb, 28 October 1853, John Milledge to Howell Cobb, 1 November 1853, John H. Lumpkin to Howell Cobb, 21 November 1853, L. Q. C. Lamar to Howell Cobb, 3 December 1853, John W. H. Underwood to Howell Cobb, 6 December 1853, Howell Cobb to Mary Ann Lamar Cobb, 21 December 1853, Cobb Papers, UGA; Lucius Q. C. Lamar to Howell Cobb, 21 September 1853, Thomas D. Harris to Howell Cobb, 13 October 1853, John T. Grant to Howell Cobb, 18 October 1853, Thomas C. Howard and H. K. Green to Howell Cobb, 3 December 1853, John H. Lumpkin to Howell Cobb, 28 December 1853, in TSC, 335–39; *Macon Georgia Journal and Messenger,* 23 November 1853, 25 January 1854; *Macon Georgia Telegraph,* 22 November, 27 December 1853; *Milledgeville Southern Recorder,* 22 November 1853, 17, 24, 31 January 1854; *Athens Southern Banner,* 24 November 1853; *Milledgeville Federal Union,* 27 December 1853; Helen I. Greene, "Politics in Georgia, 1853–1854: The Ordeal of Howell Cobb," *Georgia Historical Quarterly* 30 (September 1946): 185–211.

## 7. Kansas, Know-Nothings, and the National Democracy

1. *Journal of the Senate of the State of Georgia,* 1853, 832; *Journal of the House of Representatives of the State of Georgia,* 1853, 1003; *Congressional Globe Appendix,* 33d Cong., 1st sess., 1853–54, 302–6, 346–51, 619–21, 633–34, 716–20, 749–52; Alexander H. Stephens to Linton Stephens, 25 January 1854, Alexander H. Stephens Papers, MCSH (microfilm, EU); Robert Toombs to W. W. Burwell, 3 February 1854, in TSC, 342; *Athens Southern Banner,* 19, 26 January 1854; *Macon Georgia Journal and Messenger,* 1 February, 1 March 1854; *Milledgeville Southern Recorder,* 28 February 1854; *Savannah Republican,* 10, 11, 25 February 1854; *Columbus Enquirer,* 7, 14 February 1854; David M. Potter, *The Impending Crisis 1848–1861,* completed and edited by Don E. Fehrenbacher (New York: Harper & Row, 1976), 145–65; Robert W. Johannsen, *Stephen A. Douglas* (New York: Oxford University Press, 1973), 386–421; Roy F. Nichols, "The Kansas-Nebraska Act: A Century of Historiography," *Mississippi Valley Historical Review* 43 (September 1956): 187–316.

2. *Congressional Globe,* 33d Cong., 1st sess., 1853–54, 532, 1254; "Alexander H. Stephens to Robert Sims Burch, 15 June 1854," *American Historical Review* 8 (October 1902): 91–97; Potter, *Impending Crisis,* 165–67; William J. Cooper, Jr., *The South and the Politics of Slavery, 1828–1856* (Baton Rouge: Louisiana State University Press, 1978), 353–54; Johannsen, *Douglas,* 428–34; Thomas E. Schott, *Alexander H. Stephens of Georgia: A Biography* (Baton Rouge: Louisiana State University Press, 1988), 166–73; Roy F. Nichols, *Blueprints for Leviathan: American Style* (New York: Atheneum, 1963), 104–20; Robert R. Russel, "The Issues in the Con-

gressional Struggle over the Kansas-Nebraska Bill, 1854," *Journal of Southern History* 29 (February 1963): 187–210. All the Georgians who voted supported final passage of the Kansas-Nebraska bill; Senator Robert Toombs and Congressmen William Dent and James L. Seward were absent for the final votes.

3. *Athens Southern Banner,* 20 July 1854; *Macon Georgia Telegraph,* 6 June 1854; *Milledgeville Federal Union,* 7 February 1854; *Macon Georgia Telegraph,* 30 May 1854; Cooper, *Politics of Slavery,* 354; Potter, *Impending Crisis,* 165–67.

4. *Wilkes County Republican,* in the *Milledgeville Southern Recorder,* 18 July 1854; Alexander H. Stephens to W. W. Burwell, 26 June 1854, in TSC, 346; Schott, *Stephens,* 166–73.

5. Alexander H. Stephens to William W. Burwell, 5 May 1854, Stephens Papers, LC; *Macon Georgia Journal and Messenger,* 31 May 1854; *Milledgeville Southern Recorder,* 30 May 1854; *Athens Southern Banner,* 16 February 1854.

6. William E. Gienapp, *The Origins of the Republican Party, 1852–1856* (New York: Oxford University Press, 1987), 37–166; Michael F. Holt, *The Political Crisis of the 1850s* (New York: John Wiley & Sons, 1978), 118–71; Tyler Anbinder, *Nativism and Slavery: The Northern Know Nothings and the Politics of the 1850s* (New York: Oxford University Press, 1992), 3–126.

7. *Athens Southern Banner,* 23 November 1854; Howell Cobb to James Buchanan, 5 December 1854, in TSC, 348–49; *Milledgeville Federal Union,* 24 October, 21 November 1854.

8. Howell Cobb to Mary Ann Lamar Cobb, 6 April 1855, John H. Lumpkin to Howell Cobb, 4, 6 May 1855, Howell Cobb Papers, UGA; *Milledgeville Southern Recorder,* 31 October, 15 December 1854; *Athens Southern Banner,* 31 August 1854; *Augusta Chronicle & Sentinel,* 1 September 1854, 3 January, 16 February, 6, 10 April, 5 July 1855; *Augusta Constitutionalist,* 15, 27 August 1854; *Savannah Republican,* 10, 23 June 1854, 11, 13 January 1855; *Milledgeville Federal Union,* 16 January 1855.

9. *Macon Georgia Telegraph,* 1 August 1854; *Seventh Census of the United States, 1850,* 366, 387–91; W. Darrell Overdyke, *The Know-Nothing Party in the South* (Baton Rouge: Louisiana State University Press, 1959); Leon Cyprian Soule, *The Know Nothing Party in New Orleans: A Reappraisal* (New Orleans: Louisiana Historical Association, 1961); Jean H. Baker, *Ambivalent Americans: The Know-Nothing Party in Maryland* (Baltimore: Johns Hopkins University Press, 1977); Cooper, *Politics of Slavery,* 359–69.

10. *Savannah Republican,* 4 August 1855; *Columbus Enquirer,* 31 July 1855; "Address of the State Council of the American Party, Assembled Recently at Macon, to the People of Georgia," in the *Augusta Chronicle & Sentinel,* 7, 8 July 1855; John M. Berrien to the people of Georgia, 4 September 1855, in the *Augusta Chronicle & Sentinel,* 13 September 1855; "Chatham," in the *Milledgeville Southern Recorder,* 4

September 1855; "Melancthon," in the *Augusta Chronicle & Sentinel,* 25 May, 21 June 1855; "Sydney," in ibid., 24 May 1855; "Your Country," in the *Savannah Republican,* 19 May 1855; "Protestant," in ibid., 14 June 1855; *Augusta Chronicle & Sentinel,* 27 March, 21 September 1855; *Macon Georgia Journal and Messenger,* 31 October 1855; *Columbus Enquirer,* 24 July, 7, 28 August 1855.

11. W. W. Paine to Alexander H. Stephens, 23 February 1855, Alexander H. Stephens Papers, LC (microfilm, UGA); *Augusta Chronicle & Sentinel,* 3 June 1855.

12. *Macon Georgia Journal and Messenger,* 29 November 1854; *Milledgeville Southern Recorder,* 21 August 1855; *Savannah Republican,* 19 July 1855; "Address of the State Council of the American Party, Assembled Recently at Macon, to the People of Georgia," in the *Augusta Chronicle & Sentinel,* 7, 8 July 1855; Holt, *Political Crisis,* 163–67; Michael F. Holt, "The Politics of Impatience: The Origins of Know-Nothingism," *Journal of American History* 60 (September 1973): 309–31; Ronald P. Formisano, "Political Character, Antipartyism, and the Second Party System," *American Quarterly* 21 (Winter 1969): 683–709.

13. *Columbus Enquirer,* 17 April 1855; Charles J. Jenkins to Alexander H. Stephens, 11 May 1855, Alexander H. Stephens Papers, EU; *Milledgeville Southern Recorder,* 27 February 1855; *Augusta Chronicle & Sentinel,* 18 May 1855; Gienapp, *Origins,* 182–87; Anbinder, *Nativism,* 162–74.

14. *Savannah Republican,* 16 June 1855.

15. Letter from Jenkins, 15 June 1855, in the *Milledgeville Southern Recorder,* 19 June 1855; *Milledgeville Southern Recorder,* 6, 27 March, 22 May, 26 June, 3 July, 28 August 1855; *Augusta Chronicle & Sentinel,* 7 February, 16 May, 3, 13, 21, 29 June 1855; *Macon Georgia Journal and Messenger,* 24 January, 28 March, 6 June 1855; *Augusta Constitutionalist,* 31 May 1855; *Macon Georgia Telegraph,* 5 June 1855; *Savannah Republican,* 22 February, 23 March 1855; *Columbus Enquirer,* 29 May, 5, 19 June, 3, 10, 17 July 1855; *Milledgeville Federal Union,* 12, 19, 26 June 1855; *Columbus Corner Stone,* 9 March, 16, 23 November, 7 September 1854, 22 March, 3 May, 19 July 1855; Horace Montgomery, "The Solid South Movement of 1855," *Georgia Historical Quarterly* 26 (June 1942): 101–12.

16. *Columbus Enquirer,* 3 July 1855.

17. Basil H. Overby to J. B. Randall et al., 3 March 1855, in the *Augusta Constitutionalist,* 15 March 1855; Andrew Young to Howell Cobb, 29 April 1855, Cobb Papers, UGA; James T. Finley to Alexander H. Stephens, 13 May 1855, Stephens Papers, EU; *Macon Georgia Journal and Messenger,* 18 April 1855; *Athens Southern Banner,* 1 March, 6 July 1855; Allen P. Tankersley, "Basil Hallam Overby, Champion of Prohibition in Ante-Bellum Georgia," *Georgia Historical Quarterly* 31 (March 1947): 1–18.

18. *Milledgeville Federal Union,* 24 April 1855; *Augusta Constitutionalist,* 12 April 1855.

19. Letter from Moseley, in the *Macon Georgia Telegraph,* 15 May 1855; *Augusta Constitutionalist,* 30 August 1854; Alexander H. Stephens to Linton Stephens, 25 December 1854, Stephens Papers, MCSH; letter from Longstreet, in the *Athens Southern Banner,* 30 August 1855; Robert Toombs to T. Lomax, 6 June 1855, in TSC, 350–53; *Athens Southern Banner,* 21, 28 December 1854, 17 May, 6 September 1855; *Milledgeville Federal Union,* 12 September 1854, 1 May 1855; *Augusta Constitutionalist,* 22 March 1855; Alexander H. Stephens to Thomas W. Thomas, 9 May 1855, in Henry Cleveland, *Alexander H. Stephens, in Public and Private, with Letters and Speeches, before, during, and since the War* (Philadelphia: National Publishing, 1866), 459–71.

20. *Augusta Constitutionalist,* 24 March 1855; Alexander H. Stephens to Warren Akin, 22 April 1855, Stephens Papers, EU.

21. "A Native Whig," in the *Augusta Chronicle & Sentinel,* 18 May 1855; Charles J. McDonald to Philemon Tracy, 23 May 1855, in the *Macon Georgia Telegraph,* 5 June 1855; *Milledgeville Federal Union,* 30 January 1855.

22. "A Citizen of Georgia," in the *Augusta Constitutionalist,* 22 November 1854; "Native Whig," in the *Augusta Chronicle & Sentinel,* 19 September 1854; *Augusta Constitutionalist,* 24 March 1855.

23. *Augusta Constitutionalist,* 28 February 1856, 1 September 1854; letter from Howell Cobb, 1 June 1855, and Herschel V. Johnson to John H. Howard, 11 June 1855, in the *Athens Southern Banner,* 7, 28 June 1855.

24. *Milledgeville Federal Union,* 12 June 1855; "Equality," in the *Augusta Constitutionalist,* 16 September 1856; "Sophron," in ibid., 17 September 1856; *Milledgeville Southern Recorder,* 27 May, 10 June 1856; *Athens Southern Banner,* 29 May 1856; *Macon Georgia Telegraph,* 2, 23 September 1856; Potter, *Impending Crisis,* 199–214; Gienapp, *Origins,* 295–303; James A. Rawley, *Race & Politics: "Bleeding Kansas" and the Coming of the Civil War* (Philadelphia: J. B. Lippincott, 1969), 79–92.

25. Garnett Andrews's speech, in the *Milledgeville Southern Recorder,* 11 September 1855.

26. Garnett Andrews to Washington Poe et al., 16 July 1855, in the *Savannah Republican,* 21 July 1855.

27. Alexander H. Stephens to Linton Stephens, 5 August, 17 September 1855, Stephens Papers, MCSH; *Augusta Chronicle & Sentinel,* 8, 15, 24, 26, 31 August, 1, 4, 7, 9, 13 September 1855; *Augusta Constitutionalist,* 16, 26 June 1855; *Macon Georgia Journal and Messenger,* 30 May, 1 August, 5 September 1855; *Milledgeville Federal Union,* 11 September 1855; *Milledgeville Southern Recorder,* 24 July, 11 September 1855.

28. *Savannah Republican,* 23 October 1855; Cooper, *Politics of Slavery,* 368. The South, using Cooper's definition here, includes the eleven eventual Confederate states.

29. *Congressional Globe,* 34th Cong., 1st sess., 1855–56, 65–69; Alexander H. Stephens to Linton Stephens, 2, 29 December 1855, 8 January, 1, 4 February 1856, Stephens Papers, MCSH; Robert Toombs to Thomas W. Thomas, 9 February 1856, Robert A. Toombs Papers, DU; Thomas D. Harris to Howell Cobb, 15 October 1855, Howell Cobb to Mary Ann Lamar Cobb, 23 December 1855, 2 February 1856, in TSC, 355–56, 358–59; *Milledgeville Federal Union,* 11 November 1856; Gienapp, *Origins,* 240–47; Schott, *Stephens,* 192–94; Potter, *Impending Crisis,* 205–14.

30. *Congressional Globe Appendix,* 34th Cong., 1st sess., 1855–56, 182, 769; Alexander H. Stephens to Linton Stephens, 5 March, 14, 20 June 1856, Stephens Papers, MCSH; Gienapp, *Origins,* 295–303, 348–53.

31. *Milledgeville Southern Recorder,* 25 December 1855.

32. Gienapp, *Origins,* 248–71, 305–46, 382–401; Anbinder, *Nativism,* 194–245.

33. *Macon Georgia Journal and Messenger,* 5 March 1856; *Savannah Republican,* 19 July 1855; *Macon Georgia Journal and Messenger,* 16 July 1856; *Milledgeville Southern Recorder,* 15 July 1856; Millard Fillmore to H. V. M. Miller, 31 July 1856, in the *Milledgeville Federal Union,* 19 August 1856.

34. *Macon Georgia Journal and Messenger,* 18 June 1856; Johannsen, *Douglas,* 505–20; Roy F. Nichols, *Franklin Pierce: Young Hickory of the Granite Hills,* 2d ed., rev. (Philadelphia: University of Pennsylvania Press, 1958), 450–56; 466–69; Philip Shriver Klein, *President James Buchanan: A Biography* (University Park: Pennsylvania State University Press, 1962), 1–257.

35. *Macon Georgia Journal and Messenger,* 17 September 1856; *Savannah Republican,* 10, 11, 25 February 1854; *Milledgeville Southern Recorder,* 21 March 1854.

36. *Milledgeville Southern Recorder,* 23 September 1856; *Augusta Chronicle & Sentinel,* 8 August 1856; *Macon Georgia Journal and Messenger,* 2 July 1856.

37. *Savannah Republican,* 14 May, 12 July 1856.

38. James Buchanan's letter, 16 June 1856, in the *Macon Georgia Journal and Messenger,* 25 June 1856; *Milledgeville Federal Union,* 22 July, 5, 19 August 1856; *Macon Georgia Telegraph,* 8, 15 July 1856; Roy F. Nichols and Philip S. Klein, "Election of 1856," in Arthur Schlesinger, Jr., et al., eds., *History of American Presidential Elections, 1789–1968,* 4 vols. (New York: Chelsea House, 1971), 2:1035–39, 1041–43.

39. Alexander H. Stephens to Linton Stephens, 6 January 1855, Stephens Papers, MCSH; *Congressional Globe Appendix,* 34th Cong., 1st sess., 1855–56, 61–63.

40. *Milledgeville Federal Union,* 19 August 1856; Junius Hillyer to John H. Christy, 24 September 1856, in the *Athens Southern Banner,* 2 October 1856; *Athens Southern Banner,* 11 September 1856. The idea that territorial legislatures could exclude slavery by hostile inaction would, of course, become famous in 1858 as Stephen Douglas's Freeport Doctrine.

41. *Augusta Constitutionalist,* 9 October 1856, 12 July 1856.

42. William S. Rockwell to Howell Cobb, 20 January 1856, Cobb Papers, UGA; *Congressional Globe,* 30th Cong., 1st sess., 1847–48, 1006–7; *Congressional Globe Appendix,* 30th Cong., 1st sess., 1847–48, 844–45, 887–93, 1103–7, 1188–91; *Augusta Constitutionalist,* 29 February 1848; Don E. Fehrenbacher, *The Dred Scott Case: Its Significance in American Law and Politics* (New York: Oxford University Press, 1978), reviews the history of the problem of slavery in the territories.

43. *Augusta Constitutionalist,* 28 October 1856; *Milledgeville Federal Union,* 22 July 1856; *Augusta Constitutionalist,* 7 September 1856, 1 July 1856.

44. *Augusta Chronicle & Sentinel,* 12 September 1856, 22 August 1856; *Savannah Republican,* 21 October 1856.

45. *Savannah Republican,* 10 July 1856; *Augusta Chronicle & Sentinel,* 31 August 1856.

46. Alexander C. Walker to James Gardner, Jr., 6 August 1856, in the *Augusta Constitutionalist,* 8 August 1856; Iverson L. Harris to the Democratic Executive Committee, 30 July 1856, in ibid., 7 August 1856; Eugenius A. Nisbet to Henry G. Lamar, 1 September 1856, in the *Macon Georgia Journal and Messenger,* 10 September 1856; Charles J. Jenkins to Willis Willingham, 28 August 1856, in the *Augusta Constitutionalist,* 5 September 1856.

47. John B. Lamar to David C. Barrow, 22 July 1856, David C. Barrow Papers, UGA; *Augusta Constitutionalist,* 20 September 1856; "Sentinel," in ibid., 20 September 1856; *Milledgeville Federal Union,* 28 October 1856.

48. *Augusta Chronicle & Sentinel,* 17 October 1856, 23 August, 9 October 1856; *Savannah Republican,* 30 September 1856.

49. Nichols and Klein, "Election of 1856," in Schlesinger et al., eds., *American Presidential Elections,* 2:1094.

50. Robert Toombs to Alexander H. Stephens, 8 December 1856, Stephens Papers, EU; *Congressional Globe Appendix,* 34th Cong., 3d sess., 1856–57, 131–34; Thomas D. Harris to Howell Cobb, 14 November 1856, Cobb Papers, UGA; Alexander H. Stephens to Linton Stephens, 18 December 1856, Stephens Papers, MCSH; Thomas W. Thomas to Alexander H. Stephens, 12 January 1857, Robert Toombs to Thomas W. Thomas, 5 February 1857, in TSC, 392–94; Herschel V. Johnson to C. S. Tarpley et al., 5 December 1856, in the *Milledgeville Federal Union,* 20 January 1857; *Milledgeville Federal Union,* 11, 18 November 1856, 27 January 1857; *Augusta Constitutionalist,* 8 November 1856, 7 February 1857; *Macon Georgia Telegraph,* 18 November 1856.

51. *Macon Georgia Telegraph,* 17 March 1857; *Augusta Constitutionalist,* 18 March 1857; Alexander H. Stephens to Linton Stephens, 15 December 1856, Stephens Papers, MCSH; Howell Cobb to Mary Ann Lamar Cobb, 1, 17, 27 December 1856, John W. Forney to Howell Cobb, 26 December 1856, James Jackson to Howell Cobb,

30 December 1856, John B. Lamar to Howell Cobb, 2 January 1857 (misdated 1856 in original), Cobb Papers, UGA; Robert Toombs to Alexander H. Stephens, 1 December 1856, Howell Cobb to Mary Ann Lamar Cobb, 1 January 1857, John W. Forney to Howell Cobb, 18 February 1857, in TSC, 384, 389, 396–97; Klein, *Buchanan*, 261–69; Fehrenbacher, *Dred Scott*, 305–414; Roy F. Nichols, *The Disruption of the American Democracy* (New York: Macmillan, 1948), 52–81.

52. Kenneth M. Stampp, *America in 1857: A Nation on the Brink* (New York: Oxford University Press, 1990), 144–68; James P. Shenton, *Robert John Walker: A Politician from Jackson to Lincoln* (New York: Columbia University Press, 1961), 139–61.

53. Thomas W. Thomas to Alexander H. Stephens, 15 June 1857, in TSC, 400–401; *Augusta Constitutionalist*, 10 June 1857.

54. Howell Cobb to Alexander H. Stephens, 18 June 1857, in TSC, 403; *Macon Georgia Telegraph*, 16 June 1857; *Milledgeville Federal Union*, 23 June 1857.

55. Howell Cobb to Mary Ann Lamar Cobb, 27 June 1857, Cobb Papers, UGA; Martin J. Crawford to Alexander H. Stephens, 19 June 1857, Stephens Papers, LC; Linton Stephens to Alexander H. Stephens, 4, 16 July 1857, Stephens Papers, MCSH; Thomas W. Thomas to Herschel V. Johnson, 27 July 1857, Telamon Cuyler Collection, UGA; Robert Toombs to W. W. Burwell, 11 July 1857, Thomas R. R. Cobb to Howell Cobb, 15 July 1857, Howell Cobb to Alexander H. Stephens, 21 July 1857, in TSC, 403–7; *Milledgeville Federal Union*, 21, 28 July 1857.

56. Linton Stephens to Alexander H. Stephens, 29 June 1857, Stephens Papers, MCSH; Leroy Patillo to Howell Cobb, 10 September 1857, Cobb Papers, UGA; "Union Man," in the *Macon Georgia Journal and Messenger*, 22 July 1857; *Athens Southern Banner*, 2 April 1857; *Milledgeville Southern Recorder*, 30 June 1857; *Milledgeville Federal Union*, 30 June 1857; Joseph H. Parks, *Joseph E. Brown of Georgia* (Baton Rouge: Louisiana State University Press, 1977), 1–39.

57. Benjamin Harvey Hill to Alexander H. Stephens, 6 December 1856, in Benjamin H. Hill, Jr., *Senator Benjamin H. Hill of Georgia: His Life, Speeches and Writings* (Atlanta: H. C. Hudgins, 1891), 25; Schott, *Stephens*, 218–21; Kenneth Coleman and Charles Stephen Gurr, eds., *Dictionary of Georgia Biography*, 2 vols. (Athens: University of Georgia Press, 1983), 1:449–51; Haywood J. Pearce, Jr., *Benjamin H. Hill: Secession and Reconstruction* (Chicago: University of Chicago Press, 1928), 1–31.

58. *Macon Georgia Journal and Messenger*, 26 August 1857; *Milledgeville Southern Recorder*, 29 September 1857.

59. *Milledgeville Southern Recorder;* 22 July 1857; Benjamin H. Hill to Hines Holt et al., 20 July 1857, in ibid., 28 July 1857; "Georgia," in ibid., 18 August 1857; *Macon Georgia Journal and Messenger*, 24 June 1857.

60. *Macon Georgia Journal and Messenger*, 9 September 1857.

61. *Augusta Constitutionalist,* 7 October 1857, 29 July, 12, 19 August, 2, 24 September 1857; Alexander Stephens to the voters of the Eighth Congressional District of Georgia, 14 August 1857, in TSC, 409–20; *Athens Southern Banner,* 2, 23 July, 20 August, 24 September, 1 October 1857; *Macon Georgia Telegraph,* 25 August 1857; Stampp, *America in 1857,* 168–81.

62. *Milledgeville Southern Recorder,* 20 October 1857; Peterson Thweatt to Alexander H. Stephens, 15 September 1857, Stephens Papers, LC; Howell Cobb to Alexander H. Stephens, 3 October 1857, Stephens Papers, EU; Howell Cobb to Alexander H. Stephens, 19 October 1857, Robert Toombs to W. W. Burwell, 20 November 1857, in TSC, 425–26; Schott, *Stephens,* 234–38.

63. Howell Cobb to Alexander H. Stephens, 19 September 1857, in TSC, 423; Howell Cobb to Alexander H. Stephens, 3 October 1857, Stephens Papers, EU; Howell Cobb to Joseph E. Brown, 8 October 1857, Joseph Emerson and Elizabeth Grisham Brown Collection, UGA; Howell Cobb to Alexander H. Stephens, 3, 12, September, 9 October 1857, in TSC, 421–25.

64. *Athens Southern Banner,* 19 November 1857, Herschel V. Johnson to Alexander H. Stephens, 24 December 1857, Herschel V. Johnson Papers, DU; *Augusta Constitutionalist,* 22 July, 16 December 1857; *Macon Georgia Telegraph,* 1 December 1857, 12 January 1858; Stampp, *America in 1857,* 239–85; Potter, *Impending Crisis,* 297–319; Johannsen, *Douglas,* 576–603.

65. Thomas R. R. Cobb to Howell Cobb, 26 March 1858, Cobb Papers, UGA; Peterson Thweatt to Alexander H. Stephens, 6 April 1858, Stephens Papers, LC.

66. John W. H. Underwood to Howell Cobb, 5 February 1858, Cobb Papers, UGA; Richard D. Arnold to John W. Forney, 30 March 1858, in Richard H. Shryock, ed., "Letters of Richard D. Arnold, M.D. 1808–1876," *Papers of the Trinity College Historical Society,* double series 18–19 (1929): 87; *Congressional Globe Appendix,* 35th Cong., 1st sess., 1857–58, 124–32, 201–4, 1263–64, 1861–62; Linton Stephens to Alexander H. Stephens, 9 February, Alexander H. Stephens to Linton Stephens 4, 17 December 1858, Stephens Papers, MCSH; James Thomas to Alexander H. Stephens, 12 January 1858, M. C. Fulton to Alexander H. Stephens, 30 March 1858, Stephens Papers, LC; Thomas W. Thomas to Alexander H. Stephens, 25 December 1857, Stephens Papers, EU; Howell Cobb to John B. Lamar, 24 January, 10 March 1858, Cobb Papers, UGA; Thomas W. Thomas to Alexander H. Stephens, 12 January 1858, in TSC, 427–28; *Augusta Constitutionalist,* 25 November 1857; *Macon Georgia Telegraph,* 22 December 1857; *Milledgeville Federal Union,* 19 January, 2, 30 March 1858; Schott, *Stephens,* 241–52.

67. *Congressional Globe Appendix,* 35th Cong., 1st sess., 1857–58, 218–20, 309–12; *Macon Georgia Journal and Messenger,* 9 December 1857, 13 January 1858; *Milledgeville Southern Recorder,* 12 January, 16 February 1858; *Savannah Republican,* 9, 22, 30 January, 16 February, 26 March, 16 August 1858; Holt, *Political Crisis,* 207–

9; Potter, *Impending Crisis*, 319–20; Johannsen, *Douglas*, 603–13; Nichols, *Disruption of the American Democracy*, 158–75; Schott, *Stephens*, 243–53; Joseph H. Parks, *John Bell of Tennessee* (Baton Rouge: Louisiana State University Press, 1959), 282–331.

68. Extracts from the Democratic press, in the *Milledgeville Southern Recorder*, 18 May 1858; *Griffin American Union*, in ibid., 1 June 1858.

## 8. A White Men's Revolution

1. Abraham Lincoln to Alexander H. Stephens, 22 December 1860, in Roy P. Basler, ed., *The Collected Works of Abraham Lincoln*, 8 vols. (New Brunswick: Rutgers University Press, 1953), 4:160; Alexander H. Stephens to Abraham Lincoln, 30 December 1860, in Richard M. Johnston and William M. Browne, *Life of Alexander H. Stephens* (Philadelphia: J. B. Lippincott, 1878), 371–73.

2. Augustus Baldwin Longstreet to John C. Calhoun, 4 July 1848, in Jimmy Ray Scafidel, "The Letters of Augustus Baldwin Longstreet" (Ph.D. diss., University of South Carolina, 1976), 419; David M. Potter, "The Historian's Use of Nationalism and Vice Versa," in *The South and the Sectional Conflict* (Baton Rouge: Louisiana State University Press, 1968), 34–83.

3. *Augusta Chronicle & Sentinel*, 30 November 1854, 31 January 1855; *Augusta Constitutionalist*, 3 January 1855; Milton S. Heath, *Constructive Liberalism: The Role of the State in Economic Development in Georgia to 1860* (Cambridge: Harvard University Press, 1954), 223–28; Joseph H. Parks, *Joseph E. Brown of Georgia* (Baton Rouge: Louisiana State University Press, 1977), 45–49; Bruce W. Collins, "Governor Joseph E. Brown, Economic Issues, and Georgia's Road to Secession, 1857–1859," *Georgia Historical Quarterly* (Summer 1987): 206–10; James L. Huston, *The Panic of 1857 and the Coming of the Civil War* (Baton Rouge: Louisiana State University Press, 1987).

4. *Macon Georgia Telegraph*, 5 January 1858; *Albany Patriot*, 7 January 1858; William R. Fleming to James Gardner, Jr., 29 December 1857, James Gardner, Jr., Papers, GDAH; Robert Toombs to George W. Crawford, 29 January 1858, Robert Toombs Papers, UGA; "Caution," in the *Milledgeville Southern Recorder*, 1 December 1857, 9 February 1858; *Augusta Constitutionalist*, 2 December 1857; *Athens Southern Banner*, 10 December 1857; *Macon Georgia Journal and Messenger*, 11 November 1857, 3, 24 February, 3 March 1858; *Macon Georgia Telegraph*, 20 October, 17, 24 November, 29 December 1857; 5 January, 2 March 1858; *Milledgeville Federal Union*, 24 November 1857, 12 January 1858; Parks, *Brown*, 49–51; Collins, "Brown," 210–12.

5. *Macon Georgia Telegraph,* 9 February 1858, 19 January 1858.

6. Martin J. Crawford to Alexander H. Stephens, 8 September 1858, John W. Duncan to Alexander H. Stephens, 16 March 1859, Peterson Thweatt to Alexander H. Stephens, 20 May, 8 June 1859, Alexander H. Stephens Papers, LC (microfilm, UGA); Linton Stephens to Alexander H. Stephens, 31 May 1859, Alexander H. Stephens to Linton Stephens, 2 June 1859, Alexander H. Stephens Papers, MCSH (microfilm, EU); John H. Lumpkin to Howell Cobb, 25 October, 14 November 1858, Joseph E. Brown to Howell Cobb, 15 November 1858, John E. Ward to Howell Cobb, 21 November 1858, John H. Lumpkin to John B. Lamar, 7 March 1859, Howell Cobb to John B. Lamar, 4 November 1858, 6 April, 21 June 1859, James Jackson to Howell Cobb, 30 May 1859, Howell Cobb Papers, UGA; Joseph E. Brown to James H. Steele, 19 May 1859, Brown Family Papers; UGA; Howell Cobb to Alexander H. Stephens, 8 September 1858, in TSC, 443; *Athens Southern Banner,* 22 July 1858, 24 March, 23, 30 June 1859; *Milledgeville Federal Union,* 7 September, 15 October, 2 November 1858, 21 June 1859; *Macon Georgia Telegraph,* 23 August, 14 September 1858, 12 April, 10 May 1859; Robert W. Johannsen, *Stephen A. Douglas* (New York: Oxford University Press, 1973), 619–79; Roy F. Nichols, *The Disruption of the American Democracy* (New York: Macmillan, 1948), 200–221; Philip Shriver Klein, *President James Buchanan: A Biography* (University Park: Pennsylvania State University Press, 1962), 328–30; Thomas E. Schott, *Alexander H. Stephens of Georgia: A Biography* (Baton Rouge: Louisiana State University Press, 1988), 254–57; Parks, *Brown,* 58–88.

7. Linton Stephens to Alexander H. Stephens, 14 August 1859, Stephens Papers, MCSH; letter from Joshua Knowles, in the *Macon Georgia Journal and Messenger,* 1 June 1859; *Macon Georgia Journal and Messenger,* 13 April 1859; *Milledgeville Southern Recorder,* 14, 21, 28 June, 12, 26 July 1859.

8. *Milledgeville Southern Recorder,* 26 July 1859; Benjamin H. Hill to George M. Dudley, 25 July 1859, in the *Macon Georgia Journal and Messenger,* 10, 17 August 1859; *Milledgeville Southern Recorder,* 30 August 1859; *Griffin American Union,* in ibid., 7 June 1859; Horace Montgomery, *Cracker Parties* (Baton Rouge: Louisiana State University Press, 1950), 228–35; Luke F. Crutcher III, "Disunity and Dissolution: The Georgia Parties and the Crisis of the Union, 1859–1861" (Ph.D. diss., University of California, Los Angeles, 1974), 34–46.

9. Marc Kruman, *Parties and Politics in North Carolina, 1836–1865* (Baton Rouge: Louisiana State University Press, 1983), 180–201; Daniel W. Crofts, *Reluctant Confederates: Upper South Unionists in the Secession Crisis* (Chapel Hill: University of North Carolina Press, 1989), 37–65.

10. Iverson's speech, 14 July 1859, in the *Columbus Daily Times,* 20 July 1859; Alfred Iverson to David A. Vason, 12 September 1859, in ibid., 16 September 1859;

Don E. Fehrenbacher, *The Dred Scott Case: Its Significance in American Law and Politics* (New York: Oxford University Press, 1978), 506–32; Johannsen, *Douglas,* 685–714, 726–32.

11. *Macon Georgia Telegraph,* 25 October, 29 November, 13 December 1859; *Rome Courier,* 24 February, 10, 17, 24, 31 August, 7 September 1860; *Macon Georgia Journal and Messenger,* 5 September 1860; *Athens Southern Banner,* 13 September 1860; *Columbus Enquirer,* 13 November 1860; David M. Potter, *The Impending Crisis 1848–1861,* completed and edited by Don E. Fehrenbacher (New York: Harper & Row, 1976), 356–84; Avery O. Craven, *The Growth of Southern Nationalism, 1848– 1861* (Baton Rouge: Louisiana State University Press, 1953), 305–11; Stephen B. Oates, *To Purge This Land with Blood: A Biography of John Brown* (New York: Harper & Row, 1970), 274–361; Clarence L. Mohr, *On the Threshold of Freedom: Masters and Slaves in Civil War Georgia* (Athens: University of Georgia Press, 1986), 3–67.

12. *Milledgeville Federal Union,* 13 December 1859, 1, 15, 29, November 1859; letter from D. C. Campbell and E. J. McGeehee to the Democratic party of the state of Georgia, in ibid., 20 December 1859; Howell Cobb to John B. Lamar, 23 May 1859, James M. Smythe to Howell Cobb, 3 June 1859, Thomas R. R. Cobb to Howell Cobb, 24 August 1859, James M. Spullock to John H. Lumpkin, 16 November 1859, John H. Lumpkin to Howell Cobb, 18 November, 1859, Cobb Papers, UGA; Thomas R. R. Cobb to David C. Barrow, 17 November 1859, John H. Lumpkin to David C. Barrow, 18 November 1859, David C. Barrow Papers, UGA; Herschel V. Johnson to A. E. Cochran and James M. Spullock, 3 December 1859, Herschel V. Johnson Papers, DU; Howell Cobb to Alexander H. Stephens, 14 November 1859, in TSC, 448–49; E. J. McGeehee to Young J. Anderson, 16 February 1860, in the *Augusta Constitutionalist,* 2 March 1860; *Athens Southern Banner,* 30 June 1859; *Macon Georgia Telegraph,* 29 November 1859.

13. Joseph E. Brown to Alexander H. Stephens, 29 December 1859, J. Henley Smith to Alexander H. Stephens, 14 March 1860, Alexander H. Stephens Papers, EU; Martin J. Crawford to Alexander H. Stephens, 13 December 1859, Peterson Thweatt to Alexander H. Stephens, 30 January 1860, Alexander H. Stephens to Henry R. Casey, 9 March 1860, Stephens Papers, LC; Joseph E. Brown to Alexander H. Stephens, 5 January 1860, in TSC, 453–54; "March" and "Virginius," in the *Columbus Daily Times,* 30 January, 27 February 1860; *Milledgeville Federal Union,* 31 January 1860; *Augusta Constitutionalist,* 11, 12, 18, 21 February, 6, 8, 9, 20 March 1860; *Columbus Enquirer,* 27 March 1860; Parks, *Brown,* 94–102.

14. Howell Cobb to James M. Spullock, 14 January 1860, James M. Spullock Papers, GDAH; John H. Lumpkin to Howell Cobb, 23 January 1860, Howell Cobb to John B. Lamar, 11 February 1860, Oliver H. Prince to Mary Ann Lamar Cobb,

2 March 1860, Howell Cobb to John B. Lamar, 9 March 1860, Cobb Papers, UGA; John H. Lumpkin to David C. Barrow, 22, 30 January 1860, Mark Johnston to David C. Barrow, 8 March 1860, Barrow Papers, UGA; Howell Cobb to John B. Lamar, 15 January 1860, in TSC, 456–57; *Milledgeville Federal Union,* 24 January, 14 February, 6, 13, March 1860; *Athens Southern Banner,* 19 January, 2, 9 February 1860.

15. William McKinley to David C. Barrow, 15 March 1860, John H. Lumpkin to David C. Barrow, 17, 19 March, 1 April 1860, Barrow Papers, UGA; James H. Nisbet to Howell Cobb, 15, 17 March 1860, John B. Lamar to Howell Cobb, 16, 17 March 1860, Cobb Papers, UGA; Henry R. Casey to Alexander H. Stephens, 21 March 1860; A. J. Love to Alexander H. Stephens, 21 March 1860, J. Henley Smith to Alexander H. Stephens, 3 April 1860, Stephens Papers, LC: Howell Cobb to Isaiah T. Irvin, 20 March 1860, in the *Athens Southern Banner,* 22, 29 March 1860; *Macon Georgia Telegraph,* 17 March 1860; *Milledgeville Southern Recorder,* 20 March 1860; *Milledgeville Federal Union,* 20 March 1860; *Augusta Chronicle & Sentinel,* 17 March 1860; *Cartersville Express,* in ibid., 25 March 1860; *Griffin Southern Democrat,* in ibid., 29 March 1860.

16. Robert Toombs to Alexander H. Stephens, 10 February 1860, Alexander H. Stephens to J. Henly Smith, 24 February 1860, in TSC, 461, 463; Martin J. Crawford to Alexander H. Stephens, 19 May 1859, 8 April 1860, Peterson Thweatt to Alexander H. Stephens, 8 July 1859, Alexander H. Stephens to James A. Sledge, 25 March 1860, Henry R. Casey to Alexander H. Stephens, 17 March, 4 April 1860, Stephens Papers, LC; Robert Toombs to James M. Spullock, 17 March 1860, Spullock Papers, GDAH; Howell Cobb to John B. Lamar, 8 April 1860, Cobb Papers, UGA; Linton Stephens to James Thomas, 15 January 1859, James Thomas Papers; GDAH; Joseph Day to George R. Hunter, 27 August 1859, in the *Macon Georgia Telegraph,* 6 September 1859; *Macon Georgia Telegraph,* 2 August 1859, 24 January, 7, 14 April 1860; *Milledgeville Federal Union,* 10, 17 April, 7 June, 26 July, 25 October 1859; "A Voice from the People," in the *Augusta Constitutionalist,* 10 April 1860; *Augusta Constitutionalist,* 26 February, 1, 18, 25, 30 March, 7, 12 April 1860.

17. Henry C. Cleveland to Alexander H. Stephens, 11 May 1860, Stephens Papers, LC; John H. Lumpkin to Howell Cobb, 8 May 1860, Cobb Papers, UGA; Hiram Warner et al. to the Democratic party of Georgia, 2 May 1860, in the *Augusta Constitutionalist,* 5 May 1860; letter from Henry R. Casey, in ibid., 10 June 1860; speech of James Jackson, 7 July 1860, in the *Athens Southern Banner,* 26 July 1860; *Rome Courier,* 4, 11 May 1860; *Augusta Chronicle & Sentinel,* 27 April 1860; Potter, *Impending Crisis,* 407–12; William B. Hesseltine, ed., *Three against Lincoln: Murat Halstead Reports the Caucuses of 1860* (Baton Rouge: Louisiana State University Press, 1960), 3–110, especially 58, 85–94.

18. *Milledgeville Federal Union,* 29 May 1860; Howell Cobb to John B. Lamar, 22 May 1860, Howell Cobb to Robert Collins et al., 9 May 1860, in TSC, 480, 472. *Augusta Chronicle & Sentinel,* 16, 17 May 1860, summarizes reactions of the Georgia Democratic press.

19. Robert Toombs to Alexander H. Stephens, 5, 16 May 1860, Robert Toombs to Alexander H. Stephens, 7 May 1860, Robert Toombs to Robert Collins et al., 10 May 1860, in TSC, 469, 479, 469–70, 475–77; *Congressional Globe Appendix,* 36th Cong., 1st sess., 1859–60, 88–93; James Jackson to O. C. Gibson, 22 May 1860, in the *Athens Southern Banner,* 7 June 1860; *Milledgeville Federal Union,* 15, 29 May 1860.

20. Joseph Brown to Robert Collins et al., 12 May 1860, in the *Augusta Constitutionalist,* 19 May 1860; Eugenius A. Nisbet to Robert Collins et al., 8 May 1860, in ibid., 18 May 1860; Alexander H. Stephens to Robert Collins et al., 9 May 1860, Herschel V. Johnson to Robert Collins et al., 10 May 1860, Hiram Warner to Robert Collins et al., 9 May 1860, in ibid., 13, 17, 25 May 1860; Martin J. Crawford to Alexander H. Stephens, 11 May 1860, Francis J. Willis to Alexander H. Stephens, 19 May 1860, James P. Hambleton to Alexander H. Stephens, 23 May 1860, James D. Waddell to Alexander H. Stephens, 28 May 1860, B. Y. Martin to Alexander H. Stephens, 8 June 1860, Stephens Papers, LC; *Augusta Constitutionalist,* 5, 6, 24, 26 May 1860; *Rome Southerner* and *Marietta Advocate,* in ibid., 19, 20 May 1860.

21. Herschel V. Johnson to Alexander H. Stephens, 9, 19 June 1860, Johnson Papers, DU; Robert Toombs to Alexander Stephens, 9 June 1860, John A. Cobb to John B. Lamar, 20 June 1860, in TSC, 481–83; *Augusta Constitutionalist,* 16, 30 May, 7–10, 15 June 1860; *Milledgeville Federal Union,* 12, 26 June, 14 August 1860; *Macon Georgia Telegraph,* 8 June 1860; *Augusta Chronicle & Sentinel,* 8, 9 June 1860; *Athens Southern Banner,* 12 July 1860; Hesseltine, ed., *Three against Lincoln,* 178–278; Nichols, *Disruption of the American Democracy,* 314–33.

22. *Rome Courier,* 29 June 1860; *Augusta Chronicle & Sentinel,* 7 March, 26 May 1860, 10 February, 3 March, 10, 21 April, 2, 8–11, 21 May 1860; *Milledgeville Southern Recorder,* 1 November 1859, 8, 15 May 1860; *Rome Courier,* 16, 23 March 1860; *Columbus Enquirer,* 30 January, 12 June 1860.

23. *Augusta Chronicle & Sentinel,* 14, 17, 28 February, 21 March, 13, 16, 17, May, 9, 12, 19–21 June 1860; *Milledgeville Southern Recorder,* 24 January 1860; *Columbus Enquirer,* 15, 22 May 1860; *Rome Courier,* 29 June 1860; *Macon Georgia Journal and Messenger,* 2 May 1860; *Savannah Republican,* 12 July 1860; Hesseltine, ed., *Three against Lincoln,* 118–40; Crutcher, "Disunity and Dissolution," 87–88.

24. *Columbus Corner Stone,* 25 July 1860.

25. *Augusta Constitutionalist,* 26 July, 3 August 1860.

26. Alexander H. Stephens to J. Henly Smith, 8 August 1860, 2, 10, 15, 24 July, 12, 15, 16 September 1860, in TSC, 491, 483–89, 494–500; Herschel V. Johnson

to Alexander H. Stephens, 4, 9 July, 30 August 1860, Johnson Papers, DU; Herschel V. Johnson to J. Henly Smith, 1 September 1860, John Henley Smith Letters, GDAH; Percy S. Flippin, ed. "From the Autobiography of Herschel Johnson," *American Historical Review* 30 (January 1925): 319–22; Alexander Stephens's speech at Augusta, 1 September 1860, in Henry Cleveland, *Alexander H. Stephens, in Public and Private, with Letters and Speeches, before, during, and since the War* (Philadelphia: National Publishing, 1866), 676–94; address of James Gardner et al., 11 June 1860, in the *Macon Georgia Telegraph*, 13 July 1860; letter from E. G. Raiford, 27 August 1860, in the *Columbus Enquirer*, 11 September 1860; *Augusta Constitutionalist*, 3, 8 July, 1, 4 August, 31 October 1860; Schott, *Stephens*, 294–301; Crutcher, "Disunity and Dissolution," 93–97.

27. *Augusta Chronicle & Sentinel*, 19 September 1860, 16 June, 9 August 1860; *Savannah Republican*, 25 September 1860; *Augusta Chronicle & Sentinel*, 27 October 1860. Although Constitutional Unionists denounced cries for congressional protection, many could not resist claiming that Bell advocated the doctrine. See speech of Benjamin H. Hill at Macon, 30 June 1860, in the *Rome Courier*, 13 July 1860; *Augusta Chronicle & Sentinel*, 26 June, 3 July 1860; *Milledgeville Southern Recorder*, 22 May, 5, 12 June, 10 July 1860; *Rome Courier*, 22, 29 June, 28 September 1860; *Columbus Enquirer*, 6 March, 8, 15, 22 May, 17, 31 July 1860.

28. *Augusta Chronicle & Sentinel*, 26 July, 25 September 1860; *Milledgeville Southern Recorder*, 30 October 1860; *Augusta Chronicle & Sentinel*, 7 October 1860.

29. Howell Cobb to John B. Lamar, 5 December 1859, Cobb Papers, UGA; John J. Jones to J. Henly Smith, 10 September 1860, Smith Letters, GDAH; letter from John H. Howard, 27 September 1860, in the *Columbus Daily Times*, 2 October 1860; *Albany Patriot*, 1 November 1860; *Milledgeville Federal Union*, 31 July, 18 September, 9, 23, 30 October 1860; *Macon Georgia Telegraph*, 29 June, 6, 20 July, 3, 16 30 August, 18 October 1860; *Athens Southern Banner*, 5, 19 July, 25 October 1860; Crutcher, "Disunity and Dissolution," 96–104; Michael P. Johnson, *Toward a Patriarchal Republic: The Secession of Georgia* (Baton Rouge: Louisiana State University Press, 1977), 11–15.

30. *Columbus Daily Times*, 16 October 1860; *Augusta Chronicle & Sentinel*, 10 October 1860.

31. Linton Stephens to Alexander H. Stephens, 21 October 1860, Stephens Papers, MCSH; Hiram Warner to Herschel V. Johnson, 22 July 1860, Herschel V. Johnson to Alexander H. Stephens, 20 July, 1 October 1860, Johnson Papers, DU; letters of Benjamin H. Hill and James Gardner, in the *Rome Courier*, 26 October 1860; *Macon Georgia Telegraph*, 1 November 1860; *Macon Georgia Journal and Messenger*, 7 November 1860; *Milledgeville Federal Union*, 2 October 1860; *Columbus Enquirer*, 25 September, 9, 16, 23 October 1860; *Rome Courier*, 6 July, 19 October 1860.

32. Allen D. Candler, ed., *The Confederate Records of the State of Georgia,* 6 vols. (Atlanta: Charles P. Byrd, 1909), 1:56–57, 206–11; Potter, *Impending Crisis,* 485–94; Crutcher, "Disunity and Dissolution," 109–11, 209–18. Georgia election laws required presidential candidates to gain a majority to capture the state's electoral votes; the legislature gave Breckinridge Georgia's electoral votes.

33. Crutcher, "Disunity and Dissolution," 113–223, offers an extensive review of immediatist and cooperationist arguments.

34. Crofts, *Reluctant Confederates,* 66–360; Kruman, *Parties and Politics,* 200–221. In analyzing the arguments and evidence in Johnson, *Patriarchal Republic,* which will be dealt with further below, Crofts comments that "Johnson's arresting interpretation of Georgia loses much of its force" when Georgia is compared with the upper South, and he concludes that, compared with the upper South variety, "Georgia Unionism was a lifeless shadow" (380). I agree with Crofts and with his overall assessment that "upper South Unionism differed in kind rather than degree from lower South cooperationism" (381).

35. The forty-one sets of county resolutions found in Candler, ed., *Confederate Records,* 1:58–156, along with other county resolutions taken from newspapers, provide the best available evidence of white Georgians' views during the secession crisis. I have labeled the county resolutions as either immediatist or cooperationist based chiefly on whether the resolutions mentioned separate state secession or advocated southern conventions. I have classified some sets of resolutions that are vague or silent on these points as uncertain. I have also indicated the region in which the counties were located.

36. Troup County (black belt, cooperation) in ibid., 1:126; Lowndes County (black belt, uncertain), in ibid., 1:66; Carroll County (upcountry, immediate), in ibid., 1:85.

37. Elbert County (black belt, immediate), in ibid., 1:105; Clay County (black belt, uncertain), in ibid., 1:128; White County (mountains, cooperation), in ibid., 1:90–91; Clay County (black belt, immediate), in ibid., 1:103. Lacy K. Ford, Jr., *Origins of Southern Radicalism: The South Carolina Upcountry, 1800–1860* (New York: Oxford University Press, 1988), 338–73, analyzes themes of white equality and independence.

38. *Columbus Daily Times,* 22 March 1860; Meriwether County (black belt, cooperation), in Candler, ed., *Confederate Records,* 1:87; *Columbus Enquirer,* 11 December 1860. For similar statements that the Republican party was bent on the complete abolition of slavery, see Banks (upcountry, immediate), Dougherty (black belt, immediate), Troup (black belt, immediate), Glynn (coast, uncertain), Thomas (black belt, immediate), and Randolph (black belt, immediate) Counties, in Candler, ed., *Confederate Records,* 1:58–61, 63–64, 93–96, 108–10, 155–56.

39. Howell Cobb to the people of Georgia, 6 December 1860, in TSC, 513; John H. Howard to P. J. Philips, 8 December 1860, in the *Albany Patriot,* 3 January 1861; *Augusta Constitutionalist,* 30 November 1860.

40. "Bell Man," in the *Columbus Daily Times,* 15 December 1860; "Truth," in ibid., 17 December 1860; "A Southerner," in ibid., 10 November 1860; *Augusta Constitutionalist,* 7 December 1860.

41. Thomas R. R. Cobb to Marion Cobb, 11 October 1860 (typescript), Thomas Reade Rootes Cobb Papers, UGA; James Barrow to David C. Barrow, 15 November 1860, Barrow Papers, UGA.

42. *Columbus Sun,* in the *Albany Patriot,* 6 December 1860; *Milledgeville Southern Recorder,* 11 December 1860; Linton Stephens to Lewis J. Groce, 17 December 1860, in ibid., 1 January 1861; Alexander H. Stephens to J. Henly Smith, 12, 15, 16 September, 25 November, 31 December 1860, in TSC, 494–500, 504–5, 526–27; "A Thinker," in the *Athens Southern Watchman,* 19 December 1860; *Columbus Enquirer,* 13 November 1860; *Macon Georgia Journal and Messenger,* 21 November 1860; speech of Alexander Stephens, in William W. Freehling and Craig M. Simpson, eds., *Secession Debated: Georgia's Showdown in 1860* (New York: Oxford University Press, 1992), 52–79.

43. *Augusta Chronicle & Sentinel,* 8 November, 1 December 1860; letter from Joseph Day, 22 November 1860, in the *Macon Georgia Telegraph,* 6 December 1860; Charles J. Jenkins to J. A. Williams et al., 12 December 1860, in the *Milledgeville Southern Recorder,* 1 January 1861.

44. Speech of Benjamin H. Hill, 15 November 1860, in the *Athens Southern Watchman,* 6 December 1860; *Columbus Enquirer,* 4 December 1860; *Milledgeville Southern Recorder,* 11 December 1860. The texts in Freehling and Simpson, eds., *Secession Debated,* often differ slightly in wording from other texts that I cite; such is the case with Hill's speech. *Secession Debated* is an excellent collection, but I disagree strongly with many of Freehling and Simpson's interpretations, particularly their excessive emphasis on secessionist's anxiety over internal disloyalty to slavery and their labeling of cooperationists as "Unionists" (vii).

45. *Rome Courier,* 23 November 1860; *Savannah Republican,* in the *Weekly Chronicle & Sentinel,* 21 November 1860; Upson, Greene, Meriwether, Houston, Quitman, Sumter (all black belt, cooperation), and Milton (upcountry, cooperation) Counties, in Candler, ed., *Confederate Records,* 1:64–65, 68–79, 87–89, 123–25, 140–42, 144–54; *Savannah Republican,* 14 November, 8 December 1860; *Milledgeville Southern Recorder,* 4, 18 December 1860; *Macon Georgia Journal and Messenger,* 5 December 1860; *Rome Courier,* 4 January 1861; *Athens Southern Watchman,* 28 November, 19 December 1860; 16 January 1861; Walton County (upcountry, cooperation), in ibid., 12 December 1860; Muscogee County (black belt, cooperation), in

the *Columbus Enquirer,* 18 December 1860; letters from Lovick Pierce and "A Man in Georgia," in ibid., 25 December 1860. J. Mills Thornton III, *Politics and Power in a Slave Society: Alabama, 1800–1860* (Baton Rouge: Louisiana State University Press, 1978), 347, draws a similar conclusion about Alabama cooperationism. On Republican attitudes toward compromise, see David M. Potter, *Lincoln and His Party in the Secession Crisis* (New Haven: Yale University Press, 1942).

46. For expressions of the "overt act" argument, see "Houston," in the *Macon Georgia Journal and Messenger,* 21 November 1860; Franklin County (mountains, cooperation), in the *Athens Southern Watchman,* 12 December 1860; Floyd County (upcountry, cooperation), in the *Rome Courier,* 7 December 1860; Freehling and Simpson, eds., *Secession Debated,* 56–59.

47. Remarks of Charles J. Jenkins at the Richmond County (black belt, cooperation) meeting, in the *Augusta Chronicle & Sentinel,* 27 December 1860; *Columbus Enquirer,* 4 December 1860; Cincinnatus Peeples to James H. Silman, 3 December 1860, in the *Athens Southern Watchman,* 25 December 1860; James R. Smith to the people of Washington County, in the *Sandersville Central Georgian,* 12 December 1860; Kruman, *Parties and Politics,* 180–221; Crofts, *Reluctant Confederates.*

48. *Augusta Chronicle & Sentinel,* 15 January 1861; *Columbus Enquirer,* 11 December 1860; Young L. G. Harris to William M. McIntosh, 2 November 1860 (typescript), MacKintosh Family Papers, UGA; address of the cooperationist members of the Georgia legislature, 14 December 1860, in the *Athens Southern Watchman,* 25 December 1860; *Macon Georgia Journal and Messenger,* 14 November 1860; *Rome Courier,* 21 December 1860; Greene County (black belt, cooperation), in Candler, ed., *Confederate Records,* 1:68–79.

49. Sumter County (black belt, cooperation), in Candler, ed., *Confederate Records,* 1:147; "Forsyth," in the *Athens Southern Watchman,* 28 November 1860; Alexander H. Stephens to [?], 25 November 1860, in TSC, 505.

50. *Rome Courier,* 18 January 1861; *Macon Georgia Journal and Messenger,* 28 November 1860, 2, 16 January 1861; Herschel V. Johnson to Alexander H. Stephens, 11 November 1860, 9 January 1861, Johnson Papers, DU; Alexander H. Stephens to Linton Stephens, 8, 24, 26, 29, 30 November 1860, Linton Stephens to Alexander H. Stephens, 2 December 1860, Stephens Papers, MCSH.

51. "Georgia," in the *Athens Southern Banner,* 29 November 1860; *Albany Patriot,* 22 November 1860; *Columbus Times,* in the *Weekly Chronicle & Sentinel,* 11 November 1860; *Macon Georgia Telegraph,* 20 December 1860.

52. Henry R. Jackson to Howell Cobb, 19 December 1860, Cobb Papers, UGA.

53. *Athens Southern Banner,* 27 December 1860; Martin J. Crawford to the *Augusta True Democrat,* 25 December 1860, in the *Albany Patriot,* 3 January 1861; William C. Daniell to Robert N. Gourdin, 9 December 1860, Robert N. Gourdin

Papers, DU; Joseph E. Brown to Howell Cobb, 15 December 1860, Cobb Papers, UGA.

54. Freehling and Simpson, eds., *Secession Debated,* 5–30.

55. Message of Joseph Brown, 7 November 1860, in Candler, ed., *Confederate Records,* 1:47; "Sentinel," in the *Augusta Constitutionalist,* 13 December 1860.

56. *Athens Southern Watchman,* 1 November 1860; "Henry," in the *Milledgeville Southern Recorder,* 18 December 1860; J. Henly Smith to Alexander H. Stephens, 7 May 1860, Stephens Papers, LC; John M. Richardson to Robert N. Gourdin, 14 December 1860, Gourdin Papers, DU; George A. Smith to John B. Lamar, 5 January 1861, Cobb Papers, UGA; Robert Toombs to Alexander H. Stephens, 10 February 1860, in TSC, 462; *Columbus Enquirer,* 30 October 1860; *Savannah Republican,* in ibid., 6 November 1860.

57. Howell Cobb to Mary Ann Lamar Cobb, 10 October 1860, Cobb Papers, UGA; Thomas R. R. Cobb to Howell Cobb, 15 December 1860, in TSC, 522; Howell Cobb to Mary Ann Lamar Cobb, 26 December 1860, T. Allan to Howell Cobb, 10 December 1860, John B. Cobb to Howell Cobb, 14 December 1860, Cobb Papers, UGA.

58. *Athens Southern Banner,* 13 December 1860.

59. Message of Joseph Brown, 7 November 1860, in Candler, ed., *Confederate Records,* 1:55–56; Freehling and Simpson, eds., *Secession Debated,* 154, 155.

60. Readers familiar with the historical literature will have long ago grasped that I differ fundamentally with the interpretation of Georgia secession presented by Michael Johnson in *Patriarchal Republic.* Rather than pursue dozens of major and minor points in notes, I have decided to let the arguments and evidence presented in the text stand largely on their own—interested readers are more than capable of making their own comparisons and evaluations. But I will touch here on some of the most significant issues. Johnson interprets immediate secessionists as driven mainly by their fears and doubts about the loyalty of nonslaveholders (17–58, passim). Although the hints of distrust that appear in some of the evidence are well worth noting, to argue, as Johnson does, that Georgia seceded primarily because immediate secessionists feared other white Georgians seems to me a drastic overstatement contradicted by far more voluminous evidence, only a fraction of which I present in the text. Johnson also contends that the secession debate and the convention election represented something like a forum and a referendum on white Georgians' allegiance to slavery (xx–xxi, and, especially, 65–70). He consistently interprets both statements confirming white unity—incredibly numerous—and questioning white unity—exceedingly rare—as evidence of disunity. In other words, Johnson often insists that people meant what they did not say (especially 45–46), which leaves one wondering what, if anything, he would count as evidence against his interpretation.

Johnson treats the simple existence of cooperationism as evidence of an internal social crisis but scarcely mentions cooperationists' overwhelming emphasis on protecting slavery (52–58, 85–87). Johnson and I agree that immediate secessionists were rash and intemperate, and that their leadership took Georgia out of the Union. But I see their tactics and their arguments—none of which were novel—as utterly consistent with how Georgia politics worked. If histrionic campaigns and apocalyptic rhetoric count as prima facie evidence of an internal crisis, then white Georgians had faced such crises during every antebellum election. I do not think that either immediate secessionists or cooperationists believed that the convention campaign involved divisions among white men over the basic goal of protecting slavery. Johnson himself, at times (69–70), seems to concede this point, but his argument runs in the opposite direction. Moreover, as I read the numbers, Johnson's statistical analysis of the convention election returns (189–225) does not support many of the broad conclusions he draws in his text (63–78). (For an enlightening discussion on this point, see Crofts, *Reluctant Confederates*, 376–81). Although Johnson's interpretation is intriguing and stimulating, it does not, in my judgment, fit the evidence left by antebellum Georgians.

61. Michael P. Johnson, "A New Look at the Popular Vote for Delegates to the Georgia Secession Convention," *Georgia Historical Quarterly* (Summer 1972): 259–75, discusses the uncertainties surrounding the election results and reconstructs estimates of county voting. My tables and the discussion in this and the following paragraphs are based on Johnson's estimates of the returns (268–70), past Georgia election returns, and data from the *Eighth Census of the United States, 1860*. Probably because of a printing error, the county voting figures for immediate secession presented in Johnson's article do not add up to 44,152, but to 44,142; the county figures for the cooperation vote tally correctly.

62. In the counties that gave 61–100 percent of their vote to immediate secessionists, the total vote dropped 29.6 percent from the presidential election numbers. In competitive counties, where the immediate secession vote ranged from 40 to 60 percent, the total vote declined just 7.2 percent. The total vote in counties that gave cooperationists more than 60 percent of the vote fell off 19.8 percent from the November election.

63. Johnson, *Patriarchal Republic*, 196, found that the Pearson's correlation between the county vote for immediate secession and levels of county slave population was .239. Although Johnson generalizes about the impact of slave population levels—and other variables—on county voting, he nonetheless begins by observing that his "factor analysis" did "not indicate a strong relationship between any factor and the vote for secession" (195).

64. Ibid., 196, 199–200.

65. The total vote in these north Georgia counties dropped only slightly from the 1860 presidential election to the 1861 convention election. The vote for Breckinridge in these counties was 9,552 (62 percent); the vote for immediate secession was 5,507 (38 percent). For further discussion of voter shifts, see Johnson, *Patriarchal Republic*, 204–8.

66. Counties were ranked in quartiles based on Democratic percentage of the total vote cast in eighteen gubernatorial and presidential elections between 1835 and 1859. The 1860 presidential election, which is considered separately, was omitted, as was the anomalous 1851 Union–Southern Rights contest. The total Whig vote includes the 1852 Webster vote; the total Democratic vote includes the 1852 Tugalo vote. Some counties created in the late 1850s, of course, participated in only one or two elections before the 1861 election.

67. On this general point, see Steven A. Channing, *Crisis of Fear: Secession in South Carolina* (New York: W. W. Norton, 1970).

68. Steven Hahn, *The Roots of Southern Populism: Yeoman Farmers and the Transformation of the Georgia Upcountry, 1850–1890* (New York: Oxford University Press, 1983), 106–16, has a useful discussion of the upcountry response to the secession crisis. Hahn does not, however, attempt to deal with the confused, contradictory nature of the upcountry voting results.

69. Roy R. Doyon and Thomas W. Holder, "Secessionist Sentiment and Slavery: A Geographic Analysis," *Georgia Historical Quarterly* 73 (Summer 1989): 323–48, makes many of the same points using different methods of analysis. Among other things, Doyon and Holder show the clear east-west division in the black belt and demonstrate how useless levels of slave population were for explaining black belt voting in the convention election.

70. Candler, ed., *Confederate Records*, 1:212–69; Flippin, ed., "Autobiography of Herschel Johnson," 325–29; Johnson, *Patriarchal Republic*, 108–23; Ralph Wooster, "The Georgia Secession Convention," *Georgia Historical Quarterly* 40 (March 1956): 21–55. The vote on Nisbet's resolutions by regions was as follows: mountains, 4 to 33; upcountry, 31 to 26; eastern black belt, 45 to 39; western black belt, 49 to 17; pine barrens–wiregrass, 24 to 15; coast, 13 to 0. The final vote on the ordinance of secession by regions was as follows: mountains, 8 to 29; upcountry, 35 to 22; eastern black belt, 65 to 19; western black belt, 61 to 5; pine barrens–wiregrass, 26 to 14; coast, 13 to 0.

71. George C. Rable, *The Confederate Republic: A Revolution against Politics* (Chapel Hill: University of North Carolina Press, 1994), particularly stresses antipartyism.

# INDEX

Abolitionism, 14, 87, 89, 181, 191–93; rise
of, 35–36; as issue in 1840 election, 50–
51; as issue in 1844 election, 74–78; as
issue in 1848 election, 95, 101–2; fear of
in 1850, 158, 163, 165–66; as issue in
1856 election, 203–4; fear of in 1860–61,
218, 232–33, 236, 239–41, 320 (n. 38).
*See also* Republican party; Slavery; Slaves
Adams, John, 19
Adams, John Quincy, 23
Agriculture, 1, 5–10, 127–28; and credit,
40–41, 43; and tariff in the early 1840s,
62–63
Akin, Warren, 143, 216–17
Alabama, 169, 230, 237–38
Alabama resolutions, 97
Albany, 130–31, 137, 214
Algerine law, 181–82, 303 (n. 62)
American party, 137; development of, 189–
91; in 1855 election, 194–96; in 1856
election, 197–204; in 1857 election, 208–
10; and Lecompton constitution, 211–12;
and state banking, 214–15; transformed
into Opposition party, 216. *See also*
Constitutional Union party; Know-
Nothings; Opposition party; Whig party
Andrews, Garnett, 190, 194–95
Antipartyism, 13, 179; of State Rights party,
36, 38; of Calhounites, 48; of Whig party
in 1847–48, 89, 92, 98, 100–101; as
enduring force in state politics, 107, 111,
141; of Southern Rights party, 166; of
Know-Nothings and American party,
188–89, 197–98

Appling County, 11, 127
Apportionment, legislative, 121–25. *See also*
Legislature
Arnold, Richard D., 87, 117, 139, 211
Athens, 9, 27, 64, 135–36, 152
Atlanta, 16, 135–36, 177, 216
Augusta, 5, 8, 19, 26, 39–40, 45, 56, 133,
135–37, 149, 181, 187, 223

Baber, Ambrose, 43, 48, 148
Bacon, Major (Edwin H.?), 127, 288 (n. 22)
Bailey, David J., 90
Baker County, 130
Baldwin County, 117
Ballots, printed, 146–47, 292 (n. 62). *See
also* Voters
Bank, national, 42–44, 48, 57–58, 78, 92,
102. *See also* Bank of the United States
Banking: and panic of 1837, 38–45, 268
(n. 5); state system of, 39–40, 54–59;
Central Bank of Georgia, 39–41, 46, 52,
54–59, 271–72 (n. 27); and conflict
between state banks, 45; in *Major Jones's
Courtship,* 128–30; and panic of 1857,
214–15
Bank of the United States (BUS), 27–28,
32–33, 43–44, 57. *See also* Bank, national
Banks, Nathaniel, 196
Barbour, Philip P., 28
Barclay, Elihu S., 87
Barrow, David C., 234
Barrow, James, 234
Bartlett, Myron, 40
Bartow, Francis S., 146, 153

327